Starting and Operating a Business in California

A Step-by-Step Guide

By Michael D. Jenkins

OASIS PRESS

The Oasis Press® / PSI Research
Grants Pass, Oregon

95 AA

Published by The Oasis Press®
© 1980, 1995 by Michael D. Jenkins

This publication is designed to provide accurate and authoritative information
in regard to the subject matter covered. It is sold with the understanding that the
publisher is not engaged in rendering legal, accounting, or other professional
service. If legal advice or other expert assistance is required, the services of a
competent professional person should be sought.
> *— from a declaration of principles jointly adopted by a committee of*
> *the American Bar Association and a committee of publishers.*

The author of *Starting and Operating a Business in California* is Michael D.
Jenkins.

California State Editor: Jennifer Welburn
Series Editors: Linda Pinkham, Kathleen Doyle, and Camille Akin
Administrative Assistant: Adrienne Pueschel
Designer: Constance C. Dickinson
Typographer: Jan Olsson
Series Managing Editor: Constance C. Dickinson

Please direct any comments, questions, or suggestions regarding this book to
The Oasis Press®/PSI Research:

> Editorial Department
> 300 North Valley Drive
> Grants Pass, OR 97526
> (503) 479-9464
> (800) 228-2275

The Oasis Press® is a Registered Trademark of Publishing Services, Inc.,
an Oregon corporation doing business as PSI Research.

Library of Congress Catalog Card Number: 80-83053

ISBN 1-55571-113-8 (paperback)
ISBN 1-55571-001-8 (binder)

Printed in the United States of America
Eighth edition 10 9 8 7 6 5 4 3 2 1 0   Revision Code: 95AA

 Printed on recycled paper when available.

Table of Contents

Forms and Worksheets in this Book

Notes to Chapters 1–10

This new update of chapters 1–10 features a number of major additions, including notable additions to the sections discussing limited liability companies, estate tax planning, and emerging trends and issues. The list below identifies the most significant changes and additions to the text and gives you the chapter–section number where you will find the discussion.

- More studies confirm that failure rates among new businesses may be much lower than previously believed – 1.10
- More than 40 states have now enacted limited liability company (LLC) laws as this new type of business entity continues to catch on nationwide – 2.6
- Many states have recently repealed their bulk sales laws; yet another business trend that is rapidly spreading – 3.1, 9.14
- New 1994 OSHA regulations regarding reports of multiple injury accidents in the workplace now require employers to notify OSHA officials with 8 hours of such incidents, instead of the former 48 – 5.6
- There is a new notice, posting requirements under the Family and Medical Leave Act of 1993 – 5.8, 5.12
- The luxury tax on automobiles has been updated for indexed exemption – 7.2
- The IRS increased automobile standard mileage allowance to $0.29 (29 cents) a mile – 8.6
- There is an expanded discussion of estate tax planning and possible savings from use of bypass trusts – 8.10
- The U.S. Small Business Administration's (SBA) loan programs have expanded and updated coverage, including the SBA's new direct "microloan" program for very small businesses – 9.7
- The Federal Trade Commission's (FTC) mail order shipping rules have now expanded to also cover orders received by modem, fax, or telephone – 9.8
- Pending legislation may allow states to impose sales tax on some mail order sellers, if passed – 9.8
- Other pending legislation may increase medical insurance deduction for self-employed persons from 25% to 100%; however, income from S corporations may soon subject S corporation shareholders to self-employment tax on such income – 9.14

The author of chapters 1–10 of the entire *Starting and Operating a Business* series, is Michael D. Jenkins. Mr. Jenkins, an attorney at law and a certified public accountant, is a graduate of Harvard Law School. He has worked in Los Angeles and San Francisco as an accountant and as an attorney with a prominent San Francisco firm well known in the venture capital arena. He is a member of the State Bar of California, the American Bar Association, the American Institute of Certified Public Accountants, and the California Society of Certified Public Accountants.

How to Use this Book

0.1 Getting the Most Out of this Book

To most effectively use this book, become acquainted with the many helpful features it provides. Remember that each edition is updated annually to provide you with the most current information available. To find the most recent changes made to federal laws, refer to the Notes to Chapters 1–10: What's New page. For similar state information, refer to the Notes to State Chapter: What's New page, which immediately precedes Chapter 11.

0.2 Numbered Section Heads Correspond to Table of Contents and Index

Text

Discussions range from explaining how to start and operate your business to examining such practical issues as insurance, marketing, cash-flow management, internal financial controls, and much more. This book also explains federal and state government requirements and tax laws, as well as a number of emerging trends and issues your business may face.

Topics Noted in Margins

To make the information in this workbook easily accessible to busy people, the primary topics discussed within each numbered section are identified by "sideheads" in the margin beside the text.

Smaller Heads for Subtopics

When subsections of primary topics are discussed, the sideheads are slightly smaller.

Lists

- This small bullet helps you easily locate lists of requirements, things to do, and aspects of a particular subject or law.

Checklists

☐ Small boxes encourage you to enter a check, so that you can clearly see those items you've considered and dealt with — and those left to do.

Worksheets

Where the Action Begins

A number of worksheets are provided for you to answer questions and fill in numbers that form the basis for action plans, self-evaluation, budgeting, personnel policies, marketing feasibility studies, and the like.

The worksheets are set apart by boxes to clearly show where your interaction is required, to focus your thoughts, to record information, and to create the plans and reports that will help you establish and guide your business.

Resources

Sources and Data

Resources are set in tabular form to highlight the many agencies and companies listed to assist you.

Contacts
Addresses
Phone numbers
(listed in directory style)

Table of Contents

The detailed Table of Contents will help you quickly find any specific section of the book you wish to refer to. The first digit of the chapter–section number indicates the chapter, followed by a period and the section number.

Endnotes

The endnotes follow each chapter and are provided to assist you in accessing specific statutes, cases, regulations, and publications and to use this book as a starting place for legal research.

Index

The subject-matter index, organized alphabetically with cross-referenced entries, provides an exhaustive list of the topics, indexed not only by the terms actually used in the entries but also by various other terms you might think of instead. The Index is referenced by the chapter–section number, not by page number, to help you find the corresponding discussion in the text.

Related Resources

At the back of this book, you will find a compendium of additional resources that will save you valuable research time and money.

Appendix

The Appendix features a checklist of tax and various other major requirements for most businesses and a checklist of official government posters and notices required to be displayed by a business.

Forms

Since many business requirements depend on submitting specific forms to various government agencies, some samples of these forms are included for your reference and listed in the Table of Contents.

Post Cards

At the back of this book, you will also find post cards preaddressed to government agencies and other sources so you can request additional information, posters, and forms.

Preface

Anyone who runs a small business today, or who is thinking about starting one, knows that he or she faces serious and growing challenges. The hurdles one must get over to start or continue to operate a business seem to have grown a little higher each year since this series of books was first introduced in 1981. In particular, the government has shifted more and more responsibilities onto the shoulders of employers in recent years, a trend that seems likely to continue. As a result, many large and small firms are currently putting off expansion and hiring plans until the new Clinton universal health care proposals are finalized, since mandated health care benefits could well become the biggest financial responsibility ever thrust upon the nation's businesses — especially upon smaller businesses.

Despite the growing complexities of running a business, the slow-growth economy, and the fact that according to Dun & Bradstreet, more than 420,000 businesses failed in the last decade, small businesspeople have not been deterred. Quite to the contrary — business start ups are flourishing in this tough environment. According to an August 1993 article in *Investor's Business Daily*, for every business that failed in the "wave of creative destruction" in the 1980s, at least 15 new businesses sprang up to take its place. While many in the mass media have bemoaned the rash of takeovers, leveraged buyouts, mass layoffs, downsizing, corporate restructuring, and other wrenching changes in the 1980s and early 1990s, all this ferment seems to have provided fertile ground for new, small, and nimble businesses.

In fact, according to Dun & Bradstreet, the number of "total concerns in business" almost tripled in the 1980s to more than eight million by 1990. That compares very favorably to the 1970s, when the total number of businesses increased by just 13.8%, to 2.8 million by the end of that decade. The desire of Americans, especially many recent immigrants from all corners of the world, to start and run their own businesses seems indomitable, obstacles or no.

The publisher and I would like to think this 51-book *Starting and Operating a Business* series — which features a book for each state and the District of Columbia — might have played a significant part in empowering many of the millions of people who have started their own businesses since our first edition in 1981. A more modest view would suggest that we were merely on the leading edge of change, part of a huge expansion in the resources that have arisen in recent years to provide help to new and small firms.

We must confess, however, to being very pleased when, in April 1994, *Inc.* magazine chose *Starting and Operating a Business* as one of the best small business books available. After an exhaustive survey of hundreds of small business self-help books, as described in the cover article entitled, "In Search of the Small Business Bible," *Inc.* chose our book (series) as one of the six overall winners. We are also pleased with the award we received from the Small Business Administration "in recognition of significant contributions to the nation's small business." In fact, *Starting and Operating a Business* is featured in each of the eleven SBA Business Information Centers (BICs) in the U.S. and will also be featured in the 20 new BICs projected for the next year.

At the time we introduced this series, there were only a few useful small business self-help books available, and relatively few government resources devoted to helping new enterprises get off the ground.

Today, however, there are books and software programs offering assistance on almost every aspect of running a large, small or medium-sized business. In fact, this book series is now only part of a much larger series of business self-help books on a wide array of subjects offered by the publisher, The Oasis Press. In addition, there are now Small Business Development Centers (SBDCs) and "one-stop" business permit offices in almost every state, and while state governments are cutting services left and right, most are expected to maintain or even increase their business services and economic development and other assistance to small businesses.

Why the turnaround? State governments recognize that new and existing small businesses are the backbone of their economies and the only sector of the economy that is currently providing growth in jobs for their residents. Thus, it should not be surprising that the states are doing as much as possible to encourage business growth, expansion, and relocation.

I became involved in this trend after advising small and large businesses over the years — first as an economic and management consultant; then later, as a tax attorney; and more recently, as a certified public accountant. After years of helping many small businesses and venture capital start ups get off the ground, I had become increasingly aware of the need for a single, authoritative, and practical guide that would serve people starting and operating a business in a particular state — and acutely aware that no such guides existed, except in a few states.

Thus, in 1980, I was particularly receptive when my neighbor and publisher, Emmett Ramey, approached me with the idea of writing a nuts-and-bolts guidebook for the state of California that would guide a small business person or entrepreneur through the maze of red tape at both the federal and state levels of government, as well as provide the basic steps and advice needed to get a new business off the ground.

We decided to create an operating manual that would draw together — in a readable, usable, and nontechnical format — the practical facts of life a person needed to know when establishing a business in California. Since first publishing that California edition, we have enlisted local experts in each of the other states to work with us and coauthor the books for those states.

By and large, tax, legal, and business information is useless when it is out of date. As a result, we update each state chapter (Chapter 11) and the federal section (chapters 1–10) in this series approximately every twelve months.

So, if you want an up-to-date guide to the basic financial, legal, and tax ground rules that apply to most businesses operating in your state, the *Starting and Operating a Business* series has been designed with you in mind as a self-help tool. It is also intended to be a useful (and footnoted) reference source to the attorney who has only a limited knowledge of business taxation and the basic regulatory requirements of a large number of federal, state, and local government agencies. Accountants will also find this series a useful resource for understanding the broad scope of government regulations that affect their small business clients.

While the *Starting and Operating a Business* books provide an authoritative discussion of many legal and tax matters regarding small business, they are not intended to be a substitute for professional legal or tax advice. On the contrary, they are designed to help you focus on key points to explore in greater depth with your attorney, accountant, benefits consultant, or other adviser. By being better informed, you can use your professional advisers' time more efficiently.

Many of the items covered in this book have been added at the request of readers who have written to us with their suggestions. This series is not a "finished" project, but is under constant revision. Accordingly, as the principal author, I invite and welcome your feedback or suggestions as to improvements we might make. Your letters should be addressed either to me or my coauthor for the state chapter of this edition, in care of the publisher.

Michael D. Jenkins
July 1994

Dedication

To America's entrepreneurs — tenacious, courageous men and women — whose contribution to the variety, richness, and quality of our lives is immeasurable.

Preliminary Considerations

Part I

Chapter 1
Making the Decision to Go into Business

Chapter 2
Choosing the Legal Form of the Business

Chapter 3
Buying an Existing Business

Chapter 1

Making the Decision to Go into Business

Entrepreneurship is the last refuge of the troublemaking individual.

— James K. Glassman

1.1 Introduction

Neither this book nor any other book can tell you whether or not you should take the plunge and go into business for yourself. You alone must make that difficult decision. Before you make the decision, carefully consider some of the key points discussed in this chapter. Some of the points discussed you may not have considered yet, while others may assist you in dealing successfully with some initial problems you may face.

One of the first points to consider when starting your business is the major financial risk you will be taking. Once you have committed yourself financially, it will not be a simple or easy thing to change your mind and back out.

In addition, be aware there is a high failure rate among new businesses. Don't assume just because you are an expert in your field, you will be an automatic success. You will need to have strengths in other areas as well. In fact, statistics show that a very high percentage of those business failures result from poor management. Poor or ineffective management is usually a lack of balanced experience and competence in three areas:

- Marketing strategies — Know what kind of product or service to sell, how to target and reach your customers, and how to sell your product or service at a price that maximizes your profits.
- Technical ability — Be able to get the work done and do it right, so you will have satisfied customers. If you are going into the auto repair

business, for example, you better know a lot about how to keep autos running right, or you will not be in business very long.

- Financial knowledge — While you do not necessarily have to be a financial wizard, you do need to know how to plan and control your business' cash flow, raise or borrow the money you will need to start your business, and get through tight periods without being caught short of cash. A certain amount of financial sophistication is becoming more and more important in today's increasingly complex financial world, even for the small business owner.

If you are lacking experience or knowledge in one or more of these three critical areas, the odds of your business succeeding are greatly reduced.

This chapter engages you in the process of realistically evaluating your entrepreneurial strengths and weaknesses. It is also intended to cause you to focus on some of the typical start-up problems and choices you are likely to face, as well as assist you in dealing effectively and rationally with those issues.

Worksheets are provided at the end of the chapter. While reading the text, pick up a pencil and write in your responses when appropriate. Often, the simple process of writing down your thoughts on specific problem areas may provide significant new insights.

1.2 Advantages and Disadvantages of Owning Your Own Business

Have you realistically considered both the advantages and the disadvantages of owning and operating your own business? If not, the time to do so is before, not after, you have committed yourself.

Advantages

If you are actively considering going into business for yourself, you most likely have already thought about the potential advantages, such as:

- Being your own boss and not having to report to a superior;
- Having the independence and authority to make your own business decisions;
- Direct contact with customers, employees, suppliers, and others;
- The personal satisfaction and sense of achievement that comes with being a success, plus the recognition that goes with it;
- The opportunity to create substantial wealth and job security for yourself;
- The opportunity to be creative and to develop your own idea, product, or service;
- The chance to make a living doing something you truly enjoy; and

- Doing something that contributes to others, whether it be providing an excellent product or service, providing employment, paying dividends to stockholders, or doing something else that is useful or that creates value.

If you are like most people, you may not have thought much about the downside of going into business; however, awareness of the potential disadvantages should not discourage you from your goal of going into business for yourself, if you have a strong commitment to that goal.

Disadvantages

Seriously consider whether you and your family are prepared to handle the disadvantages that often come with being an entrepreneur.

- In many ways, you are still not your own boss. Instead of having one boss, you will have many — your customers, the government agencies to whom you must report, and in some cases, your key suppliers.
- There is a large financial risk. The failure rate is high in new businesses, and you may lose not only your own money but also that of your friends and relatives who may have bankrolled you.
- The hours are long and hard. When you start your business, you will no longer be working 9 to 5. Count on working 10- to 12- or even 15-hour days, often six or seven days a week.
- You will not have much spare time for family or social life. And you can forget about taking any long vacations for the first few years since the business is unlikely to run itself without your presence for any long length of time.
- Your income may not be steady like a salary. You may make more or less than you could working for someone else, but in either case, your income may fluctuate up and down from month to month.
- The buck stops with you. If a problem arises, there is no boss you can take it to and say: "What do we do about this?" You are the boss and all the responsibility is yours. If anything goes wrong, the cost comes out of your pocket.
- You may be stuck for years doing work you do not like. Unlike an employee, you cannot simply quit and look for a better job. It may take you years to sell the business or find some other way to get out of it without a major financial loss.
- As a business grows, the amount of activity not associated with the primary business objective will increase. You will spend more time on personnel, administrative, and legal matters and less doing what you may have wanted most to do in your business.
- Increasing legislation and litigation make owning a business very risky. You can work a lifetime to build a business only to have it lost because of a lawsuit or a new law or regulation.

1.3 Typical Characteristics of the Successful Entrepreneur

A good deal is known about what it takes to be a successful entrepreneur. For the most part, it seems the one overriding factor is a tremendous need to achieve. In short, attitude seems to have almost everything to do with success in business, while factors, such as intelligence, education, physical appearance, and a pleasing personality, are much less important. Characteristics of typical successful entrepreneurs include:

- An overpowering need to achieve, as opposed to a need to be liked or to exercise power; the form in which different individuals measure their achievement varies widely, ranging from amassing wealth to building a larger organization to creating a better mousetrap than anyone else;

- The trait of following through on a commitment, not quitting halfway through when the going gets tough: in short, perseverance;

- A positive mental attitude or the ability to remain optimistic in new and unfamiliar situations, which essentially grows out of being self-confident about one's abilities;

- Objectivity — the ability to accurately weigh and assess risks associated with a particular course of action, as well as being realistic about one's own abilities and limitations;

- A respectful attitude toward money, but a tendency to look upon money as a means for accomplishing things, or a way of keeping score in the game of business, rather than as a thing to be sought as an end in itself;

- The tendency to anticipate developments and to make things happen rather than constantly reacting to problems as they arise;

- Resourcefulness — the ability to solve unique problems in unique ways and to be able to handle things that come up for which the entrepreneur has no previous experience to rely on as a guide;

- Strong personal relations skills — the characteristics of being cheerful and cooperative, and usually getting along well with, without necessarily being close to, employees and associates;

- Well-developed communication skills, both in oral and written presentations; and

- Well-rounded technical knowledge with emphasis on the knowledge about the physical process of producing goods and services.

How do your personal characteristics stack up against the foregoing profile of the typical successful entrepreneur? If that profile doesn't sound very much like you, maybe you had better give some long, hard thought as to whether you are cut out for making it as a business owner.

Running a business is not like working for someone else. No one is there to tell you what to do when something goes wrong. You are responsible for everything.

Are you capable of handling that kind of total responsibility? Are you a self-starter, capable of planning, organizing, and carrying out projects on your own? If not, you may find that starting and running a successful business is not for you.

Running a business demands a great deal in the way of initiative, hard work, self-discipline, and resourcefulness. On the other hand, solving the problems that arise from day to day and making it all work out can be a source of immense satisfaction, as well as be financially rewarding.

Before reading further, complete Worksheet 1, which is a useful questionnaire that may help you to get a better idea of your suitability for playing the role of entrepreneur in the real world. Worksheet 1 is located at the end of this chapter.

1.4 Knowing Your Market

One of the most important questions you should ask yourself is whether you feel that you know and understand the market for the particular kind of products or services you intend to sell. Do you know who your competition is and whether the particular market you intend to appeal to is large enough for both you and the existing competition? Also, how will your products or services measure up against those of your competitors in terms of quality and price?

If your product or service is something new or unusual, you need to have a sense of whether you will be selling an item that is wanted and needed in the marketplace. Or, even if you intend to sell a product or service that you know there is a need for, you should be satisfied in your own mind that you are going to be making it available at the right place at the right time.

Few sights are sadder than the boarded-up mom-and-pop store or restaurant — in which the owners have sunk their life savings — that never got off the ground for some obvious reason, such as lack of visibility from the street, lack of substantial foot traffic by its doors, or some other fatal flaw the inexperienced owners overlooked.

To succeed, you must find the right business opportunity. If you do not have a clear idea of what business you want to go into and where you want to operate it, you will need to do some intelligent investigation of all possible opportunities that might be suitable for you.

If you already have a concept of what you want to do, you will still need to do a great deal of investigating to make sure it is as good an opportunity as it appears to be. In either case, a lot of initial research and footwork is advisable, unless you want to close your eyes and indulge in wishful thinking.

Determining Market Feasibility

In other words, to quote a well-known brokerage firm: "Investigate before you invest." This often entails doing your own marketing feasibility study before committing yourself to opening a new business.

A marketing feasibility study is simply a systematic analysis of any information you can obtain about the potential market for your product or service. This information can include the competition you face, the amount of sales you can reasonably expect to obtain in that particular market, and whether that level of sales will be adequate for your business to operate at a reasonable profit. For example, if you are planning to build homes in a small community where there is only a demand for five homes a year, and you need to build and sell ten homes a year to survive, doing a marketing feasibility study might help you realize your proposed business venture is not feasible, even if you were to capture 100% of the local housing market. Investigate first, then invest.

Alternatively, if you have several thousand dollars to spend and a well-defined idea of what it is you want to do, you can hire a professional economist or marketing consultant to do a feasibility study. In every major city, there are several firms that can do a thorough marketing and demographic study for you. Such a feasibility study can be quite valuable, but it will also be fairly expensive. Most people starting a new business tend to do their own marketing feasibility study, which is usually done very informally, if at all. The exception would be for people who create a formal, written business plan. A thorough analysis of the market for a new business' product or service is always a key portion of any such business plan. The Oasis Press publishes books and software that can assist you in creating a written business plan. See the list of publications in the back of this book for ordering information.

Before doing a marketing feasibility study, you obviously need to know what business you want to go into. When choosing your type of business, keep these thoughts in mind:

- If you see that a particular business is doing quite well and you want to go in and compete head-to-head with it, don't make the mistake of adopting a me-too approach and going in with the assumption that you can take away a lot of their business by competing on a price basis. Other than price, you better have a lot of good reasons why you think another business' customers will switch over to you. Other good reasons could include a distinctly better product, service, or location.

- Keep your eyes open for developing social, economic, and technological trends that will create new markets that you can move into at an early stage. It will help if you are a voracious reader of magazines such as *Time*, *Newsweek* (social trends); *Forbes*, *Business Week* (economic trends); or *Omni* or *Discover* (technological innovations).

An example of how observing social trends can translate into profits — in this instance stock market profits — is the case of an investment analyst in the 60s who noticed the trend toward mini-skirts and correctly anticipated that the spread of mini-skirts among women would create a boom market for panty hose. The analyst made a killing by buying shares of panty hose stock.

So how do you go about analyzing the market for your product or service once you have focused on a particular business you might want to start? Worksheet 2 will help you pinpoint the kind of information you need to develop to satisfy yourself that a good market exists for whatever it is you are planning to sell. Before you read any further, spend some time writing down your responses to each of the items on Worksheet 2.

Market Data Resources

Once you have identified your most likely potential customers, find out how to locate your business or structure and to direct your advertising and promotional efforts to most efficiently reach them. Fortunately, there is a great deal of published data you can use if you need to do this type of research. One of the best sources is *Sales and Marketing Management Magazine*, which publishes *Survey of Buying Power* each year. This survey provides breakdowns in population, households, retail sales by type of business, and total purchasing dollars for each county in the United States and for cities with a population of more than 10,000. To request information on *Survey of Buying Power*, see Statistical Information in Section 10.4.

Some of the printed sources of market information you can use in your research are:

- A.C. Nielsen market studies
- McGraw-Hill research studies from McGraw-Hill Publishing
- *National Trade and Professional Association (NTPA) Directory*
- Newspapers
- Statistical abstracts
- Trade magazines

Many of these items can be found in your local business or university library. The *NTPA Directory* can be ordered from:

National Trade and Professional Association Directory
Columbia Books
Washington, DC
(202) 898-0662

Various industry and government sources of information to consider are:

- Trade associations
- U.S. Chamber of Commerce
- U.S. Department of Commerce
- U.S. Small Business Administration

Another excellent source is the 1990 U.S. census data, which gives vast amounts of detailed information on the U.S. population and its buying habits by individual census tract. You may want to obtain a couple of useful pamphlets from your nearest U.S. Small Business Administration field office. Ask for the pamphlet entitled, *Researching Your Market*, for guidance on how to do your own market research.

Finding the Optimum Site

Even more important in your local community may be studies and future projections as to population and income trends that have been done by local groups, such as your local chamber of commerce or, in some areas, the local planning commission. If finding the optimum site to locate is important to your marketing effort, do the following:

- Talk to a knowledgeable person at your local chamber of commerce about business and other trends in the area where you intend to locate.
- Talk to a staff person at your local planning commission about census tract projections of future population growth, income trends, and economic development in the area you are considering. Also, they — or some other local agency, such as a traffic or streets department — will usually have done traffic counts showing how many cars pass certain points every day. This information can be very useful if you are opening a retail business. Also, consult any trade association, which serves your business and may have available information tailored exactly to your needs.
- Obtain a copy of the Small Business Administration's publication, *Choosing a Retail Location*.

For a complete guide to specifying, ranking, and evaluating the factors you must consider when choosing an optimum site for your new or relocating business, obtain a copy of *Company Relocation Handbook*. This handbook features a list of related reference publications and economic development organizations. Get your copy through your local book source or:

The Oasis Press
(800) 228-2275

1.5 Knowing the Business

Do you have any experience in the area of business in which you will be engaged? Of course, it is possible to learn while doing, but it helps a great deal to know a business before you start. Often, the most successful businesses are started by people who have worked in a particular line of business for years and who finally decide that they know the ropes well enough to leave their employer and start their own similar operation.

It helps to have experience in the particular business you propose to enter, but in most cases, your experience working in some other line of business will also have considerable carryover value. If you have neither type of experience, you may find you have a lot to learn once you begin the business.

A major management weakness that causes businesses to fail is the inability to get the job done and to do it right, on time, and efficiently enough to charge a competitive price for your product or service and still make a profit. For example, with the tremendous proliferation of personal computers, you may have decided to go into business repairing small computers. You may be absolutely right, but unless you have the technical capability to do such repairs, or the ability to properly select and hire employees who can do the job, you had better look for some other kind of business.

In many cases, if you know you lack the technical experience you need to open a particular kind of business, your best approach will be to get a job in that industry and work for someone else for a few years until you learn what you need to know. This may require a lot of patience, but it is definitely preferable than getting into a business you do not know well and losing your shirt in the process.

1.6 Knowing How Much Money It Will Take to Succeed

Can you afford to start a full-time business, if it will mean giving up your current employment and income? Many small businesses never really have a chance to succeed because the owners run out of money before the business becomes a viable operation. As a result, the owners often wind up having to go back to work for someone else again, disappointed and broke.

Carefully calculating and scheduling out, in as much detail as possible, the income and expenses you can reasonably expect for at least the first year of operation, as well as your living expenses and a reserve for emergencies, is a helpful step when determining how much money it will take to start and maintain your business.

You want to have enough money to last until the business reaches the point where you expect to make enough profit to live on. Remember a lot of expenses are involved in starting up almost any kind of business, and most businesses start out operating in the red for a time.

Completing worksheets 3 through 5 will help you plan your cash flow for the crucial first year of business. Worksheet 3 will help you to project your monthly sales revenue in terms of actual cash to be received. Worksheet 4 projects your monthly operating expenses for the first year of business, plus one-time, start-up expenses. Worksheet 5 is a schedule of your estimated personal living expenses during the first year.

Once you have completed worksheets 3 through 5, enter the monthly totals from the bottom line of each onto Worksheet 6, which is a summary of your cash needs. This will show you how much cash you will have to put into the business each month — and on a cumulative basis — during the first year of business. Once you have completed Worksheet 6, you will have a pretty good handle on how much money it is going to take to get your business started and approximately when you will need it.

If, under your most realistic projections, you are still running a deficit in cash flow each month at the end of the first year, you may want to do a similar projection out into the second year of operation.

If it appears you will need to borrow or raise money to keep the business operating until it gets into the black, find out well in advance how much you will be able to raise and whether or not you will be able to get that amount. If you plan to borrow, do you know how to put together a strong presentation to demonstrate to the prospective lender how you will be able to repay the loan? If not, see Section 9.7 and Chapter 10 for sources of information and help in obtaining financing for a small business.

Several books are available to help you along this process. One book, *The Loan Package*, can help you put together a loan application package for a small collateralized business loan. *Raising Capital: How to Write a Financing Proposal* can help you raise larger amounts of money for both equity and debt financing. Another book, *The Money Connection: Where and How to Apply for Business Loans and Venture Capital* provides an up-to-date list of federal, state, county, and community loan programs.

Affordable and easy-to-use software programs are also available to help your small business. Two noteworthy titles are *Small Business Expert* and *Start A Business*. Both of these programs complement this *Starting and Operating a Business* book. For more information on the software or the books above, call:

The Oasis Press
(800) 228-2275

1.7 Signing a Lease

If you will need to lease space for your business location, have you located a suitable place that is available? If so, there are a number of critical points you need to consider before you sign a lease with a landlord.

Remember that a lease is a binding legal contract, and if you agree to pay rent of $1,000 a month for two years, you are on the hook for $24,000, unless you can sublease or assign the lease to someone else, which could be difficult or impossible to do, depending on the terms of the lease. Key points to consider when signing a lease agreement include:

- What are the terms of the lease? Most businesses tend to start off by either growing rapidly or folding quickly. Thus, except in a retail or service business, you will probably be better off initially leasing on a month-to-month basis or for as short a lease term as you can get, such as three or six months, even if the monthly rent is higher than for a longer lease. You will already have enough financial problems if your business fails, without being saddled with a long-term lease obligation.

- Can you put up the kind of sign you must have on the building? A business like a restaurant can be devastated if the landlord doesn't permit a sign that is sufficiently visible to passersby.

- Will the landlord permit you to make necessary improvements and alterations to the leased premises?

- Will the local health department, fire and police departments, air pollution control authorities, and zoning rules permit operation of your particular type of business at the location you have chosen?

- Is your location in a high-crime area that will require expensive burglary insurance and security precautions?

- Is there enough parking nearby or good public transit access for customers?

- Is the location appropriate to the kind of business you will conduct? There is usually no need to locate a manufacturing operation in a busy, high-traffic area. On the other hand, retail businesses are usually heavily dependent on the number of people passing nearby on foot or by car. For example, the Pillsbury Company reportedly selects its sites for Burger King fast food restaurants by looking for locations that have at least 16,000 cars passing by each day at an average speed of about 30 miles per hour.[1]

- Does the lease provide you with an option to renew — and at what rental price — after the initial term expires?

- If the lease is for more than just a few months, do you have the right to sublease or assign the lease? If so, under what conditions or restrictions?

1.8 Will You Hire Employees?

In certain kinds of businesses, during the initial start-up phases — and perhaps even afterwards — you may be able to operate without employees by either doing all your work yourself, with the help of family members, or by contracting out certain functions to independent, outside contractors. To the extent you can do so, you may find your life is much simpler by doing it yourself or with independent contractors.

Once you hire even one employee, you take on a great many responsibilities as an employer, over and above meeting a payroll every week or two. These responsibilities include paying and filing tax returns for federal and state unemployment taxes, Social Security taxes, and income tax withholding from wages. In addition, you will need to comply with workers' compensation laws, employee health and safety laws, anti-discrimination laws, U.S. immigration law restrictions on hiring, and a variety of other federal and state labor laws and regulations that may apply once you hire employees. These and other employer requirements are discussed in Chapter 5.

This section reviews some of the legal restrictions on your hiring practices and provides you with a working outline of what you will need to consider in the way of personnel policies once your business reaches the point where you will have to hire employees.

Hiring Practices

Hiring personnel can be complicated because of the broad array of state and federal laws designed to prevent an employer from hiring on the basis of discriminatory factors, such as age, sex, race, or religion. Most of these laws affect all but the smallest employers, so you will have to be alert to most of these rules to avoid even the appearance of discrimination in your hiring practices.

While anti-discrimination rules apply to promotions, job assignments, firing, and other aspects of the employment relationship as well as to hiring, the focus here is mainly on hiring practices. This is the area where most small business owners are likely to stumble into trouble, even when they have no intention to discriminate.

Things Not to Do

All questions or information you express should relate to job qualifications only and not to extraneous factors, such as age, race, sex, or physical size or condition.

If there are special occupational requirements — for example, hard physical labor that might preclude hiring certain handicapped individuals — be sure to carefully document such unusual situations or requirements.

Help Wanted Ads

Use the list below to guide you when writing a help wanted advertisement.

- Do not mention race or national origin or any attribute of national origin, such as native language.
- Do not refer to sex classifications, such as "girl wanted."
- Avoid any type of reference to age, such as "young boy" or "recent high school graduate."

Job Application Forms

Your employment application forms should avoid any questions or information on these topics:

- Arrest record;
- Whether the applicant has ever filed for unemployment benefits;
- Place of birth or where parents were born;
- Physical characteristics, such as height or weight;

- Social Security number;
- Marital status;
- Labor union affiliation;
- Request for photograph;
- Religious affiliation;
- Mode of transportation to work;
- Sex;
- Race or national origin;
- Clubs or organizations, unless you instruct the applicant not to list organizations that indicate race or national origin; and
- Native language or how the applicant learned a foreign language.

A sample employment application form is provided for your review on page 30. If you wish to add additional questions to it, be careful not to indirectly request anything that would reflect on the applicant's race, religion, sex, age, marital status, national origin, or physical condition. Because state laws differ, check with your legal adviser or state employment department before preparing your employment application.

Employment Interviews

During interviews with potential employees, refrain from asking questions, such as:

- Are you a U.S. citizen?
- When did you attend grade school, high school, or college?
- Do you have children, and who will care for them while you are working?
- Do you have any physical or mental handicap?
- What does your spouse do for a living, and are you likely to move elsewhere?
- Would your religion prevent you from working on holidays or certain days of the week?

Federal law generally bans the use of any kind of lie detector tests in most private employment situations, except for drug manufacturers and distributors and certain security firms.[2] Many state laws are even more stringent.

In addition, questions on possible felony convictions, previous military service, and drug or alcohol addiction are not necessarily illegal in all cases, but they may entail difficulties and probably should be avoided.

Checking References

As a general rule, former employers have no legal obligation to give you any information about a former employee. As a practical matter, however, most former employers will at least verify the former employee's employment and the date of employment. Since a former employer can get into trouble for giving you negative information that they cannot substantiate, don't expect them to volunteer much information or to put anything negative in writing. For that reason, you should generally do reference checks by phone. Acceptable questions would include:

- Verifying information given by the applicant;
- Asking about the applicant's principal strong points, weak points, and degree of supervision needed;
- Asking about the applicant's attitude;
- Asking how the applicant's performance compared with others; and
- Asking if the applicant would be rehired.

Personnel Policies

Even before you hire your first employee, you will need to outline some basic personnel policies. Better yet, if you write down your policies on matters such as hours, vacation time, and sick leave and can give such a written summary to new employees, it will greatly help to clarify the employment relationship. Perhaps it will even prevent a misunderstanding that could lead to legal action against you by an employee.

Worksheet 7 provides a series of questions that will help you focus on different personnel policies that are typical in a small to medium-sized business. For a more thorough treatment of this area, and if you wish to develop a personnel policy manual for your business, you may want to obtain a copy of *A Company Policy and Personnel Workbook* from The Oasis Press.

Related Information

To supplement the information you have just read in this chapter, you may want to read the following sections which discuss more related information:

- Employee or Independent Contractor? — Section 9.11
- Fair Employment Practices — Section 5.8
- Sexual Harassment — Section 5.8
- Immigration Law Restrictions on Hiring — Section 5.9
- Hiring a Spouse as an Employee — Section 8.12
- Employee Wage-Hour and Child Labor Laws — Section 5.7
- The Americans with Disabilities Act — Section 5.11
- Mandatory Family and Medical Leave Requirements — Section 5.12

In addition, to get an overview of other legal obligations that come with the territory when you have employees, scan through Chapter 5.

1.9 Other Questions You Need to Ask

- Will or should you advertise? If you do, you need to decide what kind of advertising will be the most cost-effective for your business, whether it be newspaper ads, direct mail, radio, posters, handbills, or other forms of advertising and promotion.
- Do you understand what will be involved in purchasing, managing, and restocking your inventory of goods?
- How will you go about selling? Will you hire sales clerks or outside salespeople, or will you do most of the selling yourself?
- Will you sell to customers on credit? If so, how will you protect yourself from bad credit risks and outright deadbeats?
- How much of your personal savings are you putting at risk by going into business? Are you willing to risk losing all of it if the business is a failure?
- Can you run the business alone — or with help from family members — or would you do better with one or more partners or business associates to provide additional capital and skills and to divide up some of the responsibilities of running the business?

Again, the questions posed in this chapter are not intended to discourage you from going ahead with starting your business. Chances are you have already considered most of the points raised in this chapter and are reasonably confident that you will be able to do what is necessary to make your business work. If so, many of the questions raised above probably seem rather elementary and obvious to you, as they will to most individuals seriously considering going into business, and you will now want to proceed to the discussions in the remainder of this book.

If you have not previously given serious thought to most of the above points that are relevant to the type of business you are planning to start, now is the time to take a long, hard look at whether you are adequately prepared to embark upon such a venture.

1.10 How Likely Are You to Succeed?

One of the chief deterrents to starting your own business is the fear of failure. This fear has long been enforced by scary statistics that state approximately four out of five new businesses fail after only a short period of time. Given those kinds of frightening odds, it is surprising that anyone is brave enough to start a business.

However, a recent in-depth study of business failure rates done at the New Jersey Institute of Technology (NJIT) suggests the grim statistics on new firm failures may be little more than myth. According to the study, no more than 18% of new firms fail during the first eight years of being in business. Over half (54%) of all start ups survive over eight years with either their original owners (28%) or with a change in ownership (26%). The other 28% of new firms voluntarily terminate operations without losses to creditors.

The author of the study, Bruce A. Kirchoff, professor of entrepreneurship at NJIT and former chief economist for the U.S. Small Business Administration, states, "I suspect entrepreneurs have known the truth about survival and success for some time. While economists argue that entrepreneurs are foolish to start new businesses because the risk of failure is so high, 400,000 or more new firms are formed every year in the U.S. All these entrepreneurs cannot be stupid; they look around and talk to others and realize that their chances of survival and success are far better than academic economists have estimated. It's the economists that look foolish."[3]

According to Kirchoff, the greater survival rate is consistent with the evidence that small firms are the primary job creators in the U.S. economy. While other, even more recent, studies have suggested that most *net* new jobs are created by mid-sized businesses, rather than by either small or large businesses, a 1994 Dun & Bradstreet (D&B) study strongly backs Kirchoff's conclusion that the failure rate for new businesses is much lower than previously believed. The D&B study of 249,768 businesses that started up in 1985 showed that 177,133 (about 71%) were still going strong in early 1994.[4] The Kirchoff and D&B studies are not reasons to become foolhardy or overconfident about your prospects for success. On the other hand, they do indicate that starting your own business may not be the five-to-one long shot gamble you may have been told it was.

Endnotes

1. San Francisco *Chronicle*, Aug. 3, 1980.
2. The Employee Polygraph Protection Act, 29 U.S.C. 2001, *et seq.*
3. Kirchoff, Bruce A., Ph.D. *Assessing Firm Failure Fictions*. New Jersey Institute of Technology, 1993.
4. *Forbes,* June 6, 1994.

Worksheet 1 – Self-Evaluation Checklist for Going into Business

Under each question, check the answer that says what you feel or comes closest to it. Be honest with yourself.

Are you a self-starter?

- ☐ I do things on my own. Nobody has to tell me to get going.
- ☐ If someone gets me started, I keep going all right.
- ☐ Easy does it. I don't put myself out until I have to.

How do you feel about other people?

- ☐ I like people. I can get along with just about anybody.
- ☐ I have plenty of friends; I don't need anyone else.
- ☐ Most people irritate me.

Can you lead others?

- ☐ I can get most people to go along when I start something.
- ☐ I can give the orders if someone tells me what we should do.
- ☐ I let someone else get things moving; then I go along if I feel like it.

Can you take responsibility?

- ☐ I like to take charge of things and see them through.
- ☐ I'll take over if I have to, but I'd rather let someone else be responsible.
- ☐ There's always some eager beavers around wanting to show how smart they are. I say let them take the responsibility.

How good of an organizer are you?

- ☐ I like to have a plan before I start. I'm usually the one to get things lined up when the group wants to do something.
- ☐ I do all right unless things get too confusing; then I quit.
- ☐ Just when I'm all set, something comes along and presents too many problems, so I just take things as they come.

How good of a worker are you?

- ☐ I can keep going as long as I need to. I don't mind working hard for something I want.
- ☐ I'll work hard for a while, but when I've had enough, that's it.
- ☐ I can't see that hard work gets me anywhere.
- ☐ If I make up my mind to do something, I don't let anything stop me.
- ☐ I usually finish what I start if it goes well.
- ☐ If it doesn't go right away, I quit. Why beat my brains out?

Worksheet 1 – Self-Evaluation Checklist for Going into Business (continued)

How good is your health?

☐   I never get run down.

☐   I have enough energy for most things I want to do.

☐   I run out of energy sooner than most of my friends seem to.

Count the checks you made.

How many checks are there beside the first answer to each question? _____

How many checks are there beside the second answer to each question? _____

How many checks are there beside the third answer to each question? _____

If most of your checks are beside the first answers, you probably have what it takes to run a business. If not, you are likely to have more trouble than you can handle by yourself. You may want to find a partner who is strong on the points you are weak on. If many checks are beside the third answer, not even a good partner will be able to shore you up.

Source: U.S. Small Business Administration.

Worksheet 2 – Marketing Feasibility Study Checklist for Your Product or Service

Your Product

Briefly describe the nature of the product or service you will offer:

_____

_____

_____

Most products or services have a life cycle, beginning with very rapid growth in the introductory stage, which slows down in the maturity stage, flattens out in the saturation stage, and finally begins shrinking in the declining stage. Which stage of its market cycle do you believe your product or service is in?

☐ introductory (high growth) ☐ saturation (little or no growth)

☐ maturity (slower growth) ☐ declining (negative growth in demand)

If you believe your product is in one of the earlier, faster growing stages of its life cycle, what edge do you believe your product will have over similar products that may be introduced by new competitors who may come into the field?

_____

_____

_____

If you are entering at a fairly late stage of the product marketing cycle, why is it you believe that you can succeed in taking away others' market share with your product or service?

_____ Price _____

_____ On time : _____

_____ Hard compounds. _____

How is your product or service different in terms of quality and price from what is already on the market?

_____

_____

_____

Is there good reason to believe that your customers will recognize the difference? _____ If so, why?

_____

_____

_____

What is different about your marketing strategy or distribution strategy that will enable your product or service to succeed in a market where there is little, if any, growth?

_____

_____

_____

Worksheet 2 – Marketing Feasibility Study Checklist for Your Product or Service (continued)

Your Potential Customers

Not everyone is a potential customer. Certain age groups, income levels, geographic areas, ethnic groups, and educational levels will be more likely than others to be your customers. You need to focus on who will need your product and be most likely to buy it and then where to locate your business or how to structure your marketing approach to reach those segments of the market that you are most interested in reaching. Spell out below, as clearly as you can, who your customers are most likely to be.

The particular area from which I will be able to draw most of my customers is:

_____

_____

_____

_____

In addition, I should draw a significant number of customers from the following area or areas:

_____

_____

_____

My plan or strategy for reaching potential customers in the above areas can be summarized as follows:

_____

_____

_____

_____

The target market for my product or service, in terms of demographics, should be among the following persons (Describe your ideal customer's age, gender, educational level, and geographical location.):

_____

_____

_____

_____

In terms of income groups, my particular product or service should appeal primarily to people in the following income levels:

☐ Under $25,000 a year household income

☐ $25,000 – $35,000 a year

☐ $35,000 – $50,000 a year

☐ $50,000 – $75,000 a year

☐ $75,000 – $100,000 a year

☐ More than $100,000 a year

My product or service is likely to be more in demand by certain social, cultural, and ethnic groups than others. The groups that are most likely to be customers, if any, are:

_____

_____

_____

_____

_____

_____

_____

The groups that are least likely to be customers are:

_____

_____

_____

_____

_____

_____

Your Competition

Even though you may have done a great job in pinpointing and studying your market segment, the job isn't done until you have considered your competition.

Main competitors in my market area are (list firms by name):

1. _____

_____

2. _____

_____

3. _____

_____

4. _____

_____

5. _____

_____

6. _____

_____

Worksheet 2 – Marketing Feasibility Study Checklist for Your Product or Service (continued)

Based on my market research of statistical data, such as *Sales Marketing and Management Magazine*, the amount of buying power per business represented in my area is $ _____.

If I can generate that amount of sales, it: will ☐, will not ☐ be sufficient for me to operate successfully.

Five reasons why customers would buy from me rather than my competitors are:

1. _____
2. _____
3. _____
4. _____
5. _____

Five weaknesses my business will have when compared to my competitors are:

1. _____
2. _____
3. _____
4. _____
5. _____

To overcome these weaknesses, I will:

_____
_____
_____
_____
_____
_____
_____
_____
_____
_____
_____
_____
_____
_____
_____

Worksheet 3 – Estimated Cash Inflow from Sales for Year _____

	Jan.	Feb.	Mar.	Apr.	4-month Total
Gross Sales for Month					
Less: Credit Sales Made					
Subtotal: Cash Sales					
Plus: Collections on Prior Credit Sales					
Less: Bad Debts*					
Total: Net Cash Flow from Monthly Sales					

	May	June	July	Aug.	4-month Total
Gross Sales for Month					
Less: Credit Sales Made					
Subtotal: Cash Sales					
Plus: Collections on Prior Credit Sales					
Less: Bad Debts*					
Total: Net Cash Flow from Monthly Sales					

	Sept.	Oct.	Nov.	Dec.	4-month Total
Gross Sales for Month					
Less: Credit Sales Made					
Subtotal: Cash Sales					
Plus: Collections on Prior Credit Sales					
Less: Bad Debts*					
Total: Net Cash Flow from Monthly Sales					

Total Net Cash Flow from Monthly Sales for Year $ _____

* Consider using some percentage, say 1 or 2% of credit sale collections, to estimate your uncollectible debts.

Worksheet 4 – Estimated Business Cash Outlays for Year _____

	Jan.	Feb.	Mar.	Apr.	May
Monthly Expenses					
Rent					
Salaries and wages (except owner)					
Payroll taxes					
Advertising and promotion					
Insurance					
Federal estimated income tax					
State estimated income tax					
Owner's FICA or SE tax					
Telephone and utilities					
Inventory replacement purchase					
Interest on loans					
Maintenance					
Legal and accounting fees					
Office supplies					
Delivery expense					
Miscellaneous					
One-time Expenses					
Fixtures and equipment					
Decorating and remodeling					
Initial stock of inventory					
Utility and lease deposits					
Licenses and permits					
Other					
Total Expenses for Month					
Plus: Loan principal payment					
Less: Purchases on credit					
Plus: Payment on prior credit					
Net Monthly Cash Outlay					

June	July	Aug.	Sept.	Oct.	Nov.	Dec.	Annual Totals

Worksheet 5 – Estimated Personal and Living Expenses for Year _____

	Jan.	Feb.	Mar.	Apr.	May
Regular Payments					
Rent or house payment					
Property taxes					
Condo owner's dues					
Car payments					
Furniture and appliance payments					
Loan payments					
Health insurance					
Other insurance					
Household Expenses					
Food – restaurants					
Food – at home					
Telephone and utilities					
Water					
Personal Expenses					
Clothing and laundry					
Medical, dental, and drugs					
Education					
Dues and subscriptions					
Gifts and charity					
Gasoline and auto					
Entertainment and travel					
Miscellaneous spending					
Total Personal Expenses (Draw Required)					

June	July	Aug.	Sept.	Oct.	Nov.	Dec.	Annual Totals

Worksheet 6 – Summary of Estimated Cash Requirements for Year _____

	Jan.	Feb.	Mar.	Apr.	4-month Total
Net cash for month from sales – Worksheet 3					
Less: Net monthly cash outlay – Worksheet 4					
Subtotal: Net operating cash flow (or deficit)					
Less: Owner's draw for living & personal expenses – Worksheet 5					
Add: Money borrowed					
Add (or subtract): Equity capital paid in (or withdrawn) from the business					
Total: Net cash flow (or deficit) for month					
Cumulative* cash flow (or deficit)					

	May	June	July	Aug.	4-month Total
Net cash for month from sales – Worksheet 3					
Less: Net monthly cash outlay – Worksheet 4					
Subtotal: Net operating cash flow (or deficit)					
Less: Owner's draw for living & personal expenses – Worksheet 5					
Add: Money borrowed					
Add (or subtract): Equity capital paid in (or withdrawn) from the business					
Total: Net cash flow (or deficit) for month					
Cumulative* cash flow (or deficit)					

	Sept.	Oct.	Nov.	Dec.	4-month Total
Net cash for month from sales – Worksheet 3					
Less: Net monthly cash outlay – Worksheet 4					
Subtotal: Net operating cash flow (or deficit)					
Less: Owner's draw for living & personal expenses – Worksheet 5					
Add: Money borrowed					
Add (or subtract): Equity capital paid in (or withdrawn) from the business					
Total: Net cash flow (or deficit) for month					
Cumulative* cash flow (or deficit)					

* Add each month's net cash flow to the previous month's cumulative total.

Annual Totals: To get your total figures for the list below, add the three, four-month totals together for each item.

Net cash for month from sales – Worksheet 3 _____

Less: Net monthly cash outlay – Worksheet 4 _____

Subtotal: Net operating cash flow (or deficit) _____

Less: Owner's draw for living & personal
expenses – Worksheet 5 _____

Add: Money borrowed _____

Add (or subtract): Equity capital paid in (or
withdrawn) from the business _____

Annual cumulative cash flow (or deficit) _____

Sample Employment Application Form

Employment Application

Personal Data

Name: _____
           (last)   (first)   (middle)

Present address: _____
         (street address)   (city)   (state)   (zip)

Telephone numbers: _____ _____
            (home)   (work)

Education

High school: _____ Graduated? Yes ☐ No ☐ Location: _____

College or University: _____ Graduated? Yes ☐ No ☐ Degree(s): _____

Other (specify type): _____ Graduated? Yes ☐ No ☐ Certificate(s): _____

_____ Graduated? Yes ☐ No ☐ Certificate(s): _____

Work Experience

List below all present and previous employment, starting with the most recent.

Company name: _____ From (mo/yr): _____ Type of work: _____

Address: _____ To (mo/yr): _____ Name of supervisor: _____

_____ Reason you left: _____

Company name: _____ From (mo/yr): _____ Type of work: _____

Address: _____ To (mo/yr): _____ Name of supervisor: _____

_____ Reason you left: _____

Company name: _____ From (mo/yr): _____ Type of work: _____

Address: _____ To (mo/yr): _____ Name of supervisor: _____

_____ Reason you left: _____

Company name: _____ From (mo/yr): _____ Type of work: _____

Address: _____ To (mo/yr): _____ Name of supervisor: _____

_____ Reason you left: _____

May we contact the employers above?   Yes ☐ No ☐   If yes, list any employers you do not wish us to contact:

_____

_____

Remarks: _____

_____

_____

Worksheet 7 – Defining Your Company's Personnel Policies

Working Hours

Describe briefly the policy you will set for working hours, including:

Starting time? _____

_____

How much time will be allowed for lunch? _____

_____

Quitting time? _____

_____

Which days of the week employees will be expected to work? _____

_____

If, like many companies these days, you will adopt some kind of "flex-time" system, spell out how it will work.

_____

_____

_____

_____

Overtime

Outline your policy on overtime work. Refer to Section 5.7 of this book for legal requirements for paying overtime premiums. See also Section 11.5 regarding state wage laws. Points to consider here include:

Will you pay exempt employees (administrative or professional) overtime if they work extra hours? _____

_____

Will you require employees to obtain permission to work overtime? _____

_____

Compensation

Make a list of the job positions in the company other than your own and the compensation level for each. On a separate piece of paper, write out a specific job description for each position, outlining duties and responsibilities. Refer to sections 5.7 and 11.5 of this book for a description of hourly minimum wage requirements.

Position	Hourly Wage	Salary	Total Monthly Pay
_____	_____	_____	_____
_____	_____	_____	_____
_____	_____	_____	_____
_____	_____	_____	_____
_____	_____	_____	_____

Worksheet 7 – Defining Your Company's Personnel Policies (continued)

Vacation Policy

Describe how much paid vacation employees will have and how this may increase after a certain number of years of service. _____

_____

Will vacation time and sick leave time off be combined into a single category for employees (as some companies now do to reward employees who do not abuse sick leave and to discourage others from using sick leave as additional vacation by playing hooky)? _____

_____

Will you pay employees, who terminate, for unused vacation? (The laws of many states require you to do so.)

_____

_____

Family and Medical Leave Policy

Outline your policy for both paid and unpaid sick leave and family and medical leave. (If you have more than 50 employees, the federal Family and Medical Leave Act may apply to you. See Section 5.12.)

Sick leave: _____

_____

Family/medical leave: _____

_____

Birth or adoption of a child? _____

_____

Leaves of Absence

What will your policy be towards employees who request unpaid leaves of absence? _____

_____

_____

Time Off with Pay

Will you provide other time off with pay for such eventualities as funerals, jury duty, and training?

Funerals or family emergencies? _____

_____

Jury duty? _____

_____

Attend work-related seminars and training sessions? _____

_____

Promotions and Evaluations

Outline your policy for evaluating employees' performance and determining when promotions will be made.

_____

_____

_____

_____

_____

Fringe Benefits

Consider which employee fringe benefits you will provide and specify your policy for each.

Medical insurance: _____

_____

Long-term disability insurance: _____

_____

Life insurance: _____

_____

Dental insurance: _____

_____

Medical expense reimbursement: _____

_____

Child care benefits: _____

_____

Maternity benefits: _____

_____

Pension or profit-sharing plans: _____

_____

Paid holidays: _____

_____

Automobiles or allowances: _____

_____

Expense accounts: _____

_____

Worksheet 7 – Defining Your Company's Personnel Policies (continued)

Fringe Benefits (continued)

Education assistance programs: _____

_____

_____

_____

Employee discounts on purchases: _____

_____

Stock options (if incorporated): _____

_____

Incentive bonus plan: _____

_____

Other: _____

_____

_____

_____

Placement Fees

If you hire employees through a personnel agency or "headhunting" firm, will you pay the placement fee?

_____

_____

Other Company Policies

_____

_____

_____

_____

_____

_____

_____

_____

_____

_____

_____

Chapter 2

Choosing the Legal Form of the Business

The hardest thing in the world to understand is Income Tax.

— Albert Einstein

2.1 General Considerations

A business venture can be structured in several ways; however, the law classifies businesses so that most fall into one of three legal forms — the sole proprietorship, the partnership, or the corporation. There are also certain variations on some of these basic legal forms, such as the S corporation and the limited partnership. In addition, the limited liability company (LLC), a relatively new form of business organization, has gained legal status in more than 40 states. See Section 2.6 for more on LLCs.

If you are planning to start a business, consider the following questions when deciding your business' legal form:

- Will someone else share in ownership of the business? If so, it will not be a sole proprietorship. The choice will be between a partnership arrangement and a corporation, or possibly a limited liability company.
- How important is it to limit personal liability for debts or claims against the business? If this is a major consideration, incorporating the business would generally be the best means of limiting your liability.
- Which form of business organization will result in the least taxes? While there is no universal answer to this question, the rest of this chapter explains when it is and isn't beneficial to incorporate for tax reasons.

Before choosing the legal form of your business, it is important to realize that you may need to change to a different form at some time in the

Changing Legal Forms

future. Changing legal forms is easier to do with some forms of business than with others. As a broad generalization, it is usually a simpler matter to change from a sole proprietorship to a partnership, or to change from a sole proprietorship or partnership to a corporation, than it is to move in the opposite direction. (An LLC is usually treated like a partnership.)

For example, converting a corporation into a sole proprietorship or partnership may result in substantial individual and corporate-level taxes when the corporation is liquidated. This would occur if the value of the business, when transferred to the stockholders of the corporation, was greater than the cost or tax basis for their stock, resulting in taxable gains to the stockholders. If some of the corporate assets have value in excess of their tax basis, the corporation will also have taxable gains and will pay a corporate tax on such gains when it transfers the assets to its stockholders.

While there are almost always some expenses and complications in changing the legal form of a business, such changes are quite routine transactions. Many businesses start off as sole proprietorships, develop into partnerships, and later incorporate, if tax and other considerations indicate that it no longer makes good business sense not to be incorporated. Thus, the choice of one legal form when starting a business should not be considered a final choice.

2.2 Advantages and Disadvantages of Sole Proprietorships

The great advantage of operating a new business as a sole proprietorship is that it is simple and does not require any formal action to set it up. You can start your business today as a sole proprietorship — there is no need to wait for an attorney to draft and file documents or for the government to approve them.

Of course, you will need a business license, and a few states require you to register to do business. As a sole proprietor, you are the sole owner of your business. If married, however, your spouse will usually have a one-half interest in the business in a state which has community property laws.

Personal Liability

As the owner of the sole proprietorship, you will be personally liable for any debts or taxes of the business or other claims, such as legal damages resulting from a lawsuit. This is one reason why many entrepreneurs prefer to use a corporation rather than a sole proprietorship. Unlimited personal liability is perhaps the major disadvantage of operating a business in the form of a sole proprietorship.

Profit (or Loss) Is Yours

All of the profit or loss from your business belongs to you and must be reported on your federal income tax return, *Schedule C, Income (or Loss) from a Business or Profession*, on *Form 1040*. This can either be an advantage or a disadvantage for income tax purposes, depending on the circumstances.

If operating the business results in losses or significant tax credits, you may be able to use the tax losses or tax credits to reduce taxes on income from other sources. Or, if your sole proprietorship generates modest profits — but not more than about $60,000 to $75,000 a year — overall taxes may be less than if incorporated, assuming you need most of the income to live on.

As a sole proprietor, you are not considered an employee of your business. As a result, you will avoid having to pay unemployment taxes on your earnings from the business. Both the state and federal governments impose unemployment taxes on wages or salaries, but not on self-employment income. Note that a corporation would normally get an income tax deduction for the unemployment tax it paid on your salary, so that the actual after-tax savings from operating as a sole proprietorship would be somewhat less than the unemployment taxes you would avoid paying. Refer to sections 5.3 and 11.5 regarding the unemployment taxes you must pay for each employee.

Unemployment Tax Savings

Another advantage of a sole proprietorship is that you can shift funds in and out of your business account or withdraw assets from the business with few tax, legal, or other limitations. In a partnership or a limited liability company, you can generally withdraw funds only by agreement and, in the case of a corporation, a withdrawal of funds or property will usually be taxable as a dividend or capital gain and may violate some states' corporation laws.

Withdraw Assets Tax-Free

A major disadvantage of sole proprietorships and partnerships is they cannot obtain a number of significant tax benefits regarding group-term life insurance benefits, long-term disability insurance coverage, and medical insurance or medical expense reimbursements. To qualify for favorable tax treatment regarding such fringe benefit plans, it is necessary to incorporate. A self-employed individual is allowed to deduct 25% of his or her health insurance in computing adjusted gross income.[1] This deduction expired on December 31, 1993, but Congress will very likely extend it again.

Limited Tax Savings for Fringe Benefits

The special advantages of corporate pension and profit-sharing plans have largely been eliminated. There are now virtually no differences in the tax treatment of self-employed (Keogh) plans of sole proprietorships and partnerships, as compared with corporate retirement plans. See Section 8.3.

See the table at the end of this chapter which summarizes the key characteristics of sole proprietorships, partnerships, corporations, and limited liability companies.

2.3 Advantages and Disadvantages of Partnerships

General Partnerships

In general, any two or more individuals or entities who agree to contribute money, labor, property, or skill to a business and who agree to share in its profits, losses, and management are considered to have a partnership. You can choose to have a general partnership or a limited partnership.

Creating a partnership can be a very simple matter since the law does not require any formal written documents or other formalities for most partnerships. As a practical matter, however, it is much sounder business practice for partners in a business to have a written partnership agreement that, at a minimum, spells out their agreement on such basic issues as:

- How much and what kind of property each partner will contribute to the venture;
- What value will be placed on the contributed property;
- How profits and losses will be divided among the partners;
- When and how profits will be withdrawn;
- Whether or how certain partners will be compensated for their services to the partnership or for making capital available to the partnership; and
- How changes in ownership of interests in the partnership will be handled.

A written partnership agreement should be prepared by an attorney and, if possible, should be reviewed by a tax accountant before it is put into effect. Partnerships are a bit like marriages; they usually start out with a great deal of trust but have a high break-up rate. Be advised that partnerships are easy to get into, require a lot of patience and understanding to live with, and are often costly and painful to get out of.

Liability of Partners

As a partner, you are an agent for the partnership and can do anything necessary to operate the business, such as hire employees, borrow money, or enter into contracts on behalf of the partnership. You and each of your partners — except for a limited partner in a limited partnership — have personal liability for the debts, taxes, and other claims against the partnership.

If the partnership's assets are not sufficient to pay creditors, the creditors can satisfy their claims out of your personal assets. In addition, when any partner fails to pay personal debts, the partnership's business may be disrupted if his or her creditors proceed to satisfy their claims out of his or her interest in the partnership by seeking what is called a charging order against partnership assets.

State and Federal Tax Requirements

While a partnership must file federal and usually state information returns — *Form 1065* is the federal form — it generally pays no income tax. Instead, the partnership reports each partner's share of income or loss on the information return, and each partner reports the income or loss on *Schedule E* of his or her individual income tax return, *Form 1040*.

Certain partnerships are allowed to use a fiscal year, rather than the calendar year, for tax filing purposes; however, these partnerships may have to report and pay income taxes directly if the use of a fiscal year results in a tax-deferral benefit to their partners.[2] The exceptionally complex accounting required to determine this tax is part of the price a partnership must pay if it elects to have a fiscal tax year.

In addition, partnerships are required to file a special report, *Form 8308*, with the IRS each time a sale or exchange of an interest in the partnership occurs.[3]

Like a sole proprietor, a partner is not generally considered an employee of the partnership for income tax and payroll tax purposes. The income tax advantages and disadvantages of a sole proprietorship are equally applicable to a partnership since a partner's share of income from a partnership is treated essentially the same as income from a sole proprietorship. For example, your income from a partnership may be subject to federal self-employment tax but not to federal and state unemployment taxes as discussed in Section 2.2.

Dissolution

Unless a partnership agreement provides otherwise, a partnership usually terminates when any partner dies or withdraws from the partnership. This is in contrast to a corporation which, theoretically, has perpetual existence. Under the laws of most states, bankruptcy of a partner or the partnership itself will cause the dissolution of the partnership, regardless of any agreement.

Limited Partnerships

The law provides for a special kind of partnership in which partners have limited personal liability: the limited partnership. The limited partnership is more regulated than the more common general partnership, but it allows investors who will not be actively involved in the partnership's operations to become partners without being exposed to unlimited liability of the business' debts, if it should go out of business.

A limited partner risks only his or her investment but must allow one or more general partners to exercise control over the business. In fact, if the limited partner becomes involved in the partnership's operations, he or she may lose his or her protected status as a limited partner. The general partners in a limited partnership are fully liable for the partnership's debts. Every limited partnership must have one or more general partners as well as one or more limited partners.

State law requires certain formalities in the case of a limited partnership that are not required for other partnerships. To qualify for their special status, limited partnerships must usually file a *Certificate of Limited Partnership* with the secretary of state or other state and county offices. Establishing a limited partnership also requires a written partnership agreement. See Section 11.2 regarding special filing requirements for partnerships under state law.

2.4 Advantages and Disadvantages of Corporations

A corporation is an artificial legal entity that exists separately from the people who own, manage, control, and operate it. It can make contracts, pay taxes, and is liable for debts. Corporations exist only because state statutory laws allow them to be created.

A business corporation issues shares of its stock, as evidence of ownership, to the person or persons who contribute the money or business assets which the corporation will use to conduct its business. Thus, the stockholders or shareholders are the owners of the corporation, and they are entitled to any dividends the corporation pays and to all corporation assets — after all creditors have been paid — if the corporation is liquidated.

Limited Personal Liability

The main reason most businesses incorporate is to limit owner liability to the amount invested in the business. Generally, stockholders in a corporation are not personally liable for claims against the corporation and are, therefore, at risk only to the extent of their investment in the corporation. Likewise, the officers and directors of a corporation are not normally liable for the corporation's debts, although in some cases, an officer whose duty it is to withhold federal income tax from employees' wages may be liable to the IRS if the taxes are not withheld and paid over to the IRS as required.

Potential Loss of Limited Personal Liability

The advantage of limited liability is not always completely available through incorporation. For example, don't start a corporation on a shoestring. If your corporation is capitalized too thinly with equity capital (your money) as compared to debt capital (borrowed money), the courts may determine that your corporation is a thin corporation and hold you and your stockholders directly liable to creditors.

Failure to observe corporate formalities and the separate legal existence of the corporation can have a similar result. This is called "piercing the corporate veil" by the courts, and means if a corporation is not adequately capitalized and properly operated to protect the interests of creditors, the courts can take away the veil of limited liability that normally protects the stockholders.

Piercing the corporate veil is relatively uncommon. A much more frequent problem is that many banks and other lenders will not loan money to a small incorporated business unless someone, usually the stockholders of the corporation, personally guarantees repayment of the loan.

Despite this common business practice, the limited liability feature can still be an important protection from personal liability for other debts, such as accounts payable to suppliers and others who sell goods or services to the corporation on credit, typically without requiring any personal guarantee of payment by the owners.

Even this partial protection is a significant advantage of incorporating for most small business owners. Being incorporated can also protect you from personal liability regarding lawsuit damages not covered by your corporation's liability insurance policies; for example, someone slips on a banana peel in your store and sues the corporation for ten million dollars. To help you avoid personal liability for corporate acts, consult your attorney and keep thorough and specific records of your corporation's operations, policies, and meetings.

Unlike a sole proprietorship or partnership, a corporation has continuous existence and does not terminate upon the death of a stockholder or a change of ownership of some or all of its stock. Creditors, suppliers, and customers, therefore, often prefer to deal with an incorporated business because of this greater continuity.

Continuous Existence

Naturally, a corporation can be terminated by mutual consent of the owners or even by one stockholder in some instances.

To set up a corporation, you must file articles of incorporation with the state office that grants and approves corporate charters. See Section 11.2 for more information on state incorporating requirements.

Cost of Incorporating

Legal fees usually run between $500 and $1,000, even for a simple incorporation, and if it is necessary to obtain a permit from the state to issue stock or securities, legal fees can be much more.

Thus, it should be apparent that one of the disadvantages of incorporating is the cost involved, which will be substantial even for the simplest incorporation. In addition to the costs of establishing a corporation, there will be recurring costs, often including annual franchise or corporate income taxes.

Corporations filing their income tax returns on *Form 1120-A* or *Form 1120* will be taxed at different rates depending on the amount of their taxable income. The following table lists the current federal corporate income tax rates, which are 39% in the highest bracket.

Federal Corporate Income Taxes

Taxable Income	Tax Rate	**Corporate Tax Rate Table**
Not more than $50,000	15%	
$50,000 to $75,000	25%	
$75,000 to $100,000	34%	
$100,000 to $335,000	39%	
$335,000 to $10 million	34%	
$10 million to $15 million	35%	
$15 million to $18,333,333	38%	
More than $18,333,333	35%	

As an owner, you will most likely draw a salary from your corporation. This salary will be subject to FICA (Social Security) taxes and state and federal unemployment taxes. These unemployment taxes, however, are not imposed on your income when you own a sole proprietorship or partnership. FICA taxes are generally the same (in total) on the wages of a corporate employee/owner as would be the self-employment tax on the same amount of business income if you were a sole proprietor or a partner.

For certain types of unincorporated businesses, however, such as a firm whose income is from interest or real estate rentals, or both, there is no self-employment tax on the income. By incorporating such a firm, you would unnecessarily incur FICA (Social Security) taxes of 15.3% on your earnings from the business.

Personal Service Corporations

Certain kinds of corporations called qualified personal service corporations (QPSCs) are taxed at a flat rate of 35%, instead of the graduated tax rates listed above.[4] While it may not always be clear whether an incorporated service business is a QPSC, the IRS defines a QPSC by these characteristics:

- At least 95% of the value of its stock is held by employees or their estates or beneficiaries; and
- The employees perform services at least 95% of the time in the following fields: health, law, engineering, architecture, accounting, actuarial science, performing arts, or consulting.

Double Taxation of Corporate Earnings

Regular corporations, which are also called C corporations, have one major potential disadvantage that usually does not exist for other legal forms of doing business — the problem of potential double taxation of the earnings of the corporation. This problem arises because a C corporation must pay corporate income taxes on its taxable income. Then, the after-tax earnings may be subject to a second tax on either the individual stockholders, if the earnings are distributed as dividends, or as a corporate penalty tax, if the earnings are not distributed as dividends.

The main ways in which a corporation's earnings can be subject to double taxation are:

- Payment of taxable dividends — Shareholders will be taxed when the corporation pays dividends to them out of earnings that have already been taxed once at the corporate level. In this case, the shareholders would pay individual federal income taxes (plus state tax, in most states) on the dividends they receive. If, for example, the corporation has already paid tax at a marginal rate of 34% on its income, and individual federal income tax of roughly 40% is paid by the stockholders on the remaining 66% of corporate income that is distributed to them as dividends, then less than 40% of the profit earned by the corporation will end up in the owners' bank accounts after taxes. Even less would remain after taxes in a state that has corporate or individual income taxes, or both.

- Corporate accumulated earnings tax — Corporations that retain too much of their after-tax earnings, instead of paying out the earnings as dividends, risk being hit by the accumulated earnings tax. This tax rate can be up to 39.6% of the accumulated income.

- Certain other C corporations that are considered to be "personal holding companies" under the federal tax law are exempt from the accumulated earnings tax; however, they may instead be subject to a 39.6% personal holding company tax on their undistributed income that is derived from certain sources, such as rents, royalties, and interest or dividends received from stock investments.

- Even if a corporation avoids all of the above double taxation problems during its existence, double taxation may yet arise if the corporation is liquidated and either the value of the corporate assets or the stock is greater than the tax basis. In that case, the stockholders will usually have to pay capital gains taxes if the amount they receive in liquidation exceeds the tax basis of their shares of stock.

As a practical matter, few small incorporated businesses ever encounter actual double taxation, except when the corporation is liquidated. Most small corporations do not pay dividends, and there are many tax-planning approaches that will enable a company and its shareholders to avoid the accumulated earnings tax or personal holding company tax on their undistributed earnings.

See Section 8.9 for a discussion of various tax-planning techniques that will permit you to avoid the problems of potential double taxation listed above.

Income Splitting

By using a corporation, it may be possible to split your overall profit between two or more taxpayers so that none of the income gets taxed in the highest tax brackets. Thus, the total tax paid by the two taxpayers — you and your corporation — may be less than if all of the income were taxed to you, as in a sole proprietorship.

See Section 8.2 for a more detailed discussion of how income splitting can help reduce your income and estate taxes.

Fringe Benefit Plans

Federal and state tax laws permit you, as a corporate employer, to provide a number of different fringe benefits to employees on a tax-favored basis. These tax-favored fringe benefits include medical insurance plans, self-insured medical reimbursement plans, disability insurance, and group-term life insurance. An unincorporated business receives the same tax treatment for its employees, but not for its owners. In an unincorporated business, the payments made on behalf of the sole proprietor or partners for these fringe benefits are generally not deductible as expenses of the business, in contrast to fringe benefits paid for by a corporation for its shareholders/employees. So the tax benefits of employee fringe benefits, such as those listed above, are another reason for incorporating your business and becoming an employee of the corporation.

Note, however, that if your corporation is an S corporation, it will be treated much like a partnership for fringe benefit purposes, with regard to its shareholders who own 2% or more of its stock.[5] An exception to this partnership treatment of S corporation shareholders is for medical insurance premiums paid on their behalf, which can be deducted by the S corporation. However, the amount deducted by the corporation for medical insurance must be reported as taxable compensation income on the shareholder/employee's *Form W-2*, for income tax purposes,[6] but not for FICA (Social Security) tax purposes if the insurance plan covers employees generally.[7]

Unlike an unincorporated business, a corporation — other than an S corporation — can generally deduct the insurance premiums or other fringe benefit payments it makes on behalf of an employee who is an owner of the business, while the employee is not taxed on the value of the benefit provided. This is far more favorable than payments of salary to an employee, which are fully taxable.

The major types of fringe benefit plans, other than retirement plans, that allow for tax deductions to the corporation and no taxable income to the employee are discussed in more detail in Section 8.3.

Tax Break for Dividends Received by a Corporation

Another important tax advantage of a C corporation is that, in general, it can deduct 70% of the dividends it receives from stock investments from its federal taxable income.[8] This tax benefit, called the dividends received deduction, is discussed in more detail in Section 8.2.

Tax Break for Investing in Small Business Stock

The Clinton tax package that was enacted in August 1993 provides a major tax incentive for investing in the stock of certain small corporations. This incentive is not available for investments in unincorporated businesses or in stock of S corporations.

A noncorporate investor who purchases "qualified small business stock" after August 10, 1993 and holds it for five years or more will be allowed to exclude from his or her taxable income up to 50% of any capital gain reported on the sale of stock.[9] If the current maximum tax rate on capital gains remains at 28%, this would translate into a very low effective tax rate of only 14% on gains from qualified small business stock.

Qualified small business stock is stock of a C corporation that meets an active business test during the period the stock is held. Stock in a special entity, such as a Domestic International Sales Corporation (DISC), regulated investment company, or a real estate investment trust, is ineligible. In addition, the corporation must not have more than $50 million in gross assets before or immediately after the stock is issued to the investor.

To meet the active business test, a corporation must use at least 80% of its assets in the conduct of one or more qualified trades or businesses. Personal service firms, banks, finance or investment businesses, insurance companies, and farming businesses are not considered qualified trades or businesses; neither are companies in certain extractive industries, or in the hotel, motel, or restaurant businesses.

While this section has outlined a number of important tax advantages of incorporating a business, the picture is not all that one-sided. Some of the potential tax disadvantages of corporations are discussed in more detail in Section 8.9. Most of those disadvantages are not applicable if you elect S corporation status. Deciding whether to incorporate in this state or elsewhere is discussed in Section 9.12.

Corporate Income Tax Disadvantages

2.5 Advantages and Disadvantages of S Corporations

The first thing to understand about S corporations — formerly referred to as Subchapter S corporations — is they are just like any other corporation in terms of corporate law requirements, limited liability of shareholders, and all other corporate aspects, except regarding tax treatment. An S corporation is simply a regular corporation that meets certain requirements and which has elected to be treated somewhat like a partnership for federal income tax purposes. Most, but not all, states also allow this special tax treatment for S corporations. See Section 11.2 for a discussion of how S corporations are treated for tax purposes in this state.

Once a corporation has made an election with the IRS to be treated as an S corporation, its shareholders will generally report their share of the corporation's taxable income or loss on their individual tax returns. That is, the corporation "passes through" its income or loss and tax credits to the shareholders in proportion to their stock holdings in the corporation, much like a partnership.

The S corporation does not usually pay tax on any of its income.[10] Any domestic S corporation, however, must file *Form 1120S, U.S. Income Tax Return for an S Corporation*, regardless of any tax due. *Form 1120S* must be filed by March 15, if filing under a calendar-year basis, or the 15th day of the third month following the close of a fiscal year.

An S corporation must furnish a copy of *Schedule K-1, Shareholder's Share of Income, Credits, Deductions* to each shareholder. By not providing *Schedule K-1* before filing *Form 1120S*, the S corporation could incur penalties.

In certain instances, an S corporation may be subject to tax on "built-in gains." Built-in gains are untaxed gains on the assets of a corporation that would have been recognized as taxable if the assets had been sold at fair market value on the day a corporation became an S corporation.

Profits are deemed to be distributed to the shareholders on the last day of the corporation's tax year, whether or not the profits are actually distributed.[11] Thus, if profits of an S corporation are distributed as dividends, the distribution itself is ordinarily not taxable, so there is no double taxation of distributed profits.

The Clinton Deficit Reduction tax package enacted in August 1993 has made S corporations somewhat less attractive because it raised individual tax rates to a new maximum rate of 39.6%, up from 31%. In addition, the top corporate rate remains at 34%, except for corporations with more than ten million dollars of taxable income. These corporations now pay 35%. Shareholders of an S corporation may now pay individual income tax at a higher rate than would a C corporation in some income brackets and at a lower rate in other brackets. Thus, from a tax-rate standpoint, S corporations no longer enjoy a clear advantage over C corporations.

In addition, capital gains on sale of the stock of an S corporation will not qualify for the new 50% capital gain exclusion that is discussed in Section 2.4.

S Corporation Requirements

To qualify for S corporation treatment, your corporation must meet the following requirements:

- It must be a domestic corporation — that is, incorporated in the United States.[12]
- No shareholder can be a nonresident alien individual.[13]
- All of its shareholders must generally be individuals, although certain trusts, called Qualified Subchapter S Trusts and Grantor Trusts, may hold stock under certain circumstances. No shareholder can be a corporation or a partnership.[14]
- The corporation can have only one class of common stock and no preferred stock.[15]
- There cannot be more than 35 shareholders.[16] For this purpose, a husband and wife who are both stockholders will be counted as only one stockholder, whether or not they hold the stock in joint ownership.[17]
- The corporation cannot be a member of an affiliated group of corporations.[18] If it owns stock in a subsidiary that is considered an affiliate, it may not be able to qualify under the S corporation provisions.
- Less than 25% of the corporation's gross receipts during three successive tax years must be from passive sources, such as interest income, dividends, rent, royalties, or proceeds from the sale of securities.[19] The passive income limit does not apply at all for a brand new corporation or an existing corporation that has no accumulated earnings and profits when it elects S corporation status.[20]

Electing S Corporation Status

To become an S corporation, your company must meet the above requirements and file an election on *Form 2553* with the IRS. The election must be signed by all of the corporation's shareholders,[21] including your spouse, who may have a community property interest in stock that is in your name. The S corporation election must be filed during the first two months and 15 days of the corporation's tax year for which the election is to go into effect or at any time during the preceding tax year.[22]

Since a newly formed corporation that wants to start out as an S corporation does not have a preceding tax year, it has to file an election in the two-month and 15-day period after it is considered to have begun its first tax year. Its first tax year is considered to start when it issues stock to shareholders, acquires assets, or begins to do business, whichever occurs first. Filing of articles of incorporation with the secretary of state usually does not begin the first taxable year.

Care must be taken to file the election at the right time, which can be tricky, since it is sometimes difficult to determine when a corporation first begins to do business. There can be some horrendous tax consequences if you operate the corporation as though it were an S corporation, and the election is later determined to have been filed too early or too late.

Extreme care must also be taken if a regular C corporation elects to change over to S corporation status; this should not be done without consulting a competent tax adviser. A regular corporation that elects to become an S corporation will generally be subject to an eventual corporate-level tax on any built-in gains on its assets — assets with a value greater than their tax basis — if assets are sold for a gain within ten years.

Terminating an S Corporation Election

If it becomes desirable to revoke or terminate S corporation status after a few years, as is often the case, this can be done if shareholders owning more than half the stock sign and file a revocation form.[23] A revocation is effective for the tax year it is filed, if it is filed during the first two months and 15 days of that tax year.[24] If it is filed later in the year, it does not become effective until the next tax year.[25]

Doing anything, however, that causes the corporation to cease to qualify as an S corporation — such as selling stock to a corporate shareholder — will also terminate the election, effective on the first day after the corporation ceases to qualify as an S corporation. In that case, the company must file two short-period tax returns for the year, the first — up to the date it ceased to qualify — as an S corporation, the second as a regular taxable corporation.

Once a corporation terminates an S corporation election, it cannot re-elect S corporation status for five years, unless it obtains the consent of the IRS.[26]

Reasons for Electing S Corporation Status

For a corporation, electing S corporation status can be very advantageous in some instances, and less so, or even disadvantageous in other situations. An S corporation election should not be made without the advice and assistance of a tax professional, since it is a very complex and technical area of the tax law.

Electing S corporation treatment for a corporation is usually most favorable in these types of situations:

- Where it is expected that the corporation will experience losses for the initial year or years of doing business and where the shareholders will have income from other sources that the "passed through" losses can shelter from tax. If S corporation losses are passive losses — such as losses from real estate investments — they can only be used to offset other passive activity income, except for certain shareholders who are real estate professionals.

- Where, because of the low tax brackets the shareholders are in, there will be tax savings if the anticipated profits of the corporation are passed through to them rather than being taxed at corporate tax rates.

- Where the nature of the corporation's business is such that the corporation does not need to retain a major portion of profits in the business. In this case, all or most of the profits can be distributed as dividends without the double taxation that would occur if no S corporation election were in effect.

- Where a corporation is in danger of incurring an accumulated earnings penalty tax for failure to pay out its profits as dividends.

It will often be advantageous for your corporation to operate as an S corporation in its early years, when losses can be passed through to shareholders, or when income is not so great as to push the shareholders into higher tax brackets. Also, the nontax advantage of being incorporated and protected from personal liability if the business fails is generally most important during the early years of operation, when the risk of failure is highest.

Many businesses initially start off as S corporations, obtaining the advantage of limited liability while being taxed much like an unincorporated business. Later, when or if the profit from the business becomes very substantial, the S corporation election can be terminated, and the C corporation can be used to split income between the corporation and its stockholder/employees.

Disadvantages of S Corporation Election

While there are some significant advantages to operating as an S corporation, the S corporation election is frequently not advisable under some circumstances. Some of the possible disadvantages of operating your business in the form of an S corporation are:

- The change to S corporation status may eventually result in a large corporate-level tax on built-in gains or an immediate last in, first out (LIFO) recapture tax.

- The tax law regarding S corporations is very complex and you should expect to pay fairly substantial additional legal or accounting fees to your tax adviser, compared to what would be necessary with a regular corporation.

- S corporations are now treated almost exactly like regular corporations with respect to pension and profit-sharing plans. One important difference remains; any employee who owns 5% or more of the stock and participates in the S corporation's pension or profit-sharing plan is prohibited from borrowing from the plan, unlike a participant in a regular corporation's retirement plan.[27]

- Certain built-in gains of an S corporation may be taxed to the corporation and the shareholder for federal tax purposes.[28]

- Fringe benefit payments for medical, disability, and group-term life insurance for 2% shareholders are deductible, to the corporation, but are taxable to the shareholder/employee.[29]

- Unlike many regular corporations, very few newly electing S corporations may now have a fiscal tax year that ends earlier than September.[30]

For your convenience, a sample of *Form 2553, Election by a Small Business Corporation*, and a summary of key characteristics regarding business organization forms are provided at the end of this chapter.

2.6 Advantages and Disadvantages of Limited Liability Companies

The S corporation and the limited partnership may soon become endangered species due to the appearance of a new form of legal entity that has a number of advantages over both and that is proliferating across the country. This new type of entity is called a limited liability company (LLC). An LLC closely resembles and is taxed as a partnership, but it offers the benefit of limited liability like corporations. It is also similar to a limited partnership, except that in an LLC, all partners have the benefit of limited liability.

In 1988, the IRS concluded in Revenue Ruling 88-76 that a Wyoming limited liability company could be classified as a partnership for federal income tax purposes, despite its limited liability, because it lacked continuity of life. Under Wyoming law, LLCs have to terminate in a specified period of years, usually 30 years or less.

Another reason for this classification is because interests in the LLC were not freely transferable. This ruling was highly favorable, from a taxpayer's standpoint, because LLCs offer the corporate benefits of limited liability, while retaining the flexible flow-through tax treatment of a partnership. This is generally preferable even to an S corporation for income tax purposes.

Because this favorable IRS ruling opened the floodgates, more than four-fifths of the states have followed Wyoming's lead in adopting similar LLC laws, and approximately 45 states will probably have adopted LLC laws by early 1995.

Despite the obvious advantages of LLCs, do not be in a rush to set one up, even if you are located in one of the states that has adopted a limited liability company law. At present, if you set up an LLC in State X that allows LLCs and you do business in State Y, which does not, your LLC may not provide any limited liability protection from creditors in State Y. This is a severe risk, and one you won't face if your business is incorporated.

Under the LLC laws in almost every state, an LLC must have at least two owners, and thus is not a viable choice for a sole proprietor who wishes to change to a business entity that offers limited liability. Even if you were to create a single-owner LLC under the laws of a state that permits one-person LLCs — Arkansas, for example, permits such LLCs — the tax treatment is unclear at present. Every favorable IRS tax ruling to date on LLCs has involved a multi-owner LLC that the IRS "blessed" as being the tax equivalent of a partnership. A one-person LLC is clearly not like a partnership, so unless or until the IRS says such, an LLC is taxable as a sole proprietorship, and setting one up will have very uncertain tax consequences. Unless you want to become a pioneer, it may be prudent to shy away from creating a one-person LLC until the IRS rules on this issue. This brings to mind the old saying about how to spot a pioneer in a crowd — the pioneers are always the ones with the arrows in their backs.

In most states, LLCs can engage in any business that is permissible for a corporation to engage in, with certain limited exceptions, including professions. However, a number of states that recognize LLCs do not yet allow professional LLCs for physicians, attorneys, or other such professionals.

Another potential drawback is that a subcommittee of the U.S. House Ways and Means Committee is already looking into the possibility of enacting federal legislation that would cause LLCs to be taxed as corporations in order to prevent the loss of significant federal tax revenues. Such legislation, if enacted, would defeat the whole purpose of setting up an LLC and could even leave you in a considerable tax predicament if you put your business into an LLC and the law changed subsequently. You might even have to pay a large capital gains tax if you then decided to liquidate the LLC. Extreme caution is advised before adopting LLC status. Consult a good tax adviser before you even consider setting up an LLC, despite their obvious attractions. See Chapter 11 for more specific information on LLCs in this state.

Endnotes

1. I.R.C. § 162(l).
2. I.R.C. §§ 444 and 7519.
3. I.R.C. § 6050K.
4. I.R.C. § 11(b)(2).
5. I.R.C. § 1372(a).
6. Rev. Rul. 91-26, 1991-1 C.B. 184.
7. I.R.S. Ann. 92-16, 1992-5 I.R.B. 53.
8. I.R.C. § 243(a).
9. I.R.C. § 1202.
10. I.R.C. § 1374.
11. I.R.C. § 1366.
12. I.R.C. § 1361(b).
13. I.R.C. § 1361(b)(1)(C).
14. I.R.C. § 1361(b)(1)(B).
15. I.R.C. § 1361(b)(1)(D).
16. I.R.C. § 1361(b)(1)(A).
17. I.R.C. § 1361(c).
18. I.R.C. § 1361(b)(2)(A).
19. I.R.C. § 1362(d)(3).
20. I.R.C. § 1362(d)(3)(B).
21. I.R.C. § 1362(a)(2).
22. I.R.C. § 1362(b).
23. I.R.C. § 1362(d)(1)(B).
24. I.R.C. § 1362(d)(1)(C)(i).
25. I.R.C. § 1362(d)(i)(C)(ii).
26. I.R.C. § 1362(g).
27. I.R.C. § 4975(d).
28. I.R.C. § 1374(a).
29. Rev. Rul. 91-26, 1991-1 C.B. 184.
30. I.R.C. § 1378(a).
31. I.R.C. § 162(1).

Key Characteristics of the Various Legal Forms of Business Organization – Summary

	Proprietorship	General or Limited Partnership
Simplicity in Operation and Formation	Simplest to establish and operate.	Relatively simple and informal, except that a limited partnership must have a written agreement.
Liability for Debts, Taxes, and Other Claims	Owner has unlimited personal liability.	General partners have unlimited personal liability; limited partners are only at risk to the extent of their investment.
Federal Income Taxation of Business Profits	Taxed to the owner at individual tax rates of up to 39.6% or more, depending on exemptions and deductions which may phase out.	Taxed to partners at their individual tax rates.
Double Taxation if Profits Withdrawn from Business	No.	No.
Deduction of Losses by Owners	Yes. May be subject to "passive loss" restrictions.	Yes. But limited partner's deductions cannot exceed amount invested as a limited partner — except for real estate, in some instances. Losses are generally restricted by the "passive loss" rules.
Social Security Tax on Earnings of Owner from Business	15.3% of owner's self-employment earnings in 1994 on first $60,600 of income, plus 2.9% on earnings of more than $60,600, half of which is now deductible for income tax purposes.	15.3% of each partner's share of self-employment earnings from the business in 1994 on up to $60,600 in earnings are taxed, plus 2.9% tax on earnings over $60,600. Half of tax is deductible for income tax.
Unemployment Taxes on Earnings of Owner from Business	None.	None.
Retirement Plans	Keogh plan. Deductions, other features now generally the same as for corporate pension and profit-sharing plans. But proprietor cannot borrow from Keogh Plan.	Keogh plan. Same as for proprietorships. A 10% partner cannot borrow from Keogh Plan.
Tax Treatment of Medical, Disability, and Group-Term Life Insurance on Owners	Not deductible, except part of medical expenses may be an itemized deduction on owner's tax return, including medical insurance premiums. However, 25% of medical insurance on an owner is allowed as a deduction from adjusted gross income — at least until December 31, 1993.[31]	Not deductible, except part of medical expenses may be an itemized deduction on owner's tax return, including medical insurance premiums. However, 25% of medical insurance on an owner is allowed as a deduction from adjusted gross income — at least until December 31, 1993.
Taxation of Dividends Received on Investments	Dividends received on stock investments are fully taxable to owner.	Dividends taxable to individual partners. See proprietorship.

Limited Liability Company	Regular Corporation	S Corporation
Generally similar to a partnership, but required to file articles of organization.	Requires most formality in establishment and operation.	Same as a regular corporation but requires close oversight by a tax adviser (an additional cost).
Members are generally not liable for an LLC's debts, but they often have to guarantee loans, as a practical matter, which is similar to a corporation.	Stockholders are not generally liable for corporate debts, but often have to guarantee loans, as a practical matter, if the corporation borrows money. Also, corporate officers may be liable to the IRS for failure to withhold and pay withholding taxes on employees' wages.	Stockholders are not generally liable for corporate debts, but often have to guarantee loans, as a practical matter, if the corporation borrows money. Also, corporate officers may be liable to the IRS for failure to withhold and pay withholding taxes on employees' wages.
Taxed to owners at their individual tax rates, unless the IRS treats the LLC as a corporation.	Taxed to the corporation, at rates higher than those of individuals — maximum of 34% or 39% in 1993, except for very large corporations.	Taxed to individual owners at their individual rates — certain gains are taxable to the corporation as well.
No, unless the LLC is treated as a corporation.	Yes, but not on reasonable compensation paid to owners who are employees of the corporation.	No, in general.
Yes, generally, if treated as a partnership by IRS. No, if treated as a corporation by IRS.	No. Corporation must carry over initial losses to offset future profits, if any.	Yes, in general, for federal tax purposes. But not for state tax purposes in all states. Loss for a shareholder limited to investment in stock plus amount loaned to the corporation. Losses may be subject to "passive loss" restrictions.
Not clear yet. Probably same as for a partnership, if treated as partnership by IRS. Same as a corporation, if the LLC is treated as a corporation.	Owner/employee of corporation pays 7.65% on his or her salary and corporation pays 7.65%. Total Social Security (FICA) tax on employer and employee is 15.3% of employee's first $60,600 of wages (in 1994). Employee and corporation each pay 1.45% on wages above $60,600.	Owner/employee of corporation pays 7.65% on his or her salary and corporation pays 7.65%. Total Social Security (FICA) tax on employer and employee is 15.3% of employee's first $60,600 of wages (in 1994). Employee and corporation each pay 1.45% on wages above $60,600.
Not clear yet, but probably none, if treated as a partnership for income tax purposes by IRS.	Yes. State and federal unemployment taxes apply to salaries paid to owners.	Yes. State and federal unemployment taxes apply to salaries paid to owners.
Not clear yet, but probably same as a partnership, if treated as a partnership by IRS.	Corporate retirement plans are no longer significantly better than Keogh plans. Deduction limits are same now as for Keogh, but participants can borrow from plan.	Plans now essentially identical to regular corporate retirement plans, except that shareholder/employee (5% shareholder) of S corporation cannot borrow from plan.
Not clear yet, but probably same as a partnership, if treated as a partnership by IRS.	Corporations may be allowed to deduct corporation medical insurance premium or reimbursements paid under medical reimbursement plan. Generally not taxable to the employee, even if employee is an owner. Similar treatment for disability and group-term life insurance plans.	Fringe benefits for 2% shareholders are deductible by corporation, but must be included in income of the shareholder who may be allowed to deduct 25% of medical insurance from adjusted gross income.
Dividends taxable to individual members, if the LLC is treated as a partnership.	Dividends are taxable to the corporation. However, 70% of the dividends received are generally free of federal income tax (unless stock is purchased with borrowed money), an important tax advantage.	Dividends taxable to individual shareholders of the S corporation, as in the case of a partnership.

Instructions for Form 2553: Sample

Department of the Treasury
Internal Revenue Service

Instructions for Form 2553
(Revised September 1993)
Election by a Small Business Corporation
Section references are to the Internal Revenue Code unless otherwise noted.

Paperwork Reduction Act Notice.—We ask for the information on this form to carry out the Internal Revenue laws of the United States. You are required to give us the information. We need it to ensure that you are complying with these laws and to allow us to figure and collect the right amount of tax.

The time needed to complete and file this form will vary depending on individual circumstances. The estimated average time is:

Recordkeeping	6 hr., 13 min.
Learning about the law or the form	2 hr., 59 min.
Preparing, copying, assembling, and sending the form to the IRS	3 hr., 13 min.

If you have comments concerning the accuracy of these time estimates or suggestions for making this form more simple, we would be happy to hear from you. You can write to both the **Internal Revenue Service**, Attention: Reports Clearance Officer, T:FP, Washington, DC 20224; and the **Office of Management and Budget**, Paperwork Reduction Project (1545-0146), Washington, DC 20503. **DO NOT** send the tax form to either of these offices. Instead, see **Where To File** below.

General Instructions

Purpose.—To elect to be an "S corporation," a corporation must file Form 2553. The election permits the income of the S corporation to be taxed to the shareholders of the corporation rather than to the corporation itself, except as provided in Subchapter S of the Code. For more information, get **Pub. 589**, Tax Information on S Corporations.

Who May Elect.—A corporation may elect to be an S corporation only if it meets **all** of the following tests:

1. It is a domestic corporation.

2. It has no more than 35 shareholders. A husband and wife (and their estates) are treated as one shareholder for this requirement. All other persons are treated as separate shareholders.

3. It has only individuals, estates, or certain trusts as shareholders. See the instructions for Part III regarding qualified subchapter S trusts.

4. It has no nonresident alien shareholders.

5. It has only one class of stock (disregarding differences in voting rights). Generally, a corporation is treated as having only one class of stock if all outstanding shares of the corporation's stock confer identical rights to distribution and liquidation

proceeds. See Regulations section 1.1361-1(l) for more details.

6. It is not one of the following ineligible corporations:

   a. A corporation that owns 80% or more of the stock of another corporation, unless the other corporation has not begun business and has no gross income;

   b. A bank or thrift institution;

   c. An insurance company subject to tax under the special rules of Subchapter L of the Code;

   d. A corporation that has elected to be treated as a possessions corporation under section 936; or

   e. A domestic international sales corporation (DISC) or former DISC.

7. It has a permitted tax year as required by section 1378 or makes a section 444 election to have a tax year other than a permitted tax year. Section 1378 defines a permitted tax year as a tax year ending December 31, or any other tax year for which the corporation establishes a business purpose to the satisfaction of the IRS. See Part II for details on requesting a fiscal tax year based on a business purpose or on making a section 444 election.

8. Each shareholder consents as explained in the instructions for Column K.

See sections 1361, 1362, and 1378 for additional information on the above tests.

Where To File.—File this election with the Internal Revenue Service Center listed below.

If the corporation's principal business, office, or agency is located in ▼	Use the following Internal Revenue Service Center address ▼
New Jersey, New York (New York City and counties of Nassau, Rockland, Suffolk, and Westchester)	Holtsville, NY 00501
New York (all other counties), Connecticut, Maine, Massachusetts, New Hampshire, Rhode Island, Vermont	Andover, MA 05501
Illinois, Iowa, Minnesota, Missouri, Wisconsin	Kansas City, MO 64999
Delaware, District of Columbia, Maryland, Pennsylvania, Virginia	Philadelphia, PA 19255
Florida, Georgia, South Carolina	Atlanta, GA 39901
Indiana, Kentucky, Michigan, Ohio, West Virginia	Cincinnati, OH 45999
Kansas, New Mexico, Oklahoma, Texas	Austin, TX 73301

Alaska, Arizona, California (counties of Alpine, Amador, Butte, Calaveras, Colusa, Contra Costa, Del Norte, El Dorado, Glenn, Humboldt, Lake, Lassen, Marin, Mendocino, Modoc, Napa, Nevada, Placer, Plumas, Sacramento, San Joaquin, Shasta, Sierra, Siskiyou, Solano, Sonoma, Sutter, Tehama, Trinity, Yolo, and Yuba), Colorado, Idaho, Montana, Nebraska, Nevada, North Dakota, Oregon, South Dakota, Utah, Washington, Wyoming	Ogden, UT 84201
California (all other counties), Hawaii	Fresno, CA 93888
Alabama, Arkansas, Louisiana, Mississippi, North Carolina, Tennessee	Memphis, TN 37501

When To Make the Election.—Complete and file Form 2553 **(a)** at any time before the 16th day of the third month of the tax year, if filed during the tax year the election is to take effect, or **(b)** at any time during the preceding tax year. An election made no later than 2 months and 15 days after the beginning of a tax year that is less than 2½ months long is treated as timely made for that tax year. An election made after the 15th day of the third month but before the end of the tax year is effective for the next year. For example, if a calendar tax year corporation makes the election in April 1994, it is effective for the corporation's 1995 calendar tax year. See section 1362(b) for more information.

Acceptance or Nonacceptance of Election.—The Service Center will notify the corporation if its election is accepted and when it will take effect. The corporation will also be notified if its election is not accepted. The corporation should generally receive a determination on its election within 60 days after it has filed Form 2553. If box Q1 in Part II is checked on page 2, the corporation will receive a ruling letter from the IRS in Washington, DC, that either approves or denies the selected tax year. When box Q1 is checked, it will generally take an additional 90 days for the Form 2553 to be accepted.

Do not file Form 1120S until the corporation is notified that its election has been accepted. If the corporation is now required to file **Form 1120**, U.S. Corporation Income Tax Return, or any other applicable tax return, continue filing it until the election takes effect.

Care should be exercised to ensure that the IRS receives the election. If the corporation is not notified of acceptance or nonacceptance of its election within 3 months

Cat. No. 49978N

Instructions for Form 2553: Sample (continued)

of date of filing (date mailed), or within 6 months if box Q1 is checked, please take follow-up action by corresponding with the Service Center where the corporation filed the election. If the IRS questions whether Form 2553 was filed, an acceptable proof of filing is: **(a)** certified or registered mail receipt (timely filed); **(b)** Form 2553 with accepted stamp; **(c)** Form 2553 with stamped IRS received date; or **(d)** IRS letter stating that Form 2553 has been accepted.

End of Election.— Once the election is made, it stays in effect for all years until it is terminated. During the 5 years after the election is terminated under section 1362(d), the corporation (or a successor corporation) can make another election on Form 2553 only with IRS consent. See Regulations section 1.1362-5 for more details.

Specific Instructions

Part I

Part I must be completed by all corporations.

Name and Address of Corporation.— Enter the true corporate name as set forth in the corporate charter or other legal document creating it. If the corporation's mailing address is the same as someone else's, such as a shareholder's, please enter "c/o" and this person's name following the name of the corporation. Include the suite, room, or other unit number after the street address. If the Post Office does not deliver to the street address and the corporation has a P.O. box, show the box number instead of the street address. If the corporation changed its name or address after applying for its EIN, be sure to check the box in item G of Part I.

Item A. Employer Identification Number.— If the corporation has applied for an employer identification number (EIN) but has not received it, enter "applied for." If the corporation does not have an EIN, it should apply for one on **Form SS-4**, Application for Employer Identification Number, available from most IRS and Social Security Administration offices.

Item D. Effective Date of Election.— Enter the beginning effective date (month, day, year) of the tax year requested for the S corporation. Generally, this will be the beginning date of the tax year for which the ending effective date is required to be shown in item I, Part I. For a new corporation (first year the corporation exists) it will generally be the date required to be shown in item H, Part I. The tax year of a new corporation starts on the date that it has shareholders, acquires assets, or begins doing business, whichever happens first. If the effective date for item D for a newly formed corporation is later than the date in item H, the corporation should file Form 1120 or Form 1120-A, for the tax period between these dates.

Column K. Shareholders' Consent Statement.— Each shareholder who owns (or is deemed to own) stock at the time the election is made must consent to the election. If the election is made during the corporation's tax year for which it first takes effect, any person who held stock at any time during the part of that year that occurs before the election is made, must consent to the election, even though the person may have sold or transferred his or her stock before the

election is made. Each shareholder consents by signing and dating in column K or signing and dating a separate consent statement described below.

An election made during the first 2½ months of the tax year is effective for the following tax year if any person who held stock in the corporation during the part of the tax year before the election was made, and who did not hold stock at the time the election was made, did not consent to the election.

If a husband and wife have a community interest in the stock or in the income from it, both must consent. Each tenant in common, joint tenant, and tenant by the entirety also must consent.

A minor's consent is made by the minor or the legal representative of the minor, or by a natural or adoptive parent of the minor if no legal representative has been appointed.

The consent of an estate is made by an executor or administrator.

If stock is owned by a trust that is a qualified shareholder, the deemed owner of the trust must consent. See section 1361(c)(2) for details regarding qualified trusts that may be shareholders and rules on determining who is the deemed owner of the trust.

Continuation sheet or separate consent statement.— If you need a continuation sheet or use a separate consent statement, attach it to Form 2553. The separate consent statement must contain the name, address, and employer identification number of the corporation and the shareholder information requested in columns J through N of Part I.

If you want, you may combine all the shareholders' consents in one statement.

Column L.— Enter the number of shares of stock each shareholder owns and the dates the stock was acquired. If the election is made during the corporation's tax year for which it first takes effect, do not list the shares of stock for those shareholders who sold or transferred all of their stock before the election was made. However, these shareholders must still consent to the election for it to be effective for the tax year.

Column M.— Enter the social security number of each shareholder who is an individual. Enter the employer identification number of each shareholder that is an estate or a qualified trust.

Column N.— Enter the month and day that each shareholder's tax year ends. If a shareholder is changing his or her tax year, enter the tax year the shareholder is changing to, and attach an explanation indicating the present tax year and the basis for the change (e.g., automatic revenue procedure or letter ruling request).

If the election is made during the corporation's tax year for which it first takes effect, you do not have to enter the tax year of any shareholder who sold or transferred all of his or her stock before the election was made.

Signature.— Form 2553 must be signed by the president, treasurer, assistant treasurer, chief accounting officer, or other corporate officer (such as tax officer) authorized to sign.

Part II

Complete Part II if you selected a tax year ending on any date other than December 31

(other than a 52-53-week tax year ending with reference to the month of December).

Box P1.— Attach a statement showing separately for each month the amount of gross receipts for the most recent 47 months as required by section 4.03(3) of Revenue Procedure 87-32, 1987-2 C.B. 396. A corporation that does not have a 47-month period of gross receipts cannot establish a natural business year under section 4.01(1).

Box Q1.— For examples of an acceptable business purpose for requesting a fiscal tax year, see Revenue Ruling 87-57, 1987-2 C.B. 117.

In addition to a statement showing the business purpose for the requested fiscal year, you must attach the other information necessary to meet the ruling request requirements of Revenue Procedure 93-1, 1993-1 I.R.B. 10 (updated annually). Also attach a statement that shows separately the amount of gross receipts from sales or services (and inventory costs, if applicable) for each of the 36 months preceding the effective date of the election to be an S corporation. If the corporation has been in existence for fewer than 36 months, submit figures for the period of existence.

If you check box Q1, you must also pay a user fee of $200 (subject to change). Do not pay the fee when filing Form 2553. The Service Center will send Form 2553 to the IRS in Washington, DC, who, in turn, will notify the corporation that the fee is due. See Revenue Procedure 93-23, 1993-19 I.R.B. 6.

Box Q2.— If the corporation makes a back-up section 444 election for which it is qualified, then the election must be exercised in the event the business purpose request is not approved. Under certain circumstances, the tax year requested under the back-up section 444 election may be different than the tax year requested under business purpose. See **Form 8716**, Election To Have a Tax Year Other Than a Required Tax Year, for details on making a back-up section 444 election.

Boxes Q2 and R2.— If the corporation is not qualified to make the section 444 election after making the item Q2 back-up section 444 election or indicating its intention to make the election in item R1, and therefore it later files a calendar year return, it should write "Section 444 Election Not Made" in the top left corner of the 1st calendar year Form 1120S it files.

Part III

Certain Qualified Subchapter S Trusts (QSSTs) may make the QSST election required by section 1361(d)(2) in Part III. Part III may be used to make the QSST election only if corporate stock has been transferred to the trust on or before the date on which the corporation makes its election to be an S corporation. However, a statement can be used in lieu of Part III to make the election.

Note: *Part III may be used only in conjunction with making the Part I election (i.e., Form 2553 cannot be filed with only Part III completed).*

The deemed owner of the QSST must also consent to the S corporation election in column K, page 1, of Form 2553. See section 1361(c)(2).

Page 2   ✪ *Printed on recycled paper*   *U.S. Government Printing Office: 1993 — 301-628/80221

Form 2553 – Election by a Small Business Corporation: Sample

Form **2553** (Rev. September 1993) Department of the Treasury Internal Revenue Service	**Election by a Small Business Corporation** (Under section 1362 of the Internal Revenue Code) ▶ For Paperwork Reduction Act Notice, see page 1 of instructions. ▶ See separate instructions.	OMB No. 1545-0146 Expires 8-31-96

Notes:
1. *This election, to be an "S corporation," can be accepted only if all the tests are met under **Who May Elect** on page 1 of the instructions; all signatures in Parts I and III are originals (no photocopies); and the exact name and address of the corporation and other required form information are provided.*
2. *Do not file **Form 1120S**, U.S. Income Tax Return for an S Corporation, until you are notified that your election is accepted.*

Part I   Election Information

Please Type or Print	Name of corporation (see instructions)	**A** Employer identification number (EIN)
	Number, street, and room or suite no. (If a P.O. box, see instructions.)	**B** Date incorporated
	City or town, state, and ZIP code	**C** State of incorporation

D Election is to be effective for tax year beginning (month, day, year) . . . . ▶ _____ / _____ / _____

E Name and title of officer or legal representative who the IRS may call for more information

F Telephone number of officer or legal representative (_____) _____

G If the corporation changed its name or address after applying for the EIN shown in **A**, check this box . . . . ▶ ☐

H If this election takes effect for the first tax year the corporation exists, enter month, day, and year of the **earliest** of the following: (1) date the corporation first had shareholders, (2) date the corporation first had assets, or (3) date the corporation began doing business . . . . ▶ _____ / _____ / _____

I Selected tax year: Annual return will be filed for tax year ending (month and day) ▶ . . . .

If the tax year ends on any date other than December 31, except for an automatic 52-53-week tax year ending with reference to the month of December, you **must** complete Part II on the back. If the date you enter is the ending date of an automatic 52-53-week tax year, write "52-53-week year" to the right of the date. See Temporary Regulations section 1.441-2T(e)(3).

J Name and address of each shareholder, shareholder's spouse having a community property interest in the corporation's stock, and each tenant in common, joint tenant, and tenant by the entirety. (A husband and wife (and their estates) are counted as one shareholder in determining the number of shareholders without regard to the manner in which the stock is owned.)	**K** Shareholders' Consent Statement. Under penalties of perjury, we declare that we consent to the election of the above-named corporation to be an "S corporation" under section 1362(a) and that we have examined this consent statement, including accompanying schedules and statements, and to the best of our knowledge and belief, it is true, correct, and complete. (Shareholders sign and date below.)*		**L** Stock owned		**M** Social security number or employer identification number (see instructions)	**N** Share-holder's tax year ends (month and day)
	Signature	Date	Number of shares	Dates acquired		

*For this election to be valid, the consent of each shareholder, shareholder's spouse having a community property interest in the corporation's stock, and each tenant in common, joint tenant, and tenant by the entirety must either appear above or be attached to this form. (See instructions for Column K if a continuation sheet or a separate consent statement is needed.)

Under penalties of perjury, I declare that I have examined this election, including accompanying schedules and statements, and to the best of my knowledge and belief, it is true, correct, and complete.

Signature of officer ▶ _____   Title ▶ _____   Date ▶ _____

See Parts II and III on back.   Cat. No. 18629R   Form **2553** (Rev. 9-93)

Form 2553 – Election by a Small Business Corporation: Sample (continued)

Form 2553 (Rev. 9-93) Page **2**

Part II Selection of Fiscal Tax Year (All corporations using this part must complete item O and one of items P, Q, or R.)

O Check the applicable box below to indicate whether the corporation is:

1. ☐ A new corporation adopting the tax year entered in item I, Part I.
2. ☐ An existing corporation retaining the tax year entered in item I, Part I.
3. ☐ An existing corporation changing to the tax year entered in item I, Part I.

P Complete item P if the corporation is using the expeditious approval provisions of Revenue Procedure 87-32, 1987-2 C.B. 396, to request: **(1)** a natural business year (as defined in section 4.01(1) of Rev. Proc. 87-32), or **(2)** a year that satisfies the ownership tax year test in section 4.01(2) of Rev. Proc. 87-32. Check the applicable box below to indicate the representation statement the corporation is making as required under section 4 of Rev. Proc. 87-32.

1. Natural Business Year ► ☐ I represent that the corporation is retaining or changing to a tax year that coincides with its natural business year as defined in section 4.01(1) of Rev. Proc. 87-32 and as verified by its satisfaction of the requirements of section 4.02(1) of Rev. Proc. 87-32. In addition, if the corporation is changing to a natural business year as defined in section 4.01(1), I further represent that such tax year results in less deferral of income to the owners than the corporation's present tax year. I also represent that the corporation is not described in section 3.01(2) of Rev. Proc. 87-32. (See instructions for additional information that must be attached.)

2. Ownership Tax Year ► ☐ I represent that shareholders holding more than half of the shares of the stock (as of the first day of the tax year to which the request relates) of the corporation have the same tax year or are concurrently changing to the tax year that the corporation adopts, retains, or changes to per item I, Part I. I also represent that the corporation is not described in section 3.01(2) of Rev. Proc. 87-32.

Note: *If you do not use item P and the corporation wants a fiscal tax year, complete either item Q or R below. Item Q is used to request a fiscal tax year based on a business purpose and to make a back-up section 444 election. Item R is used to make a regular section 444 election.*

Q Business Purpose—To request a fiscal tax year based on a business purpose, you must check box Q1 and pay a user fee. See instructions for details. You may also check box Q2 and/or box Q3.

1. Check here ► ☐ if the fiscal year entered in item I, Part I, is requested under the provisions of section 6.03 of Rev. Proc. 87-32. Attach to Form 2553 a statement showing the business purpose for the requested fiscal year. See instructions for additional information that must be attached.

2. Check here ► ☐ to show that the corporation intends to make a back-up section 444 election in the event the corporation's business purpose request is not approved by the IRS. (See instructions for more information.)

3. Check here ► ☐ to show that the corporation agrees to adopt or change to a tax year ending December 31 if necessary for the IRS to accept this election for S corporation status in the event: (1) the corporation's business purpose request is not approved and the corporation makes a back-up section 444 election, but is ultimately not qualified to make a section 444 election, or (2) the corporation's business purpose request is not approved and the corporation did not make a back-up section 444 election.

R Section 444 Election—To make a section 444 election, you must check box R1 and you may also check box R2.

1. Check here ► ☐ to show the corporation will make, if qualified, a section 444 election to have the fiscal tax year shown in item I, Part I. To make the election, you must complete **Form 8716**, Election To Have a Tax Year Other Than a Required Tax Year, and either attach it to Form 2553 or file it separately.

2. Check here ► ☐ to show that the corporation agrees to adopt or change to a tax year ending December 31 if necessary for the IRS to accept this election for S corporation status in the event the corporation is ultimately not qualified to make a section 444 election.

Part III Qualified Subchapter S Trust (QSST) Election Under Section 1361(d)(2)**

Income beneficiary's name and address	Social security number
Trust's name and address	Employer identification number

Date on which stock of the corporation was transferred to the trust (month, day, year) . . . . ► / /

In order for the trust named above to be a QSST and thus a qualifying shareholder of the S corporation for which this Form 2553 is filed, I hereby make the election under section 1361(d)(2). Under penalties of perjury, I certify that the trust meets the definitional requirements of section 1361(d)(3) and that all other information provided in Part III is true, correct, and complete.

_____   _____
Signature of income beneficiary or signature and title of legal representative or other qualified person making the election   Date

**Use of Part III to make the QSST election may be made only if stock of the corporation has been transferred to the trust on or before the date on which the corporation makes its election to be an S corporation. The QSST election must be made and filed separately if stock of the corporation is transferred to the trust after the date on which the corporation makes the S election.

✪ *Printed on recycled paper*   *U.S. Government Printing Office: 1993 — 301-628/80216

Notes

Chapter 3

Buying an Existing Business

Trust in Allah. But always tie your camel.

— Arab proverb

3.1 General Considerations

Obviously, it may not be necessary for you to build your business from
the ground up. If you wish to go into a particular type of business, you
may find an appropriate existing business that is for sale. Buying an
existing business can have considerable advantages over starting one
from scratch, and one of the most important of these is the chance to start
out with an established customer base. It is also sometimes possible to
have the seller stay on as an employee or consultant for a transitional
period to help you become familiar with the operation of the business.

Other advantages of purchasing a going business include:

- You may be able to take a regular draw or salary right from the start, if
it is a profitable operation. This is usually not the case in a start-up
operation, which typically starts off losing money.

- Your risk is frequently less when you buy an established, profitable
business. You know that it has a viable market if it is already profitable.
Your main risk would be that something would change after you
acquire the business, such as new competition or product obsolescence,
and this would adversely affect your business. Another risk is that you
will mismanage the business.

- Getting started is simpler. By buying an established business, you can
focus your attention on giving good service and operating profitably.
Since most facilities, operating systems, and employees will already
be in place, your efforts will not be diluted by remodeling the
premises, trying to hire employees, setting up accounting systems,

acquiring initial inventory, and the like. With an existing business, in most cases, you should be able to step right into an operation that has already been established by someone else.

While there are some definite advantages to buying an established business, as compared to starting a new business, it can also be a lot more complicated and involves many potential pitfalls that you must avoid. The watchword in buying any kind of business should be *caveat emptor* — let the buyer beware.

Because the process of buying and selling businesses is very complicated even for experts, do not attempt it without retaining the services of a reliable attorney and, usually, a good accountant. Even skilled professionals, however, can generally only protect you from certain legal, financial, or tax pitfalls that arise in connection with the purchase of a business. Many of the potential problems that would not become obvious until it is too late can only be spotted in advance, if at all, by the exercise of your good judgment and as a result of your doing the necessary homework. Important pitfalls you should look out for in connection with buying an existing business are discussed in Section 3.3.

3.2 Finding a Business for Sale

How do you go about finding a business that is for sale? You have a number of ways to approach the problem, none of which are ideal, so you will probably want to use two or more of the approaches discussed below to find and buy an existing business.

Advertisements

The business opportunities section of your local newspaper, regional magazine, or trade association journal can be a major source of leads to businesses that are for sale. Such ads often do not tell you very much about the nature of the business, but at least they can be a starting point in your search. In many cases, the ads will have been placed by a business broker rather than the owner. The business broker will often be representing people who are seeking to sell their businesses.

Business Brokers and Realtors

Business brokers and realtors can be excellent sources in your search for a business that is for sale. The main drawback of going through a business broker or realtor is that his or her fee (paid by the seller) is usually a percentage, often 10%, of the sales price of the business; so the broker or realtor, like the seller, is trying to get the highest possible price for the business. At the same time, the seller will usually want more than he or she would if the sale were made without a broker, since he or she knows that the broker will take a healthy commission out of the negotiated sales price.

Your local chamber of commerce can usually tell you a great deal about the local business community and also provide you with leads to firms that are for sale.

Local Chambers of Commerce

Professionals, such as accountants, attorneys, and bankers, can often provide leads regarding good businesses even before they are on the market. Frequently, a business client will tell his or her accountant, attorney, or banker that he or she is planning to sell out or retire, long before making any formal attempt to put the business up for sale. So, if you have friends who are accountants, attorneys, or bankers, take them to lunch and tell them what you have in mind. Typically, they will have a vested interest in finding a friendly buyer for a retiring client's business, since they may loose that account if the firm is sold to buyers who have their own professional advisers.

Accountants, Attorneys, and Bankers

Certified public accountants (CPAs) can be excellent sources of leads. Not only will they usually not charge you any kind of finder's fee, but they usually know which of their clients' businesses are little gold mines. In some cases, a CPA who has a very profitable client who wishes to sell out may even want to go into the business with you as a financial partner, leaving the day-to-day operations to you. In these cases, you can generally be sure that if the CPA is putting up his or her money, he or she has studied the client's business carefully and feels that it is a real money-maker. In short, the CPA will have already done much of the prescreening for you.

Often, if you see a small business you think you might like to buy, the simplest approach will be to talk to the owner and see if he or she is interested in selling. While an owner may have had no serious thoughts about selling the business before, the appearance of an interested potential buyer is not only somewhat flattering, but it may even cause him or her to decide to sell out to you. Many businesses are bought and sold this way.

The Direct Approach

3.3 What to Look for Before You Leap

One of the first questions you may want to ask is: "Why are you selling your business?" Often, the response will be the owner wants to retire or is in poor health. While such an explanation may be true in many cases, it is also quite likely to be a well-rehearsed cover story. The real reason may be the business is in a declining neighborhood and the owner has been robbed several times recently and wants out. Or, the owners of a profitable little corner grocery store may be anxious to sell out while they can because they have learned that a major chain-store supermarket will

Why Is the Business for Sale?

be opening in the neighborhood in a few months. Another common reason behind a planned sale is that the business is either losing money or is not sufficiently profitable to make continuing worthwhile.

Whatever the real reason behind the owner's attempt to sell the business, you are unlikely to discover it without rolling up your sleeves and doing some independent and in-depth investigation. Perhaps the best way to find that needle in the haystack is to talk to a number of other businesspeople in the vicinity of the business you are investigating, particularly competitors in the same business. The business' suppliers can also be a source of important information.

Even if you are very diligent and thorough, you may not be able to discover the hidden reason — if there is one — underlying an owner's desire to sell out. You may simply have to rely on your intuition in deciding whether the seller's reason for getting out of the business is the real reason. Just remember that in most cases a good and profitable small business is not something that most people walk away from, unless there is a very good reason to do so or the price offered is too good to turn down.

What Kind of Reputation Does the Business Have?

One of the great advantages of taking over an existing business can be the opportunity to enjoy the reputation and goodwill that the existing owner has built up with customers and suppliers over the years. On the other hand, you may be much better off starting your own business from scratch than acquiring a business that has a poor reputation because of inferior work or merchandise or inferior service. It could take you years of hard work and reduced profits to overcome a former owner's poor reputation.

Even if the present owner has an excellent business reputation, you will want to know whether or not that goodwill is based on personal relationships built up between the owner and customers. These types of relationships aren't easily transferable. If the business relies heavily on a few key customers with whom the owner has very favorable business arrangements based on personal relationships, you may find those business arrangements could be lost when you attempt to take the owner's place. In short, satisfy yourself the goodwill you are buying is not based solely on personal relationships.

How Profitable Is the Business Now?

Unless you have some very good reasons to believe that you can operate the business more profitably than the current owner, you should not purchase a going business that does not produce a satisfactory profit under its current ownership. Thus, it is extremely important to find out how the business has fared financially for the last few years. This is where the services of a good accountant, who has knowledge of the particular type of business, will be invaluable.

Insist on having the seller make available the business' financial and business records to your accountant. Be particularly wary of a business that keeps poor records. Often, the most reliable sources of financial information can be the owner's income tax and sales tax returns, since it is not very likely that a business owner will report more income than was actually earned for tax purposes.

If the owner is not willing to make financial records available, make it clear that you are not willing to negotiate any further. Buying a business is a lot like buying a used car; you want to make sure it runs before you pay for it.

Assets and Liabilities

You will need to review both the tangible and intangible assets of the business to see if they are worth the price you will be paying and also to determine just what assets you will be acquiring under the sales agreement.

Personally inspect the business premises, and look for things like obsolete or unsalable inventory, out-of-date or rundown equipment, or furniture or fixtures that you may have to repair or replace. Also, determine whether the business is able to expand at its present location or if it is already too cramped. What you determine might require you to buy or lease additional facilities, if you wish to expand.

Review the terms of any leases. Some businesses close because of the imminent expiration of a favorable long-term lease or because the landlord plans to either raise the rent drastically or not renew the lease at all when the current lease expires.

If you will be acquiring the accounts receivable of the business, review them in detail. An aging of the accounts should be performed to determine how long various receivables have been outstanding. As a general rule, the longer a given receivable has been outstanding, the more likely it will prove to be uncollectible.

If a few large accounts of credit customers make up a significant portion of the receivables, you will want to particularly focus on those accounts and perhaps even have credit checks run on those customers. The bankruptcy of a major credit customer can ruin an otherwise successful business.

Part of your job in investigating a business that you want to buy is to find out what makes it tick — and make sure you will be getting whatever it is. For example, a business that has well-developed customer or mailing lists should ordinarily include those lists in the sales agreement. If there is a favorable lease, make sure it can and will be assigned to you. If patents, trademarks, trade names, or certain skilled employees are vital to the business, be sure that you will get them as part of the package.

You also need to be aware of potential problems with the government that the seller is experiencing or expects to experience in the near future, such as zoning problems or new environmental restrictions that may hamper the business' profitability.

Hidden Liabilities

Liabilities of the business may not always show up on its accounting records. There may be any number of hidden claims against the business, such as security agreements encumbering the accounts receivable, inventory, or equipment; unpaid back taxes of various kinds; undisclosed lawsuits or potential lawsuits; or simply unpaid bills.

If you are going to assume the liabilities of the business, the written agreement of sale should specify exactly which liabilities are being assumed and the dollar amount of each.

Other examples of hidden liabilities to look out for are:

- Pension liabilities — You may be taking on significant termination liability as a successor employer if the seller maintains or contributes to a pension fund and has unfunded pension fund liabilities.

- Vacation liabilities — If you are a successor employer, you may be liable for accrued but unpaid vacation leave of employees, which can be a significant hidden liability in some cases.

- Environmental liabilities — In many instances, environmental law imposes liability for past environmental abuses on current land owners or lessors. Many banks and savings and loans have recently learned about this the hard way, after foreclosing on land which had been contaminated over the years by toxic substances, and being held liable for clean-up costs as the contamination problems came to light.

  Many companies, when buying land or other companies that own land, now require the sellers to make detailed representations and warranties concerning environmental matters and to undertake extensive and costly environmental audits as a condition to buying a business. See Section 9.9 for a more detailed discussion of these issues.

If you intend to buy a corporation, you will be well advised to buy the business assets from the corporation rather than purchase its stock. The latter approach will subject the business to all hidden or contingent liabilities of the old corporation, whether or not you have agreed to pay for any liabilities of the corporation that predated the sale.

One exception to this general rule would be for a corporation that had substantial tax loss or tax credit carryovers that you might be able to utilize if you bought the stock of the corporation rather than the assets. Be aware, however, the tax law is a minefield when it comes to taking over someone else's tax loss or credit carryovers.

So before you do so, seek good advice from a tax attorney or tax accountant. If you don't, you may find that the carryovers you thought you were acquiring have evaporated like a mirage.

A change in ownership of more than 50% of the stock of a corporation in a three-year period will generally result in a severe restriction on the amount of its prior net operating losses that can be deducted in any subsequent taxable year.

3.4 Should You Consider a Franchise Operation?

Many small businesses, particularly fast food restaurants and print shops, are operated under franchises from a large national company (a franchisor). There can be substantial advantages to operating a franchised business, such as the benefits of national advertising, training programs, and assistance in setting up and running the business. If you are investigating a franchise, determine whether the franchise can be transferred to you, and if so, provide for the transfer as part of the sale in the sales agreement.

Carefully review the franchise agreement with the help of your attorney to determine whether the franchisor must approve the transfer, what the costs of operating are under the franchise, and the other terms of the agreement.

If the franchisor is not a well-known and respected company, contact your local Better Business Bureau or an appropriate state agency to see if they have any information regarding the history, ethics, and reputation of the franchisor. You do not want to sign on with one of the less-than-reputable franchising operations that charge substantial franchising fees for very little in the way of useful services.

The Federal Trade Commission (FTC) and a number of states provide franchising laws and regulations that offer you protection. These laws and regulations mandate the timing and content of the various disclosures which the franchisor must make to you, as the potential franchisee. You or your attorney should make sure that you ask for all of these disclosures on a timely basis, and be wary of any franchisor who does not provide these disclosures to you unless you ask for them.

A number of excellent publications, including *Franchise Bible* by Erwin J. Keup, can be obtained to help you evaluate various franchise opportunities. *Franchise Bible* explains what the franchise system entails and presents how both the franchisor and the franchisee should approach a franchising venture or opportunity.

For more information on *Franchise Bible* and additional franchise publications, refer to Section 10.9.

If you acquire a franchise, either from the franchisor or as a transfer from another franchisee, you may be able to amortize (write off) the cost of acquiring the franchise, under certain circumstances, for federal income tax purposes. Consult your tax adviser as to whether or not this will be possible in your case. If it is amortizable, you may want to allocate a significant part of the purchase price for the business to the cost of the franchise, which could save you major tax dollars in the long run.

Once you have focused on a particular franchise opportunity, you will find the checklist located at the end of this chapter very useful for evaluating the franchise operation.

3.5 Negotiating the Purchase

The Purchase Price

No book can tell you how much you should pay for the business you are planning to buy. You are on your own on that one. If, however, you have done your homework thoroughly in investigating the business in question and have talked to bankers and other businesspeople about what the normal purchase price for a business of that type and size should be, you should have a fairly good basis for determining whether the purchase price is a reasonable one.

For example, you may find that small businesses of the type you are considering generally sell for about one and one-half times their annual gross sales. That could be very important to know if the seller is asking three times last year's gross sales.

Even if you conclude the purchase price is a fair one, or even a bargain, you still must decide whether the price is one you can afford. Assuming that you can get the purchase price together, will it so deplete your liquid resources that you will not have enough working capital to make the business go or put you in a bind if income from the business drops off while you are at the learning stage? Or, if you are financing a substantial part of the purchase price, will your operating budget be able to stand the cost of making the payments on the debt and still leave enough for you to live on?

Remember, just because you can get the purchase price or down payment together does not necessarily mean that you can afford to buy a particular business even when the price is right.

Disclosure of Financial Information

At an early stage in the negotiations, specify that you want access to tax returns, books of account, and other financial records of the business, and make it clear that you have no interest in continuing the negotiations unless the seller cooperates fully in this respect.

Additionally, be sure this condition is expressed in any informal "memorandum of understanding" or letter of agreement between you and the seller that is written up before the final contract of sale.

Allocation of Purchase Price

One very important item that is often omitted in business sales agreements, perhaps because it is not absolutely necessary, is a provision in the agreement that shows how the parties agree to allocate the purchase price between the various assets that are being acquired.

For tax purposes, however, it is often very important to both you, as the purchaser, and the seller to have a written allocation agreement.

Since you and the seller usually have opposing interests in making an agreed allocation, the courts and IRS have generally been willing to abide by any allocation agreement between the parties.

The passage of the Clinton Deficit Reduction tax legislation on August 10, 1993 has greatly simplified the allocation process and made it easier, on an after-tax basis, to acquire a business when a significant portion of its assets are intangibles.[1]

Under the 1993 tax law, a broad new category of amortizable assets, called "Section 197 Intangibles," has been created. Section 197 Intangibles may be amortized over a 15-year period for assets purchased after August 10, 1993. Taxpayers may elect to have the new law apply retroactively to acquisitions of intangible assets that occurred after July 25, 1991. Consider amending your tax returns if you have recently purchased a business, after the latter date, and acquired any intangible assets that were not amortizable under prior law.

Before passage of this new law, a business buyer would seek to allocate as much of the purchase price as possible to depreciable tangible assets and amortizable intangible assets, such as technical know-how, customer lists, or covenants not to compete. In addition, buyers usually sought to minimize the portion of the purchase price allocated to other intangible items, such as goodwill or going concern value, which could never be amortized.

However, there was often little choice but to allocate most of the purchase price to intangibles because the value of tangible assets, such as office equipment and furniture and a few supplies, made up only a small portion of the purchase price. Since the IRS clearly would not accept a purchase price allocation that put a $50,000 value on $5 worth of paper clips, buyers were forced to become creative and try to define some asset, such as a customer base or insurance renewals list, and allocate some part of the purchase price to that asset.

In the past, when a buyer attempted to write off the cost of such intangible assets, the IRS often disallowed the amortization deduction. To sustain the deduction, the buyer often had to litigate the issue with the IRS and prove to a court that the intangible assets had a short, reasonably ascertainable economic life, and could thus be amortized for tax purposes. The courts frequently allowed taxpayers to write off various types of intangible assets over various periods of time, but only when the taxpayers convincingly demonstrated that such assets lost their economic value over a given period. The costs of such litigation, however, are usually prohibitive for small businesses.

Thankfully, the new law should put an end to most such disputes with the IRS over intangible assets. For the first time ever, the tax law allows goodwill and going concern value to be amortized as Section 197 Intangibles over 15 years. Also included in the definition of Section 197 Intangibles are:

- Workforce in place;
- Information base;
- Any license, permit, or other right granted by a governmental unit or agency;

- Know-how, such as patents, copyrights, formulas, designs, patterns, or similar items (special rules apply to computer software and interests in films, tapes, books, and videos);
- Any customer-based intangible, such as customer lists, depositor lists, subscribers, and insurance expirations;
- Any supplier-based intangible, such as favorable supplier contracts;
- Covenants not to compete; and
- Any franchise, trademark, or trade name.

Computer software is considered an intangible asset, but it is generally not subject to the 15-year amortization requirement of Section 197. Software that is readily available for purchase by the general public is not considered a Section 197 Intangible asset and can now be amortized over three years rather than the five-year period that previously applied.[2] Other computer software is a Section 197 Intangible asset only if acquired in a transaction that involves the purchase of a whole business or a substantial portion of a business.

Section 197 will benefit most business buyers by preventing many disputes with the IRS regarding the purchase price of a business and by allowing amortization of the cost of intangible assets that were not deductible in the past. The new law, however, is not entirely favorable. Previously, business buyers who were allowed to amortize certain intangibles were often able to do so over a period of only a few years, which was far better than the new 15-year amortization requirement.

Allocation Agreements Are Still Important

Do not assume that the new law makes a purchase price allocation agreement unnecessary or unimportant. Certain assets that might be acquired in a business purchase, such as land, are still not depreciable or amortizable, so it will be advisable to try to allocate as little as possible to the cost of land in a purchase price allocation agreement. Also, it will still be advantageous to allocate as much as possible of the purchase price to inventories or depreciable assets whose costs can be written off in a time frame shorter than the 15-year amortization period for Section 197 Intangibles.

A tax deduction you can take today or in the near future is almost always worth a great deal more than a tax deduction 15 years from now.

Required Filing

Tax regulations require both you and the seller to file *Form 8594* with the IRS any time a business is bought or sold.[3] *Form 8594* reports certain information about the purchase price allocation. Penalties for failure to file this form can be extremely large. Needless to say, the information on your *Form 8594* and that of the seller's should be identical, or you both will be inviting IRS audits.

In most cases, whatever value of an asset you and the seller agree on is binding for tax purposes. So, it is very important from a tax standpoint to negotiate the best possible allocation of the purchase price among the assets you acquire and have that allocation reflected in the contract of sale.[4]

3.6 Closing the Deal

The legal procedures involved in buying an existing business are rather complex. To ensure you are protected as fully as possible from liabilities you have not agreed to assume, have your attorney take the steps described below.

Legal Steps in Buying a Business

In many states, the purchaser of a retail or wholesale establishment or certain other types of businesses must prepare a notice to creditors of bulk transfer and file it in counties where the business operates and publish it in a general circulation newspaper before the purchase of the business. If this is not properly done, the seller's unsecured creditors may be able to attach the property that you thought you were buying free and clear. Since 1989, however, more than half the states have decided that their bulk sale or bulk transfer laws were a nineteenth-century anachronism and an unnecessary burden on commerce; these states have repealed such laws outright. See Section 9.14 for more details regarding the increasing number of bulk sale law repeals.

File Bulk Transfer Notice

Before closing the purchase, your attorney should check with the secretary of state's office to determine whether anyone has recorded a security interest — a lien or chattel mortgage — against the personal property of the seller's business. Naturally, if the transaction involves a purchase of real property, you should also have a title search performed to see if the seller has good title and if there are any recorded mortgages or other claims against the property that the seller has not disclosed to you.

Check Security Interests

For a fee, the secretary of state's office (or its equivalent) will provide a listing of any security interests that have been recorded as a lien against the assets of the business you are buying.

As a condition of the sale, have the seller obtain the necessary form that certifies all state employment taxes have been paid by the seller from the appropriate state agency. If you fail to withhold enough of the purchase price to cover any of the seller's unpaid employment taxes, you may be liable to the state for those taxes. See Section 11.3 for specifics on state requirements.

Get Tax Releases

Similarly, require the seller to obtain and provide you with a sales and use tax certification showing that all outstanding sales and use tax payments due have been made by the seller. You do not want to end up paying for the seller's unpaid sales or use taxes.

File *Form 8594* with the IRS regarding the purchase price allocation and other information in connection with the transaction. The penalty for intentional disregard of this filing requirement is 10% of the amount that was not correctly reported, which could mean up to 10% of the entire purchase price. Don't forget to file *Form 8594*.

File with IRS

Retain a Lawyer

Do not attempt to buy or sell a business without the assistance of an attorney to review and structure the deal. Preferably, the attorney should be one who specializes in business law practice rather than a litigation specialist or general practitioner. Obtain competent tax advice, either from your attorney or from an accountant, when negotiating and structuring aspects of the deal, such as the allocation of the purchase price and the disposition of any employee benefit plans carried on by the seller for the employees of the business.

Use an Escrow

In general, both you and the seller will be protected — from the time the sales agreement is signed until the deal closes — if an escrow is used to handle the sale of the business. The escrow holder, which is usually an escrow company or escrow department of a financial institution, will hold the agreement, escrow instructions, funds, and important documents until all conditions for closing the deal or releasing the funds or documents are fulfilled.

When the deal closes, the escrow holder will disburse the funds to the seller and deliver the documents of title to you. If the deal is not completed, the escrow instructions will specify how the items held in escrow are to be distributed to the parties.

Your attorney or the seller's attorney may also act as escrow holder, but you probably will not want the seller's attorney to act in that role in most cases, for obvious reasons.

Build in Holdbacks

If the seller has made misrepresentations to you in the contract of sale regarding assets that do not exist, or the like, you may always seek satisfaction by suing for damages. In view of the cost, delay, and uncertainty in bringing a lawsuit, however, you would generally be far better off if there were some simple way you could merely offset any such overstated asset or understated liability against the purchase price, retroactively.

To make this possible, seek to structure the deal so part of the purchase price is held back for some period, say a year, just in case such a contingency arises. Then, if you discover false representations as to assets or liabilities, it will be relatively simple — compared to bringing a lawsuit against a seller who may have skipped town — to have your claim deducted from the amount held back. Discuss with your attorney the possibilities of structuring the transaction so you either:

- Give the seller a note as part of the purchase price, with a right to reduce the principal amount of the note if certain contingencies occur; or
- Have part of the cash payment price held in escrow for six months or more after the sale occurs.

3.7 Summary Checklist for Buying an Existing Business

☐ Why does the present owner want to sell the business? **Investigation**

☐ Will the reputation of the business be helpful or harmful if you take it over?

☐ Obtain tax returns, bank deposit records, and other financial records.

☐ If the business is not currently very profitable, why do you think you can run it more profitably than the present owner?

☐ Thoroughly investigate the business' financial records and history, its reputation, and any factors that might unfavorably impact on its future. You may need the help of an accountant or other experts.

☐ Review or have reviewed the provisions of key contracts, leases, franchise agreements, or any other legal arrangements which have a significant effect on the business. Be sure you are not assuming an unfavorable lease or contract or losing the benefits of a favorable one.

☐ Make sure that the purchase price is fair. Even if it is, can you afford it? Will you have enough working capital to run the business properly after you pay the purchase price? **Negotiations**

☐ Insist on getting accurate financial information and access to the supporting data, early in the negotiations.

☐ Push for an allocation of the purchase price to specific assets in the sales agreement. Seek to maximize the amounts allocable to depreciable assets and any noncompetition covenant. Seek to minimize allocations to goodwill or land purchased.

☐ Look for hidden liabilities, such as pending lawsuits, accrued vacation liabilities, unfunded pension plan liabilities, or potential exposure to environmental clean-up costs.

☐ Retain an attorney to participate in drawing up the sales agreement. **Closing the Transaction**

☐ If your state still has a bulk sales law, comply with the requirements of the Bulk Transfer Act, if it applies to the particular type of business being acquired.

☐ Be sure that the acquired property is not subject to any recorded security interests or other liens beyond those disclosed by the seller.

☐ Have the seller obtain and furnish a certification that all employment taxes due have been paid.

☐ Have the seller obtain and furnish a certification that all sales and use taxes due have been paid.

☐ Seek to hold back part of the purchase price as security to reimburse yourself for any misrepresentations as to assets or liabilities by the seller.

☐ Prepare *Form 8594*, and file it with the IRS.

☐ See Section 11.3 for state law considerations.

Other Tax Considerations

☐ Determine whether the sale of the business will result in a sales tax liability with respect to part or all of the purchase price. If so, is there a way to reshape the transaction to reduce or avoid sales tax? For example, allocate more of the purchase price to assets not subject to sales tax and less to assets that are.

☐ If you are buying a corporation that has not been paying income taxes because it has carryovers of net operating losses or investment tax credits, be aware you may be able to use only a small portion of those carryovers to shelter the income of the business once you become the owner.

☐ If the seller has a favorable experience rating for unemployment tax purposes, make sure you act promptly so that you can succeed to that rating as a successor employer.

☐ If you are acquiring intangible assets, including previously non-deductible intangibles, such as goodwill or going concern value, you may now amortize the cost of most such intangible assets over 15 years, under recent tax legislation.

Endnotes

1. I.R.C. §197.
2. I.R.C. §167(f)(1).

3. Temp. Treas. Regs. 1.1060-1T(h)(2).
4. I.R.C. §1060(a).

Checklist for Evaluating a Franchise

The Franchise

YES NO

☐ ☐ After studying it paragraph by paragraph, did your lawyer approve the franchise contract you are considering?

☐ ☐ Does the franchise call upon you to take any steps which are, according to your lawyer, unwise or illegal in your state, county, or city? If yes, what are the steps? _____

_____

☐ ☐ Does the franchise give you an exclusive territory for the length of the franchise? or

☐ ☐ Can the franchisor sell a second or third franchise in your territory?

☐ ☐ Is the franchisor connected in any way with another franchise company handling similar merchandise or services? If yes, what is your protection against this second franchisor organization?

_____

_____

☐ ☐ Can you terminate the franchise contract? Under what circumstances can you do it and at what cost to you, if you decide for any reason at all that you wish to cancel it?

_____

_____

☐ ☐ If you sell your franchise, will you be compensated for the goodwill you have built into the business?

The Franchisor

How many years has the firm offering you a franchise been in operation? _____

☐ ☐ Does the firm have a reputation for honesty and fair dealing among the local firms holding its franchise?

☐ ☐ Has the franchisor shown you any certified figures indicating exact net profits of one or more going firms?

☐ ☐ Have you personally checked these certified figures with the franchisor?

☐ ☐ Will the firm assist you in the following areas?

YES NO		YES NO	
☐ ☐	A management training program?	☐ ☐	Capital?
☐ ☐	An employee training program?	☐ ☐	Credit?
☐ ☐	A public relations program?	☐ ☐	Merchandising ideas?

☐ ☐ Will the firm help you find a good location for your new business?

☐ ☐ Is the franchising firm adequately financed so it can carry out its stated plan of financial assistance and expansion?

Checklist for Evaluating a Franchise (continued)

YES NO
☐ ☐ Is the franchisor a one-person company? or

☐ ☐ Is the franchisor a corporation with an experienced management trained in-depth (so that there would always be an experienced person at its head)?

Exactly what can the franchisor do for you which you cannot do for yourself? _____

_____

_____

☐ ☐ Has the franchisor investigated you carefully enough to assure itself that you can successfully operate one of the franchises at a profit both to the franchisor and to you?

☐ ☐ Does your state have a law regulating the sale of franchises? and

☐ ☐ Has the franchisor complied with that law?

You – The Franchisee

How much equity capital will you have to have to purchase the franchise and operate it until your income equals your expenses? _____

Where are you going to get the capital? _____

_____

☐ ☐ Are you prepared to give up some independence of action to secure the advantages offered by the franchise?

☐ ☐ Do you really believe you have the innate ability, training, and experience to work smoothly and profitably with the franchisor, your employees, and your customers?

☐ ☐ Are you ready to spend much or all of the remainder of your business life with this franchisor, offering its product or service to your public?

Your Market

☐ ☐ Have you made any study to determine whether the product or service which you propose to sell under franchise has a market in your territory at the prices you will have to charge?

Will the population in the territory given you increase ☐, remain static ☐, or decrease ☐ over the next five years?

Will the product or service you are considering be in greater demand ☐, about the same ☐, or in less demand ☐ five years from today?

What competition already exists in your territory for the product or service you contemplate selling:

From nonfranchise firms? _____

From franchise firms? _____

Source: *Franchise Opportunities Handbook*, U.S. Department of Commerce, Washington, D.C., 1982.

Starting the Business

Part II

Chapter 4
A Trip through the Red Tape Jungle:
Requirements that Apply to Nearly All New Businesses

Chapter 5
The Thicket Thickens:
Additional Requirements for Businesses with Employees

Chapter 6
Businesses that Require Licenses to Operate

Chapter 4

A Trip through the Red Tape Jungle: Requirements that Apply to Nearly All New Businesses

The difference between a taxidermist and a tax collector is that the taxidermist leaves the skin.

— Old American proverb

4.1 General Considerations

This chapter outlines the most common governmental requirements and other red tape that virtually everyone starting a new business must attend to. The requirements discussed will also generally apply if you have bought an existing business, unless you have acquired the stock of an incorporated business. Items covered in this chapter will generally apply even if your business has no employees. If you expect to have one or more employees, a large number of additional legal requirements will affect your business immediately. Chapter 5 covers the additional requirements that apply to new businesses that have employees. This chapter does not discuss the special licenses that many types of businesses are required to have. If you do not know whether the type of business you are considering going into requires a special license or licenses from federal, state, or local government agencies, refer to Chapter 6 and Section 11.6.

4.2 Choosing a Name for the Business

The name you choose for your business can be important from a business image standpoint and also in communicating to the public what you have to offer. Most small businesses should select a name that, at least in part, clearly describes the product or service provided. If you ignore this basic common-sense rule, you run the risk of losing many potential customers for the simple reason they will pass right by without realizing what you do. A fanciful or whimsical name is fine from an image standpoint, but it should also give the public a clear idea of what it is your business provides in the way of goods or services. For example, if you call your restaurant "The Comestible Emporium," a lot of hungry people will probably drive right by without realizing that you serve food.

It is advisable, however, from the standpoint of protecting your business' name as a trademark or service mark under federal or state law, to adopt a name that is also partially arbitrary or nondescriptive, in conjunction with a name that is descriptive of the services or goods provided. An example would be the "21 Club Restaurant." The reason for selecting a name that is partially whimsical or arbitrary is that trademarks or service marks that are merely descriptive of the goods or services cannot be legally protected from use by others unless it can be proven that the name has acquired a secondary meaning, which is very difficult to establish for a new small business.[1]

You also need to think of the possible consequences of putting your name out before the public. You may want to consider using some sort of fictitious name (see Section 4.10) for your business, rather than your name. There is nothing illegal or shady about using a fictitious business name. If you put your name on the business and the venture goes belly up, as some new businesses do, many people in the community will automatically associate your name with the defunct or bankrupt business. This may make it very difficult if you try to start another business or to obtain credit in the same community in the future.

Once you have settled on a name for your business, you or preferably your attorney, should find out whether the same name, or a confusingly similar name, has already been preempted by someone else. This involves making an inquiry with the state's secretary of state's office to find out whether the name is already being used in the state. Inquiry should also be made of the county clerk, in each county where you will do business, to see if another business is already using the same or a confusingly similar name in the county and has filed a fictitious business name statement. If so, you may have to choose a different name. See Section 9.5 for more information on trademark protection.

4.3 Local Business Licenses

Almost every business will need city or county business licenses, or both. These licenses can be obtained at the local city hall or county offices. Failure to obtain a license when you start business will usually result in a penalty when the local government eventually catches up with you; therefore, obtaining the necessary licenses should be among the first steps taken when you start a business.

Some cities and counties impose a gross receipts, income, or payroll tax on most businesses. Certain types of businesses, such as restaurants, may also be required to obtain special permits from local health authorities and fire or police departments.

If your business will construct its own building, it will be necessary to consult your local city or county zoning ordinances. A building permit must be obtained for both new construction and remodeling in most areas.

In addition, whether or not you plan to carry on any construction activity or do any remodeling, you will need to make certain that the business activity you intend to carry on does not violate any zoning regulations or any ordinances regarding hazardous activities. You may also be required to obtain a use permit from the city or county planning commission.

4.4 State Licenses

Most states impose license fees or taxes on a wide range of businesses, occupations, and professions. The fees often vary widely among the different types of businesses and occupations, ranging from relatively nominal to substantial amounts or rates, depending upon the activity. The many different types of licenses and permits are usually granted based on some combination of requirements such as registration, bonding, education, experience, and passage of licensing examinations.

Since you may not legally operate any of these regulated businesses or professions without being licensed, you should find out whether there is a state licensing requirement for the business you plan to start. If so, determine whether and how you will be able to comply with the licensing requirements.

See Section 11.6 for a partial listing of businesses, occupations, and professions that must be licensed under the laws of this state.

4.5 Federal Licenses

Most new small businesses are unlikely to require any type of federal permit or license to operate, unless they are engaged in rendering investment advice, making alcohol or tobacco products, preparing meat products, or making or dealing in firearms. Federal permits or licenses would also be necessary to commence certain large-scale operations, such as a radio or television station or a common carrier and the production of drugs or biological products. If you wish to engage in any of the foregoing activities, all of which are heavily regulated, consult an attorney regarding regulatory requirements well in advance.

4.6 Estimated Taxes

Individual

As a sole proprietor or partner in a partnership, you will have to make advance payments of estimated federal — and possibly state — income taxes and federal self-employment tax once your business begins to turn a taxable profit. Individual estimated tax payments are due in four annual installments on April 15, June 15, September 15, and January 15 of the following year for an individual whose tax year is the calendar year. Any remaining unpaid federal tax is due with your tax return on April 15 of the following year — which is also the date when the first estimated tax installment is due for that year. You will file *Form 1040-ES* with your federal estimated tax payments. During a year, you must make estimated tax payments equal to 90% of the current year's tax or 100% of the prior year's tax, whichever is less.

Certain high-income taxpayers, however, are not allowed to base their payments on the prior year's tax. Starting in 1994, taxpayers with more than $150,000 of adjusted gross income in the prior year may base their payments on 110% of the prior year's tax.[2]

Corporate

If your business is incorporated, the corporation will generally have to make corporate estimated tax payments, if it has taxable income, as early as the fourth month of its first tax year. For tax years beginning after December 31, 1993, your corporation must pay estimated tax equal to 100% of its current year tax or 100% of its tax for the prior year, whichever is less. A large corporation — one which had one million dollars or more of taxable income in one of the three preceding years — may not base its estimates on the prior year's tax. Estimated tax installments are due on April 15, June 15, September 15, and December 15, for a corporation with a calendar year for its taxable year.

Federal estimated tax payments should be computed on *Form 1120-W* — which can be obtained, along with other federal tax forms, from any IRS office — and must be deposited in a bank that is authorized to accept federal tax deposits. The corporate estimated tax deposits must be accompanied by federal tax deposit coupons. Your corporation will be issued one coupon book that contains coupons with your corporate tax identification number already preprinted on them. These coupons can be used for deposits of all types of federal taxes. On each coupon, you must indicate, by checking the applicable box, the kind of tax being deposited and the calendar quarter to which payroll tax deposits are to be applied. The boxes on the coupon indicate the form name for the type of tax being paid.

Federal Tax Deposits

Type of Tax	Box to Darken on Coupon
Payroll tax deposits	941
Federal unemployment tax	940 (or 940-EZ)
Corporate income tax estimates (and year-end payments)	1120

The tax deposit coupon instructions also require you to darken an appropriate quarterly box (1st, 2nd, 3rd, or 4th quarter). While this is fairly straightforward for payroll tax deposits (simply darken the box for the appropriate calendar quarter), the requirements are somewhat less logical in the case of corporate estimated income tax deposits.

For income tax deposits (*Form 1120*), darken the first quarter box for all current year estimated income tax deposits, regardless of the quarter to which the deposit relates. However, when making income tax deposits that relate to the prior taxable year (such as a payment made with extension request *Form 7004* or the final tax payment that is made at the time of filing the *Form 1120* corporation income tax return), darken the fourth quarter box instead.

The coupon books will be sent to you automatically when you file *Form SS-4*, which requests a tax identification number for the corporation. When you receive your coupon book, a reorder form, *Form 8109A*, will be provided so you can request additional coupon books for the current year, if needed.

A penalty may be imposed for failure to make deposits directly to an authorized government depository bank. In the past, when tax deposit cards were unavailable, it was common practice to mail payments to the Internal Revenue Service accompanied by a letter indicating the nature of the tax payment and requesting additional tax deposit cards. This method of paying business taxes is no longer acceptable. Thus, it is important to mail the reorder form in time to receive additional coupon books before you run out; however, the IRS will sometimes send you blank coupons for temporary use. Refer to Section 11.4 regarding state filing requirements for individual and corporate estimated income taxes.

4.7 Miscellaneous Tax Information Returns

As a general rule, every person engaged in a trade or business must report to the IRS any payments of $600 or more made to any person during the calendar year, for items such as rent, compensation for services, commissions, interest, and annuities, plus other items of fixed or determinable

Reporting Payments to Individuals

income.[3] To make these filings, you will use a series of 1099 forms. A number of additional tax reporting requirements are listed below. Be aware there are stiff new penalties for failure to comply with them.

Obtaining Social Security Numbers

It is necessary to obtain the name and Social Security number or other tax identification number of any person to whom you make payments of $600 or more. There is a $50 penalty for failure to obtain their tax identification number — unless you have a reasonable excuse, such as their refusal to give you the number.[4] If they do refuse to give you the number, you must withhold 31% of whatever amount you owe them and deposit it with the IRS, or you will be subject to a penalty for failure to withhold.[5]

Reporting Sales to Direct Sellers

In addition, you must report sales of $5,000 or more of consumer products to any individual who is engaged in direct selling — that is, selling in any way other than through a permanent retail establishment.[6] This will mainly apply to sales made to people in direct sales organizations, such as Tupperware, Amway, or Shaklee. It would also apply in many other situations, such as where the person you sell to sells the goods by mail order. Use *Form 1099-MISC* to report these sales.

1099 Forms

Reportable payments you make that are in excess of $600 per year are usually filed for each payee on *Form 1099-MISC* (information return) or *Form 1099-INT* (for interest); a duplicate must be sent to the payee. In addition, you must prepare and file a *Form 1096* return summarizing all the information on the 1099-MISC forms and on the other forms in the 1099 series. Each of these forms is due by February 28 each year, for the prior calendar year, and a copy must also be sent to the recipient of the payment by January 31.

Be aware that instructions for *Form 1099* say you should use your personal Social Security number rather than your business' employer identification number on the form. Putting down the wrong taxpayer identification number in such a case will subject you to a penalty.

Payments of compensation in excess of $600 made to nonemployees — independent contractors — are also reportable on *Form 1099-MISC*. Businesses must also report royalty payments of $10 or more made to any person.

Penalties

There are stiff IRS penalties for not filing the above 1099 forms. The penalty for not filing or not giving a 1099 to a payee is $50 per failure. Since there is a separate penalty for not giving a copy of the 1099 to the payee, as well as for not filing a copy with the IRS, it can cost you $100 for each person for whom you fail to prepare 1099s.[7] The $50 penalty for late-filed 1099s, and certain other information returns, can be reduced to $30, if you file more than 30 days late but before August 1 of the year the filing is due. Or, if you file within 30 days after the due date, the penalty can be reduced to only $15.

In addition, if you erroneously, but in good faith, treat a person as an independent contractor, and it is later shown that the person was actually an employee, you will only be liable as an employer for 20% of the employee's Social Security tax that should have been withheld and for income tax withholding equal to 1.5% of what you paid the individual provided that you properly filed *Form 1099-MISC* with the IRS.[8] If you failed to file *Form 1099-MISC* for that person, the amount of withholding tax you are liable for is doubled.[9]

Fortunately, a number of important exemptions from the 1099 filing requirements will eliminate most of the people or companies to whom you are likely to make payments of $600 or more. You do not have to report:

Exemptions for 1099 Filings

- Payments to corporations — except certain corporations in the medical field;[10]
- Payments of compensation to employees that are already reported on their W-2s;[11]
- Payments of bills for merchandise, telegrams, telephone, freight, storage, and similar charges;[12]
- Payments of rent made to real estate agents;[13]
- Expense advances or reimbursements to employees that the employees must account to you (the employer) for;[14] and
- Payments to a governmental unit.[15]

If your business is incorporated, your corporation will have to file a *Form 1099-DIV* for each person to whom it pays dividends of $10 or more each year.[16] You must also file *Form 1099-INT* for each person to whom you pay $10 or more in interest on bonds, debentures, or notes issued by the corporation in registered form.[17] *Form 1099-DIV* or *Form 1099-INT* is also required for any other payment of dividends or interest on which you are required to withhold tax. Payments reported on *Form 1099-DIV* and *Form 1099-INT* must also be reported on the *Form 1096* summary. *Form 1099-S* must be given to recipients of the proceeds from the sales of real estate, in general.

Reporting Dividends and Interest

Any business that receives a payment of more than $10,000 in cash, in cash equivalents — such as cashier's checks or traveler's checks — or in foreign currency in one transaction, or in two or more related transactions, is required to report the details of the transactions within 15 days to the IRS[18] and to furnish a similar statement to the payor by January 31 of the following year.[19] The form for reporting such "suitcase" transactions is *Form 8300*.

Reporting Large Cash Transactions

The penalties for noncompliance are generally the same as for not filing 1099s, except that in cases of intentional failure to file, there is an additional penalty equal to the higher of $25,000 or the amount of the cash or cash equivalent received in the transaction, up to $100,000.[20] In addition to the requirement that you file 1099s with the IRS, you may have to file similar forms with the state.

Reporting Mortgage Interest Received

Federal law requires that you give *Form 1098* to any individual from whom you receive $600 or more in mortgage interest during the year, in the course of your trade or business. *Form 1098* has the same filing requirements as *Form 1099*.[21]

Reporting on Magnetic Media

Note that the IRS permits you to file *Form 1098* and *Form 1099*, as well as certain other information returns, on magnetic media (computer tapes or disks) rather than the actual paper forms, if very specific formats for the computer tape or disk are met. The IRS requires that certain information returns be filed on magnetic media, if your business files 250 or more such returns for a calendar year.[22] These include *Form 1098*, all of the 1099 series and W-2 series of information returns, and various others, such as *Form 5498* and *Form 8027*.

A "hardship waiver" to excuse you from having to file in magnetic media format may be granted under certain circumstances, if you file a request on *Form 8508* at least 90 days in advance of the due date.

Failure of a taxpayer to file an information return on magnetic media — or on a machine-readable form where magnetic media filing is not required — when required to do so is treated as a failure-to-file and can result in the imposition of applicable penalties for failure to file, as noted earlier.

If your business finds it will be required to file information returns on magnetic media, there are many data processing firms and computer programs you can buy that will encode the data for you, at a relatively small cost, in a way that meets the IRS's highly technical specifications.

4.8 Sales and Use Tax Permits

With a limited number of exceptions, every business that sells tangible personal property, such as merchandise, to customers must obtain a seller's permit from the state sales tax agency. Usually, a separate permit must be obtained for each place of business where property subject to tax is sold. See Section 11.4 for a discussion of the state's sales and use tax laws and permit requirements. Some states have a gross income or a gross receipts tax rather than a sales tax.

In general, as a wholesaler or manufacturer, you will not have to collect sales tax on goods you sell to a retailer for resale, if the retailer holds a valid seller's permit and provides you with a resale certificate in connection with the transaction. Likewise, if your business, as a retailer, buys goods for resale, you need not pay sales tax to the wholesalers if you provide them with resale certificates. You may buy blank resale certificate forms at most stationery stores in states where such certificates are required.

The sales and use tax laws typically require a business that sells or leases tangible personal property to keep complete records of the gross receipts from sales or rentals whether or not the receipts are believed to be taxable. You must also keep adequate and complete records to substantiate all deductions claimed on sales and use tax returns and of the total purchase price of all tangible personal property bought for sale, lease, or consumption in the state.

4.9 Real Estate Taxes

Property Taxes

As a rule, you do not need to worry about contacting the county tax assessor's office regarding payment of any real property taxes on real property acquired for your business. They will usually contact you by mailing a property tax bill to the owner of record. See Section 11.4 for a general description of how state or local real property and personal property taxes are assessed and collected.

FIRPTA Withholding Tax on Purchase of Real Property

In addition to local property taxes, U.S. citizens and residents who acquire U.S. real estate from foreign persons — including partnership interests or stock in certain firms owning U.S. real property — must withhold up to 10% of the purchase price and remit it to the IRS under the Foreign Investment in Real Property Tax Act (FIRPTA). If you fail to withhold the tax, you are liable for it. This is a potentially dangerous tax trap for unsuspecting American buyers of real estate, since it is often difficult to determine whether a seller is a foreign person.

While there is an exception for residences costing $300,000 or less — if you will live in it for at least 50% of the time for two years — it is far safer to obtain a certificate of nonforeign status from the seller if there is any possibility that the seller is a nonresident alien or a foreign company.

To protect yourself when purchasing real estate — or your client, if you are in the real estate business — you should require, as a condition of closing the transaction, that the seller provide you with an affidavit certifying whether or not the seller is a nonresident alien or a foreign company.

If the seller refuses to sign the affidavit and provide the required information, you should withhold 10% of the gross purchase price and transmit it to the IRS within ten days of the sale along with IRS *Form 8288* and *Form 8288-A*. This can be a real problem in a highly leveraged deal where less than 10% of the purchase price is paid in cash at the closing.

Some states have adopted similar withholding provisions with regard to purchases of real estate within such states where the seller is a nonresident of the state.

In short, if the seller is a foreign person, you will owe the IRS 10% of the purchase price if you fail to withhold the tax, unless you received a certificate of nonforeign status from the seller.

4.10 Fictitious Business Name Statement

Almost every state has laws requiring any person who regularly transacts business in the state for profit under a fictitious business name to file and publish a fictitious business name statement. For a sole proprietorship or partnership, a business name is generally considered fictitious unless it contains the surname of the owner or all of the general partners and does not suggest the existence of additional owners. Use of a name that includes words like "company," "associates," "group," "brothers," or "sons" will suggest additional owners and will make it necessary for a business to file and publish a fictitious business name statement.

Putting a name that would be considered fictitious on your company letterhead, on your business cards, in advertising, or on your products will be considered a use of the name.

Many newspapers will provide the form for filing, publish the notice, and file the required affidavit. See Section 11.4 regarding specific requirements for filing a fictitious business name statement in this state.

4.11 Insurance — A Practical Necessity for Businesses

Insurance, like death and taxes, is an inevitable necessity for the owner of any small business. For almost any business, even one that has no employees, insurance coverage for general liability, product liability, fire and similar disasters, robbery, theft, and interruption of business should be considered.

If your business will have employees, workers' compensation insurance is usually mandatory under state law. Employee life, health, and disability insurance have also become virtual necessities in many businesses and professions, if you wish to be competitive with other firms in hiring and retaining capable employees.

Fidelity bonding should be considered for employees who will have access to the cash receipts or other funds of the business. If you have an employee pension or profit-sharing plan subject to the Employee Retirement Income Security Act of 1974 (ERISA), employees involved in administering the plan or handling its funds are required to be covered by a fidelity bond.[23] See Section 5.5 for further information.

Insurance Agents

Since it isn't realistic to expect you to become a sophisticated comparison shopper for insurance while you are trying to get a business off the ground, seek out a good insurance agent whom you can trust and rely upon to give you good advice. There is no easy way to find such an agent, just as there is no sure way of finding a good lawyer or accountant. In general, the best approach will be to ask friends, lawyers, accountants, or other businesspeople you know to refer you to a topflight insurance agent.

Agents who have earned the Chartered Life Underwriter (CLU) designation will, as a rule, be more experienced and capable than those without the CLU credential. This can be an additional factor to consider when selecting your insurance agent.

Agents who deal primarily in property and casualty insurance will not usually have CLU on their business cards. Instead, they may have the initials CPCU — Chartered Property/Casualty Underwriter — after their name, which is a similar mark of distinction in the field of property/casualty insurance.

Another good tip in finding an insurance agent is to analyze your own insurance needs. There are several how-to books that can help you analyze your risks and compare insurance prices. One such book is the *Buyer's Guide to Business Insurance*, which is available from The Oasis Press for $19.95. Companion software, *The Insurance Assistant*, is also available.

Insurance Consultants

If you cannot find an agent with whom you feel comfortable, call an insurance consultant. Be sure the consultant is a member of the Society of Risk Management Consultants. To belong to the group, the individual or firm cannot be an insurance broker. These consultants are insurance experts and can give you an objective analysis on risk management and insurance.

Society of Risk Management Consultants
300 Park Avenue
New York, NY 10022
(800) 765-SRMC

The usual hourly fees may seem high, but most new businesses probably will not need an excessive amount of time. Most will bill in quarter-hour increments.

You will probably recoup the consultant's fee several times over in premium savings in just the first year alone. Be wary, however, of a consultant who wants to increase the number of hours by offering to create specifications and provide additional services.

Once you have met with an independent consultant and know what is needed, shop for the insurance you need from insurance brokers. Don't let them bid up the amount of coverage or add on additional types of insurance.

Use the insurance consultant as you would an attorney or physician — follow his or her advice.

4.12 Requirements Specific to the Legal Form of the Business

Sole Proprietorships

There are no significant government regulatory requirements that apply specifically to sole proprietorships; although, as a sole proprietor of a business, you will need to attach a form *Schedule C* to your individual federal tax return, on which you will report the income or loss from your business.

If your sole proprietorship shows a profit, you will usually have to pay a self-employment tax equal to 15.3% of your net self-employment income from the business or at least on the first $60,600 of such income, plus an additional 2.9% on self-employment income of more than $60,600 in 1994. The self-employment tax is computed on *Schedule SE*, which must also be attached to your federal income tax return. See Section 11.4 for how to report business profits on your state income tax returns.

Partnerships

Like a sole proprietor, as a partner, you will have to pay a self-employment tax on your share of your partnership's net self-employment income. Net self-employment income usually includes all partnership income less all partnership deductions allowed for income tax purposes. Some types of income, such as interest, may or may not be considered self-employment income. The source of your income and your involvement in the activity from which your income is received will determine whether it is self-employment income.

If your earnings from self-employment is $400 or more for the year, you will have to figure self-employment tax on *Schedule SE* of your federal *Form 1040*. The self-employment tax is a Social Security and Medicare tax for those who work for themselves.

Schedule E of your federal *Form 1040* deals with your personal income tax and includes all other taxable income, such as royalties, rentals, and interest. You report your share of partnership ordinary income or loss on *Schedule E*.

In addition, your partnership must file a partnership information return, federal *Form 1065*, reporting the partnership's income and each partner's share of income and other items. The partnership must also file *Form SS-4* with the IRS to obtain a federal employer identification number, even if it has no employees. See Section 11.4 for state partnership return filing requirements, and the end of this chapter for a sample *Form SS-4*.

When a partner buys, sells, or exchanges a partnership interest, the partnership must file a special information return if the partnership's assets include unrealized receivables or substantially appreciated inventory that might cause the seller to have ordinary gain, rather than all capital gain, on the sale or exchange.[24] Statements also have to be sent to the partners involved in the transaction.[25]

A limited partnership, to qualify as such, is usually required to file a *Certificate of Limited Partnership* with the secretary of state or other state agency. In most states, a limited partnership should also file certified copies in each county where it does business or owns real estate.

Corporations

Corporations are subject to the following requirements. These requirements are not applicable to other legal forms of business organization.

- Filing articles of incorporation;
- Adopting a set of bylaws;
- Observing other corporate formalities on a regular basis, such as the election of directors by shareholders and appointment of officers by action of the board of directors;
- Filing federal income tax returns on *Form 1120* — or *Form 1120-S* for an S corporation — and state income or franchise tax returns in most states where they do business. See Section 11.4 for various filings, taxes, and fees required of corporations that are incorporated or doing business in this state;
- Reporting certain information relating to the transfer of tax-free property under Internal Revenue Code Section 351 on the corporation's income tax return for that year;[26]
- Filing *Form SS-4* with the IRS to obtain an employer identification number, even if there are no employees; and
- Qualifying with the secretary of state to do business, if the corporation was organized under the laws of another state.

Limited Liability Companies

A limited liability company (LLC) must file articles of organization — similar to articles of incorporation — with the secretary of state or other appropriate state agency, and pay any applicable filing fees. See Section 11.2 for filing requirements in this state. In addition, tax treatment of an LLC will generally be the same as for a partnership, if it is properly structured.

4.13 Checklist of Requirements for Nearly All New Businesses

☐ Obtain local business licenses.

☐ Check on local zoning ordinances, regulations, and other land use restrictions.

☐ Determine if your particular business requires a state license to operate.

☐ Determine whether any type of federal permit or license is required.

☐ Be prepared to make estimated income tax payments almost immediately after starting business or incorporating.

☐ Apply for a sales and use tax seller's permit if you will sell tangible personal property.

☐ File sales and use tax returns, if you must collect sales or use tax.

☐ File with the county clerk and publish a fictitious business name statement if the business operates under a fictitious name, and then file an affidavit of publication with the county clerk (in most states).

☐ Locate a good insurance agent or retain and meet with an insurance consultant regarding fire, accident, liability, theft, and other types of commercial insurance. Then obtain the necessary insurance coverage.

☐ If you purchase real estate, you must withhold up to 10% of the purchase price and remit it to the IRS if the seller is a foreign individual or foreign-owned company, under the Foreign Investment in Real Property Tax Act.[27] Otherwise, you should insist upon receiving an affidavit that the seller is not a nonresident alien, with his or her taxpayer identification number, unless you are certain that he or she is a U.S. citizen or resident.

☐ For a sole proprietorship, report any self-employment income on *Schedule SE* of federal *Form 1040*, and report income or loss on *Schedule C* of *Form 1040*.

☐ A partnership files *Form 1065* reporting partnership income. Each partner reports his or her share of self-employment income on *Schedule SE* of *Form 1040* and income or loss from partnership operations on *Schedule E* of *Form 1040*.

☐ For a limited partnership, file a *Certificate of Limited Partnership* with the secretary of state and copies in counties where the partnership has places of business or real estate (in most states).

☐ For an LLC, file articles of organization and, if treated as a partnership, file partnership tax returns and report each owner's share of income or loss on the owners' tax returns. If treated as a corporation, comply with all corporate tax filing requirements.

☐ For a corporation, file articles of incorporation, adopt bylaws, and observe necessary corporate formalities. File federal income tax return *Form 1120*; *Form 1120-S* for an S corporation. If property is transferred to the corporation tax-free under Internal Revenue Code

Section 351, report required information relating to the transfer on the corporation's income tax return for that year.

☐ For a corporation, limited liability company, or a partnership, apply for a federal employer identification number on *Form SS-4*, even if the business has no employees. See sample at the end of this chapter.

☐ File annual tax information returns, *Form 1096* and the *Form 1099* series, for payments of $600 or more for items such as rent, interest, and compensation for services, and send 1099s to the payees.

☐ File *Form 1098* for mortgage interest of $600 or more your business receives in a year from an individual.

☐ Also, report any cash payments or cash equivalents of more than $10,000 that you receive to the IRS within 15 days. Such filing may have to be done on computer-readable magnetic media.

☐ If your business is a corporation, be sure to obtain an adequate supply of federal tax deposit coupons in time to make your corporate estimated tax payments.

The above requirements apply to any business, whether it has employees or not. There are many additional requirements for businesses that do have employees, and these are covered in the next chapter. See Section 11.4 for a checklist of additional state law requirements that apply to nearly all new businesses.

4.14 Securities Laws

Inherent in the choice of the legal form of the business is the potential application of federal and state securities laws, if the new business is to have more than one owner or should it become necessary to raise capital for an existing business. Because of the potentially dire consequences of violating federal or state securities laws, it is important to consult with your attorney as early as possible when considering issuing or transferring a security. Corporate stock and limited partnership interests generally are considered securities, and even a general partnership interest can be a security in appropriate circumstances, as can certain types of debt instruments.

Registration of Securities

Since the Securities Act of 1933, federal law has required registration as a prior condition to the issuance or transfer of securities. The law exempts various types of securities and certain types of transactions. The most important of these exemptions for small businesses have been the exemption for securities sold to persons residing within a single state and transactions by an issuer not deemed to involve any public offering. The Securities and Exchange Commission (SEC) from time to time has issued regulations exempting small securities issues, attempting to balance the needs of small businesses to raise capital against the public policy of protecting investors. In 1982, the commission adopted Regulation D as its primary method of regulation of securities offerings by small businesses, although not to the exclusion of other exemptions which might apply.

Rule 504 Exemption

Rule 504 under Regulation D exempts the issuance of securities by an entity if the aggregate offering price of all exempt securities sold by the entity during a twelve-month period does not exceed one million dollars — not more than $500,000 of securities can be offered and sold without registration under some states' securities laws.[28] The securities cannot be offered or sold by any form of general solicitation or general advertising, and the securities so acquired cannot be resold without registration or an exemption from registration.

This rule does not require any specific information to be given to the purchasers of the securities; however, since the anti-fraud provisions of the securities laws apply even though the transaction is exempt from registration, it is helpful to memorialize in writing the material information regarding the offering.

Rule 505 Exemption

Rule 505 exempts offers and sales of securities if the offering price for all exempt securities sold over a twelve-month period does not exceed five million dollars.[29] To obtain this exemption, the issuer must reasonably believe that there are not more than 35 purchasers exclusive of accredited investors.

Examples of accredited investors include banks, insurance companies, a natural person whose net worth at the time of purchase exceeds one million dollars, or a person who has individual income in excess of $200,000 — or $300,000 jointly with a spouse — in each of the two most recent years and expects the same in the current year. Exceptions are also made for certain large investors, including corporations, partnerships, or business trusts with total assets in excess of five million dollars, unless formed for the specific purpose of acquiring the securities.

For purposes of Rule 505, the issuer must furnish extensive information and certified financial statements to the investors, unless securities were sold only to accredited investors. The prohibition against advertising and solicitation applies to this rule, as do the anti-fraud provisions of the securities laws.

Rule 506 Exemption

Rule 506 provides exemptions similar to those under Rule 505, including the 35-purchaser limitation, with the same exception for accredited investors described above.[30] However, Rule 506 requires that an issuer of securities must reasonably believe, immediately before making a sale to a nonaccredited investor, that the investor is sufficiently knowledgeable to adequately evaluate the merits and risks of the investment. Alternatively, the issuer can rely on the knowledge and experience of a person who represents the investor. The other main difference between Rule 505 and Rule 506 is that there is no five million dollar or other maximum size limitation on the amount of securities that can be issued in a Rule 506 offering.

Regulation D Filing Requirements

Issuers utilizing any of the above exemptions must file *Form D* with the SEC generally no later than 15 days after the first sale of securities and at other specified times thereafter. Rule 507 disqualifies any issuer found to have violated the *Form D* filing requirement from future use of the Regulation D exemptions, if the issuer has been enjoined by a court for violating the notice filing requirement — but apparently will not disqualify prior issuances of securities merely due to failure to file *Form D*.[31]

The exemptions available under the federal securities laws are more liberal than those available under the securities laws of many states. In connection with any issuance or transfer of securities, it is necessary to consider the possible application of securities laws in the state where the business entity is established or operates, and, if different, the states where purchasers of the securities live. See Section 11.2 for further information concerning state securities laws.

Going Public Easier for Small Businesses

Through its 1993 Regulation S-B, the SEC provides a new set of rules designed to make it easier and simpler for small businesses to raise capital in the public market. Regulation S-B is an integrated system of rules, forms, and reporting requirements designed especially for small firms, which have traditionally found the costs and complexity of "going public" to be prohibitive. To make a public offering of securities that qualifies under the streamlined procedures of Regulation S-B, an issuing company must meet all the following requirements:

- A company must be a U.S. or Canadian company and cannot be an investment company.
- A company's revenues must be less than $25 million per year.
- The aggregate value of a company's outstanding securities (not counting those held by affiliated companies or persons) must not exceed $25 million.
- If the issuer is a majority-owned subsidiary of another corporation, the parent company must also meet the above criteria.

Endnotes

1. *Armstrong Paint and Varnish Works v. New and U-Enamel Corp.* 305 U.S. 315 (1938); *Carter-Wallace, Inc. v. Proctor and Gamble Co.* 434 F.2d 794 (9th Cir. 1970). The author wishes to acknowledge Henry C. Bunsow, esq. of the San Francisco patent and trademark law firm of Townsend and Townsend for alerting him to this important point.

2. I.R.C. § 6654.

3. I.R.C. § 6041(a).

4. I.R.C. § 6724(d)(3).

5. I.R.C. § 3406(a).

6. I.R.C. § 6041A(b).

7. I.R.C. §§ 6721–6722.

8. I.R.C. § 3509(a).

9. I.R.C. § 3509(b).

10. Treas. Regs. § 1.6041-3(c).

11. Treas. Regs. § 1.6041-3(a).

12. Treas. Regs. § 1.6041-3(d).

13. Treas. Regs. § 1.6041-3(e).

14. Treas. Regs. § 1.6041-3(i).

15. I.R.C. § 6041(a) requires filing of information returns for payments made to another "person." As defined in IRC § 7701(a)(1), "person" does not include governmental bodies.

16. I.R.C. § 6042(a).

17. I.R.C. § 6049(a).

18. I.R.C. § 6050I.

19. I.R.C. § 6722.

20. I.R.C. § 6721.

21. I.R.C. § 6050H.

22. Rev. Proc. 93-24, 1993-1 C.B. 555.

23. 29 U.S.C. § 1112 (§ 412 of ERISA).

24. I.R.C. § 6050K(a).

25. I.R.C. § 6050K(b).

26. Treas. Regs. § 1.351-3.

27. I.R.C. § 1445(a).

28. 17 C.F.R. § 230.504.

29. 17 C.F.R. § 230.505.

30. 17 C.F.R. § 230.506.

31. Rule 507, as interpreted in Securities Act Release No. 6825, March 14, 1989 (17 C.F.R. § 230.507).

Form SS-4 – Application for Employer Identification Number: Sample

Form **SS-4** (Rev. December 1993) Department of the Treasury Internal Revenue Service	**Application for Employer Identification Number** (For use by employers, corporations, partnerships, trusts, estates, churches, government agencies, certain individuals, and others. See instructions.)	EIN OMB No. 1545-0003 Expires 12-31-96

Please type or print clearly.

1 Name of applicant (Legal name) (See instructions.)

2 Trade name of business, if different from name in line 1	**3** Executor, trustee, "care of" name
4a Mailing address (street address) (room, apt., or suite no.)	**5a** Business address, if different from address in lines 4a and 4b
4b City, state, and ZIP code	**5b** City, state, and ZIP code

6 County and state where principal business is located

7 Name of principal officer, general partner, grantor, owner, or trustor—SSN required (See instructions.) ▶

8a Type of entity (Check only one box.) (See instructions.)
- ☐ Sole Proprietor (SSN) ____
- ☐ REMIC ☐ Personal service corp.
- ☐ State/local government ☐ National guard
- ☐ Other nonprofit organization (specify) ____
- ☐ Other (specify) ▶ ____
- ☐ Estate (SSN of decedent) ____
- ☐ Plan administrator-SSN ____
- ☐ Other corporation (specify) ____
- ☐ Federal government/military
- (enter GEN if applicable) ____
- ☐ Trust
- ☐ Partnership
- ☐ Farmers' cooperative
- ☐ Church or church controlled organization

8b If a corporation, name the state or foreign country (if applicable) where incorporated ▶ | State | Foreign country |

9 Reason for applying (Check only one box.)
- ☐ Started new business (specify) ▶ ____
- ☐ Hired employees
- ☐ Created a pension plan (specify type) ▶ ____
- ☐ Banking purpose (specify) ▶
- ☐ Changed type of organization (specify) ▶ ____
- ☐ Purchased going business
- ☐ Created a trust (specify) ▶ ____
- ☐ Other (specify) ▶

10 Date business started or acquired (Mo., day, year) (See instructions.) | **11** Enter closing month of accounting year. (See instructions.)

12 First date wages or annuities were paid or will be paid (Mo., day, year). **Note:** *If applicant is a withholding agent, enter date income will first be paid to nonresident alien (Mo., day, year)* ▶

13 Enter highest number of employees expected in the next 12 months. **Note:** *If the applicant does not expect to have any employees during the period, enter "0."* ▶ | Nonagricultural | Agricultural | Household |

14 Principal activity (See instructions.) ▶

15 Is the principal business activity manufacturing? ☐ Yes ☐ No
If "Yes," principal product and raw material used ▶

16 To whom are most of the products or services sold? Please check the appropriate box. ☐ Business (wholesale)
☐ Public (retail) ☐ Other (specify) ▶ ☐ N/A

17a Has the applicant ever applied for an identification number for this or any other business? ☐ Yes ☐ No
Note: *If "Yes," please complete lines 17b and 17c.*

17b If you checked the "Yes" box in line 17a, give applicant's legal name and trade name, if different than name shown on prior application.
Legal name ▶ Trade name ▶

17c Enter approximate date, city, and state where the application was filed and the previous employer identification number if known.
Approximate date when filed (Mo., day, year) | City and state where filed | Previous EIN

Under penalties of perjury, I declare that I have examined this application, and to the best of my knowledge and belief, it is true, correct, and complete. | Business telephone number (include area code)

Name and title (Please type or print clearly.) ▶

Signature ▶ Date ▶

Note: *Do not write below this line.   For official use only.*

Please leave blank ▶	Geo.	Ind.	Class	Size	Reason for applying

For Paperwork Reduction Act Notice, see attached instructions. Cat. No. 16055N Form **SS-4** (Rev. 12-93)

Instructions for Form SS-4: Sample

Form SS-4 (Rev. 12-93)   Page **2**

General Instructions

(Section references are to the Internal Revenue Code unless otherwise noted.)

Purpose

Use Form SS-4 to apply for an employer identification number (EIN). An EIN is a nine-digit number (for example, 12-3456789) assigned to sole proprietors, corporations, partnerships, estates, trusts, and other entities for filing and reporting purposes. The information you provide on this form will establish your filing and reporting requirements.

Who Must File

You must file this form if you have not obtained an EIN before and

● You pay wages to one or more employees.

● You are required to have an EIN to use on any return, statement, or other document, even if you are not an employer.

● You are a withholding agent required to withhold taxes on income, other than wages, paid to a nonresident alien (individual, corporation, partnership, etc.). A withholding agent may be an agent, broker, fiduciary, manager, tenant, or spouse, and is required to file **Form 1042,** Annual Withholding Tax Return for U.S. Source Income of Foreign Persons.

● You file **Schedule C,** Profit or Loss From Business, or **Schedule F,** Profit or Loss From Farming, of **Form 1040,** U.S. Individual Income Tax Return, and have a Keogh plan or are required to file excise, employment, or alcohol, tobacco, or firearms returns.

The following must use EINs even if they do not have any employees:

● Trusts, except the following:

1. Certain grantor-owned revocable trusts (see the Instructions for Form 1040).

2. Individual Retirement Arrangement (IRA) trusts, unless the trust has to file **Form 990-T,** Exempt Organization Business Income Tax Return (See the Instructions for Form 990-T.)

● Estates

● Partnerships

● REMICS (real estate mortgage investment conduits) (See the instructions for **Form 1066,** U.S. Real Estate Mortgage Investment Conduit Income Tax Return.)

● Corporations

● Nonprofit organizations (churches, clubs, etc.)

● Farmers' cooperatives

● Plan administrators (A plan administrator is the person or group of persons specified as the administrator by the instrument under which the plan is operated.)

Note: *Household employers are not required to file Form SS-4 to get an EIN. An EIN may be assigned to you without filing Form SS-4 if your only employees are household employees (domestic workers) in your private home. To have an EIN assigned to you, write "NONE" in the space for the EIN on* **Form 942,** *Employer's Quarterly Tax Return for Household Employees, when you file it.*

When To Apply for A New EIN

New Business.—If you become the new owner of an existing business, **DO NOT** use the EIN of the former owner. If you already have an EIN, use that number. If you do not have an EIN, apply for one on this form. If you become the "owner" of a corporation by acquiring its stock, use the corporation's EIN.

Changes in Organization or Ownership.—If you already have an EIN, you may need to get a new one if either the organization or ownership of your business changes. If you incorporate a sole proprietorship or form a partnership, you must get a new EIN. However, **DO NOT** apply for a new EIN if you change only the name of your business.

File Only One Form SS-4.—File only one Form SS-4, regardless of the number of businesses operated or trade names under which a business operates. However, each corporation in an affiliated group must file a separate application.

EIN Applied For, But Not Received.—If you do not have an EIN by the time a return is due, write "Applied for" and the date you applied in the space shown for the number. **DO NOT** show your social security number as an EIN on returns.

If you do not have an EIN by the time a tax deposit is due, send your payment to the Internal Revenue service center for your filing area. (See **Where To Apply** below.) Make your check or money order payable to Internal Revenue Service and show your name (as shown on Form SS-4), address, kind of tax, period covered, and date you applied for an EIN.

For more information about EINs, see **Pub. 583,** Taxpayers Starting a Business and **Pub. 1635,** EINs Made Easy.

How To Apply

You can apply for an EIN either by mail or by telephone. You can get an EIN immediately by calling the Tele-TIN phone number for the service center for your state, or you can send the completed Form SS-4 directly to the service center to receive your EIN in the mail.

Application by Tele-TIN.—Under the Tele-TIN program, you can receive your EIN over the telephone and use it

immediately to file a return or make a payment. To receive an EIN by phone, complete Form SS-4, then call the Tele-TIN phone number listed for your state under **Where To Apply. The** person making the call must be authorized to sign the form (see **Signature block** on page 3).

An IRS representative will use the information from the Form SS-4 to establish your account and assign you an EIN. Write the number you are given on the upper right-hand corner of the form, sign and date it.

You should mail or FAX the signed SS-4 within 24 hours to the Tele-TIN Unit at the service center address for your state. The IRS representative will give you the FAX number. The FAX numbers are also listed in Pub. 1635.

Taxpayer representatives can receive their client's EIN by phone if they first send a facsimile (FAX) of a completed **Form 2848,** Power of Attorney and Declaration of Representative, or **Form 8821,** Tax Information Authorization, to the Tele-TIN unit. The Form 2848 or Form 8821 will be used solely to release the EIN to the representative authorized on the form.

Application by Mail.—Complete Form SS-4 at least 4 to 5 weeks before you will need an EIN. Sign and date the application and mail it to the service center address for your state. You will receive your EIN in the mail in approximately 4 weeks.

Where To Apply

The Tele-TIN phone numbers listed below will involve a long-distance charge to callers outside of the local calling area, and should be used only to apply for an EIN. THE NUMBERS MAY CHANGE WITHOUT NOTICE. Use 1-800-829-1040 to verify a number or to ask about an application by mail or other Federal tax matters.

If your principal business, office or agency, or legal residence in the case of an individual, is located in:	Call the Tele-TIN phone number shown or file with the Internal Revenue Service center at:
Florida, Georgia, South Carolina	Attn: Entity Control Atlanta, GA 39901 (404) 455-2360
New Jersey, New York City and counties of Nassau, Rockland, Suffolk, and Westchester	Attn: Entity Control Holtsville, NY 00501 (516) 447-4955
New York (all other counties), Connecticut, Maine, Massachusetts, New Hampshire, Rhode Island, Vermont	Attn: Entity Control Andover, MA 05501 (508) 474-9717
Illinois, Iowa, Minnesota, Missouri, Wisconsin	Attn: Entity Control Stop 57A 2306 E. Bannister Rd. Kansas City, MO 64131 (816) 926-5999
Delaware, District of Columbia, Maryland, Pennsylvania, Virginia	Attn: Entity Control Philadelphia, PA 19255 (215) 574-2400

Instructions for Form SS-4: Sample (continued)

Form SS-4 (Rev. 12-93)   Page **3**

| Indiana, Kentucky, Michigan, Ohio, West Virginia | Attn: Entity Control Cincinnati, OH 45999 (606) 292-5467 |

Kansas, New Mexico, Oklahoma, Texas — Attn: Entity Control Austin, TX 73301 (512) 462-7843

Alaska, Arizona, California (counties of Alpine, Amador, Butte, Calaveras, Colusa, Contra Costa, Del Norte, El Dorado, Glenn, Humboldt, Lake, Lassen, Marin, Mendocino, Modoc, Napa, Nevada, Placer, Plumas, Sacramento, San Joaquin, Shasta, Sierra, Siskiyou, Solano, Sonoma, Sutter, Tehama, Trinity, Yolo, and Yuba), Colorado, Idaho, Montana, Nebraska, Nevada, North Dakota, Oregon, South Dakota, Utah, Washington, Wyoming — Attn: Entity Control Mail Stop 6271-T P.O. Box 9950 Ogden, UT 84409 (801) 620-7645

California (all other counties), Hawaii — Attn: Entity Control Fresno, CA 93888 (209) 452-4010

Alabama, Arkansas, Louisiana, Mississippi, North Carolina, Tennessee — Attn: Entity Control Memphis, TN 37501 (901) 365-5970

If you have no legal residence, principal place of business, or principal office or agency in any state, file your form with the Internal Revenue Service Center, Philadelphia, PA 19255 or call (215) 574-2400.

Specific Instructions

The instructions that follow are for those items that are not self-explanatory. Enter N/A (nonapplicable) on the lines that do not apply.

Line 1.—Enter the legal name of the entity applying for the EIN exactly as it appears on the social security card, charter, or other applicable legal document.

Individuals.—Enter the first name, middle initial, and last name.

Trusts.—Enter the name of the trust.

Estate of a decedent.—Enter the name of the estate.

Partnerships.—Enter the legal name of the partnership as it appears in the partnership agreement.

Corporations.—Enter the corporate name as set forth in the corporation charter or other legal document creating it.

Plan administrators.—Enter the name of the plan administrator. A plan administrator who already has an EIN should use that number.

Line 2.—Enter the trade name of the business if different from the legal name. The trade name is the "doing business as" name.

Note: *Use the full legal name on line 1 on all tax returns filed for the entity. However, if you enter a trade name on line 2 and choose to use the trade name instead of the legal name, enter the trade name on all returns you file. To prevent processing delays and errors,* **always** *use either the legal name only or the trade name only on all tax returns.*

Line 3.—Trusts enter the name of the trustee. Estates enter the name of the executor, administrator, or other fiduciary. If the entity applying has a designated person to receive tax information, enter that person's name as the "care of" person. Print or type the first name, middle initial, and last name.

Line 7.—Enter the first name, middle initial, last name, and social security number (SSN) of a principal officer if the business is a corporation; of a general partner if a partnership; and of a grantor owner, or trustor if a trust.

Line 8a.—Check the box that best describes the type of entity applying for the EIN. If not specifically mentioned, check the "other" box and enter the type of entity. Do not enter N/A.

Sole proprietor.—Check this box if you file Schedule C or F (Form 1040) and have a Keogh plan, or are required to file excise, employment, or alcohol, tobacco, or firearms returns. Enter your SSN (social security number) in the space provided.

Plan administrator.—If the plan administrator is an individual, enter the plan administrator's SSN in the space provided.

Withholding agent.—If you are a withholding agent required to file Form 1042, check the "other" box and enter "withholding agent."

REMICs.—Check this box if the entity has elected to be treated as a real estate mortgage investment conduit (REMIC). See the Instructions for Form 1066 for more information.

Personal service corporations.—Check this box if the entity is a personal service corporation. An entity is a personal service corporation for a tax year only if:

● The principal activity of the entity during the testing period (prior tax year) for the tax year is the performance of personal services substantially by employee-owners.

● The employee-owners own 10 percent of the fair market value of the outstanding stock in the entity on the last day of the testing period.

Personal services include performance of services in such fields as health, law, accounting, consulting, etc. For more information about personal service corporations, see the instructions for **Form 1120**, U.S. Corporation Income Tax Return, and **Pub. 542**, Tax Information on Corporations.

Other corporations.—This box is for any corporation other than a personal service corporation. If you check this box, enter the type of corporation (such as insurance company) in the space provided.

Other nonprofit organizations.—Check this box if the nonprofit organization is

other than a church or church-controlled organization and specify the type of nonprofit organization (for example, an educational organization.)

If the organization also seeks tax-exempt status, you must file either **Package 1023** or **Package 1024,** Application for Recognition of Exemption. Get **Pub. 557,** Tax-Exempt Status for Your Organization, for more information.

Group exemption number (GEN).—If the organization is covered by a group exemption letter, enter the four-digit GEN. (Do not confuse the GEN with the nine-digit EIN.) If you do not know the GEN, contact the parent organization. Get Pub. 557 for more information about group exemption numbers.

Line 9.—Check only **one** box. Do not enter N/A.

Started new business.—Check this box if you are starting a new business that requires an EIN. If you check this box, enter the type of business being started. **DO NOT** apply if you already have an EIN and are only adding another place of business.

Changed type of organization.—Check this box if the business is changing its type of organization, for example, if the business was a sole proprietorship and has been incorporated or has become a partnership. If you check this box, specify in the space provided the type of change made, for example, "from sole proprietorship to partnership."

Purchased going business.—Check this box if you purchased an existing business. DO NOT use the former owner's EIN. Use your own EIN if you already have one.

Hired employees.—Check this box if the existing business is requesting an EIN because it has hired or is hiring employees and is therefore required to file employment tax returns. **DO NOT** apply if you already have an EIN and are only hiring employees. If you are hiring household employees, see **Note** under **Who Must File** on page 2.

Created a trust.—Check this box if you created a trust, and enter the type of trust created.

Note: *DO NOT file this form if you are the individual-grantor/owner of a revocable trust. You must use your SSN for the trust. See the instructions for Form 1040.*

Created a pension plan.—Check this box if you have created a pension plan and need this number for reporting purposes. Also, enter the type of plan created.

Banking purpose.—Check this box if you are requesting an EIN for banking purposes only and enter the banking purpose (for example, a bowling league for depositing dues, an investment club for dividend and interest reporting, etc.).

Instructions for Form SS-4: Sample (continued)

Form SS-4 (Rev. 12-93)   Page **4**

Other (specify).—Check this box if you are requesting an EIN for any reason other than those for which there are checkboxes, and enter the reason.

Line 10.—If you are starting a new business, enter the starting date of the business. If the business you acquired is already operating, enter the date you acquired the business. Trusts should enter the date the trust was legally created. Estates should enter the date of death of the decedent whose name appears on line 1 or the date when the estate was legally funded.

Line 11.—Enter the last month of your accounting year or tax year. An accounting or tax year is usually 12 consecutive months, either a calendar year or a fiscal year (including a period of 52 or 53 weeks). A calendar year is 12 consecutive months ending on December 31. A fiscal year is either 12 consecutive months ending on the last day of any month other than December or a 52-53 week year. For more information on accounting periods, see **Pub. 538,** Accounting Periods and Methods.

Individuals.—Your tax year generally will be a calendar year.

Partnerships.—Partnerships generally must adopt the tax year of either (1) the majority partners; (2) the principal partners; (3) the tax year that results in the least aggregate (total) deferral of income; or (4) some other tax year. (See the Instructions for **Form 1065,** U.S. Partnership Return of Income, for more information.)

REMICs.—Remics must have a calendar year as their tax year.

Personal service corporations.—A personal service corporation generally must adopt a calendar year unless:

● It can establish a business purpose for having a different tax year, or

● It elects under section 444 to have a tax year other than a calendar year.

Trusts.—Generally, a trust must adopt a calendar year except for the following:

● Tax-exempt trusts,

● Charitable trusts, and

● Grantor-owned trusts.

Line 12.—If the business has or will have employees, enter the date on which the business began or will begin to pay wages. If the business does not plan to have employees, enter N/A.

Withholding agent.—Enter the date you began or will begin to pay income to a nonresident alien. This also applies to individuals who are required to file Form 1042 to report alimony paid to a nonresident alien.

Line 14.—Generally, enter the exact type of business being operated (for example, advertising agency, farm, food or beverage establishment, labor union, real estate agency, steam laundry, rental of coin-operated vending machine, investment club, etc.). Also state if the business will involve the sale or distribution of alcoholic beverages.

Governmental.—Enter the type of organization (state, county, school district, or municipality, etc.).

Nonprofit organization (other than governmental).—Enter whether organized for religious, educational, or humane purposes, and the principal activity (for example, religious organization—hospital, charitable).

Mining and quarrying.—Specify the process and the principal product (for example, mining bituminous coal, contract drilling for oil, quarrying dimension stone, etc.).

Contract construction.—Specify whether general contracting or special trade contracting. Also, show the type of work normally performed (for example, general contractor for residential buildings, electrical subcontractor, etc.).

Food or beverage establishments.—Specify the type of establishment and state whether you employ workers who receive tips (for example, lounge—yes).

Trade.—Specify the type of sales and the principal line of goods sold (for example, wholesale dairy products, manufacturer's representative for mining machinery, retail hardware, etc.).

Manufacturing.—Specify the type of establishment operated (for example, sawmill, vegetable cannery, etc.).

Signature block.—The application must be signed by: (1) the individual, if the applicant is an individual, (2) the president, vice president, or other principal officer, if the applicant is a corporation, (3) a responsible and duly authorized member or officer having knowledge of its affairs, if the applicant is a partnership or other unincorporated organization, or (4) the fiduciary, if the applicant is a trust or estate.

Some Useful Publications

You may get the following publications for additional information on the subjects covered on this form. To get these and other free forms and publications, call 1-800-TAX-FORM (1-800-829-3676).

Pub. 1635, EINs Made Easy

Pub. 538, Accounting Periods and Methods

Pub. 541, Tax Information on Partnerships

Pub. 542, Tax Information on Corporations

Pub. 557, Tax-Exempt Status for Your Organization

Pub. 583, Taxpayers Starting A Business

Pub. 937, Employment Taxes and Information Returns

Package 1023, Application for Recognition of Exemption

Package 1024, Application for Recognition of Exemption Under Section 501(a) or for Determination Under Section 120

Paperwork Reduction Act Notice

We ask for the information on this form to carry out the Internal Revenue laws of the United States. You are required to give us the information. We need it to ensure that you are complying with these laws and to allow us to figure and collect the right amount of tax.

The time needed to complete and file this form will vary depending on individual circumstances. The estimated average time is:

Recordkeeping . . . . . . 7 min.

Learning about the law or the form . . . . 18 min.

Preparing the form. . . . . 44 min.

Copying, assembling, and sending the form to the IRS . 20 min.

If you have comments concerning the accuracy of these time estimates or suggestions for making this form more simple, we would be happy to hear from you. You can write to both the **Internal Revenue Service,** Attention: Reports Clearance Officer, PC:FP, Washington, DC 20224; and the **Office of Management and Budget,** Paperwork Reduction Project (1545-0003), Washington, DC 20503. **DO NOT** send this form to either of these offices. Instead, see **Where To Apply** on page 2.

Printed on recycled paper   *U.S. Government Printing Office: 1993 — 363-331/99125

Chapter 5

The Thicket Thickens: Additional Requirements for Businesses with Employees

Man is a thinking animal, a talking animal, a tool-making animal,
a building animal, a political animal, a fantasizing animal. But in
the twilight of a civilization, he is chiefly a taxpaying animal.

— Hugh MacLennan

5.1 General Considerations

As the previous chapter indicated, there is a considerable amount of governmental red tape involved in starting almost any new business. If your business will have any employees — even if it is incorporated and you are the only employee — the level of government regulation and red tape will multiply several times over in a typical case. This chapter outlines the bases you must cover, in addition to those described in Chapter 4, if you start a business that will have employees.

5.2 Social Security and Income Tax Withholding

Once you go into business and begin paying salary or wages to employees, you will find that you have been appointed, as an agent of the government, to collect taxes from your employees. In addition to various payroll taxes, you will also be required to collect income taxes and Social Security (FICA) tax from employees' wages.

The first order of business is to apply for a federal employer identification number (EIN) with the IRS. This number will be used to identify your

Employer Identification Number

business on payroll and income tax returns and for most other federal tax purposes. To apply for an EIN number, you need to file a completed *Form SS-4* at the earliest possible time, especially if you have employees. This will ensure that you will get tax deposit coupons in time for depositing federal payroll taxes or corporate income tax. Corporations and partnerships must file *Form SS-4* even if they have no employees. A sample of this form is located at the end of Chapter 4.

The IRS can provide you with a business tax kit that is specifically put together for new employers. You can also obtain *Circular E, Employer's Tax Guide*, an IRS publication that explains federal income tax withholding and Social Security tax requirements for employers. *Circular E* contains up-to-date withholding tables that you must use to determine how much federal income tax and Social Security tax is to be withheld from each employee's paycheck.

Employer Social Security Tax

In addition to withholding Social Security tax from an employee's paycheck — at the rate of 7.65% on gross wages up to $60,600, 1.45% on wages in excess of $60,600 in 1994 — the employer must also pay an equal amount of employer's Social Security tax. The withheld federal income tax, withheld employee Social Security tax, and employer's Social Security tax are lumped together and paid to the IRS at the same time. In some cases, these taxes can simply be mailed in with your payroll tax return (*Form 941* series) at the end of the calendar quarter or year; however, if you have significant amounts of these taxes to pay, you will generally be required to deposit the taxes with a federal tax deposit form, a precoded coupon, at an authorized commercial bank or a federal reserve bank. As a rule, the greater the amount of taxes due, the sooner they must be paid.

The complex tax deposit deadlines of previous years have been totally revised and considerably simplified and revised under recent IRS regulations. Rules for how and when federal income and Social Security taxes are to be mailed in or deposited are summarized briefly as follows:

Type of Depositor	Deadline
Small depositor — An employer with less than $500 of combined income and Social Security taxes for the calendar quarter.[1]	Deposit by last day of month following the end of the quarter, or mail with *Form 941* return by then.
Monthly depositor — An employer, who for the 12-month period ending June 30th of the preceding calendar year, reported $50,000 or less of employment taxes.[2]	Deposit by 15th day of the following month.
Semi-weekly depositor — All other employers:[3]	
For Wednesday–Friday semi-weekly period:	Deposit on or before next Wednesday.
For Saturday–Tuesday semi-weekly period:	Deposit on or before next Friday.

Some exceptions to the above tax deposit schedules do exist. For example, any employer with $100,000 of employment taxes accumulated at the end of any day — for the current month or semi-weekly period only, whichever applies — must deposit those taxes in an authorized bank by the end of the next banking day, subsequently becoming a semi-weekly depositor.[4] Shortfalls in required deposits will result in underpayment penalties. No penalty, however, will be imposed if the shortfall does not exceed 2% of the required deposit (or $100, if greater) provided the shortfall is made up within specified periods. For a more detailed explanation of federal tax deposits, see IRS *Notice 109*. Deposits of payroll and withholding taxes may be mailed to a depository bank, if postmarked at least two days prior to the tax deposit due date. But tax deposits of $20,000 or more by employers making more than one deposit a month must reach the bank by the due date, regardless of the postmark date.[5]

New Employees

When a new employee is hired, give the employee a federal *Form W-4*. He or she must then complete and return the form to you. When completed, *Form W-4* provides the employee's Social Security number and the number of withholding exemptions the employee is claiming. The number of exemptions is used to determine how much income tax you must withhold from his or her wages. You keep *Form W-4*. Neither it nor the information on it is filed with the IRS, except in the case of an employee who claims more than ten withholding exemptions, or who claims exemption from income tax withholding.

By January 31 of each year, you must furnish each employee with copies of *Form W-2, Annual Wage and Tax Statement*, showing the taxable wages paid to an employee during the preceding calendar year and the taxes withheld, including state income tax. By February 28, the original of *Form W-2* and a summary form, *Form W-3*, should be filed with the IRS.

Independent Contractors

A person who performs services for your business does not necessarily have to be your employee. In many cases, you can structure your legal relationships with persons who provide services to you so they are considered independent contractors for tax and other legal purposes. From an employer standpoint, it is preferable to treat someone as an independent contractor rather than as an employee of your business because you do not have to pay Social Security tax or federal or state unemployment taxes on his or her compensation. An independent contractor is considered to be self-employed for tax purposes and pays self-employment tax.

In addition, you don't have to withhold income and payroll taxes from compensation paid to independent contractors or file payroll tax returns with respect to their compensation. You must, however, file a *Form 1099-MISC* for each independent contractor to whom you make payments of $600 or more during a calendar year (with certain exceptions) or, in the case of a direct seller of consumer goods, for each such direct seller to whom you sell $5,000 of goods during a year.

Because of the obvious advantages employers obtain by treating their employees as independent contractors, the IRS has been very aggressive in attempting to reclassify so-called independent contractors as employees where they perform functions in a manner that is more typical of an employer/employee relationship. Requiring businesses to file *Form 1099-MISC* is an attempt by the IRS to identify those businesses that may be improperly treating employees as independent contractors.

Before you decide to treat anyone who works for you as an independent contractor, consult your tax adviser because there can be serious consequences if those individuals are reclassified as employees by the IRS. See Section 9.11 for a discussion of the risks involved.

Each state has its own withholding taxes. For information on the withholding tax requirements for this state, see Section 11.5.

5.3 Unemployment Taxes

With relatively few exceptions, all businesses with employees must pay both federal and state unemployment taxes. These taxes are imposed entirely on you, the employer. Theoretically, the federal unemployment tax is 6.2% of the first $7,000 of annual wages per employee.[6] In actuality, however, the rate is usually only 0.8% because a credit for up to 5.4% is given for state unemployment taxes paid and for a favorable experience rating for state unemployment tax purposes.[7]

The state unemployment tax rate for an employer can be either more or less than the basic rate, depending upon the amount of unemployment claims by former employees. The more unemployment benefits claimed by your former employees, the higher your unemployment tax rate will be, within certain limits.

Federal Unemployment Tax

Your business will be required to pay federal unemployment tax (FUTA) for any calendar year in which it pays wages of $1,500 or more[8] or if it has one or more employees for at least a portion of the day during any 20 different calendar weeks during the year.[9] Needless to say, this will cover almost any business that has one employee, even if that employee is part-time.

If the FUTA liability during any of the first three calendar quarters is more than $100, you must deposit the tax with a federal tax deposit coupon, *Form 8109*, at an authorized bank during the month following the end of the quarter. If the tax is $100 or less, you are not required to make a deposit, but you must add it to the taxes for the next quarter. For the fourth quarter, if the undeposited FUTA tax for the year is more than $100, deposit the tax with a tax deposit coupon at an authorized bank by January 31. If the balance due is $100 or less, either deposit it with the coupon or mail it to the IRS with your federal unemployment tax return, *Form 940*, by January 31. *Form 940* is not due until February 10 if all of the FUTA tax for the prior year has already been deposited when due.

The IRS also provides *Form 940-EZ*, a greatly simplified FUTA return for certain small employers. In general, the small employers who can use *Form 940-EZ* are those:

- Who pay unemployment tax to only one state;
- Who pay state unemployment taxes by the *Form 940-EZ* due date; and
- Whose wages subject to FUTA are also taxable for state unemployment tax purposes.

The state also imposes an unemployment tax which meshes closely with the federal unemployment tax. Refer to Section 11.5 for details on state unemployment taxes, rates, returns, and registration as an employer.

5.4 Workers' Compensation Insurance

A business is generally required by state law to obtain workers' compensation insurance for its employees. This means that you, as an employer, may have to immediately seek out and obtain a workers' compensation insurance policy covering all your employees, or you will be subject to possible legal sanctions. Workers' compensation insurance coverage provides various benefits to an employee who suffers a job-related injury or illness.

Many insurance companies offer workers' compensation coverage, though many may be reluctant to write a policy that covers only one or a few employees, unless it is tied to other types of insurance policies. See Section 11.5 for a description of other formal requirements applicable to employers under the workers' compensation laws.

5.5 Compliance with ERISA — Employee Benefit Plans

If you have employees and provide them with fringe benefits, such as group insurance — other than workers' compensation — or other types of employee welfare plan benefits, or if you adopt a pension or profit-sharing retirement plan, you will almost certainly have to comply with at least some aspects of the Employee Retirement Income Security Act of 1974 (ERISA).

There are criminal penalties for willful failure to comply with two types of ERISA requirements: 1) reporting to government agencies, and 2) disclosure to employees.[10] In addition, there are a number of different types of civil penalties, which are incredibly numerous and complex, for unintentional failures to comply with ERISA requirements.[11] In short, compliance with ERISA is not a simple matter.

This section lays down some relatively simple and straightforward guidelines you, as a layperson, can follow in trying to recognize when you might have an ERISA compliance obligation. If you recognize your need to be in compliance, call your attorney, accountant, or benefit consultant for help. ERISA deals with two kinds of employee benefit plans: pension plans and welfare plans.

Pension Plans

Pension plans under ERISA are pretty much what you might expect — tax qualified retirement plans including both pension and profit-sharing plans (including Keogh plans), plus other types of benefit programs that defer payments until after employment has terminated.[12]

Because these compliance requirements are so very complex and are constantly in a state of flux, no attempt to spell them out in detail is made here. Instead, the basic ERISA compliance requirements for most pension and profit-sharing plans are summarized in the table on page 22.

If your business maintains a pension or profit-sharing plan, it should be obvious from this summary of basic ERISA compliance requirements that you need some expert help from an attorney, accountant, or pension consulting firm — or all of them — if you are going to be able to properly comply with the requirements of ERISA and avoid potential fines and other civil and criminal penalties.

The cost of maintaining these plans has unfortunately multiplied several times over since the passage of ERISA in 1974, followed by a labyrinth of ERISA regulations issued by several different federal agencies. In short, unless you make substantial contributions to and obtain significant tax savings from an employee retirement plan, it may not be worth having because of the heavy costs of compliance with ERISA.

Welfare Plans

Welfare plans under ERISA include most other types of employee benefit plans that are not considered pension plans.[13] These include typical fringe benefit plans adopted by small firms, such as health insurance, long-term disability, group-term life insurance, and accidental death insurance plans. ERISA compliance for welfare plans is usually less of a burden than for pension plans, but is required for almost every business that provides any kind of benefits for employees of the type mentioned above.

A number of so-called fringe benefits that are in the nature of payroll practices, such as paid holidays, vacation pay, bonuses, overtime premium pay, and most kinds of severance pay arrangements, are usually not considered to be either pension or welfare plans under ERISA.[14] Thus, these kinds of payroll practices are not subject to ERISA at all. Compliance requirements for reporting and disclosure under ERISA are briefly discussed below.

Summary Plan Descriptions

The one ERISA compliance requirement that applies to most small businesses is the requirement for you to prepare a summary plan description

(SPD) for distribution to all employees covered by any type of welfare plan you sponsor, such as typical health, accident, life, or disability insurance plans.[15] An SPD must contain more than 20 specific items of information listed in the U.S. Department of Labor Regulations,[16] including an ERISA rights statement which must be copied more or less verbatim from the regulations.

An SPD must be prepared for each plan and distributed to covered employees within 120 days after the plan is first adopted.[17] Each new employee must be given a copy of the SPD within 90 days after becoming a participant in the plan.[18] Since an SPD must be prepared for each employee plan subject to ERISA, even a very small business may find that it has to produce three or four of these documents, each of which must meet detailed technical requirements.

One important consideration in taking out insurance coverage for employees should be a firm commitment from the insurance company or brokers that they will prepare the necessary SPDs for the insurance plans they are selling you. Otherwise, you may need to have your attorney or benefit consultant prepare the SPDs, which can result in substantial professional fees.

Other than the need for you to prepare SPDs and distribute them to employees, there are no significant ERISA requirements that apply to most kinds of insured-type welfare plans that cover fewer than 100 employees.[19] You must, however, make available the insurance policies and other plan documents for inspection by your employees and you must furnish copies to them upon request.[20]

Additional ERISA Requirements

If your business should grow to have 100 or more employees who are covered by a plan, or if you adopt any type of uninsured funded welfare plan, you will suddenly become subject to a whole array of additional ERISA requirements, including:

- Filing a copy of the SPD with the U.S. Department of Labor;[21]
- Filing an annual return/report or registration (*Form 5500* series) with the IRS each year;[22]
- Preparing and distributing a summary annual report to covered employees each year;[23]
- Preparing a summary of material modifications of the plan, if necessary, and filing it with the U.S. Department of Labor and distributing it to covered employees;[24] and
- Filing a terminal report if the plan is terminated.[25]

Bonding and Withholding Requirements

Besides the ERISA reporting and disclosure requirements listed in the summary on page 22, you should be aware of two other points regarding ERISA: the bonding requirement and withholding requirements on pension or profit-sharing plan distributions. If any of your employees are deemed to handle assets of an employee benefit plan that is subject to

ERISA, they must be covered by a fidelity bond.[26] Consult your attorney or benefit consultant to see if any required bonding needs to be paid regarding any benefit plans you maintain for your employees. This is particularly important if you have a pension or profit-sharing plan.

Secondly, withholding is mandatory on distributions of pension, profit-sharing, and IRA benefits.[27] There is an exception for certain periodic distributions on which the recipient elects, in advance, not to have any tax withheld.

In addition to reporting and disclosure requirements under ERISA, there are other federal reporting and recordkeeping requirements for certain types of fringe benefit plans.[28] For example, employers maintaining educational assistance programs, group legal services plans, and so-called cafeteria plans are currently required to file annual reports with the IRS on *Form 5500* or *Form 5500-C/R* and, if needed, to maintain records to show that those plans qualified for tax purposes for each year after 1984.[29]

5.6 Employee Safety and Health Regulations

As has been discussed in Section 5.4, employers are required by state law in many states to carry workers' compensation insurance for the protection of employees who develop job-related illnesses or who are injured on the job. In addition, there are comprehensive and far-reaching federal laws that set safety standards designed to prevent injuries arising from unsafe or unhealthy working conditions. The primary federal law regulating job safety, the Occupational Safety and Health Act of 1970 (OSHA), imposes several reporting and recordkeeping obligations for employers.

Federal OSHA

Over the years, the Occupational Safety and Health Administration has issued reams of regulations and standards for workplace safety. If you have employees, you will need to consult an attorney, preferably one with OSHA expertise, to determine what, if any, steps you must take to comply with federal and state safety standards at your place of business. Otherwise, you may be subject to fines and other legal sanctions if any employee is injured on the job or OSHA inspectors find that you are not in compliance with applicable safety standards at your place of business.

You should also contact the nearest regional U.S. Department of Labor – OSHA office and request information on any free consultative services or publications the office may have available. Many state occupational safety and health agencies provide confidential, on-site consultations for no charge. These consultations point out state compliance issues at your place of business without fining or penalizing you for any discovered violations.

OSHA requires that you post a permanent notice to employees regarding job safety.[30]

Under OSHA, it is necessary to keep a log of industrial injuries and illnesses.[31] Records maintained under an approved state OSHA plan can be used to satisfy this federal requirement.[32] The information in the log must also be summarized and posted prominently in your workplace from February 1 to March 1.[33] This requirement has been eliminated for most retail, financial, insurance, and service firms,[34] but not for:

- Building material and garden supply stores;
- General merchandise stores;
- Food stores;
- Hotels and other lodging places;
- Repair, amusement, and recreation services; and
- Health services.[35]

Under OSHA, a supplementary record must be prepared after a recordable injury or illness occurs, using federal *Form 101* or any of the substitutes state law permits to be used for this purpose.[36]

Neither of the above recordkeeping forms are ordinarily filed with the government. Instead, these records must be retained and kept available for inspection for five years.[37] In addition, special recordkeeping requirements will generally apply if your employees are exposed to toxic substances, asbestos, radiation, or carcinogens on the job.

You can obtain more detailed information on OSHA recordkeeping requirements by calling the nearest OSHA office (usually listed in the phone book under U. S. Government – Department of Labor) and asking for the booklet entitled, *Recordkeeping Requirements for Occupational Injuries and Illnesses*.

OSHA exempts any employer with ten or fewer employees from most of its reporting and recordkeeping requirements;[38] however, these small employers are not exempt from keeping a log of all injuries and accidents or reporting job-related fatalities and multiple injuries.

Federal OSHA reporting requirements include:

- The Bureau of Labor Statistics may require certain selected employers, including small employers, to report certain summary information on job-related injuries and illnesses annually on an occupational injuries and illness survey form.[39]
- In the event of a fatality or an accident resulting in the hospitalization of three or more employees, you must notify the area OSHA director within eight hours, describing the circumstances of the accident, the extent of any injuries, the number of fatalities, and other information.[40] There are penalties in the event you fail to give notice as required.[41]

See Section 11.5 for a discussion of laws this state may have that govern employee safety and health.

5.7 Employee Wage-Hour and Child Labor Laws

Not all businesses nor all employees of a given business are covered by federal and state wage-hour and child labor laws. The coverage of these laws is a crazy quilt patchwork of exceptions. Thus, there is no simple way to tell you whether your business will be subject to one or more of the federal and state laws relating to minimum wage, overtime pay, and child labor, or, if it is, which employees are covered and which are not. To find out which laws apply to your business, contact your attorney or the local wage-hour office.

Federal Wage-Hour Laws

The Federal Fair Labor Standards Act (FLSA) includes a number of requirements regarding compensation of employees covered under the act. There are two major requirements you need to know about — the minimum wage and overtime requirements.

Minimum Wage Requirement

The minimum wage provisions of the FLSA set an hourly minimum wage that you must pay to an employee. The current federal minimum wage is $4.25 per hour.[42] Certain states provide for a minimum wage in excess of the federal requirement or that applies to some employees who are not covered under the federal minimum wage law. Refer to Section 11.5 for the requirements in this state.

Overtime Pay Requirement

The overtime pay requirement rule states you must pay a covered employee at one and one-half times the employee's regular hourly rate for any hours worked in excess of 40 in a week.[43] The regular hourly rate cannot be less than the minimum wage. For the overtime pay requirement, the FLSA takes a single workweek as its measuring period and does not permit averaging of hours over two or more weeks. For example, if an employee works 30 hours one week and 50 hours during the next, he or she must receive overtime compensation (time and one-half) for the 10 overtime hours worked in the second week, even though the average number of hours worked in the two weeks is 40.

Note that the FLSA only requires overtime pay based on the number of hours worked during a week and not for working long hours on a particular day.

The above rules generally apply to salaried workers as well as to those paid on an hourly basis. To determine the regular hourly rate for a salaried employee, it is necessary to divide the employee's weekly salary by the number of hours in his or her regular workweek (40 or less).

Employee Exemptions

Executives, administrators, professionals, and outside salespeople are not covered by federal wage-hour laws and thus are not entitled by law to a minimum wage or to any pay for overtime hours worked.[44] The theory behind this exemption is apparently the view that these types of employees are independent and sophisticated enough to take care of themselves and do not need to be protected by the government from possible exploitation by their employers.

Under the Code of Federal Regulations, Title 29, Section 541.5, an employee qualifying for the exemption as an outside salesperson must meet the two requirements listed below.

- The employee customarily and regularly works away from the employer's place of business while making sales or obtaining orders or contracts for services or for the use of facilities for which a consideration will be paid by the client or customer.
- The employee cannot do any other kind of work for the company, besides that of selling, for more than 20% of the usual workweek put in by the company's nonexempt employees; for example, the outside salesperson or exempted employee could do receptionist work for only 8 hours of each 40-hour workweek.

Various indicators of an employee's bona fide status as an outside salesperson include:

- A contractual designation or job title that reflects involvement in sales;
- Significant compensation on a commission basis;
- Special sales training; and
- Little or no direct or constant supervision in carrying out daily tasks.

Small Enterprise Exemption

Employees of certain small companies, other than those enterprises engaged in commerce, are exempt from coverage under the wage-hour laws. Translated from the legalese, this means certain smaller businesses that do not significantly affect the flow of goods and services in interstate commerce are exempted from FLSA overtime and minimum wage requirements.

An "enterprise engaged in commerce" is one that "has employees engaged in commerce or in the production of goods for commerce, or that has employees handling, selling, or otherwise working on goods or materials that have been moved in commerce or produced for commerce by any person," and "is an enterprise whose annual gross volume of sales made or business done is not less than $500,000."[45]

All of which means that, if your firm does less than a half million dollars in sales a year, it will generally be exempt from FLSA overtime and minimum wage requirements.[46]

Even if you are exempt from the FLSA wage-hour rules, state wage-hour laws may apply and may be more stringent than federal laws in many states.

Numerous other exemptions from the wage-hour laws are based on the type of business, the nature of the work performed by the employee, where the work is done, and other factors.[47] Before you assume your employees are covered by the FLSA, consult your attorney, or at least call the local wage-hour office on an anonymous basis and ask for an informal and nonbinding opinion over the phone.

Detailed Records Required

Possibly, the most important thing you should be aware of, if you have employees subject to FLSA standards, is the need to keep detailed records of hours worked, the type of work, and wages or salary paid.

Under the law, if an employee files a claim against you for alleged failure to pay required wages in the past, you will need to be able to produce proof that you met the statutory requirements. Keeping detailed pay and work records for each employee is the only way to protect yourself against such claims for back pay. In addition, the FLSA requires employers to preserve such records for up to three years.

Poster Requirement

If you have employees whose wages, hours, and working conditions are subject to FLSA regulations, you will need to post the official wage- hour poster that is provided by the U.S. Department of Labor. In addition, you will most likely be required to post an official wage-hour poster for this state. For a discussion of the basic wage-hour and other significant labor law requirements under the law, refer to Section 11.5.

Child Labor Laws

Both the FLSA and various state laws regulate or prohibit the employment of children in businesses, with very few exceptions. If you intend to hire children to work in your business — other than hiring your own children, which is usually permitted, except in hazardous situations — you need to be aware of the following basic child labor law provisions.

As a general rule, the FLSA prohibits the employment of children under 16 years of age;[48] however, there are a number of exceptions to this rule.[49] In addition, all children under age 18 are excluded from certain occupations that are designated as hazardous by the secretary of labor.[50] Children under 16 years of age cannot be hired under any of the following circumstances:

- To work in any workplace where mining, manufacturing, or processing operations take place;
- To operate power machinery, other than office equipment;
- To operate or serve as a helper on motor vehicles — with certain exceptions for vehicles not exceeding 6,000 pounds gross weight, during daylight hours;
- To work in public messenger services; and
- To work in the following occupations: transportation, warehousing or storage, communications or public utilities, or construction — except in sales or office work.[51]

Children 14 or 15 years of age can be hired in other occupations not considered to be hazardous, but there are numerous limitations on the hours and times when they may work, particularly when schools are in session.

A few occupations, such as delivering newspapers and doing theatrical work, are exempt from the federal child labor laws, even for children under 14 years of age.[52]

Most states also strictly regulate the employment of children. See Section 11.5 regarding state child labor laws in this state. Thus, if you intend to employ children under 18 years of age in a business, you will probably need legal guidance as to the conditions under which they may work, if at all, under federal and state child labor laws.

5.8 Fair Employment Practices

As an employer, you will also need to be alert to your obligations under a number of federal and state laws that prohibit discrimination in employment on the basis of sex, age, race, color, national origin, religion, or on account of mental or physical handicaps. These anti-discrimination laws are not just limited to hiring practices, but relate to almost every aspect of the relationship between an employer and employee, including compensation, promotions, type of work assigned, and working conditions.

In addition to outlawing discrimination in employment, companies contracting for business with the federal government are generally required to adopt affirmative action programs in the employment of minorities, women, people with disabilities, and Vietnam veterans.

Affirmative action programs are employment programs that go beyond elimination of discrimination. Under such programs, employers consciously make an effort to hire more women and minority group members and to upgrade the pay and responsibility levels of women and other groups that have historically been subject to patterns of discrimination.

Affirmative action programs are generally required for businesses that are government contractors. On the other hand, most other businesses are only required to refrain from discriminating in employment.

If your small business employs fewer than 15 employees and is not working on government contracts or subcontracts, the federal anti-discrimination laws listed on the following page will generally not apply to you. The one exception to this would be the Equal Pay Act of 1963, which requires equal pay for equal work for women and men. This act is applicable to employers with two or more employees.

**Federal
Anti-Discrimination Laws**

Employers Subject to Federal Anti-Discrimination Laws

Name of Law	Employers Who Are Covered	What the Law Requires
Title VII of the Civil Rights Act of 1964 and Americans with Disabilities Act (ADA)	Employers with 15 or more employees during 20 weeks of a calendar year	No discrimination in employment practices based on race, religion, disability or national origin
Pregnancy Discrimination Act	Same as for Title VII above	Equal treatment for pregnant women and new mothers for all employment-related purposes, including fringe benefits
Executive Order 11246 as amended	Employers with federal contracts or subcontracts of $10,000 or more	No discrimination in employment practices based on race, sex, color, religion, or national origin
Equal Pay Act of 1963	Nearly all employers with two or more employees	Equal pay for women and men doing similar work
Age Discrimination in Employment Act of 1967, as amended	Employers with 20 or more employees during 20 or more weeks in a calendar year	No discrimination in hiring or firing on account of age, for persons age 40 or older
Rehabilitation Act of 1973	Employers with federal contracts or subcontracts of $2,500 or more	No discrimination in employment practices on account of mental health or physical handicaps
Vietnam-Era Veteran Readjustment Assistance Act of 1974	Employers with federal contracts or subcontracts of $10,000 or more	Affirmative action programs for certain disabled veterans

Employers who violate any of the above laws may be sued by either the complaining individuals or by the various government enforcement agencies, or both.

Formal Compliance Requirements

Small businesses are not required to do a lot of paperwork or filling out of forms when it comes to federal anti-discrimination laws. An employer with more than 100 employees, however, must file *Form EEO-1* with the Equal Employment Opportunity Commission (EEOC) each year.[53]

As an employer you are required to keep detailed records — and should, for your own protection — as to the reasons for hiring or not hiring, promoting or not promoting, any employee or job applicant. In the event it is ever necessary to demonstrate that your firm has not discriminated against any group or individual member of a group in violation of federal laws, these records will provide the needed documentation.

Besides these requirements, there are a number of official posters you may be required to post in your place of business. These may include:

Type of Poster	Who Must Post	Source of Poster	
Civil rights poster regarding sexual, racial, religious, and ethnic discrimination or because of physical or mental disability (*WH Publication 1088*)	Employers with 15 or more employees during 20 weeks of the year or with federal contracts or subcontracts of $10,000 or more[54]	EEOC offices, the nearest Office of Compliance	**Display Posters**
Age discrimination poster	Employers with 20 or more employees who work 20 or more weeks a year[55]	EEOC offices	
Notice to employees working on government contracts (*WH Publication 1313*)	Any employer performing government contract work subject to the Service Contract Act or the Public Contracts Act	U.S. Department of Labor, Employment Standards Division	
Poster required under the Vietnam Era Veterans Readjustment Assistance Act	Employers with federal contracts or subcontracts of $10,000 or more	From the federal contracting officer administering the contract	
Poster explaining the Family and Medical Leave Act of 1993	Employers with 50 or more employees during 20 weeks of the year	U.S. Department of Labor, Wage and Hour Division	

To obtain these posters, contact each of the appropriate federal agencies and request a copy of their required poster.

Sexual Harassment

You need to be keenly aware of your potential liability for sexual harassment in the workplace, another increasingly significant area of the anti-discrimination laws under Title VII of the Civil Rights Act. While the federal Civil Rights Act does not specifically refer to sexual harassment as a form of discrimination, the courts and the EEOC have long accepted it as such. There are two types of sexual harassment under Title VII, as it has been interpreted over the years.

One type of sexual harassment is where tangible job benefits are granted or withheld based on an employee's receptiveness to unwelcome requests or conduct. For example, a male supervisor tells a female employee to meet him in the hot tub of his mountain chalet on a Saturday afternoon to discuss a business contract. She refuses to meet him at his place and later receives a bad rating from him for a "poor attitude and unwillingness to work overtime," which costs her a raise or promotion. The female employee in such a case has been denied a tangible job benefit due to sexual harassment.

The second type of sexual harassment involves a hostile work environment; that is, a situation in which the work environment is oppressive and hostile to members of one sex. This occurs when such conditions either unreasonably interfere with the individual's work performance or create an intimidating, hostile, or offensive environment. This type of harassment may not have any economic effects on the individual, and management or supervisory personnel may not be involved. Nevertheless, an employer who allows such a condition to persist may still be liable if management was aware of the harassment by co-workers — or even by customers — and fails to take appropriate actions to remedy the situation.

Merely having a company policy that prohibits sexual harassment at your company won't automatically stop such activity or protect the firm from liability if harassment occurs, but the absence of such a policy makes such conduct somewhat more likely to occur and will also tend to strengthen an employee's claim against you if your firm is sued for allowing such acts to occur. Adopt a sexual harassment policy that not only prohibits such conduct, but which sets up a grievance mechanism for employees who are victims of any such harassment, and communicate this company policy strongly and clearly to your employees.

In addition to federal civil rights case law, the statutes of many states, or the regulations of many state civil rights commissions, now specifically prohibit sexual harassment in the workplace. Some of these laws go well beyond the protections afforded under federal law. For a more detailed discussion of anti-discrimination laws in this state, refer to Section 11.5.

5.9 Immigration Law Restrictions on Hiring

The Immigration Reform and Control Act of 1986 represents a major governmental requirement regarding the relationship between an employer and employee. Under this law, you are prohibited from hiring illegal aliens, and depending on the number of any prior violations, you are subject to fines of $250 to $20,000 for each illegal alien hired after November 6, 1986. At the same time, the act also prohibits employment discrimination on the basis of citizenship status and national origin; you may not fire or fail to hire anyone on the basis of foreign appearance, language, or name.

For all employees hired after November 6, 1986, you are required to verify their eligibility for employment within three business days of each new hire. As an employer, you will need to fill out and retain *Form I-9*. The employee fills out the top portion of the form, indicating whether he or she is a citizen or national of the United States; an alien lawfully admitted for permanent residence; or an alien authorized by the U.S. Immigration and Naturalization Service (INS) to work in the United States.

On the back portion of *Form I-9*, there are three separate lists of various forms of identification and employment eligibility documents the employee must provide for you. In Section 2 of the form, you must record the documents you have examined, such as a passport or certificate of naturalization. These papers must include either one document in List A or one each in lists B and C. Both you and the employee must sign the form under penalty of perjury, and you must retain the completed form and make it available if the INS or U.S. Department of Labor requests it during an inspection.

You may obtain copies of *Form I-9* and a related *Employer's Handbook* from the nearest office of the U.S. Immigration and Naturalization Service. A sample *Form I-9* is also included at the end of this chapter. For more information on employer responsibilities, call:

U.S. Immigration and Naturalization Service
(800) 755-0777

The U.S. Department of Justice also has a hotline number you can call to hear prerecorded taped messages regarding the type of documents you can request to establish identity and work eligibility. The messages also offer tips on how to avoid discrimination when completing *Form I-9*. To hear these messages, call:

Office of Special Counsel for Immigration-Related
** Unfair Employment Practices (OSC)**
U.S. Department of Justice
(800) 255-8155

5.10 Restrictions on Layoffs of Employees

If your business grows to where you have 100 or more full-time employees — or the equivalent, based on 40-hour workweeks — at a single location, you may be subject to the potentially onerous provisions of the plant closing law called the Worker Adjustment and Retraining Notification Act, or WARN Act.[56] This act would affect you if you laid off 50 or more employees, or one-third of the work force, in a 30-day period. It applies to virtually any plant closing or major layoff for any reason, with a few obvious exceptions, such as due to an earthquake or flood, or due to a labor dispute, such as a strike or lockout for which no notice need be given.

The WARN Act

A "layoff" under this act includes any of the following:

- A permanent termination of employment;
- A layoff of an employee for more than six months; or
- A loss of half the employees' working hours for six consecutive months.

In case of any major layoff or shutdown, the law requires you to give at least 60 days advance notice. If you give less than that, you are required to pay the laid-off workers for 60 days minus the actual number of days' notice you gave. The law requires you to notify the labor union that represents the employees, or, if none, the individual employees by mailing the notice to their last known address or including it in their pay envelope. You must also notify the local city or county government and state labor agency of the planned shutdown or cutback.

The WARN Act doesn't generally prohibit a company from making lay-offs or shutting down a money-losing plant, but it makes it more costly for the employer to do so, and also gives local unions and politicians time to find some way to attempt to coerce or persuade a company into main-taining its operations, even if it is no longer economically viable.

The WARN law does impose stiff restrictions on a firm's ability to sell off, reorganize, merge, or consolidate operations, if such a decision would adversely affect the jobs of 50 or more employees. In other words, if your foreign competition renders your plant obsolete, you will not be allowed to sell it off to a competitor, if doing so would cost 50 or more employees their jobs. The act has made it much more costly to take a risk on building a plant in the United States — if it fails, you may have to close shop rather than restructure or sell.

As a result, there is considerable litigation over what does and does not constitute a mass layoff or shutdown under the WARN Act.

5.11 The Americans with Disabilities Act

In 1990, Congress enacted a revolutionary and wide-reaching piece of legislation, the Americans with Disabilities Act (ADA), which is designed to make both the workplace and most public facilities much more accessible to disabled persons.

The ADA and related regulations, which are being phased in over several years, will have a significant impact on a great many businesses, both in terms of employment practices and in terms of removing architectural barriers and other physical features that have limiting effects on the lives of disabled persons.[57]

Anti-Discrimination Rules Regarding the Disabled

Title I of the ADA prohibits discrimination against any "qualified indi-vidual with a disability" in all aspects of employment, including hiring and discharging of workers, compensation, and benefits. Title I applies to employers who employ 15 or more employees during 20 weeks of any calendar year. In addition, you must reasonably accommodate employ-ees' or applicants' disabilities, which may mean modifying facilities, restructuring work schedules, or transferring disabled workers to vacant positions for which they are qualified, in appropriate circumstances. You are not required to accommodate a disabled worker, however, if doing so would impose an "undue hardship" on your business.

One area that is now significantly affected in the hiring process is the limitation on medical screening of applicants. Under the ADA, companies can no longer screen out prospective employees with disabilities because the applicant has an elevated risk of an on-the-job injury or a medical condition that might be aggravated because of job demands. The law specifically bans questions about a job applicant's physical or mental condition either on an employment application form or during a job interview. This would include general questions such as, "Do you have any mental or physical conditions that would prevent you from performing your job functions?"

Medical exams are still allowed, but they are greatly restricted. Pre-offer exams are prohibited, but an offer may be conditioned upon the satisfactory results of a medical examination. Results, however, cannot be used to withdraw an offer, unless they show that the individual in question is not able to perform the tasks required by the position.

The definition of "disabled" under the ADA includes people with AIDS, those who test positive for the HIV virus, and rehabilitated drug abusers and alcoholics; however, the ADA does not:

- Prohibit voluntary tests, such as employer-sponsored cholesterol or blood pressure tests; or
- Require employers to hire persons who are drug users or who have contagious diseases.

The ADA is neutral on the issue of drug testing of employees, in effect leaving that up to regulation by the states.

Medical Screening Tests

Title III of the ADA requires practically all businesses to make their facilities accessible to disabled employees and customers. Examples of various accessibility requirements with regard to public accommodations include:

- One designated parking space for the disabled must be provided for every 25 or fewer spaces. A lesser ratio applies if there are more than 100 total spaces.
- Hotels and motels must have 5% of their rooms accessible to wheelchairs and another 5% must be equipped with devices such as visual alarms for the hearing-impaired.
- Access ramps must be in place where the floor level changes more than one-half of an inch.
- Elevators must be provided in three-story or taller buildings and in those with more than 3,000 square feet per story.
- In retail or grocery stores, checkout aisles must be at least 36 inches wide. This is wide enough for wheelchairs.
- Theaters and similar places of assembly for 50 or more persons must have at least three wheelchair spaces dispersed throughout the seating area.

Public Accommodations for the Disabled

Tax Incentives

Companies spending money to remove architectural and transportation barriers to the disabled can deduct up to $15,000 a year of such expenses.[58] In addition, small firms — those with gross receipts under one million dollars or fewer than 30 full-time employees — who spend between $250 and $10,250 a year on access for the disabled, can claim a tax credit for up to 50% of the cost of such expenditures, a maximum annual credit of $5,000.[59]

For more information on the ADA, contact:

Equal Employment Opportunity Commission or
2401 E Street
Washington, DC 20506
(202) 663-4900 or
(800) 669-4000 (information)
(800) 669-3362 (publications)

Civil Rights Division
U.S. Department of Justice
(800) 514-0301

5.12 Mandatory Family and Medical Leave Requirements

The Family and Medical Leave Act of 1993 became effective on August 5, 1993. This new law applies to all companies — as well as nonprofit entities — that have 50 or more employees during 20 or more calendar workweeks during the current or preceding calendar year.[60] As a result, many companies, who employ roughly half of all employees in the United States, are now subject to the family leave law's requirements.

The new act requires covered employers to:

- Offer their employees twelve weeks of unpaid leave after the birth or adoption of a child; to care for a seriously ill child, spouse, or parent; or for an employee's own serious illness.
- Maintain health care coverage for an employee who is on a leave of absence as described above; and
- Guarantee that employees will be able to return to either the same job or to a comparable position after the leave.
- Post a notice, which may be obtained from the U.S. Department of Labor – Wage and Hour Division, explaining the rights of employees under the Family and Medical Leave Act of 1993.[61]

A serious illness must be verified by a physician's certification, and as the employer, you may require a second medical opinion if desired. An employee is required to provide you with 30 days notice for foreseeable leaves of absence for a birth, adoption, or planned medical treatment.

One major exception to the law's coverage is a provision that exempts certain "key employees" from coverage. Key employees are defined as the highest-paid 10% of the employer's workforce and those whose leave of absence would cause significant economic harm to the employer. Also exempted from the law's provisions are employees who haven't worked at least one year for the employer and who haven't worked at least 1,250 hours, or 25 hours a week, in the preceding twelve months. In addition, you are given the option of substituting an employee's accrued paid leave, if any, for any part of the twelve-week period of family leave.

A number of states, such as California and Hawaii, have also enacted similar family leave laws. Refer to Chapter 11 for information on any such laws that have been adopted in this state.

Endnotes

1. Treas. Regs. §31.6302-1(f)(4).
2. Treas. Regs. §31.6302-1(b)(2).
3. Treas. Regs. §31.6302-1(b)(3).
4. Treas. Regs. §31.6302-1(c)(3).
5. I.R.C. §7502(e)(3).
6. I.R.C. §§3301(1) and 3306(b)(1).
7. I.R.C. §§3301(1) and 3302(b).
8. I.R.C. §3306(a)(1)(A).
9. I.R.C. §3306(a)(1)(B).
10. 29 U.S.C. §1131.
11. 29 U.S.C. §1132; I.R.C. §§4971, 4975, 6057–6059, and 6652.
12. 29 U.S.C. §1002(2); 29 C.F.R. §2510.3-2.
13. 29 U.S.C. §1002(1); 29 C.F.R. §2510.3-1.
14. 29 C.F.R. §2510.3-1(b); 29 C.F.R. §2510.3-2(b).
15. 29 C.F.R. §2520.104b-2.
16. 29 C.F.R. §2520.102-3.
17. 29 C.F.R. §2520.104b-2(a)(2).
18. 29 C.F.R. §2520.104b-2(a)(1).
19. 29 C.F.R. §2520.104-20.
20. 29 U.S.C. §1024(b)(4); 29 C.F.R. §2520.104b-1.
21. 29 C.F.R. §2520.104a-3.
22. 29 C.F.R. §2520.104a-5.
23. 29 C.F.R. §2520.104b-10.
24. 29 C.F.R. §§2520.104a-4 and 2520.104b-3.
25. 29 U.S.C. §1021(c).
26. 29 U.S.C. §1112.
27. I.R.C. §3405(a).
28. I.R.C. §6039 D.
29. Announcement 86-20, I.R.B. 1986–87, 34.
30. 29 C.F.R. §1903.2.
31. 29 C.F.R. §1904.2.
32. 29 C.F.R. §1904.10.
33. 29 C.F.R. §1904.5.
34. 29 C.F.R. §1904.16.
35. 29 C.F.R. §1904.12.
36. 29 C.F.R. §1904.4.
37. 29 C.F.R. §1904.6.
38. 29 C.F.R. §1904.15.
39. 29 C.F.R. §§1904.15 and 1904.21.
40. 29 C.F.R. §1904.8 as amended, April 1, 1994.
41. 29 C.F.R. §1904.9.
42. 29 U.S.C. §206(a)(1).
43. 29 U.S.C. §207(a)(1).
44. 29 U.S.C. §213(a)(1).
45. 29 U.S.C. §203(s).
46. 29 U.S.C. §207(a)(1).
47. 29 U.S.C. §213.
48. 29 U.S.C. §§203(1) and 212.
49. 29 U.S.C. §213.
50. 29 C.F.R. §570.50–570.71.
51. 29 C.F.R. §570.33.
52. 29 U.S.C. §213(c) and (d).
53. 29 C.F.R. §1602.7.
54. 29 C.F.R. §1601.30.
55. 29 U.S.C. §627 and 29 C.F.R. §1627.10.
56. 29 U.S.C. §§2101–2109.
57. 42 U.S.C. §§12101 *et seq.* and 29 C.F.R. §1630.
58. I.R.C. §190.
59. I.R.C. §44.
60. 29 C.F.R. §825.104(a).
61. 29 C.F.R. §825.300(a).

Summary of Basic ERISA Compliance Requirements for Pension Plans

Item	Provided to
Summary plan description.	U.S. Department of Labor; participants; beneficiaries
Annual return/report (*Form 5500, 5500-EZ,* or *5500-C/R*).	IRS (now required even for a simple one-person Keogh plan)
Schedule A, Form 5500 series (insurance information).	IRS
Schedule B, Form 5500 series (actuarial information prepared and signed by an enrolled actuary for "defined benefit" plans only).	IRS
Schedule SSA, Form 5500 series (registration statement).	IRS
Form W-2P (report of periodic plan benefit payments made during the year).	IRS; recipient of distribution
Form 1099-R (report of total distribution of benefits during the year).	IRS; recipient of distribution
Form W-3 or *W-3G* (transmittal of *Form W-2P* and *Form 1099-R*).	IRS
Form PBGC-1 (premium payment of required plan termination insurance — for "defined benefit" plans only).	Pension Benefit Guaranty Corporation (a government agency that insures pension plans of corporate employers)
Summary annual report.	Participants; beneficiaries
Individual deferred vested benefit statement to separated employee.	Former participant in plan
Summary of material modifications to a plan.	U.S. Department of Labor; participants; beneficiaries
Terminal report (when plan is terminated).	U.S. Department of Labor; participants; beneficiaries
Written explanation of joint and survivor annuity and financial effect of not electing to receive it (if plan provides benefits in the form of an annuity).	Participants
Written explanation of reasons for denying benefit claim and description of appeal procedures.	Person claiming entitlement to plan benefits
Various documents and information to be provided on request.	U.S. Department of Labor; participants
Various formal notices upon occurrence of certain events.	IRS; U.S. Department of Labor; Pension Benefit Guaranty Corporation; participants

Form I-9 – Employment Eligibility Verification: Sample

EMPLOYMENT ELIGIBILITY VERIFICATION (Form I-9)

1 EMPLOYEE INFORMATION AND VERIFICATION: (To be completed and signed by employee.)

Name: (Print or Type) Last	First	Middle	Birth Name

Address: Street Name and Number	City	State	ZIP Code

Date of Birth (Month/Day/Year)	Social Security Number

I attest, under penalty of perjury, that I am (check a box):

- ☐ 1. A citizen or national of the United States.
- ☐ 2. An alien lawfully admitted for permanent residence (Alien Number A _____).
- ☐ 3. An alien authorized by the Immigration and Naturalization Service to work in the United States (Alien Number A _____ . or Admission Number _____ , expiration of employment authorization, if any _____).

I attest, under penalty of perjury, the documents that I have presented as evidence of Identity and employment eligibility are genuine and relate to me. I am aware that federal law provides for imprisonment and/or fine for any false statements or use of false documents in connection with this certificate.

Signature	Date (Month/Day/Year)

PREPARER/TRANSLATOR CERTIFICATION (To be completed if prepared by person other than the employee). I attest, under penalty of perjury, that the above was prepared by me at the request of the named individual and is based on all information of which I have any knowledge.

Signature	Name (Print or Type)		
Address (Street Name and Number)	City	State	Zip Code

2 EMPLOYER REVIEW AND VERIFICATION: (To be completed and signed by employer.)

Instructions:
Examine one document from List A and check the appropriate box, **OR** examine one document from List B **and** one from List C and check the appropriate boxes. Provide the *Document Identification Number* and *Expiration Date* for the document checked.

List A — Documents that Establish Identity and Employment Eligibility	List B — Documents that Establish Identity **and**	List C — Documents that Establish Employment Eligibility
☐ 1. United States Passport ☐ 2. Certificate of United States Citizenship ☐ 3. Certificate of Naturalization ☐ 4. Unexpired foreign passport with attached Employment Authorization ☐ 5. Alien Registration Card with photograph	☐ 1. A State-issued driver's license or a State-issued I.D. card with a photograph, or information, including name, sex, date of birth, height, weight, and color of eyes. (Specify State)_____ ☐ 2. U.S. Military Card ☐ 3. Other (Specify document and issuing authority) _____	☐ 1. Original Social Security Number Card (other than a card stating it is not valid for employment) ☐ 2. A birth certificate issued by State, county, or municipal authority bearing a seal or other certification ☐ 3. Unexpired INS Employment Authorization Specify form # _____
Document Identification # _____	*Document Identification* # _____	*Document Identification* # _____
Expiration Date (if any)	*Expiration Date (if any)*	*Expiration Date (if any)*

CERTIFICATION: I attest, under penalty of perjury, that I have examined the documents presented by the above individual, that they appear to be genuine and to relate to the individual named, and that the individual, to the best of my knowledge, is eligible to work in the United States.

Signature	Name (Print or Type)	Title
Employer Name	Address	Date

Form I-9 (05/07/87)
OMB No. 1115-0136

U.S. Department of Justice
Immigration and Naturalization Service

Form I-9 – Employment Eligibility Verification: Sample (continued)

Employment Eligibility Verification

> **NOTICE:** Authority for collecting the information on this form is in Title 8, United States Code, Section 1324A, which requires employers to verify employment eligibility of individuals on a form approved by the Attorney General. This form will be used to verify the individual's eligibility for employment in the United States. Failure to present this form for inspection to officers of the Immigration and Naturalization Service or Department of Labor within the time period specified by regulation, or improper completion or retention of this form, may be a violation of the above law and may result in a civil money penalty.

Section 1. Instructions to Employee/Preparer for completing this form

Instructions for the employee.

All employees, upon being hired, must complete Section 1 of this form. Any person hired after November 6, 1986 must complete this form. (For the purpose of completion of this form the term "hired" applies to those employed, recruited or referred for a fee.)

All employees must print or type their complete name, address, date of birth, and Social Security Number. The block which correctly indicates the employee's immigration status must be checked. If the second block is checked, the employee's Alien Registration Number must be provided. If the third block is checked, the employee's Alien Registration Number *or* Admission Number must be provided, as well as the date of expiration of that status, if it expires.

All employees whose present names differ from birth names, because of marriage or other reasons, must print or type their birth names in the appropriate space of Section 1. Also, employees whose names change after employment verification should report these changes to their employer.

All employees must sign and date the form.

Instructions for the preparer of the form, if not the employee.

If a person assists the employee with completing this form, the preparer must certify the form by signing it and printing or typing his or her complete name and address.

Section 2.   Instructions to Employer for completing this form

(For the purpose of completion of this form, the term "employer" applies to employers and those who recruit or refer for a fee.)

Employers must complete this section by examining evidence of identity and employment eligibility, and:
- checking the appropriate box in List A *or* boxes in both Lists B and C;
- recording the document identification number and expiration date (if any);
- recording the type of form if not specifically identified in the list;
- signing the certification section.

NOTE: Employers are responsible for reverifying employment eligibility of employees whose employment eligibility documents carry an expiration date.

Copies of documentation presented by an individual for the purpose of establishing identity and employment eligibility may be copied and retained for the purpose of complying with the requirements of this form and no other purpose. Any copies of documentation made for this purpose should be maintained with this form.

Name changes of employees which occur after preparation of this form should be recorded on the form by lining through the old name, printing the new name and the reason (such as marriage), and dating and initialing the changes. Employers should not attempt to delete or erase the old name in any fashion.

RETENTION OF RECORDS.

The completed form must be retained by the employer for:
- three years after the date of hiring; or
- one year after the date the employment is terminated, whichever is later.

> Employers may photocopy or reprint this form as necessary.

U.S. Department of Justice
Immigration and Naturalization Service

OMB #1115-0136
Form I-9 (05/07/87)
☆ U.S.G.P.O. 1987- 183-918/69085

For sale by the Superintendent of Documents, U.S. Government Printing Office
Washington, D.C. 20402

Chapter 6

Businesses that Require Licenses to Operate

The bureaucrat who smiles when something serious has gone wrong
has already found someone to blame it on.

— Anonymous

6.1 General Licensing

Almost any kind of business activity you engage in will require a city or county business license, which is usually fairly simple to obtain. In addition, some types of businesses will have to obtain licenses from the federal government to operate, while other businesses, occupations, and professions are also licensed and regulated by the state.

Even though there are tremendous variations regarding the requirements for obtaining necessary federal and state licenses, these requirements generally relate to educational attainments, experience in the particular field, passage of examinations, submission of detailed applications, meeting financial or bonding requirements, or some combination of the foregoing, plus payment of a licensing fee or tax.

In addition to the federal and state licensing requirements, certain local city or county permits may have to be obtained. For example, if you will be in the food business, you may have to get a license from the county health department; or, if your business would like to do any construction or remodeling, you might have to get approval from your local planning commission.

Before you begin to operate any kind of business, find out whether you will be required to obtain any special government licenses or permits, since in most cases, you must obtain the particular license before commencing operation.

This chapter and Section 11.6, respectively, provide a partial listing of the federal and state licensing requirements you are most likely to encounter as a small business owner. Because the number of activities that may require federal or state licenses is so large, no attempt has been made to try to list all of them in this book.

Thus, the lists of licensing agencies and businesses that require licenses found in this chapter and in Chapter 11 should be helpful in alerting you, as a small business owner, to possible licensing needs, but you should remember that these lists are not complete and are not a substitute for individualized legal advice.

6.2 Federal Licenses

If you are starting a small business, it is relatively unlikely that you will need any type of license or permit from the federal government; however, the following is a list of the federal licensing requirements you might possibly encounter:

Federal Licensing Requirements

Activity	Federal Agency
Rendering investment advice	Securities and Exchange Commission
Providing ground transportation as a common carrier	Interstate Commerce Commission
Preparation of meat products	Food and Drug Administration
Production of drugs or biological products	Food and Drug Administration
Making tobacco products or alcohol	Treasury Department, Bureau of Alcohol, Tobacco, and Firearms
Making or dealing in firearms	Treasury Department, Bureau of Alcohol, Tobacco, and Firearms
Radio or television broadcasting	Federal Communications Commission

For a partial listing of businesses and professions required to be licensed in this state, see Section 11.6.

Operating the Business

Part III

Chapter 7

Excise Taxes

Taxation without representation is tyranny.

— Patrick Henry

Taxation with representation is worse.

— Will Rogers

7.1 General Considerations

Both federal and state tax laws impose excise or similar taxes on a number of different types of businesses, products, services, and occupations. These taxes are usually imposed without any assessment or notice to the taxpayer. Thus, it is up to you to find out if you are subject to any of these taxes and, if so, to obtain the proper tax return forms and pay the tax on time.

It is not uncommon for a small business to operate for several years without the owner ever being aware of the need to pay excise taxes. Then comes the day of reckoning, when a formal notice is received from the government demanding immediate payment of several years' worth of back taxes on some particular item subject to excise tax, plus interest and penalties for not filing the returns and not paying the tax. This can be a disastrous surprise, especially since the business owner has not factored the cost of paying the excise into the price of his or her goods or services.

This chapter is designed to alert you in advance to the types of federal and state excise — and similar — taxes that you may need to know about. Some excise taxes, such as those on telephone service and insurance companies, are not discussed below since they are passed along or absorbed by the telephone company, insurance company, or other large institution with which your business may deal, and you have no obligation to file any returns or make any direct payment to the government of such taxes.

See Section 11.7 for a summary of various state excise taxes that may affect your business.

7.2 Federal Excise Taxes

Federal excise taxes on many products and transactions have been repealed over the last 20 years, so these taxes are much less pervasive now than in the past. The excise tax that the largest number of small businesses are likely to be subject to is the motor vehicle highway use tax on vehicles of more than 55,000 pounds gross weight.[1] *Form 2290* must be filed by owners of trucks and buses subject to the highway use tax. If you want information about the highway use tax, request a copy of IRS *Publication 349* from any IRS office.

The federal government imposes a number of excise taxes on various types of business activities. Some excise taxes are on the production or sale of certain goods. Some are on services or the use of certain products or facilities. Still others are imposed on businesses of a certain type.

Most federal excise taxes are reported on *Form 720, Quarterly Federal Excise Tax Return*, the most common excise tax form. Environmental taxes on petroleum and 42 designated chemical substances are reported on *Form 6627* and attached to *Form 720*. Federal excise taxes can be broken down into several major categories:

- The motor vehicle highway use tax — This tax is imposed on vehicles of more than 55,000 pounds gross weight.[2]

- Retailer taxes on certain fuels[3] — The federal gasoline tax is $0.183 (18.3 cents) per gallon on gasoline, and the tax on diesel is $0.243 (24.3 cents) per gallon.

    In addition, both of the taxes are increased by $0.01 (one-tenth of one cent) per gallon by the Leaking Underground Storage Tank Trust Fund Tax. A reduced tax rate applies to qualified methane and ethanol fuel.

Other retail excise taxes are imposed on sales of:
- Heavy trucks and trailers;[4]
- Tires and tubes;[5]
- Recreation equipment, such as bows, arrows, fishing rods, reels, lures, and creels;[6] and
- Firearms and ammunition.[7]

Other excise taxes exist on the following as well:

- Air transportation — If you are in the business of transporting people by air, you may have to collect an excise tax;[8]
- Telephone and teletype services;[9]
- Wagering;[10]
- Coal mined in the United States;[11]
- Alcohol and tobacco products;[12] and
- Manufacturers of certain vaccines — Certain vaccines manufactured or imported into the United States are subject to an excise tax in order to create a Vaccine Injury Compensation Trust Fund, a no-fault program for compensating persons who are injured by, or die from, certain vaccines.[13]

There are also several environmental excise taxes, such as:

- An excise tax on ozone-depleting chemicals;
- An oil spill liability excise tax of $0.05 (5 cents) a barrel;[14] and
- Environmental taxes on petroleum products, various chemicals, and hazardous wastes.[15]

Luxury Taxes

A luxury tax applies to retail purchases of passenger automobiles costing more than $30,000.[16] The tax is equal to 10% of the amount by which the purchase price exceeds $30,000. For example, the luxury tax on a new $35,000 automobile would be 10% of $5,000 — the excess of $35,000 over $30,000, or $500. The $30,000 threshold amount is indexed for inflation that has occurred since December 31, 1990, and is set at $32,000 in 1994.

The luxury tax does not apply to:

- Vehicles of more than 6,000 pounds unloaded gross weight; or
- Any vehicle, such as a taxicab, that is used exclusively in the active conduct of a trade or business of transporting people or property for compensation or hire.

The luxury tax on automobiles is collected by the retailer who sells the item. This luxury tax only applies to the first retail sale of an item. For example, if you buy a used $50,000 automobile, there is no luxury tax on the purchase.

Other luxury taxes on boats, aircraft, furs, and jewelry were repealed on August 10, 1993, retroactive to January 1, 1993. If you paid luxury taxes on any of those items in 1993, you are entitled to a refund of the tax from the retailer who collected it from you.

For further information on excise taxes and other federal taxes, you may wish to obtain IRS *Publication 334, Tax Guide for Small Business*, or for more detailed information on excise taxes, IRS *Publication 510, Excise Taxes*.

Endnotes

1. I.R.C. § 4481(a).
2. Id.
3. I.R.C. §§ 4041, 4081, and 4091.
4. I.R.C. § 4051.
5. I.R.C. § 4071(a).
6. I.R.C. § 4161(a) and (b).
7. I.R.C. § 4181.
8. I.R.C. §§ 4261(a) and 4271(a).
9. I.R.C. § 4251.
10. I.R.C. §§ 4401 and 4411.
11. I.R.C. § 4121(a).
12. I.R.C. §§ 5001, 5041(b), 5701, and 5801–5822.
13. I.R.C. §§ 4131–4132.
14. I.R.C. §§ 4611(c)(2) and 4681.
15. I.R.C. §§ 4611 and 4661.
16. I.R.C. §§ 4001–4012.

Chapter 8

Planning for Tax Savings in a Business

The words of such an act as the income tax merely dance before
my eyes in a meaningless procession: cross-reference to cross-
reference, exception upon exception — couched in abstract terms
that offer no handle to seize hold of — leave in my mind only
a confused sense of some vitally important, but successfully
concealed, purport, which it is my duty to extract, but which
is within my power, if at all, only after the most inordinate
expenditure of time. I know that these monsters are the result of
fabulous industry and ingenuity, plugging up this hole and
casting out that net against all possible evasion; yet at times
I cannot help recalling a saying of William James' about certain
passages of Hegel: that they were no doubt written with a
passion of rationality; but that one cannot help wondering
whether to the reader they have any significance save that the
words are strung together with syntactical correctness.

— Judge Learned Hand

referring to the 1939 Internal Revenue Code, a statute which was almost
childlike in its simplicity compared to our current tax law.

8.1 General Considerations

One of the most shocking and unpleasant realizations of many successful small business owners comes when they realize they have acquired
an unwanted silent partner — a partner who contributes nothing to the
business but who often lays claim to half or more of the owner's hard-
earned profits. That silent partner, of course, is the government income

tax collector, and this chapter is a summary of many of the best and most effective legal ways to reduce that silent partner's share of the profits from your business.

This chapter is not intended to be a substitute for professional tax advice regarding your individual situation. Because the tax laws are so enormously complex, a technique that may work brilliantly in most cases might be useless or even disastrous in your particular tax situation. This chapter will provide you with a working understanding of some of the key ways to plan for tax savings and to avoid tax pitfalls in your business.

After you have read this chapter, you may want to talk to your tax adviser about one or more of the ideas discussed, if you feel they might be useful for applying to your business. Your tax adviser should be able to tell you whether a particular idea will work in your situation. If it will, he or she can help you implement it.

Tax attorneys and accountants often have a very heavy workload and a large number of clients to serve. An unfortunate result of this situation is your tax adviser may tend to spend most of the time responding to inquiries by clients and meeting tax deadlines rather than taking the initiative in seeking out ways to minimize your taxes. Thus, by having some understanding of what you would like to do in the way of reducing taxes on your business income, you can propose ideas to your tax advisers and maximize the effectiveness of their expert knowledge and advice. In tax planning, as in so many areas of life, it pays to be assertive. "The wheel that squeaks is the one that gets the grease."

8.2 Using a Corporation as a Tax Shelter

One of the most effective ways to reduce your taxes, in many cases, is to incorporate your business. Incorporation is most likely to be advantageous if the business is generating about $75,000 or less in annual profits and salary for the owner — or per owner, if there is more than one. There are three basic ways, other than the adoption of employee fringe benefit plans, that incorporation can reduce your taxes on business income:

- Leaving profits in the corporation
- Income-splitting
- Investing in stock

Leaving Profits in the Corporation

If you are able to leave your first $75,000 of annual profits in your corporation, the profits will generally be taxed at corporate rates that are lower than your individual income tax rates. This provides a strong incentive for you to leave at least that much taxable income in the corporation rather than pay it all out to yourself as salary. At taxable income levels above $75,000, corporate income is taxed at roughly the same rates as individual income, except at very high income levels of $335,000 or more. Refer to the table of corporate income tax rates in Section 2.4 and compare those rates with the personal income tax rates for your filing status. Be careful about leaving too much profit in your corporation. Sections 8.5 and 8.9 discuss the potential benefits and risks of having your profits accumulate in your corporation.

Income Splitting

By using a corporation, it is also possible to split your overall profit between two or more taxpayers, so that none of the income gets taxed in the highest tax brackets. For example, with an overall economic profit of $100,000, an incorporated business may be able to reduce its taxable income to $50,000 by paying (and deducting) a $50,000 salary to its owner, as an officer/employee of the corporation. The corporation would pay tax only on the remaining $50,000 profit, at a maximum federal tax rate of only 15%, while the owner would pay tax on the $50,000 salary received.

Because of the progressive tax rate structure under the federal income tax laws, the tax on the $100,000 income divided between the owner and his or her corporation would typically be much less than if the whole $100,000 were taxable to the owner. In 1993, for example, a single individual would pay $26,522 in federal income taxes on $100,000 of taxable income, while if the income were split evenly between the owner and his or her corporation, the corporation's tax would be $7,500 and the owner's $11,127, a savings of $7,895 — assuming the corporation is not a personal services corporation subject to a 35% flat rate of tax.

Another way to split the income of a business between multiple taxpayers is for you to make your children part owners of the business. Ideally, the children should be given an interest in the business when it is started, since the value of the gifts to them will often be minimal for gift tax purposes at that time.

It is frequently more feasible to split corporate income with your children by giving them some of the corporation's stock. This approach, however, will work only if your corporation has filed for an S corporation election on *Form 2553* with the IRS. The taxable income of a corporation that qualifies as an S corporation is taxable to its shareholders — in proportion to the stock they own in the corporation — and is generally not taxed to the corporation.

By giving a number of shares of stock in such an S corporation to one or more of your children, part of the taxable income of the business can often be shifted to the children[1] and taxed at their low tax brackets — assuming, as is usually the case, that the children do not have a lot of taxable income from other sources.

If, however, the parents attempt to shift too much income to the children by drawing no salary or too little salary from the corporation, the IRS has the power to reallocate the corporation's income to the parents to reflect the value of services rendered to the corporation. Shifting significant income to your children will not work if the children are under 14 years of age.[2]

Investing in Stocks

By investing accumulated corporate funds in dividend-paying stocks of other corporations, you can take advantage of the 70% deduction that corporations are entitled to on the dividends they receive.[3] Because this special deduction makes most dividends received by a corporation — other than those received by an S corporation — practically tax-free to the recipient corporation, your incorporated business can be an excellent place to hold stocks you wish to invest in, if you do not need the dividend income to live on.

Before you get too excited about putting your whole stock portfolio into your incorporated business, take these potential drawbacks into account:

- If you decide to later withdraw your corporate dividends or the stocks themselves, the withdrawal will usually be taxable to you as ordinary income[4] or perhaps, if you liquidate the corporation, as capital gains.[5] Capital gains are taxed at a maximum rate of 28% for individuals.[6]

- If you should accumulate more than $250,000 — $150,000 for professional and certain personal service firms — in after-tax earnings in your corporation, including the 70% of dividends that the corporation doesn't pay income tax on, and invest part of those earnings in liquid, nonbusiness investment assets like stocks, you may be inviting an IRS audit and a potential penalty tax for unreasonably accumulating earnings and profits in the corporation.[7] See the discussion of the accumulated earnings tax in Section 8.9.

- If too much of your corporation's income is in the form of dividends and other passive types of investment income, the corporation may be classified as a personal holding company for tax purposes, and this can have drastic tax consequences, as outlined in Section 8.9.[8] As long as more than 40% of your corporation's gross income is from sales of goods and services, however, as a general rule, you should not have to be concerned about personal holding company taxes.[9]

- Putting your personal assets that are not needed in the business into your corporation will subject those assets to the risk of the business. That is, anything you put into the corporation will be subject to the claims of the corporation's creditors if it goes bankrupt. If you put all of your assets into the corporation, you will in effect have given up the benefits of limited liability.

- If your corporation borrows money to invest in or carry stock investments, the 70% dividend exclusion will be reduced in part by the interest paid on the borrowed funds.[10]

Your accountant will probably be the best person to consult for determining how and whether you can use a corporation to reduce taxes on your business profits.

8.3 Retirement Plans and Other Fringe Benefits

One advantage of being your own boss, either as a sole proprietor, a partner, or a shareholder of a closely held corporation, is the opportunity to be able to set up a Keogh plan or corporate retirement plan. In a C corporation, you can also obtain insurance and other important fringe benefits as an officer and employee of the corporation on a tax-favored basis. Some of the ways you can benefit from using retirement plans and other tax-favored fringe benefits are outlined in this section.

There are three types of tax-favored retirement plans:

Tax Advantages of Retirement Plans

- Corporate pension and profit-sharing plans;
- Keogh pension and profit-sharing plans for unincorporated business; and
- Individual Retirement Accounts (IRAs), which may be set up by any individual who has earned income, including an employee.

IRAs are of limited interest to most business owners, since the maximum annual contribution to an IRA is $2,000 a year — $2,250 if you have a nonworking spouse. Even these small deductions may not be available if you are a participant in a Keogh or corporate retirement plan and your adjusted gross income is over $50,000 — $35,000 if you are a single person. Accordingly, the discussion below focuses on corporate and Keogh retirement plans.

The primary tax advantages of the three types of tax-qualified retirement plans — corporate, self-employed (Keogh), and IRA — are these:

- Amounts contributed, up to certain limits, are deductible from the income of the corporation or individual taxpayer.[11] This deduction can be as much as 25% of the individual's compensation for the year (not counting the plan contribution) or $30,000, whichever is less. Even larger contributions can be made by so-called defined benefit plans.
- Contributed funds can be invested by pension or profit-sharing plans on a tax-free basis.[12] The qualified retirement trust that is usually set up to hold the retirement funds is exempt from state and federal income taxes on its income or capital gains from investments in stocks, bonds, savings accounts, gold, silver, real estate, and other passive investments. Note, however, that gold, silver, and other collectibles can no longer be purchased as investments by individually directed retirement plans or by an IRA. The only exception is for certain gold and silver coins minted by the United States.[13]
- When trust funds are paid out to you at retirement, you may be in a lower tax bracket than when you made the contributions to the plan. Thus, not only do you get to defer payment of any tax on amounts contributed to the plan until you retire, but the tax you finally pay at retirement is apt to be at a lower rate than you would have paid when you were working.

- Receipt of all your retirement plan funds in a lump sum at retirement, or in certain other circumstances, may often qualify for special low tax rates if the distribution is from a corporate or Keogh plan but not from an IRA.

Corporate and noncorporate Keogh retirement plans are almost identical under the tax law in all major respects, except for the ability to borrow one's retirement funds from the plan, which will be subject to an excise or penalty tax in the case of a Keogh. It does not pay to incorporate your business just for pension and profit-sharing plan purposes. If you decide to establish a retirement plan, there are several practical points you should consider before reaching a decision.

Model SEP Plans from Financial Institutions

If you are setting up a Simplified Employee Pension (SEP) plan for yourself, or a Keogh plan, consider obtaining a "canned" plan from a bank, savings and loan, insurance company, or mutual fund. Usually, these preapproved plans will be suitable for you unless you have a significant number of employees to cover under your Keogh, in which case, you probably should be incorporated anyway. The great advantages of getting a canned SEP or Keogh plan from a financial institution are cost and simplicity. Most such institutions will charge you only $10–$25 to adopt their plan. Their profit comes from investing your funds for a management fee, in the case of a mutual fund; or maintaining your deposits in interest-bearing accounts, in the case of a bank or savings and loan.

By contrast, hiring a lawyer or benefit consultant to draw up a customized SEP or Keogh plan for you could cost anywhere from a few hundred to a few thousand dollars in fees. In addition, since the pension laws seem to be rewritten every time Congress meets, you may find yourself paying hundreds or even thousands of dollars each year to your attorney or benefit consultant to revise or amend a custom-designed plan, just to keep it in compliance with the never-ending changes in the tax and other laws affecting pension plans.

Model SEP and Keogh Plans from Stockbrokerages

If you are not content to invest your SEP or Keogh funds in or with a financial institution, you can still participate in a canned plan offered by some stockbrokerage firms. These plans usually permit you to direct your own stock and bond investments.

Model Corporate Plans

If you are setting up a corporate retirement plan, it is also possible to obtain canned prototype plans from banks, if you allow them to act as trustee — or from insurance companies, if you buy their insurance or managed fund accounts through the plan. These plans usually have variable terms that can be tailored somewhat to suit your needs, unless you want to do something out of the ordinary, such as allow each participant to direct the investment of his or her portion of the plan's funds. Other institutions, such as stockbrokerages and mutual funds, also offer corporate plans.

Even if you do need something unusual that requires a customized retirement plan for your corporation, you will probably find it more cost-effective to have a benefit consulting firm draw up the plan for you. This way, your attorney would only be involved in reviewing the plan and obtaining approval of the plan from the IRS. Typically, benefit consultants or pension consultants will charge only a fraction of what a law firm would charge to draw up the plan, and the larger benefit consulting firms are generally quite competent. Most of their fees come from helping you administer the plan under ERISA after it is set up — a service you will need anyway.

Customized Plans

Simplified Employee Pension (SEP) plans have gotten very little use since they were created by Congress several years ago; however, they now offer most of the attractive features of typical Keogh and corporate plans with virtually no administrative costs. This is in contrast to a Keogh or corporate plan that may cost up to $2,000 or $3,000 a year to maintain for only five or ten employees.

Saving with SEPs

A SEP is basically a glorified individual retirement account (IRA), but it is one where you contribute to each employee's IRA account an amount of up to 15% of an employee's compensation with a maximum of $30,000 — $22,500, as a practical matter.

The amount contributed is not taxed to the employee and can be invested in any type of IRA account the employee chooses. SEPs can be set up by corporations, partnerships, or sole proprietorships. Participants can still contribute up to $2,000 a year to their SEP/IRA or to another IRA plan.

SEP participants with taxable income in excess of $25,000 (single) or $40,000 (married filing jointly), however, will have their IRA deductions reduced or eliminated.

The main existing drawback of an SEP is that any distributions from the plan at retirement are taxed as ordinary income. The special five-year averaging — which can result in a lower tax rate — for lump sum distributions from a Keogh or corporate qualified plan is not available for IRAs or SEPs. Even so, they strongly merit consideration as an alternative to Keogh or corporate retirement plans, due to their relative simplicity.

An increasingly popular form of qualified retirement plan is the Section 401(k) plan. This type of plan generally permits employees to elect to have a percentage of their salary — with various limitations — deducted from their paychecks, free of income tax, and deposited on their behalf in a profit-sharing-type plan. In many cases, as an additional incentive to employees to make such tax-favored savings, you, as an employer, may provide some degree of matching contribution to the plan on behalf of the employee.

Section 401(k) Plans

For example, a typical situation would be where you contribute $0.50 (50 cents) for every dollar the employee elects to have withheld from his or her pay. Your contribution is placed in the 401(k) plan and is tax-free to the employee.

Various Nonretirement Fringe Benefit Plans

The federal tax laws are replete with a whole host of tax-favored employee fringe benefits, which are characterized as being deductible to you and nontaxable to the employee. Some of the most common and important nontaxable fringes are discussed below.

Medical Insurance Plans

The corporation that maintains a medical insurance plan, such as Blue Cross or a prepaid health care plan, is permitted to deduct the premiums it pays to the insurer. In addition, the employee is not required to include either the cost of the premiums or the benefits provided by the insurer in his or her taxable income, as a general rule.[14]

Self-Insured Medical Reimbursement Plans

A corporation can set up a plan under which the corporation directly reimburses employees for medical expenses or even for such expenses as dental care, orthodontic work, and prescription eyeglasses or contact lenses.[15] If the plan satisfies tax law requirements prohibiting discrimination in favor of highly paid employees, the reimbursements paid can be deducted by the corporation and are not taxable to the recipients.[16]

Such plans are often set up in addition to medical insurance plans, either to cover deductibles that the insurance does not pay or to cover particular types of medical or dental costs that the insurance plan does not provide for. The costs of cosmetic surgery are no longer deductible as medical expenses.

Disability Insurance

Payment by a corporation of disability insurance premiums is deductible by the corporation and is not taxed to the employees covered by the insurance — except in the case of an S corporation.[17]

If an employee becomes disabled and receives disability benefits under a policy that the employer has paid the premiums for, the benefits will be included in the employee's income for tax purposes. On the other hand, if an individual, such as a sole proprietor or partner, has paid his or her own premiums for disability insurance, any disability benefits received are tax-free.[18]

Group-Term Life Insurance

Your corporation may set up a group-term life insurance plan and deduct the insurance premiums it pays on behalf of employees. To the extent the life insurance coverage on an employee does not exceed $50,000 under the plan during the taxable year, the premiums paid by you are not taxable income to the employee.[19]

Even to the extent an employee's coverage exceeds $50,000, the amount the employee must include in taxable income from the additional insurance premiums paid by you for the excess coverage is sometimes considerably less than the premium actually paid and deducted.

Unless your business is a C corporation, it cannot deduct the premiums for your own coverage under a group life insurance plan because you are not considered an employee of the business for tax purposes.

The following fringe benefits are excludable both from income and employment taxes (FUTA and FICA) for you and the employee:

Section 132 Excludable Fringe Benefits

- No-additional-cost services provided to an employee — These services consist of benefits such as free airline, rail, or bus transportation provided by companies in those industries; rooms for hotel employees; or free phone service for telephone company employees.

- Employee discounts — Service companies can provide their services to employees at up to a 20% discount. For companies selling goods, the discount may not exceed the employer's gross profit percentage multiplied by the usual selling price of the item to customers.

- Working condition fringes — These fringe benefits are tax-free, up to the amounts that would have been deductible if paid by the employee. Benefits include such items as a company car or plane used for business purposes; subscriptions to trade or professional publications; on-the-job training; business travel; and others.

- Qualified transportation fringes — These benefits include employer-provided transit passes and commuter transportation worth up to $60 a month and parking provided to employees worth up to $155 a month. Parking fringes are not available to self-employed individuals.

- Minor fringes — These benefits are items that are considered to be minimal to justify the administrative costs for them, such as using the company's copier machine or having a secretary type a personal letter.

- On-premises athletic facilities — Providing and operating facilities such as gyms, pools, tennis or golf courses on the business premises, for employees, their spouses, and dependents is a nontaxable fringe benefit.[20]

If meals are provided on-premises to employees, for your convenience as the employer, the value of such meals is usually not taxable to the employee for income tax purposes;[21] however, you can deduct 50% of the cost of furnishing such meals.

Meals on Premises

You may pay educational expenses on behalf of an employee — free of employment taxes or income tax to the employee — if the purpose of such education meets one of the two following tests: 1) the education maintains or improves skills required by the job, and 2) the education meets requirements set by you or applicable laws, where such requirements are imposed as a condition of the retention of employment or rate of compensation.

Educational Assistance Plans

You may also set up tax-qualified educational assistance plans to provide other — not necessarily job-related — educational benefits for employees, in amounts up to $5,250 a year per employee.[22] To qualify, such a plan must be in writing, disclosed to employees, and no more than 5% of benefits paid under the plan can go to 5% owners of the firm or their spouses or dependents. This tax benefit expired on June 30, 1992, but has been retroactively extended again for the period from June 30, 1992 through December 31, 1994.

Dependent Care Plans

Dependent care plans are one of the most popular and rapidly growing types of employee fringe benefit plans in recent years, providing up to $5,000 a year of dependent care benefits for children or elderly dependents per employee. Not more than 25% of benefits provided, however, can be on behalf of 5% owners of the employer company, and other technical nondiscrimination rules also apply.[23]

Stock Option Plans

Companies have devised, or Congress has provided, a number of different stock option plans with various tax advantages, all of which are designed to encourage employees to acquire a proprietary stake in the companies they work for. Major types of such plans include:

- Nonqualified stock options — In this plan, you usually grant favored employees options to acquire stock of the company at a bargain price during a period of several years. Such an option is usually not a taxable event; although, the excess of the value over the option price of the stock received, when the option is eventually exercised, is then taxed as ordinary compensation income in most cases — unless the stock is restricted or forfeitable.

- Incentive stock options (ISOs) — ISOs are options granted under a plan that meets IRS requirements, where the term of the option is limited and the option price is not less than the value of the stock at the day the option is granted. That is, with an ISO, there is no bargain element built into the option. If the stock is worth $20 a share the day the option is granted to the employee, the option must be at an exercise price of no less than $20. Thus, the employee will not stand to profit from exercising the option unless the value of the stock subsequently rises to above $20 a share — which is good incentive for the employee to help make the company as profitable as possible. If certain requirements are met, the employee does not recognize taxable income when he or she exercises an ISO and may qualify for subsequent capital gains treatment if the stock received from exercise of the option is sold at a gain.[24]

- Employee stock purchase plans — Under a tax-qualified employee stock purchase plan, a company may allow employees to purchase its stock, directly from the company, for up to a 15% discount from the fair market value of the stock. The employee is not taxed when exercising the right to purchase stock under such a plan and may receive capital gain treatment when the stock is eventually sold at a gain.[25]

Flexible Spending Plans

In the last few years, the flexible spending plan, or flex plan, has become another increasingly popular type of tax-favored employee benefit plan.

Each of the three flex plans below are designed to permit employees to choose how much to spend on a tax-free basis for various employee benefits, such as health care or dependent care. Flex plans are for employees only and cannot cover sole proprietors, partners in a partnership, or 2% shareholders in an S corporation.

Premium-conversion accounts are the simplest kind of flex account. They primarily are set up to allow employees to pay for their share of health, disability, or group-term life insurance premiums with untaxed dollars by deducting specified amounts out of their regular paychecks to pay for such coverage. The amounts the employees agree to have withheld from their salaries or wages to pay such insurance premiums are excluded from their taxable income, but deductible by the corporation or unincorporated employer. Such plans, in effect, convert part of wages directly into insurance payments, without having the government first remove a slice for taxes. Premium-conversion accounts are practical for even the smallest companies with only one or two employees.

Premium-Conversion Accounts

Flexible reimbursement accounts are accounts where an employee may agree to contribute a specified amount to each year and draw on the account to pay for health care expenses not covered by the company. Health care expenses could include medical insurance deductibles, vision care, dental coverage, or for up to $5,000 a year for dependent care expenses.

Flexible Reimbursement Accounts

Here is how these accounts work: Before the start of each year, the employees must estimate their medical and dependent care costs for the coming year that they want paid out of their accounts. The amount designated by an employee is withheld from his or her paycheck during the year (tax-free). As expenses are incurred during the year for health and dependent care, the employee submits requests for reimbursement out of the account to the plan administrator, up to the specified maximum. Employers may choose to supplement or match amounts employees choose to have withheld from their pay, as an additional tax-free benefit to the employee.

Flexible reimbursement accounts may stand alone, or may be combined with premium-conversion accounts. They are feasible for fairly small employers as well; although, administrative costs may tend to be greater than for premium-conversion accounts.

Cafeteria plans are more complex and are rarely adopted by companies with fewer than 50 employees. Under a cafeteria plan, a company gives employees a menu of benefit choices, provides a fixed number of tax-free dollars per employee each year, and allows the employees to each select or buy the particular benefits desired, such as:

Cafeteria Plans

- 401(k) contributions
- Health insurance

- Life insurance
- Disability insurance
- Vision or dental care, or both
- Vacation time

If the costs of the benefits selected exceeds the dollar amount provided by you, the employee may fund the balance with salary reduction amounts through premium-conversion or reimbursement accounts, or both, also on an untaxed basis.

Under flex plans, the golden rule is "use it or lose it." Any amount in an employee's account that is not utilized by the employee during the year is forfeited, and reverts back to you at the end of the year. Flex plans are required to meet nondiscrimination tests to ensure that highly compensated employees do not receive a disproportionate share of the benefits provided.[26] For more information on flex plans, contact:

Employers Council on Flexible Compensation
927 15th Street NW, Suite 1000
Washington, DC 20005
(202) 659-4300

8.4 Sheltering Profits on Export Sales

Many small and large American businesses have an unfortunate tendency to look at the United States as their only market and to ignore the vast potential markets for their products or services that lie outside the borders of this country. One way in which Congress has taken constructive steps to encourage more exports and to make American goods and services more competitive in foreign markets is to provide a form of indirect tax subsidy to American firms that export.

While this export subsidy has not succeeded in stemming the unfavorable trend in the balance of trade the United States has experienced in recent years, it does provide a very attractive tax benefit for U.S. companies that export. If your business is one of the many small firms that does sell its goods or services overseas, you may be able to qualify for this tax incentive by setting up either a Domestic International Sales Corporation (DISC) or a Foreign Sales Corporation (FSC).

In general, a DISC will allow you to accumulate profits earned from export sales in a specially treated corporation, free of U.S. taxes until you eventually choose to distribute the deferred income. An FSC will allow you to accumulate such income, whether or not distributed, free (in part) of U.S. corporate taxes. For an FSC, the exempt foreign trade income will not even be taxed when paid out as a dividend, if the shareholder is a corporation.[27] For small companies, DISCs may often be much simpler to operate and preferable to the FSCs, at least for the first few years of operation.

A DISC is usually just a separate dummy corporation that has no employees and does not carry on any sort of business, except on paper.

The tax law allows a U.S. firm that has qualified export receipts to set aside part of its profits on the export transactions by paying a so-called sales commission to a DISC.[28] As a corporation without any employees, the DISC does not actually do anything to earn the commissions; your firm pays the DISC the largest commission permitted by the tax law on each qualifying export sale. It is usually advisable to have a written commission agreement between your firm and the DISC for legal purposes, although this is not required for tax purposes.

The commission that can be paid to the DISC on an export sale is the larger of 4% of the gross sales price or 50% of the profit on the sale[29] — so long as the commission does not create a loss on the sale for your firm.[30] In addition, the DISC's commission income can be increased by 10% of certain export promotion expenses, if any, incurred by the DISC.[31] As you might suspect, some fairly elaborate tax accounting rules determine how much profit you have on an export sale, for purposes of computing the DISC's maximum commission.[32]

The tax benefits for your business arise because you or your business owns the DISC stock, and the commissions your business pays to the DISC are deducted from the business taxable income, while the DISC pays no tax on income it receives.

However, about 6% (or $1/17$) of the DISC's income each year is taxed to its corporate (but not individual) shareholders,[33] so the DISC will usually pay about 6% of its income back as a dividend to the business that owns the stock of the DISC — which is usually, but not necessarily — your corporation that paid the DISC the commissions. Thus, 94% (or $16/17$) of the income that is shifted to the DISC as export sales commissions escapes federal income tax indefinitely, until the DISC either pays out the accumulated income as dividends or is disqualified and loses its status as a DISC.[34]

For deferred DISC income that accumulates after 1984, however, each DISC shareholder must compute the amount of additional tax it would pay each year if all the deferred DISC income were taxed and pay the IRS interest on the deferred tax.[35] This interest will apparently be tax-deductible if paid by a corporation. The interest rate is based on the going rate for one-year T-bills.

Conceptually, having a DISC can be thought of as taking $100 of pre-tax income out of your left-hand pocket and putting it in your right-hand pocket, then putting $6 back into the left-hand pocket. You do not have to pay tax on the $94 that remains in the right-hand pocket as long as you leave it there. In fact, there are even legal ways in which you can borrow the $94 and put it back in the left-hand pocket (your business) without paying tax on it — another example of having your cake and eating it too.[36] But as long as you keep the $94 in the right-hand pocket, you pay interest on the tax saved.

Another advantage of having a DISC is that the DISC can continue to accumulate its undistributed profits year after year without fear of incurring an accumulated earnings tax, since a DISC is exempt from the accumulated earnings tax as well as the regular federal income tax.[37]

FSCs — In a Nutshell

A Foreign Sales Corporation (FSC) is somewhat similar to a DISC, but it will probably be too great of an administrative burden for it to be worthwhile for your small business to consider. Unlike a DISC, an FSC cannot be a dummy or paper corporation set up in the United States. Instead, it must meet all of the following requirements:

- It must be a foreign corporation, incorporated in a U.S. possession or in a foreign country that, in general, has arrangements to swap tax information with the IRS.
- There can be no more than 25 shareholders in an FSC.
- An FSC cannot issue preferred stock.
- An FSC must maintain a foreign office, at which there is a permanent set of tax records, including invoices.
- The FSC's board of directors must include at least one person who is not a resident of the United States — although the nonresident member can apparently be a U.S. citizen.
- An FSC cannot be part of a controlled group of corporations that also includes a DISC. That is, you can set up either an FSC or a DISC, but not both.[38]

Summary

Here is a brief summary of this section on DISC and FSC tax benefits.

- If your business will be engaged or is engaged in selling goods or services abroad, consult your tax adviser as to the advisability of establishing a DISC or FSC to shelter a large portion of your export profits.
- Both DISCs and FSCs are extremely complex entities to establish and administer, although a DISC will probably be much less of a headache for a small business to operate than an FSC. In either case, you will need to hire some very sophisticated accounting talent, so unless you earn some fairly substantial export profits, the administrative costs of having a DISC or FSC may well exceed any tax savings you will generate.
- State tax treatment of DISCs and FSCs is discussed in Section 11.8.

8.5 Planning for Withdrawal of Corporate Funds with Minimum Tax Cost

Because of the many tax and other advantages of operating a corporation, there is a good chance you will choose, either initially or later on, to incorporate your business. If you do, and your business becomes profitable to the extent that it has significant profits even after paying you the largest salary that can be justified as "reasonable compensation" under the circumstances, you will eventually be faced with the problem of how to remove the accumulated profits from the corporation without excessive tax costs. That is, unless you decide to liquidate the corporation at some point and operate as an unincorporated business or decide to sell your stock to someone else. The proceeds you receive from liquidation or selling your stock would probably result in capital gains tax in most cases, in addition to a tax at the corporate level upon liquidation. For a definition of unreasonable compensation, see Section 8.9.

If the corporation simply pays dividends to you, this activity will normally be a tax disaster because the dividends you receive will probably be taxable to you as ordinary income at federal income tax rates up to 39.6% or somewhat more. Since the corporation will have already paid tax on the money it distributes to you as dividends, double taxation will result. If both you and the corporation are in the maximum tax brackets, the result can be an effective tax rate of approximately 60% (federal corporate and individual taxes) on the income that is paid out as dividends and an even higher rate if there are also state income taxes. There are better ways to get the money out of the corporation.

Personal Loans from the Corporation

Your corporation can often serve as a bank for your short-term financial needs; however, if you continually borrow from your corporation, the IRS can in some cases treat the loans as dividends to you, which is just what you want to avoid. Or, if your corporation has an accumulated earnings problem, as described in Section 8.9, the existence of loans to shareholders can make it very difficult to argue that the corporation is accumulating earnings for the reasonable needs of the business. So, while a loan from your corporation can be a very good way to tap its funds on a temporary basis, it is not a long-term solution.

If you do borrow, you should normally pay interest if the loan is greater than $10,000. The interest rate should not be less than the applicable federal rate established by the IRS.[39] This rate is announced by the IRS each month of the year for transactions that occur during the following month.

Preliminary Structuring

A number of different ways of structuring your corporation at its inception can give you a great deal of potential flexibility in getting money out of the corporation for yourself or family members later at no tax cost or, at worst, as only partially taxable. Some of these approaches can also make it possible to keep a great deal of the value of the corporation's stock out of your taxable estate for estate tax and inheritance tax purposes. Discuss the structuring of your corporation with your tax adviser before you form the corporation. Here are some of the strategies you might explore.

Putting Stock in Names of Spouse and Children

When the corporation is formed, consider putting a substantial part of the stock in the name of your spouse or children, or both. Later, when or if the business has prospered and the stock has become valuable, it may be possible to bail out a large chunk of the corporation's accumulated profits at a child's lower tax rates by having the corporation redeem (purchase) all of the stock of your spouse or child.

The redemption will usually be treated as a sale for a capital gain if your spouse or child agrees to notify the IRS if he or she reacquires any interest in the corporation within ten years after the redemption.[40] Working as an employee of the corporation would be an "interest" that would prevent the spouse or child from receiving favorable capital gains treatment. So if you want your son or daughter to work for you in the business, do not count on being able to redeem his or her stock as a capital gain.

Note that while capital gains are taxed at only slightly lower rates than ordinary income, it is still very desirable to have a stock redemption qualify for capital gains treatment, because part of the money received will be a nontaxable recovery of the shareholder's tax basis in the stock that is being redeemed. This is usually not the case if the redemption payment is treated as an ordinary income dividend.

Such redemption of stock as a capital gain could even be made on an installment basis.[41] For example, if your daughter had all her stock redeemed by the corporation for $150,000, the corporation could pay the $150,000 price, plus interest, in 15 annual installments of $10,000 each, so that your daughter would not have a "bunching" of all the capital gain on the sale in one tax year. Instead, the capital gains tax would be spread over a 15-year period, and the corporation should be able to deduct interest paid on the note held by the daughter.

Constraints in Community Property States

Unfortunately, this tactic does not work as well in community property states if you attempt to redeem your spouse's stock. Under the community property laws, half of your stock will generally be treated as owned by your spouse. This makes it difficult to completely terminate his or her interest, unless all of the stock that is community property is first split in half between you by agreement, so that you each own your shares as separate property.

Even in that case, your spouse may be considered to have reacquired a community property interest in your separately owned stock if you continue to work for the corporation and the value of the stock increases on account of your efforts. Thus, if you live in a community property state, you probably should not count on trying to redeem your spouse's interest in the corporation as a capital gain. The states that have community property laws are Arizona, California, Idaho, Louisiana, Nevada, New Mexico, Texas, Washington, and Wisconsin.

Gifts of Stock to Children

Even if the corporation never redeems your children's stock, it is useful to put some of the stock in their names when you form the corporation — especially at a time when a gift to them of the stock will be subject to little or no gift tax because of its low value. When you die many years later, the stock owned by your children may then be very valuable and will not be included in your estate in most instances, which could save your children a great deal in estate and inheritance taxes. The federal gift tax laws now permit you to make gifts worth up to $10,000 per child per year free of federal gift tax. If you are married, you and your spouse can jointly make gifts of up to $20,000 per year per child; however, you may be subject to state gift taxes in some states.

Until the Revenue Reconciliation Act of 1989 was passed, it was considered astute tax planning — when setting up a new corporation — to capitalize the company with both equity capital (stock) and debt capital (an interest-bearing note from the corporation to you); however, such a tactic can now be a tax trap.

Debt Capitalization Pitfall

This type of structuring can still be done without adverse tax consequences, but only if the assets you are transferring to the corporation are cash or other assets on which you would not have a taxable gain if sold at current fair market value. Otherwise, under the 1989 law, any notes or other debt capital you take back from the corporation will cause you to pay tax on appreciated assets (land, equipment, etc.) that you transfer to the corporation in return for the stock and debt instruments.

If, however, the only asset you are putting in the corporation to start it up is, for example, cash, you will not be affected by the 1989 tax law change mentioned in the preceding paragraph. As an illustration, if you plan to put $10,000 in the corporation to get the business started, you might take back stock for $5,000 and a $5,000 note when the corporation is set up, rather than having the corporation issue you stock for the whole $10,000. While the note is outstanding, you will be able to siphon off some funds from the corporation as interest on the note, which the corporation can deduct. By contrast, if the corporation distributed profits to you as dividends on its stock, it would result in double taxation of those profits, since, unlike interest, the corporation cannot deduct dividends it pays.

Debt Capitalization Still Can Be Advantageous

More importantly, when the note becomes due, the corporation will repay you the $5,000 principal of the note; if things have been handled properly, you should pay no tax on that $5,000. In contrast, if the corporation attempted to return part of your investment in the stock, whatever you received would probably be fully taxable to you as a dividend, even if you surrendered some of your stock in a redemption. Lending the corporation part of its start-up capital allows you to withdraw part of your investment without paying tax.

Thus, there are considerable advantages in partially capitalizing your corporation with debt in the form of a note or notes that you will hold from the corporation. You will need competent tax advice before you do so, however, since there are hundreds of court cases that have tried to define when debt instruments will be considered debt and when they will be considered stock. For example, if you capitalize your corporation with more than $3 of debt for each $1 of stock — say a $6,000 note and $2,000 of stock — the note (debt) may be treated as though it were stock for tax purposes. Thus, if the corporation paid you interest or principal on the note, whatever payments you received would be treated as dividends to you, and the corporation's deduction for the interest payments would be disallowed. So tread very lightly in lending money to your corporation. See Section 8.9 for more on the distinction between debt and equity for tax purposes.

Post-Incorporation Planning

Whether or not you take advantage of the above planning suggestions at the time you incorporate, there are a number of other ways you can get cash out of your corporation at a low tax cost later on.

Leasing to the Corporation

Instead of putting your own money into the corporation so it can buy property it needs, keep the money outside the corporation, and buy the property yourself and lease it all at a reasonable rental to the corporation. This way, you will be able to directly obtain the tax depreciation and other benefits of owning the property. At the same time, by keeping the property out of the corporation, you will be putting less of your assets at risk in the business, especially if the corporation goes broke. Also, if the leased property is real estate, it will probably appreciate in value.

You can personally and directly benefit from that appreciation, including the increased rent you will be able to charge the corporation as inflation continues. Furthermore, if you have used straight-line depreciation and sell the property at a gain, all of the gain will be capital gain. By contrast, if the corporation sells real property at a gain, 20% of the straight-line depreciation is recaptured as ordinary income.[42] Although a corporation's capital gains are currently taxed at the same rate as ordinary income, Congress restored preferential tax rates for individuals' capital gains in 1990, and it may do the same for corporations in the future.

Trusts for Your Children

You could make a gift of business property — or the funds to buy it — to a trust and have a bank or other independent trustee negotiate a reasonable lease of the property to the business, with the rental income going to the trust for distribution to your children. Upon the trust's termination, or earlier, such as when your children reach specified ages, the property and accumulated income can be distributed to the children, or if a child does not live until age 21, revert to you at his or her death.

This can be a useful way of taking cash out of the corporation for the benefit of your children, who have lower tax brackets; however, since the IRS regularly attempts to attack these types of arrangements, you should go into this only with the help of an astute tax adviser. Be aware that the Tax Reform Act of 1986 eliminated nearly all the tax advantages of trusts for children under 14 years of age.

DISC Deferrals

Consider setting up a DISC corporation if your corporation has foreign sales. You can then hold the DISC stock yourself or give it to your children.

This will not only enable you to indefinitely defer federal income taxes on part of the profits from export sales, it will also, in effect, allow you or your children to siphon off part of the profits on export sales — dividends paid by the DISC — in a manner that allows your corporation to deduct those dividends, thereby avoiding double taxation.

Consider adopting corporate pension or profit-sharing plans and various corporate fringe benefit plans. These types of benefit plans, in appropriate circumstances, can provide deferred retirement benefits or current insurance benefits to you tax-free — or on a tax-deferred basis, in the case of retirement plans — while reducing the corporation's current taxable income. See the discussion of these kinds of employee benefit plans in Section 8.3.

Benefit Plans

8.6 Deducting Expenses Related to Your Business

One major advantage of operating your own business is the opportunity it may give you to deduct the costs of certain activities or luxuries as business expenses. Some of these deductions are discussed below.

Some of the tax benefits that were available in the past, however, such as costs of attending foreign conventions [43] and treating part of your home as a business office [44] have been severely curtailed, and there are strict recordkeeping requirements for others. [45] For instance, deductions for attending foreign conventions are now completely disallowed, unless you can show that:

- It is just as reasonable for the convention to be held abroad as it would be to hold it in North America; and
- The meeting is directly related to your trade or business.

If these two requirements are met, you must then meet the general requirements for traveling outside the United States. Deductions for conventions or seminars on cruise ships are limited to $2,000, and other travel by "luxury water transportation" is deductible only up to certain per diem amounts. [46] For more on office-in-the-home expenses, refer to Section 8.14.

It is still possible to deduct business travel expenses, entertainment of your clients or customers, and business-related meals; however, you can only deduct 50% of qualifying business meals and entertainment. Consequently, this 50% rule considerably complicates recordkeeping for these types of expenses.

Travel, Entertainment, and Meal Expenses

For instance, if you stay in a hotel on a business trip and charge your meals to your room, you are required to separately break out your meal expenses for tax purposes because your meal expenses are only 50% deductible.

If you are an employee of your business, the 50% disallowance of meal and entertainment expenses does not apply to you individually, if your company reimburses you for the expenses; it applies only at the company level.

Detailed Records Required

To claim any of these kinds of deductions, you must keep daily, detailed records of such expenditures, including bills, receipts, and the following information for each expense:

- The relationship of the expenditure to the business;
- The time when the expense was incurred;
- Where the money was spent, and to whom it was paid;
- The amount of the expenditure; and
- The identities of the persons involved, including persons entertained.[47]

The law requires that taxpayers keep "adequate records or . . . sufficient evidence corroborating the taxpayer's own statement."[48] It is strongly recommended that you pick up a daily expense record book or diary and enter all expenses for travel, meals, and entertainment you think should be deductible. Include the above information for each item.

Not All Expenses Deductible

Not all expenses for entertaining clients or customers will be deductible, even if you keep meticulous records. As a general rule, your records must show that you were engaged in a substantial and bona fide business discussion during or immediately before or after the entertainment.[49] Expenses of entertaining people just to create a good impression on them, in the hope they might send some business your way in the future, are classified as goodwill entertainment, and you cannot deduct them for tax purposes.

The rule allowing quiet business meals with clients or potential customers to be deductible, even if no business is discussed, has been repealed.[50] For more information on business-related expenses you can deduct, contact your local IRS office and request *Publication 463, Travel, Entertainment, and Gift Expenses.*

Automobile Expenses

If you use an automobile more than 50% of the time for business purposes, you will generally be able to deduct a percentage of the costs of owning and operating the car, if you can substantiate the business mileage. The expenses of using the car for commuting to and from work and for personal travel are not deductible.[51]

For example, if your business purchases a new car for your use as a business car, and 80% of the mileage on the car can be shown to be for business trips, and only 20% for commuting to work and other personal use, you should be able to deduct 80% of the gas, oil, insurance, and maintenance costs relating to the car. You can also depreciate the cost of the car, less 20% for personal use.

Rules are even more drastic for any automobile, airplane, boat or computer not kept in your place of business if you can't establish a business-use percentage in excess of 50%. Automobile depreciation is stretched out over at least six years, straight-line: 10% the first year; 20% a year thereafter, for four years; and 10% the final year. For boats, planes, or computers, it can be stretched out for longer periods.[52] There are also strict dollar limits on maximum annual depreciation deductions for so-called luxury automobiles costing more than about $15,000. For luxury automobiles, the maximum annual depreciation deduction allowed is limited to the amounts below.

Luxury Automobile Depreciation

1993 Acquisitions	**1994 Acquisitions**
$2,860 for the first year	$2,960 for the first year
$4,600 for the second year	$4,700 for the second year
$2,750 for the third year	$2,850 for the third year
$1,675 for each succeeding year	$1,675 for each succeeding year

These restrictions don't apply to business vehicles such as ambulances, hearses, taxis, delivery vans, or heavy trucks.[53]

Exemptions

If you drive an inexpensive economy car on business, it may be simpler and more advantageous to elect to deduct a flat $0.29 (29 cents) per mile for 1994[54] for your business mileage rather than keep records of your various kinds of automobile expenses. If you use this method, you can still deduct tolls and parking incurred on business trips. If you drive an expensive car, you will probably get much larger tax deductions by reporting your actual operating expenses, plus depreciation, than by electing the mileage allowance. Be sure to keep an accurate record of your business mileage so you can substantiate the car was used for business purposes.

Mileage Deduction

Form 4562 of your annual tax return requires you to answer a number of detailed questions if you claim an automobile deduction.

8.7 Choosing the Best Taxable Year for a Corporation

If your business is an S corporation or is considered a personal service corporation, you will generally have no choice but to operate on a calendar-year basis, and you can skip over the following discussion of how to select a taxable year. If, however, your business is incorporated and is neither an S corporation or a personal service corporation in which the services performed are "substantially performed" by owner/employees,[55] you will have an opportunity to choose any tax fiscal-year period you desire during your initial year of operation as a corporation. There are significant tax deferral and savings opportunities in selecting the right year end.

Unfortunately, in some cases, it will be necessary to be able to project with some accuracy how much your corporation will earn or lose each month for several months to a year ahead. If you expect to have start-up losses and show an overall net profit for your first year as an incorporated business, one good rule is to cut off your first taxable year at the end of the month in which you first get back to break even for the year-to-date.

For example, assume your first tax year starts on January 1, 1995, and you show a cumulative tax loss of $20,000 at the end of June. You then have taxable income of $10,000 a month in July, August, and September, and expect profits to continue. If you chose June 30 as your tax year end, you would have a $20,000 loss for your first tax period ending June 30, 1995. For federal income tax purposes, it is no problem, since you can carry over the loss and use it to offset $20,000 of taxable income during the next tax year. Some states, however, do not allow a carryover of losses.

Another approach would be to choose an August 31 year end, so that you would show no taxable income for your first year, assuming the corporation continued to net $10,000 a month.

If you do not mind paying some tax earlier, it might pay, in the above example, to wait until the end of October, November, or even December to cut off the first tax year. This would enable the corporation to isolate $20,000 to $40,000 or so of profit in a tax period subject to low federal corporate income tax rates, which are only 15% on the first $50,000 of corporate income.

If you do so, however, you are making an assumption that the corporation will be in a higher tax bracket in the following year, which cannot be known with any certainty. In addition, the existence of tax credits would somewhat complicate the simple picture portrayed above. Obviously, your accountant can help you decide which tax year will produce the best result.

Start-up Losses Must Be Capitalized, Not Deducted

Remember, when projecting your start-up losses, you can't immediately deduct preopening expenses; instead, you must capitalize those costs and write them off (straight-line) over 60 months.[56] For example, if you are starting a restaurant and are paying salaries to a manager and to employees being trained before the day the restaurant opens for business, you might well think those expenses are immediately deductible. Not so! All such preopening expenses must be capitalized, and you can't begin to amortize them until opening day.

Another planning approach in adopting a year end, which may sometimes conflict with the above strategy, is to adopt a January 31 year end. If you structure your employment contract with your corporation so that you receive a substantial part of your compensation in January each year, you can, in effect, defer the bonus to your following tax year, while the corporation can deduct it — if paid in January — for its fiscal year ending just after the bonus is paid. Naturally, the corporation will be required to withhold income tax from your bonus, but at reduced rates, compared to regular monthly salary payments. Federal income tax withholding on bonuses is at a flat rate of only 28%.

Benefits of Adopting January 31 Year End

If you have a seasonal business, you may want to defer taxes by selecting a tax year that ends just before your most profitable season begins. For example, if you are in the business of selling Christmas tree ornaments and do most of your business from October through December each year, you might choose a September 30 tax year end.

Seasonal Businesses

Remember, though, that tax considerations are not the only factors to take into account in choosing a fiscal year. If taking an annual inventory is a major task, consider adopting a year end that occurs when inventory is at a low ebb and when business is slow, if possible. You may also find that you will get somewhat quicker and better service from your CPA firm for annual tax returns, audits, etc. if you pick a fiscal year that ends several months before or after December. Most CPAs are at their busiest during their annual tax season from about February to May, preparing 1040s and doing audits for their many clients who have December year ends.

8.8 Selecting Tax Accounting Methods

Rely on your tax accountant's advice when choosing which tax accounting methods you should adopt in your business. This section is provided for your information in case you are not sure whether your accountant has recommended the method that will produce the best results for you.

The two overall tax accounting methods most commonly used are the cash method and the accrual method. There are, however, other special overall methods, plus a number of special kinds of accounting elections a business can make with regard to particular items, such as installment sales, inventory valuations, and deduction of accrued vacation pay.

The cash receipts and disbursements method of accounting, called the cash method, is the simplest accounting method in use. Under this method, you include income only as it is actually or constructively received.

Cash Method

Likewise, you only become entitled to deductions when you actually pay expenses — except for certain special items like depreciation or amortization of certain kinds of expenditures — rather than when you receive bills for the expenses. Thus, you usually do not have to report your year-end accounts receivable in income for the year and cannot deduct your year-end accounts payable. This will normally allow you to defer some taxable income each year if your year-end receivables are larger than accounts payable and other accrued but unpaid expenses. Obviously, this gives you some flexibility, too, if you want to pay off a number of payables at year end to reduce your taxable income for the current year.

The cash method is the method used by most individual taxpayers and by businesses in the real estate, financial, and service fields, where inventories of goods are not material factors in producing income.

Businesses with significant inventories, such as manufacturers and wholesale or retail firms, are usually required to use an accrual method of tax accounting.[57] In some cases, however, it is possible even for those businesses to use a hybrid accounting method — accounting for income and the cost of goods sold on an accrual method — while using the cash method to report selling expenses and administrative expenses.

The Tax Reform Act of 1986 disallowed use of the cash method for C corporations — regular corporations — and for partnerships that have C corporations as partners. One exception is for small firms with an average gross receipts of five million dollars or less during the three preceding years.[58] Another exception is made for larger firms in the farming business and for certain employee-owned qualified personal service corporations in fields such as law, medicine, accounting, architecture, or consulting.

Sole proprietorships, S corporations, and partnerships with no C corporation partners are not affected by these restrictions, unless they are considered tax shelters, and may remain on the cash method if that is a permissible accounting method for their particular type of business. Firms that are forbidden from using the cash method must adopt the more complex accrual method of accounting.

Accrual Method

As noted above, most large corporations and businesses with significant inventories are required to report income on the accrual method of accounting for tax purposes. This method requires you to report income when income is earned rather than when you receive it. Similarly, expenses can be deducted when all events have occurred that fix the amount and the fact of your business' liability for a particular expense, even if it is paid in a subsequent tax year. However, if economic performance required of the other party does not occur until a subsequent tax year, you may not be able to deduct an accrued expense until economic performance occurs.

For example, if you sign a contract with your accountant in 1995 to prepare your tax return in 1996, "economic performance" does not occur until 1996, and you may be unable to accrue the deduction in 1995, unless you meet several requirements, such as recurring expenses or performance occurs within a reasonable time after the end of the tax year.[59]

Even though the accrual method may not be required for your business, you may find it preferable to use, if most or all of your income is from cash sales and you pay a large part of your expenses on a delayed credit basis. In this case, you would have few, if any, receivables at year end but might have substantial accrued payables you could deduct in the current year without having to actually make payment before year end.

Accrual of bonuses to employees, in an incorporated business, is a good example of a deduction that can be accelerated by a business using the accrual method. But expenses owed to you or a related owner of the business can't be deducted until actually paid.[60]

If your business is engaged in heavy construction work on a long-term contract basis, it may be difficult to tell in advance whether a particular contract will result in a profit or loss, since many unforeseen difficulties may arise. The tax regulations recognize this problem and allow such contractors to utilize special methods of accounting which may delay the time at which profit or loss is recognized on a long-term contract. They are:

Special Accounting Methods Long-Term Contracts

- The percentage of completion method; and
- The completed contract method.[61]

The Tax Reform Act of 1986, however, and subsequent legislation has eliminated the use of the completed contract method of accounting for most large companies, except for certain ship contracts and for some home construction and other residential building contractors.

Fortunately, small businesses, whose average annual gross receipts for the three preceding years do not exceed ten million dollars, are still allowed to use completed contract accounting for tax purposes, at least for contracts that are estimated to take no more than two years to complete.[62]

Even those completed contract method deferrals that survive the new restrictions are now mostly considered tax preference items under the alternative minimum tax rules.[63] In other words, heads you lose, tails the tax collector wins.

If your business makes casual or occasional sales of personal property — other than merchandise held for sale — or makes sales of real estate it owns, the profit on any such sale can, in general, be reported on the installment basis as and when payments are received, rather than in the year of sale.[64] The installment method of reporting, however, is not available for "dealers," such as retailers, in personal or real property, except for certain dealers in real property. This is an election that sellers of residential lots or time-shares may make to use the installment method. The

Installment Sales

catch is that the dealer making such an election must agree to pay interest on any tax that is deferred by using installment reporting.[65]

In the case of nondealer sales of property for more than $150,000, if the total face amount of all installment notes exceeds five million dollars for the year, at the end of the year, the seller must pay interest on the deferred tax liability.[66] Sales of personal-use property or of farm property, for any amount, are exempt from the interest-on-deferred-tax provisions.[67]

Inventory Valuation Methods

If you maintain substantial inventories, discuss with your accountant the pros and cons of using the last-in-first-out (LIFO) method of valuing year-end inventories[68] versus the more common and simpler first-in-first-out (FIFO) method.

FIFO Method

Under the FIFO method, the cost of ending inventory is calculated under the assumption that the first items of inventory bought were the first ones to be sold, so that only the most recently purchased items are assumed to be left in inventory at the end of each year. This usually means the highest-cost items, in times of inflation. That is, if a company turns all its inventory over every three months each year, FIFO assumes, in effect, that the inventory remaining on hand at December 31 was all bought in the last three months of the year, rather than at some earlier date when prices may have been lower.

Most companies use the FIFO method because:

- FIFO is much simpler to use in terms of maintaining accounting records;
- When prices of goods are generally rising, FIFO has the effect of making a company's net income appear to be greater than if the more conservative LIFO method were used — but it also tends to inflate the amount of a company's taxable income; and
- Their accountants never mention to them that there is an alternative method (LIFO) of inventory accounting that can be used.

LIFO Method

In contrast to FIFO, the LIFO method assumes that the items in your ending inventory are the first or oldest ones that were acquired. Thus, under LIFO, ending inventory values for many of the items of inventory will be based on what that item cost in the very first year in which the business began using the LIFO method. The difference in inventory valuation can be dramatic if, for example, a business using LIFO for ten years was paying $10 each ten years earlier for the widgets it keeps in inventory versus a current price of $75 per widget. Under LIFO, the widgets would still be carried on the accounting records at a cost of $10 apiece versus $75 under FIFO.

Accordingly, the difference in inventory cost, or $65 per widget in the above example — called the LIFO reserve — would be the amount of taxable income per widget that the company has deferred over the ten years. Thus, for a company with large amounts of capital invested in inventories, it is easy to see how LIFO can result in a huge tax saving.

At present, using the LIFO method is extremely complex, and the tax savings may in some cases be offset by increased accounting fees incurred and additional management time spent in attempting to comply with the LIFO tax regulations. The tax requirements for using LIFO, however, are somewhat relaxed for those small businesses with less than five million dollars a year in sales.[69]

Any firm with inventories may elect to use either FIFO or LIFO. If a firm is already using FIFO, it may be able to change over to LIFO, if a number of technical requirements set by the IRS are met. Or, a company using LIFO may also change over to FIFO. Note, however, that if a firm uses LIFO and changes to FIFO for some reason, it will usually have to pay a large amount of tax, when it recaptures the LIFO reserve described above, at the time of the changeover. Any such changes in inventory accounting methods should not be attempted without the assistance of a competent tax adviser. If your C corporation already uses LIFO inventory accounting and elects S corporation status, your corporation will be required to pay tax, in four annual installments, on the LIFO reserve at the time of the changeover to an S corporation.[70]

Regardless of whether a company uses LIFO or FIFO for inventory accounting, it generally must allocate a wide range of its indirect costs to inventory, rather than simply deducting them as expenses, under the IRS's uniform capitalization rules. The practical effect of this is that any such costs that have been absorbed into the cost of inventory on hand at the end of the tax year do not get deducted currently for tax purposes. Manufacturing and processing operations of any size are subject to these complex capitalization rules. Fortunately, the uniform capitalization rules do not apply to a wholesale or retail business in any year when the company's annual gross receipts for the preceding three years have averaged ten million dollars or less.[71]

Vacation Pay Accrual Method

If you accrue employees' vacation pay for internal business purposes, you normally can only deduct your liability for such accruals when an employee actually uses his or her vacation pay. The only exception is for accrual-basis taxpayers, where vacation pay is vested at the end of a tax year and paid within two and a half months afterwards.

8.9 Tax Problems Unique to Corporations

While this book has outlined some of the many tax and other advantages inherent in operating a corporation, you need to be aware of a number of traps in the tax law if you go overboard in trying to take advantage of the tax benefits bestowed on corporations.

As is emphasized in this chapter, the most basic goal in corporate tax planning for many high-income individuals is to leave as much profit in the corporation as possible so it can be taxed at the relatively low corporate tax rates and later withdrawn tax-free or at capital gains rates, such as by selling or having the corporation redeem the stock or by liquidating the corporation.

The government's role is to prevent the taxpayer from reaching these goals except where the corporation has good business reasons — as opposed to the individual's tax and investment reasons — for virtually everything it does. In attempting to plug up all the possible loopholes taxpayers might use to take advantage of low corporate rates, the tax law contains a whole array of penalties for corporations:

- That unreasonably accumulate earnings;[72]
- That are used as "incorporated pocket books" for holding personal investments;[73] or
- That are capitalized too heavily with debt.[74]

These and other operating problems of corporations under the tax law are briefly outlined below to give you a sense of what the limits are and how far you can go in utilizing corporate tax advantages. None of these problems are significant concerns for S corporations.

Penalty Tax on Accumulated Earnings

The accumulated earnings tax might well be called the scourge of the overly successful small corporation.[75] This tax potentially applies to almost every corporation that accumulates more than $250,000[76] in after-tax profits (with certain adjustments),[77] unless the corporation can demonstrate that it needs to retain the profits for use in its business operations.[78]

Your corporation can accumulate up to $250,000 — $150,000 for professional and certain personal service firms — in earnings without having to be concerned about this penalty tax.[79] If additional accumulations cannot be justified as being made for the "reasonable needs of the business," however, the corporation will be faced with the choice of paying out the excess earnings as dividends or paying the accumulated earnings tax. The tax is imposed at the rate of 39.6% on the improperly accumulated earnings.[80] Since this is a tax that is imposed in addition to the corporate income tax, it is one you probably do not ever want to be forced to pay.

As long as you are able to keep plowing profits back into your business; buying more facilities, equipment, and inventory; and maintaining needed working capital, you will not have much cause for worry about the accumulated earnings tax. If, however, you reach a point where the corporation has more liquid funds than it needs, and you are beginning to look for places to invest the surplus cash, like real estate or the stock market, that should serve as a signal to you that there may be a potential accumulated earnings problem. In that case, you will need some good tax advice as to what you can do to protect the corporation from imposition of the penalty tax.

Fortunately, there are a number of acceptable reasons that can justify accumulating funds that are not currently being used in the corporation's business. Some of the more important ones include:

- Setting up a reserve to redeem enough of the stock of a shareholder (yourself, for example) who dies, in order to enable the individual's estate to pay certain expenses related to his or her death — estate and inheritance taxes, funeral expenses, and expenses of administering the estate.[81] This reserve can only be created by the corporation after the death of a shareholder, prior to the repurchase of the shareholder's stock;

- Creating a fund to allow for a bona fide plan to replace facilities or expand the business, including the acquisition of another business;[82]

- Creating a reasonable reserve fund to pay potential uninsured product liability claims;[83]

- Accumulating funds to retire indebtedness created in connection with the business of the corporation;[84] and

- Setting up a defined benefit pension plan with an initial "past service liability" to be funded over a number of years.

A number of ways also exist to reduce the accumulated earnings without paying them out as dividends. Some typical examples would be to redeem part of the stock of the corporation, such as the stock of one of your children. This will not only reduce accumulated earnings but will reduce the amount of excess cash not needed in the business.

Another useful approach is to have the corporation purchase real estate that it might currently be leasing. This can sometimes be particularly advantageous where you are the landlord who is leasing the property to the corporation, as suggested in Section 8.5. This tactic technically will not reduce the corporation's accumulated earnings, but will use up excess cash that would otherwise raise questions by IRS auditors.

Another effective solution if you have an accumulated earnings problem is to convert your C corporation to an S corporation, if that is possible. S corporations are not subject to the accumulated earnings tax because all their earnings are deemed to be distributed to shareholders.

If a closely held corporation gets a large proportion of its gross income, usually 60% or more, in the form of personal holding company income,[85] such as dividends, interest, rents, and royalties, it will generally be considered a personal holding company for tax purposes.[86]

Other kinds of income considered personal holding company income include income received by a service business from anyone (other than the corporation) who has the right under a contract to designate a particular individual to perform the contracted services. The person designated, however, must own at least 25% of the corporate stock.[87] Also, payments a corporation receives from a 25% shareholder for use of its property is personal holding company income.[88] This puts a damper on schemes such as having your corporation buy a yacht and charter it to you.

As a rule, if a corporation comes within the definition of a personal holding company, the tax law imposes a 39.6% penalty tax on any personal holding company income not distributed as a dividend.[89]

Most actively conducted small businesses will not need to be very concerned about being treated as personal holding companies since they will seldom get 60% or more of their gross income from passive sources like dividends and interest.

The kind of small business most likely to have a personal holding company problem is the incorporated personal service business — when the corporation enters into contracts and agrees to provide the services of an employee who is a major shareholder.

The best way to avoid this problem is to specify in the contract that the corporation reserves the right to designate the person who will provide the services. You will need to consult your tax adviser, however, before entering into any such personal service contract since the tax rules in this area are quite subtle and the tax penalty is very heavy if the income under the personal service contract is considered to be personal holding company income.

Another type of operating company that frequently encounters personal holding company tax problems is the developer of computer software that generates much of its income from software licensing agreements.

While the Tax Reform Act of 1986 included a special exemption from the personal holding company provisions for corporations actively engaged in the computer software business, the terms of this exception are quite technical and many software firms will only be able to qualify for this relief with very careful planning.[90]

Possible Treatment of Corporate Debt as Stock

As discussed in Section 8.5, there are two significant advantages to putting part of your investment in an incorporated business into the corporation in the form of debt, rather than all of it in exchange for stock. These advantages are:

- The interest paid to you is normally deductible by the corporation, unlike dividends paid on its stock.
- Repayment of the money you loaned to the corporation allows you to take part of your investment out of the corporation free of tax.

Because the use of debt in structuring a closely held corporation is so advantageous, Congress has taken steps to limit the extent to which you can use debt to capitalize a corporation and still enjoy these advantages.[91]

Over the last two decades, the IRS has proposed several sets of new and complex regulations as to when loans to a corporation by its shareholders will be treated as equivalent to an investment in its stock — in which case interest payments will not be deductible by the corporation and principal payments would be taxable to the recipient.

These regulations raised such a storm of protest each time they were proposed that the IRS finally withdrew them. So, to determine what constitutes debt and stock, guidelines are used from hundreds of different court decisions. Nevertheless, there are a few generally accepted ground rules that you should follow to avoid having corporate debt reclassified by the IRS as equity or stock:

- The loan should not have any equity-type features, such as interest or payments, pegged to the corporation's income.
- The loan should be made at a reasonable interest rate, such as the rate at which the IRS imputes interest between related parties.
- The corporation's total debts — other than trade accounts payable — should not be more than about three times its net worth.
- The loan should be documented by a written note and should have a specified maturity date. All interest and principal payments on the note should be made on time.

If you follow each of the above rules, you will generally avoid the problem of having debt reclassified as stock. If you fail to comply with one or more of those rules when lending money to your corporation, the loan may be treated as a stock investment. This can be a serious tax trap if, when the loan is to be repaid, you are unaware that the repayment to you may constitute taxable income.

The most basic tax problem resulting from incorporating a business is the possibility of double taxation of the business income if it is paid out as dividends. That is, if the corporation has any profit after payment of salaries and other expenses, it must pay tax on those profits, unless it is an S corporation. Then, if those profits left after taxes are distributed to stockholders as dividends, the stockholders must also pay tax on the dividends they receive.

Fortunately, the problem of double taxation is generally quite manageable and most small incorporated businesses never pay dividends. The owners normally are also the officers of the corporation and can take enough income out in the form of salary and fringe benefits to live on, usually leaving some profit in the corporation to be plowed back into the business.

Also, as outlined briefly in Section 8.5, there are a number of better ways to get the accumulated profits out of the corporation than by paying dividends.

If you own an incorporated business or own a portion of its stock and are actively involved in operating the business, you will be an employee of the corporation and will draw a salary. Drawing a large salary from the corporation may enable you to withdraw much of the profits of the business without any problem of double taxation, since the corporation can deduct reasonable compensation it pays to you as your salary.[92]

Thus, taking salary out of the corporation is preferable to taking money out in the form of dividends, since the corporation cannot deduct dividends it pays. The salary you receive, if reasonable, is deductible by the corporation; however, the key word here is reasonable. If you try to take too much income out of the corporation as salary, including bonuses and fringe benefits like pension and profit-sharing contributions, the IRS may try to treat part of your salary as unreasonable compensation. If you are fortunate enough to be worried about the one-million-dollar limitation on executive compensation that went into effect in 1994, you can relax. That limitation will only apply to executives of publicly held corporations. So unless your company has gone public, you don't need to be concerned about this limitation.[93]

There are no hard and fast rules as to how much compensation is reasonable, but if you are taking no more than the officers in similar businesses of the same size are paid, you should not have any problem establishing that your compensation from the corporation is reasonable under the circumstances.

If, however, the IRS does succeed in treating part of your compensation as excessive, there will be two serious tax consequences:

- The deduction by the corporation for the unreasonable portion of your salary will be disallowed.
- Part of your salary will be reclassified as dividend income, and thus pension and profit-sharing plan contributions based on that salary may not be fully deductible, which could even result in disqualification of your pension or profit-sharing plan.

8.10 Estate Planning in Connection with Your Business

As the owner of part or all of even a moderately successful business, you may find that after a few years, the value of your business accounts for a very large portion of your personal net worth. As such, your business will probably be the most important single asset you have to be concerned with for estate planning purposes, both during your lifetime and at the time of your death. No attempt will be made here to go into the intricacies of the estate-planning possibilities that may be available; instead, the fundamental approaches you need to be aware of are outlined below. Discuss how to relate these concepts to your own situation with your tax adviser and attorney.

Income Splitting

A useful method of reducing lifetime income taxes is to split the taxable income from your business between two or more persons or entities. Usually a corporation, particularly an S corporation, is a useful vehicle for doing this; you can split income between you and your children by giving them stock in the corporation. A corporation that has not elected S corporation treatment can also be used to split income between you and the corporation. See Section 8.2.

Often, the best time to remove potential wealth from your taxable estate at death is by giving your children part of the stock in your incorporated business when the business is formed — when the value of the stock is likely to be negligible. If you wait until the business has become a valuable and profitable enterprise, gifts of stock at that time may result in substantial taxable gifts for gift tax purposes, even though the tax cost of those gifts may not be felt until you die, in some cases. You can currently make gifts of up to $10,000 ($20,000 if married) per year to each of your children completely free of federal gift taxes.

Reducing Estate and Gift Taxes

Assuming that you want part of your stock in your incorporated business to pass to your children at your death, it obviously makes sense to give them a portion of the stock — but not enough to affect your control of the corporation — during your lifetime. By doing this, there will be little or no gift tax cost if it is done when the business is started. Thus, they will already own the stock when you die, and that valuable asset will have passed to them free of death taxes in most instances. In addition, as noted above, lifetime gifts of stock to your children may also save on income taxes.

If you have one or more partners or business associates who also own a part of the business, it is very important that you enter into a buy-sell agreement with them that spells out what happens if one of you dies, becomes disabled, or wants to sell his or her interest in the business.

Buy-Sell Agreements

Often, these agreements are funded by life insurance on the owners, so that if you die, the business or the other owners will collect the life insurance proceeds and use those funds to buy out your interest in the business. Otherwise, your surviving family members might find it very difficult to sell the interest in the business they inherit from you, except at a give-away price.

Many small business owners ignore the need for buy-sell agreements or, like having a will drawn up, they keep putting it off. When one of the partners or shareholders dies, the survivors may have a problem in raising enough cash to pay the death taxes. This is only one of the problems that may arise when there is no buy-sell agreement.

The few hundred dollars you may spend in legal fees to have a buy-sell agreement with your business partners or associates drawn up is probably one of the best investments you and your associates will ever make.

Thanks to the estate tax unlimited marital deduction, enacted by Congress in 1982, any assets you leave to your spouse are treated as a deduction from the amount of your estate that is subject to federal estate tax. Thus, if you leave all of your assets to your spouse when you die, it is generally

Unlimited Estate Tax Marital Deduction

possible to avoid all federal estate tax at that time. However, those assets will increase the size of your surviving spouse's estate later, when he or she also dies, thus pyramiding the estate tax on the second spouse's death. Keep in mind that estate tax rates go up as the size of a taxable estate increases.

This exemption from the estate tax also applies to pension benefits you leave to your spouse when you die, unless the accrued value of your pension benefits exceeds $750,000 (less in some instances). If so, your estate will have to pay a special 15% excise tax on the amount over $750,000.[95]

If you are married, and if you and your spouse have a combined net worth of more than $600,000, you may be able to save a much as several hundred thousand dollars of estate tax by having wills drawn up that provide for creation of a "bypass trust" (or "credit shelter trust") for the other spouse when one of you dies. No tax will be saved, or need be paid, on the first death; however, up to $600,000 can be left in trust (still tax-free) at that time for the survivor, instead of passing everything under the unlimited marital deduction to the surviving spouse. This $600,000 amount — plus any investment growth — will be entirely excluded from the estate of the other spouse later, when he or she dies.

Because the federal estate tax often takes close to 50% of the net estate on the death of the second spouse, having set aside $600,000 in a trust — plus any appreciation on that amount — at the first death will quite clearly result in a very large estate tax savings, thus greatly increasing the after-tax amount you can leave to your children. For a relatively small expenditure in legal fees to draw up such wills and trust, this is one of the most easily attainable, and yet most substantial tax benefits you will ever be able to achieve, with almost no downside — except that you won't be around to see your heirs enjoy it.

The Oasis Press/PSI Research publishes a software program, *Small Business Expert*, which includes a tax-planning module that allows you to do quick and easy what-if estate tax scenarios. You can instantly calculate and illustrate how much estate tax you could save by using a bypass trust as suggested above, based on assumptions you input about your net worth and several other key factors. *Small Business Expert* is available from:

The Oasis Press
(800) 228-2275

Since not all state inheritance tax laws permit an unlimited marital deduction, it can create inheritance tax problems in those states if you leave too much property to your spouse. Refer to Section 11.8 for details regarding this state's marital deduction rules under its inheritance tax laws.

Wills or trusts executed before September 13, 1981 may not qualify for the unlimited estate tax marital deduction.[96] If you have such a will or trust, you need to have it updated immediately, unless your state has enacted protective legislation to ensure that such older wills of its residents qualify for the federal unlimited marital deduction.

8.11 Targeted Jobs Tax Credit

Are you aware that if you hire members of certain economically disadvantaged groups, the federal government will pay you a subsidy of up to $2,400 in the form of tax credits per employee? Unfortunately, most employers, particularly small businesses, seem to be unaware of this substantial tax subsidy.

Part of the reason so many employers fail to take advantage of this tax incentive appears to be on account of a Catch-22 in the way the program works. To qualify for the targeted jobs tax credit for hiring a disadvantaged category person, he or she must be certified as such by a designated state employment security agency, and the certification must be received by the employer (or requested in writing) at least one day before the employee begins work.[97]

At the same time, state and federal anti-discrimination laws make it very difficult for you as an employer to ask prospective job applicants if they belong to any of the disadvantaged groups that are eligible for the targeted jobs tax credits, since to do so could be considered a discriminatory hiring practice.

Your best bet is to check first with your local state employment department or division to find out how to take advantage of state and federal job credit programs. The department will either refer you to the proper agency or organization that can assist you, or the department itself will help you find an individual who qualifies under this program and matches your specific job requirements.

Targeted Groups

The targeted group individuals for whom you can claim the jobs tax credit are:

- Vocational rehabilitation referrals — These referrals are for certain disabled individuals who have completed rehabilitation programs. Tax credits aside, disabled individuals often are extremely good and conscientious employees.

- Economically disadvantaged youths — These individuals are between 18 and 22 years of age and are certified as members of economically disadvantaged families.

- Economically disadvantaged Vietnam veterans.

- Supplemental Security Income (SSI) recipients — SSI recipients are people who are 65 or older, or blind, or have a disability and who don't own much or have a lot of income. SSI payments are not just for adults; they can also go to disabled and blind children.

- General assistance recipients — These persons receive state or local welfare payments.

- Economically disadvantaged ex-convicts.

- Youths participating in a cooperative education program — Youths in this category are between 16 and 20 years of age and have not finished high school.
- Eligible work incentive program employees.
- Qualified summer youth employees — These economically disadvantaged youths are 16 or 17 years old and are hired to work between May 1 and September 15. They cannot have been previously employed by you.

On the first $6,000 you pay an eligible target group employee, you will earn tax credits of 40% of the wages. This is limited to $3,000 of wages for qualified summer youth employees during the first 90 days they work for you.

Here is how the federal targeted jobs tax credits apply for eligible and certified new employees:

Category of Employee	Federal Tax Credit	Minimum Work Period
All qualified employees as listed above	40% of wages on first $6,000 of wages or a maximum credit of $2,400 per employee	90 days or 120 hours
Qualified summer youth employees	40% of first 90 days' wages for up to $3,000 of wages or maximum credit of $1,200	14 days or 20 hours

Drawbacks

One drawback with all of these tax credits is that you must reduce the wages you can deduct dollar-for-dollar for credits you claim.[98] That is, if you pay someone $1,000 and claim a $400 targeted jobs tax credit, you can only deduct $600 for wage expense, not the full $1,000. The credit is not allowed for wages paid to strikebreakers.

The targeted jobs credit expired on December 31, 1994, but may, once again, be extended by Congress. The Clinton administration, however, appears to oppose extending the targeted jobs credit.

8.12 Hiring a Spouse as an Employee

If you run an unincorporated business and your spouse works with or for you, there are three ways your spouse can be treated for tax purposes:

- As an employee;
- As a partner in the firm; or
- As an unpaid employee in a family business.

Social Security Tax

Congress, by enacting the Omnibus Budget Reconciliation Act of 1987, ended the exemption from Social Security (FICA) taxes for wages paid to a spouse, parent, or minor child — with the exception of a child under 18 years of age. There are, however, still some advantages to having your spouse be a paid employee of your proprietorship, as described below.

If your spouse works for you without pay and has no other income from an outside job, the most the two of you can put into an individual retirement account (IRA) is $2,250. If you start compensating your spouse, even as little as $2,000 a year, you should each qualify for a $2,000 IRA deduction or a total of $4,000 a year, rather than only $2,250. Note that IRA deductions may be limited if either of you is an active participant in another retirement plan.

Individual Retirement Account for Spouse

You can deduct any medical insurance premiums that you pay for employees, but you can only deduct a limited portion, if any, of your own medical insurance premiums. If your spouse works for you, however, you can put your spouse on the payroll and provide a medical expense reimbursement plan or medical insurance for your spouse and his or her family — which includes you — you can then deduct the payments or premiums in full since your spouse is an employee.[99] See Section 11.8 regarding state tax exemptions and other implications of hiring a spouse as an employee.

Medical Insurance

8.13 How to Save on Unemployment Taxes

The unemployment tax rate you pay as an employer is one of the few taxes where you have some control over the rate you pay. The state maintains a reserve account for each employer, in which it monitors the unemployment taxes you pay in and the unemployment benefits it pays out to your former employees. The more benefits the state pays to your former employees, the higher your individual company's tax rate will be and vice versa.

So it pays for you to have as few former employees as possible who are collecting unemployment benefits, since these are charged to your reserve account.

To succeed in keeping down the unemployment claims charged to your account, you need to challenge any former employees' claims that appear to be unjustified. Often, you will be surprised to learn that an employee you had fired for stealing or who had quit on you has filed for benefits and has lied about his or her reasons for leaving. In general, an ex-employee can't collect unemployment from you if he or she left your employment for one of these reasons:

- Refusal to work;
- Voluntarily quitting;
- Inability to continue work due to illness or injury; or
- Misconduct, such as theft, not showing up for work, or the like.

An employee who leaves your employ for virtually any other reason, such as being fired for incompetence, can generally collect benefits, which will cost you money by raising your unemployment tax rate. Here

Reducing Claims

are some tips on how you can keep down the number of unemployment claims filed against your account.

- When you are hiring, be aware of the cost you may have if you lay off these people in the future. You may hire a number of new employees for an expansion or new project with the view that if things don't work out as planned, you will simply lay them off and cancel the project with no further cost. Count the cost. Remember that if you do have to lay them off, you may pay a much higher unemployment tax rate for several years.

- Document in writing your reasons for firing an employee, if for reasons such as theft, insubordination, absence, or intoxication on the job. This will buttress your argument that the fired employee is not entitled to benefits if he or she should file a claim.

- Be aware that if you change an employee's hours of work and he or she quits as a result, it will be considered involuntary dismissal and the employee will probably be eligible for benefits. So it pays to have a written agreement signed by the employee to work any shift or hours that are required, if needed. Then, if the employee quits, it will not be due to a change in job conditions in the eyes of the law.

- If you decide to fire someone for misconduct, do it on the spot. If you keep them on at your convenience until you find a replacement, it will not usually be considered a discharge for misconduct, and the fired employee will most likely be eligible for benefits.

- If new employees do not work out, consider firing them before they have worked three months. In most states, a person has to work for you at least three months before they can earn unemployment benefits that are chargeable to your reserve account.

In general, it pays to keep a close eye on your employer reserve account and be aware of who is filing benefit claims that will cost you money. Contest any claims that you feel are not legitimate.

8.14 Deductions for Office-in-the-Home Expenses

If you use part of your residence for business purposes, you may be able to deduct part of your office-in-the-home expenses; however, the rules are rather stringent, and the general rule is that office-in-the-home expenses are not deductible for tax purposes, unless you meet a number of very technical requirements.

There are several types of situations under which you may be able to claim deductions for part of your rent or expenses related to ownership of your residence, as well as other occupancy expenses, despite the home-office deduction limitations.

If you use part of your residence exclusively for business purposes and on a regular basis, you may be able to claim office-in-the-home deductions, if you also qualify under one of these tests: [100]

- You use a portion of your home as your principal place of business.
- You use your home as a place to meet clients, customers, or patients.
- Your home office is a separate structure that is not attached to your house or living quarters.

Exclusive-Use Tests

The ability to treat a home office as your "principal place of business" has been sharply limited by the U.S. Supreme Court's 1993 decision in the *Soliman* case. Under this holding, even if your home office is your *only* office, it won't qualify if it is not also your *most important* place of work. In *Soliman*, the Supreme Court disallowed home-office deductions of a physician who had no office other than a room in his home, where he kept his business records and made business-related phone calls. Most of his actual work was done at various hospitals where he performed services as an anesthesiologist.

As a result, the rule for determining whether your home office is your principal place of business now depends on two primary considerations:

- The relative importance of the activities performed at each work location; and
- The amount of time spent at each location.

Two special exceptions are made where part of a home is regularly, but not exclusively, used for business purposes.

Nonexclusive Uses that Qualify

- Storage of inventory — A wholesaler or retailer who uses part of a home to store inventory that is being held for sale; if the dwelling unit is the taxpayer's sole fixed location of the trade or business; or
- Day care facility — Part of the home is used for day care of children, physically and mentally handicapped persons, or individuals age 65 or older.

If you can show that a portion of your residence qualifies as a home office, you have cleared the first hurdle. But note that even if you don't meet any of the above requirements, these rules will not disallow your deductions that are otherwise allowed for tax purposes, such as interest on your home mortgage, real estate taxes, or casualty losses from damage to your residence. Also, business expenses that are not home-related, such as business supplies, cost of goods sold, wages paid to business employees, and other such operating expenses, are not affected by the limitation on home office-related deductions.

If the business use of your home qualifies under one of the above tests, then you may be able to deduct part of the home office expenses that are allocable to the portion of your home that is used in your business, in addition to home mortgage interest, property taxes, and casualty losses.

For example, if 15% of your home is used exclusively and regularly as your principal place of business, you could possibly deduct up to 15% of your occupancy costs, such as gas, electricity, insurance, repairs, and similar expenses, as well as 15% of your rent or depreciation expense on 15% of the tax basis of your house. The IRS and the tax court don't agree on the deductibility of certain other types of expenses, such as lawn care.

Deductions Limited to Income

Note, however, that the amount of qualifying home office expense you can actually deduct for the year is limited to the gross income from your home business, reduced by regular operating expenses (wages, supplies, etc.) and an allocable portion (15% in the above example) of your mortgage interest, property taxes, and casualty loss deductions. If you still have net business income after taking those deductions, then you may deduct the allocable portion of your home office expenses, up to the amount of such net income.

Any portion of your home office expenses that aren't deducted due to the income limit in one year can be carried over to future years until usable, if ever. Thus, it pays to keep track of any such disallowed expenses, in case your home-based business becomes more profitable in the future, and you are then able to deduct the carried-over expenses from earlier years.

Your federal individual return, *Schedule C*, no longer asks you whether expenses for business use of a home are being deducted. Instead, you must determine a tentative profit or loss on *Schedule C*, without taking into account home use expenses. Home office expenses are now computed separately on *Form 8829*. On this form, you must compute the amount of deductible expenses for business use of the home, which (if any) can then be deducted from the net *Schedule C* income. This will make it impossible, or at least illegal, for taxpayers filing *Schedule C* to simply bury the home office expenses in with other business expenses.

Potential Tax Trap

The downside of taking home office deductions is a potential tax bite when you sell your home. For example, if 15% of your home has been used for business and you sell your home for a gain, you will have to pay tax on 15% of the gain, even if you reinvest in a new house, or even if you qualify for the once-in-a-lifetime $125,000 exclusion of gain — for persons over age 55 — when you sell the house. Thus, a few hundred dollars of home office deductions now, could later result in many thousands of dollars of tax on the "business" part of your house, if you sell it for a gain a few years down the road. For more information on the deductibility of home-office expenses, obtain IRS *Publication 587, Business Use of Your Home.*

Endnotes

1. I.R.C. § 1366(e).
2. I.R.C. § 1(g).
3. I.R.C. § 243(a).
4. I.R.C. §§ 301 and 302(d).
5. I.R.C. § 331.
6. I.R.C. § 1(h).
7. I.R.C. § 531.
8. I.R.C. § 542.
9. I.R.C. § 542(a)(1).
10. I.R.C. § 246A.
11. I.R.C. §§ 219 and 404(a).
12. I.R.C. § 501(a).
13. I.R.C. § 408(m).
14. I.R.C. §§ 105–106.
15. I.R.C. § 105(b).
16. I.R.C. § 105.
17. I.R.C. § 106.
18. I.R.C. § 104(a)(3).
19. I.R.C. § 79(a).
20. I.R.C. § 132.
21. I.R.C. § 119.
22. I.R.C. § 127.
23. I.R.C. § 129.
24. I.R.C. § 422.
25. I.R.C. § 423.
26. I.R.C. § 125.
27. I.R.C. § 245(c)(1).
28. I.R.C. §§ 991–997.
29. I.R.C. § 994(a).
30. Treas. Regs. § 1.994-1(e).
31. I.R.C. § 994(a).
32. Treas. Regs. § 1.994.
33. I.R.C. § 995(b)(1)(F)(i) (as amended by The Tax Reform Act of '86).
34. I.R.C. § 995.
35. I.R.C. § 995(f).
36. Rev. Rul. 75-430, 1975-2 C.B. 313; Rev. Rul. 76-284, 1976-2 C.B. 236.
37. Treas. Regs. § 1.991-1(a).
38. I.R.C. § 922(a)(1).
39. I.R.C. § 7872.
40. I.R.C. § 302(c)(2) permits the complete termination of the interest of a family member in a corporation by means of a stock redemption to qualify for capital gains treatment, if certain conditions are met.
41. I.R.C. § 453(g).
42. I.R.C. § 291(a).
43. I.R.C. § 274(h).
44. I.R.C. § 280A.
45. I.R.C. § 274(d).
46. I.R.C. § 274(m)(1).
47. I.R.C. § 274(d).
48. I.R.C. § 274(d), as amended by Pub. L. No. 99-44.
49. I.R.C. § 274(a)(1)(A).
50. I.R.C. § 274(e)(1). (Repealed as of 1-1-87.)
51. I.R.C. § 262; Treas. Regs. § 1.212-1(f).
52. I.R.C. § 280F(b)(2).
53. I.R.C. § 280F(d)(5)(B).
54. Rev. Proc. 93-51, § 5.01, 1993-42 I.R.B. 30.
55. I.R.C. § 441(i).
56. I.R.C. § 195.
57. Treas. Regs. § 1.446-1(c)(2)(i).
58. I.R.C. § 448.
59. I.R.C. § 461(h).
60. I.R.C. § 267(a)(2).
61. Treas. Regs. § 1.451-3.
62. I.R.C. § 460.
63. I.R.C. § 56(a)(3).
64. I.R.C. § 453(b).
65. I.R.C. §§ 453(1)(2)(B) and 453(1)(3).
66. I.R.C. § 453A(b).
67. I.R.C. § 453A(b)(3).
68. I.R.C. § 472.
69. I.R.C. § 474.
70. I.R.C. § 1363(d).
71. I.R.C. § 263A(b)(2)(B).
72. I.R.C. § 531.
73. I.R.C. § 541.
74. I.R.C. § 385.
75. I.R.C. § 531.
76. I.R.C. § 535(c)(2).
77. I.R.C. § 535(a) and (b).
78. I.R.C. § 537(a).
79. I.R.C. § 535(c)(2).
80. I.R.C. § 531.
81. I.R.C. § 537(a)(2).
82. Treas. Regs. §§ 1.537-1(b)(1) and 1.537-2(b)(2).
83. I.R.C. § 537(b)(4).

84. Treas. Regs. § 1.537-2(b)(3).

85. As defined in I.R.C. § 543.

86. I.R.C. § 542.

87. I.R.C. § 543(a)(7).

88. I.R.C. § 543(a)(6).

89. I.R.C. § 541.

90. I.R.C. § 543(d).

91. I.R.C. § 385.

92. I.R.C. § 162(a)(1).

93. I.R.C. § 162(m).

94. I.R.C. § 2056.

95. I.R.C. § 4980A(d).

96. Economic Recovery Tax Act of 1981, Pub. L. No. 97-34, § 403(e)(3).

97. I.R.C. § 51.

98. I.R.C. § 280C(a).

99. Rev. Rul. 71-588, 1971-2 C.B. 91.

100. I.R.C. § 280A(c)(1).

Chapter 9

Miscellaneous Business Pointers

Money is not the root of all evil. The lack of money is the root of all evil.

— Reverend Ike

9.1 General Considerations

This chapter contains helpful information on a variety of topics of interest to many small businesses, ranging from basic information on accounting, auditing, cash flow management, and sources of financing, to useful tax and business tips and a comprehensive discussion of the very wide range of environmental laws that may affect your business. Also covered are other matters you may have to consider, such as consumer credit laws, the pros and cons of using independent contractors, key areas of pending legislation, and developing legal and economic trends that may have an impact on you in the near future.

9.2 Accounting — Some Basics

Maintaining good accounting records is a must for any small business. Without accurate and up-to-date records, you will be operating your business without vitally important information. Meaningful financial statements can only be prepared if the underlying records of transactions are accurate and current.

Accounting Systems

It may help to think of your accounting system as being like an airplane's radar system. If you are not getting current and correct feedback from either system, you will not have enough time to react to prevent a potential crash.

Single-Entry Method

While most schools and colleges teach only the double-entry method of bookkeeping, which provides a series of checks and balances in recording income and expenditures, some small business owners use a single-entry method of accounting.

If you are not knowledgeable about double-entry bookkeeping and handle most of the funds directly yourself, you may find that a single-entry system is acceptable for your needs and much simpler to use. The single-entry method is only slightly more involved than keeping a checkbook record of cash income and disbursements and usually consists of three basic records:

- A daily cash receipts summary — This summary may come from a cash register tape or sales slips. It will not only give you a total of your daily cash receipts, but it will break down your sales by product, by salesperson, or by store, depending on how much detail you need.
- A monthly cash receipts summary — This is simply a monthly summary of the daily cash receipts.
- A monthly cash disbursements report — This is a report on expenses and other payments, such as debt repayments, purchases of capital assets, or distributions of profits.

A number of simplified write-it-once systems for all different kinds of businesses are available at office supply stores.

Double-Entry Method

While a single-entry system is easy to use, it is not a complete accounting system because it focuses mainly on profit and loss and does not provide a balance sheet. For all but the very smallest of businesses, a single-entry accounting system is likely to be inadequate. Even if your business is very small, but expects to grow, it is usually advisable to start out with a full set of books, using the double-entry method.

You can avoid many future problems if you get a CPA to help you set up the accounting system for your business. He or she will tailor a chart of accounts to your specific needs and build in internal controls to record all transactions and to reduce the possibilities of employee theft or embezzlement that might go undetected with a poorly designed system.

If you use a personal computer in your business, there are any number of general ledger accounting software packages you can buy if your accounting needs are fairly straightforward and if you have a reasonable understanding of how double-entry accounting works. For a very small business, there are adequate software packages available for under $100.

Accounting Firm Services

If you are going to use an outside accounting firm to prepare financial statements, they can provide three different levels of service — compilations, reviews, and audits.

Compilations

Most financial statements prepared for small businesses are compilations because they are far less expensive than an audit or review. In a compilation, the outside accountant has no obligation to do any investigation unless something looks suspicious or misleading. Generally, all an accountant is required to do in preparing compilation statements is to take the financial data you give him or her and present it in a manner that conforms with generally accepted accounting principles (GAAP).

In a compilation, the accountant expresses no opinion on the accuracy of the information presented. The accountant is simply taking what you gave him or her and putting it in a proper financial statement format. It is important for you to remember that regardless of what type of assurance your accountant expresses, you are ultimately the one responsible for ensuring your financial statements are prepared accurately.

Reviews

A review involves some limited analysis or testing of the financial records, but the certified public accountant (CPA) expresses only a very limited opinion as to the accuracy of the information in the financial statements. A review is somewhat less expensive than an audit, but more expensive than a compilation. Most small businesses hire a CPA firm to do a review only if their bankers or other lenders or financial backers insist on a review rather than a compilation.

Audits

An audit is invariably the most involved and most expensive level of service in connection with financial statements. An accounting firm that audits financial statements must not only verify that your financial statements are presented fairly and in accordance with GAAP, but it also checks and verifies some or all of the accounts to satisfy itself that they are real.

To verify accounts, an accounting firm can request confirmations of bank accounts or receivable and payable account balances from banks, customers, and vendors to uncover possible errors or fraud in recordkeeping. Because audits are relatively expensive, many small businesses elect to have review or compilation statements done; however, lenders or bonding companies often insist that you have a certified audit.

Depreciation

The Tax Reform Act of 1986 effectively repealed the highly favorable accelerated cost recovery system (ACRS) tax depreciation system that was in force from 1981 until the end of 1986. In January 1987, taxpayers learned to live with another whole new complex system of depreciation. Unfortunately, it is still necessary to know the former ACRS rules for assets acquired during the 1981–86 period, as well as the old depreciation rules for items acquired before 1981, to compute current depreciation on those assets.

The Modified ACRS System

The modified ACRS (MACRS) law from 1986 does not provide depreciation tables, unlike the previous ACRS system. Instead, all assets (with a few special exceptions) placed in service after 1986 are assigned to 3-, 5-, 7-, 10-, 15-, or 20-year recovery period categories, except for real estate, which must be depreciated over 39 years — 27.5 years for residential rental property.[1]

Under the MACRS system, most personal property is depreciated under the 200% declining balance method over a specified number of years — called a recovery period. The only exceptions are for 15- or 20-year property, for which the 150% declining balance method is used. Real estate may only be depreciated under the straight-line method.

Assets other than real estate are mostly assigned to the various recovery periods that vary from industry to industry and are far too voluminous and technical to reproduce in a book of this nature. MACRS, however, specifically assigns some types of assets to recovery classes. For example, autos and light trucks are five-year property. The MACRS provisions have also reduced the maximum annual depreciation deductions on luxury automobiles as discussed in Section 8.6.

One small ray of sunshine in the MACRS tax depreciation nightmare is a liberalization of the former $10,000 first-year expending election for tangible personal property. You may elect to expense up to $17,500 in cost of furniture and equipment in the year such assets are placed in service.[2] For example, if the only depreciable items you buy in 1994 are $15,000 of office equipment, you may be able to deduct the full $15,000 in 1994. Note, however, that this special deduction is not allowed to the extent that it would create a loss for your trade(s) or business(es) for the year. Also, the deduction is phased out if you acquire more than $200,000 of eligible property during the tax year.

Internal Accounting Controls

Poor internal accounting controls and recordkeeping procedures are a weakness for many small business owners. Lax procedures are frequently to blame when a secretary or bookkeeper departs for Brazil with thousands of dollars of stolen or embezzled funds belonging to his or her employer. Ideally, you would consult a good accountant to set up and review your internal financial controls; however, that will cost you a good deal of money, so before you do so, you may want to do your own review of your internal controls, utilizing the checklist located at the end of this chapter.

9.3 Cash-Flow Management

Cash flow is the lifeblood of any business organization; yet, small business operators are often so concerned with other matters, they don't pay attention to managing their cash resources properly. Good cash management can make a significant contribution to the competitiveness and profitability of your business. Poor cash management is one of the main causes of business failures, particularly among smaller firms, since a cash shortage due to poor planning can set off a chain reaction of disastrous consequences, even in a profitable business.

Cash-flow management has two aspects: 1) projecting future cash flow, and 2) controlling and maximizing the cash available from operations at all times.

Perhaps the most important part of cash-flow management is accurately projecting your business' near- and long-term cash needs and making your business decisions reflect those needs. Often, to project what your sales will be in coming months, it will be necessary to rely on what has happened in the past — what percentage will be credit sales and when your receivables are likely to be collected.

Projecting Cash Flow

Similarly, you have to estimate and project what you will have to pay out in the way of payroll, rent, taxes, servicing debts, purchasing inventory, and paying off existing payables, plus extraordinary outlays you can anticipate.

The purpose of making these detailed projections of expected cash inflows and outflows is to point out any future cash shortages or deficits, so you can take steps in advance to prevent such occurrences. For example, if your projections indicated you were going to experience a severe cash crunch in about three months, you might take any of a number of steps to avert it, such as:

- Seeking to raise new capital;
- Borrowing money;
- Liquidating some of your inventory by cutting prices; or
- Cutting back on planned expenditures.

If you have a computer, microcomputer models are available to assist you in preparing projections of cash flows. If you don't own a computer, your accountant may have such models available to assist you.

If you are able to increase available cash by speeding up collections, delaying payments, or by other means, you can use the extra cash to reduce your borrowings — thus saving interest expenses — or you can invest the surplus cash to earn interest. Either way, improving your cash flow should increase your net earnings and should also help you avert cash shortages.

Controlling and Maximizing Cash Flow

Here are some basic ways to improve your business' cash flow.

- Bill your customers promptly. The later they receive the bill, the later you will usually collect for a particular sale.
- If you know that certain large customers must receive bills by certain days of the month so you can get paid in that month, try to bill them before those deadlines.
- Deposit your cash receipts daily, if possible.
- Keep close tabs on credit customers. Send them past due notices as soon as payments become overdue.

- If you can do so without hurting business, add late charges to overdue accounts.

- Never pay bills until just before they become due, unless there is a worthwhile discount for quick payment.

- Try to keep inventories as lean as possible. Even if you occasionally lose a small sale because you are temporarily out of an item, you should be far ahead of the game by substantially reducing the amount of cash you have tied up in inventory.

- Look for items in your inventory that are moving slowly or not at all. Consider slashing the price on those articles to convert them to cash and also to reduce the cost of storing them or having them take up valuable shelf space.

- Consider leasing equipment items instead of buying.

- Do not pay more on your estimated income taxes than you have to. You may qualify — without incurring interest charges or late payment penalties — under one or more exceptions that will allow you to delay paying much of your tax for the year until the tax return is due. If you realize that you have already overpaid your corporate estimated tax for the year, there is a procedure for obtaining a refund prior to the time when you can file a return.[3]

- If your business has a net operating loss for tax purposes that can be carried back to prior years, a procedure exists for filing a claim for a quick refund of the prior years' taxes. File it as early as you can because the IRS no longer pays interest on these refunds.

- Instead of keeping all your business cash in a local bank account, consider putting a significant portion of your cash in an out-of-town money market-type fund that pays interest and allows you to write checks against the account. Since you continue to earn interest on funds on deposit until the checks clear, consider using a fund in a distant part of the country, since it will take longer for your checks to clear when you make payments to local firms.

9.4 Protecting Your Assets

Starting a new business is almost always a risky proposition, and if the business fails, you may be forced into bankruptcy and could lose everything except what the bankruptcy laws allow you to keep. This is one reason why many small businesses incorporate at the outset, since a corporation will generally limit your liability to business creditors to the amount you invest in the corporation, plus any loans to the corporation you guarantee.

Accordingly, if you incorporate, be cautious about committing too much of your personal assets to the business. For example, instead of putting a building or piece of land you own into the corporation, it may be better —

and may save income and property taxes — for you to keep the property and lease it to the corporation. Even if you incorporate, the leases or bank loans you find it necessary to guarantee on behalf of the corporation could still wipe out your personal assets if the business folds. Thus, it often makes sense to have your corporation set up a tax-qualified pension or profit-sharing plan and to have it contribute as much as possible to the plan on your behalf. Not only does this provide substantial tax savings and deferral, but the law in most states will in many cases protect your account under such a plan from your creditors or the corporation's creditors.

So, if you can build up a significant retirement fund in your corporation's pension plan, you have at least some degree of assurance that the failure of the business or a disastrous lawsuit will not touch that nest egg. In a divorce, however, your spouse may be able to claim his or her share of the pension plan account.

9.5 Protecting Trade Names and Trademarks

If you intend to use some type of distinctive trade name for your business or trademark for your product or in advertising your services, consider taking steps to protect the use of the name or mark by registering it under state or federal law, or both. When considering your trade name or trademark, it may be necessary to perform a search, which can be expensive, to determine whether someone else has already registered the same or a very similar name or symbol. You do not want to open yourself up to a lawsuit for infringement. Since not every trade name can be registered, you will need to consult a trademark attorney if you are interested in protecting a particular name used by your business.

Advantages to Trade Name or Trademark Registration

Federal registration of a name confers a number of significant benefits to registering your trade name or trademark, including:

- Nationwide notice to others of your exclusive right to use the name or mark.
- Prima facie evidence of the validity of the registration and your exclusive right to use the mark throughout the country.
- With certain exceptions, registration gives you an unquestionable right to use the name or mark.
- If you prove in court that someone violated your rights under the Trademark Act of 1946,[4] you will be entitled to recover their profits and damages from its use.
- The right to sue in federal court for trademark infringement regardless of the amount at stake and whether or not there is diversity of citizenship — that is, regardless of whether you and the defendant operate in the same or different states.

- The right to have customs officials halt importation of counterfeit goods using your trademark.

Federal registration is permitted only if you will use the trade name or trademark in more than one state.

9.6 Section 1244 Stock

If you invest directly in a small corporation by transferring money or property (other than securities) to the corporation in exchange for its common stock — or preferred stock, if issued after July 18, 1984 — the stock will usually qualify as Section 1244 stock.[5] If it does, and the stock later becomes worthless or you sell it at a loss, Section 1244 of the Internal Revenue Code permits you to deduct up to $50,000 of your loss — $100,000 for a couple filing a joint return — as an ordinary deduction instead of as a capital loss for that year. This can be very important, since you can fully deduct an ordinary loss from your taxable income, while capital losses can only be used to offset capital gains, if you have any, or $3,000 of ordinary income per year until your capital losses are used up.[6] The $50,000/$100,000 limit on the amount of loss that can qualify for ordinary loss treatment is an annual limitation.

Any stock issued by a small business corporation will generally qualify as Section 1244 stock unless the corporation obtained half or more of its gross receipts from passive kinds of income, such as interest, dividends, and the like, in the five years before your loss is incurred.[7] A corporation qualifies as a small business corporation if the total invested in its stock is one million dollars or less.[8]

If the stock issued by your corporation meets the requirements of Section 1244, it will automatically qualify for ordinary loss treatment, up to the first one million dollars of stock issued. You should be aware, however, that capital contributions you make, where no stock is received by you for such money, will not qualify for ordinary loss treatment.[9]

See Section 11.9 as to whether state law also provides favorable tax treatment for losses on stock in a small business corporation.

9.7 U.S. Small Business Administration and Other Government Loans

If you need to borrow money for your business and cannot obtain regular bank financing, don't overlook the possibility of obtaining a loan through the U.S. Small Business Administration (SBA). Many small business owners are under the impression that it is virtually impossible to obtain an SBA loan unless a member of a minority group; this is not the case. Although the SBA does make special efforts to provide financing for minority-owned businesses, only a relatively small percentage of SBA loans are made to minority firms. Furthermore, a very high percentage of applications for SBA loans are approved when applications are properly submitted, often within three to six weeks.

SBA Loan Programs

The SBA, an agency of the U.S. government, guarantees intermediate and long-term loans to small firms, and to a limited extent, also makes direct loans to some small businesses. The SBA is not allowed to grant such financial assistance unless the borrower is unable to obtain private-sector financing on reasonable terms. The SBA does not compete with banks or other lenders; instead, it works with private lenders to assure availability of capital to potentially profitable small firms. Contrary to what you may have heard on late-night television infomercials, the SBA does *not* have a grant program for starting a small business.

For your business to qualify for SBA financial assistance, it must come within the current definition of a small business. In general, these are the types of small businesses eligible for SBA financing:

- Manufacturers with a maximum of 500 to 1,500 employees, depending upon the industry in which the applicant is engaged;
- Retailers with less than $3.5 million in annual sales — up to $13.5 million for some types of retailers;
- Wholesaling firms with 100 or fewer employees;
- General construction firms, whose annual sales have averaged less than $9.5 million for the last three fiscal years; lower limits apply to various special trade construction firms;
- Service firms with annual receipts not in excess of $3.5 to $14.5 million, depending on the industry; and
- Other definitions apply for businesses engaged in activities, such as agriculture and transportation.

Private lenders that are eligible to make SBA-guaranteed loans or participate in SBA financing packages include banks, savings and loans, and certain other lenders. The SBA has several types of loan programs for small businesses, the largest of which is the 7(a) Loan Program.

Guaranteed Loans

Most SBA financing actually consists of loans by banks or other lenders that are guaranteed by the SBA. This enables the small business to obtain such loans at reasonable interest rates because the bank's risk is largely eliminated. SBA-guaranteed loans are tied to the bank prime rate, as published in *The Wall Street Journal*, at a rate of 2.25% above prime rate for loans of less than seven years, or 2.75% above prime for loans of seven or more years. The SBA charges lenders a 2.0% guarantee fee on the portion of a loan that is guaranteed. Lenders are allowed to charge this fee to the borrower.

The SBA has recently adopted an alternate standard for the 7(a) Loan Program, under which a prospective borrower that does not qualify as a small business under the various standards listed above, may now qualify as such if its net worth is no more than six million dollars and if it had annual after-tax net income of two million dollars or less in each of the two preceding years.

As the borrower, you put up a reasonable amount of equity or collateral. These loans are usually secured by fixed assets, real estate, and inventory and are limited in term to 7 years for working capital loans or 10 years for purchasing fixed assets. Construction loans can be for as long as 25 years.

Under this program, the bank or other private lender deals with the SBA, and you deal with the bank, not the SBA. You will, however, need to do the following in applying for such a loan or any other SBA financing:

- Define the amount you need to borrow and the purposes for which the funds will be used.
- Describe the collateral you will offer as security.
- Determine from a bank that a conventional loan is not available.
- Prepare current financial statements, preferably with your accountant's assistance. These would include, at a minimum, a relatively current balance sheet and an income statement for the previous full year and for the current year up to the date of the balance sheet.
- Prepare personal financial statements of the owners, partners, or stockholders owning more than 20% of the stock of the company.

Direct Loans

If you are unable to obtain sufficient conventional financing or SBA-guaranteed loan funds, it may be possible, in rare instances, to obtain a direct loan from the SBA. When made, these direct loans are usually offered on a participation basis with a bank or other lender, where the bank oversees the loan payments and loan servicing on behalf of itself and the SBA. In recent years, the SBA has largely ceased making direct loans because it has had only minimal funds available, from time to time. Even when it does occasionally have funds to lend, there are always far more qualified applicants than funds to lend to them. Consequently, you will have very little chance of obtaining such a direct loan.

In 1992, however, the SBA began, as part of its direct loan program, to make "microloans" at slightly below-market interest rates to veterans, business owners with disabilities, and persons desiring to start companies in economically depressed areas. These loans, ranging from as little as $100 to a maximum of only $25,000, are intended to help very small businesses, particularly those run by minorities, women, and low-income people, who generally have a difficult time raising capital. As such, microloans are designed to empower people, such as single mothers, disabled individuals, and public housing tenants, to become self-employed and self-supporting. The SBA's microloans are modeled after microloan programs that have been operated for a number of years by nonprofit agencies in the United States and in a number of Third World countries, generally with great success. For the smallest microloans — often only a few hundred dollars — no collateral is generally required, only a good character reference or a good reputation in the community.

The SBA microloan program is generally run in cooperation with local nonprofit organizations. To find an SBA microlender, contact an SBA district office or:

SBA Answer Desk
(800) 827-5722

New legislation frequently adds to and modifies the number and scope of SBA loan programs. Other such programs include:

Other SBA Programs

- Seasonal lines of credit;
- Economic opportunity loans for entrepreneurs who are physically handicapped or members of a minority group;
- Short-term contract loan guarantees;
- Energy loans to small firms to install, sell, service, develop, or manufacture solar energy or energy-saving devices; and
- Disaster recovery loans to firms harmed by natural disasters.

Since the nature, scope, and availability of funds under these numerous programs are constantly changing, consult your bank or local SBA offices if you think your firm may qualify under one of these special financial assistance programs.

The U.S. Department of Housing and Urban Development (HUD) makes Urban Development Action Grants (UDAG) to cities in economically distressed areas. The cities are then able to use these UDAG funds to make second-mortgage loans to private developers who are able to leverage these loans by borrowing at least five times such amounts — three times in small towns — from private sources. The purpose of such loans is to encourage new investment and development in depressed areas.

U.S. Department of Housing and Urban Development

The Economic Development Administration (EDA) of the U.S. Department of Commerce makes direct loans and offers loan guarantees to businesses in areas with low family incomes or areas suffering from high unemployment. The purpose of these loans is to promote creation or retention of jobs for the residents living in these areas.

U.S. Department of Commerce

To qualify for this financing, your business must be located in an EDA redevelopment area and you need to demonstrate that the venture will directly benefit local residents and will not create local over-capacity for the industry in question. Application for EDA loan assistance is a long and complex process, taking much longer for processing than typical SBA loans.

Farmers Home Administration

The Farmers Home Administration (FmHA) can perhaps be thought of as an SBA for rural areas. It offers insured and guaranteed loans to develop business and industry in nonurban areas with populations of under 50,000. Like the SBA program, FmHA loan guarantees are for up to 90% of the total amount of the loan and are made for up to 30 years for financing real estate acquisition, 15 years for machinery and equipment, and 7 years for working capital. FmHA loan guarantees are not available for agricultural production.

Unlike SBA loan guarantees, there is no dollar limit on FmHA loan guarantees, nor does the FmHA make direct loans. Applicants for FmHA loan guarantees must not only have adequate collateral and good business histories, they must also demonstrate that the project will have a favorable economic impact and will create new jobs in the area — not merely shifting business activity and jobs from one area to another. Preference is given:

- To businesses who are expanding rather than transferring into an area;
- To projects in open country areas or towns with populations of under 25,000; and
- To business owners who are military veterans.

Other Federal Loan Programs

Other major federal loan programs are provided through the Federal Land Bank Association, Production Credit Association, and the Federal Intermediate Credit Bank. These organizations offer loans to businesses that provide services to farmers. These loans can be for purchasing land and equipment and for obtaining start-up working capital.

SBICs and MESBICs

In addition to direct loans and guarantees from government agencies, don't overlook possible loans or equity financing from Small Business Investment Companies (SBICs) and Minority Enterprise Small Business Investment Companies (MESBICs). Both are licensed and regulated by the SBA to provide equity capital, long-term loans, and management assistance to small businesses.

SBIC and MESBIC loans are usually subordinated to loans from other creditors and are typically made for five- to seven-year terms. Both types of investment companies are privately owned and thus tend to favor loans to established companies with significant net worth rather than new business start ups.

You may have to give up a large part of the equity in your business if you obtain SBIC financing. An SBIC is not permitted to control a company (50% or greater ownership) it lends to, but typically an SBIC lender will insist on debt that is convertible into common stock, warrants, and options, which may give it up to 49% ownership in your company. An SBIC will also want seats on your board of directors, will impose controls and restrictions on the way your business operates, and may insist upon salary limits for the principal owners. SBIC financing does not come without a price.

MESBICs serve only those small firms that are owned by members of economically or socially disadvantaged minority groups.

Business Development Corporations are Local Development Companies (LDCs) and Certified Development Companies (CDCs) organized by local residents to promote economic development in their particular communities. These entities do not make working capital loans or loans to purchase free-standing equipment.

Business Development Corporations

Instead, LDCs or CDCs will arrange for SBA-guaranteed bank loans and sale of SBA-guaranteed debentures for up to 90% financing for 25 years for land acquisition, building construction, or renovation and purchase of fixed assets, such as machinery and equipment. For information on what state business loan programs may be available in this state, refer to Section 11.9.

9.8 Mail Order Sales

If your business involves selling goods by mail order, become familiar with Rule 435.1, a regulation issued by the Federal Trade Commission (FTC).[10] This federal regulation requires any business soliciting mail order sales to be prepared to ship the merchandise within 30 days after an order is received, unless it has clearly stated in its solicitation that orders will not be shipped for a longer period. Otherwise, the solicitation will be considered as an unfair and deceptive trade practice. In addition, if you receive an order and for some reason you cannot ship it within 30 days, or the period stated in your solicitation, you must:

- Immediately notify the customer and offer to either cancel the order and receive a refund or consent to the delay in shipment.
- Indicate when you will be able to ship or that you do not know when you will be able to ship the order.
- Provide other required information to the customer, which will vary in content depending upon when you expect to be able to ship.

Since March 1, 1994, the coverage of Rule 435.1 has been extended to all orders you receive, including those received by modem, fax, or telephone, in addition to those received by mail.

If you are going into the mail order business and want a single source of information on state and federal mail order laws, obtain the *Mail Order Legal Guide,* by Erwin J. Keup, from your book source or:

The Oasis Press
(800) 228-2275

Rule 435.1 is fairly complex and difficult to understand, but you need to understand and be familiar with it if you sell goods by mail order. For a free guide on this FTC rule, contact the FTC at the number listed below and request *A Business Guide to the Federal Trade Commission's Mail Order Rule.*

Federal Trade Commission
(202) 326-2222

State Sales and Use Taxes

If you sell across state lines to customers in states where you have no offices, employees, or other presence, the sale is usually not subject to sales tax in either state, since it is an interstate sale; however, technically, such sales are subject to use tax in the customer's state. A use tax is sort of a shadow of the sales tax and, in most states, applies where the sales tax doesn't.

The U.S. Supreme Court and other courts generally have not supported attempts of the various states to force out-of-state retailers to collect use tax on mail order or other sales made to residents of the taxing state, so that most mail order firms tend to treat such interstate sales as being tax-free, or tell the customers that it is up to them to report the purchase and pay the use tax, which they rarely do.

Unfortunately, in the last few years, many states have enacted new and broader sales and use tax laws. Many of these laws require out-of-state retailers, who advertise in the local media or send substantial amounts of direct mail/catalog solicitations into the state, to register as retailers subject to sales or use tax in the state and to treat such direct sales as taxable. The U.S. Supreme Court has finally ruled that these aggressive new sales tax laws are unconstitutional in the 1992 case of *Quill Corporation v. North Dakota.* Thus, it appears most of the broad new mail order sales and use tax laws — which have been adopted in some 34 states and are targeted to hit out-of-state mail order firms — may be invalid. While this is good news for mail order retailers, the bad news is the court also indicated in its decision that Congress could, if it chose to do so, constitutionally enact legislation that would permit the states to require use tax collection on mail order and similar sales by out-of-state retailers.

In fact, just such a bill has already been introduced in the U.S. Senate by Senator Dale Bumpers (D) of Arkansas, inaptly named the "Tax Fairness for Main Street Business Act of 1994." This bill, if enacted, would grant states the right to enact laws requiring out-of-state sellers of tangible personal property to collect and remit state and local sales-use taxes if the following requirements were met:

- The seller is subject to the personal jurisdiction of the taxing state;
- The tangible personal property has a final destination in the state in question;
- The seller's gross receipts from sales of such property in the twelve months ending September 30 of the calendar year before the year of the sale exceeded $100,000 in the taxing state or $3 million in the United States as a whole; and

- The taxing state collects and administers all of the local sales-use taxes imposed on behalf of its local jurisdictions, such as cities and counties.

Where a state has nonuniform local sales tax rates, the proposed legislation would give the seller the choice of either collecting tax at the appropriate rate in each local jurisdiction, or collecting tax at a flat statewide rate, based on an average rate determined by the state, rounded to the nearest 0.25%. Each state passing such a law would have to maintain a toll-free help line, which small mail order sellers could call at any time to determine the appropriate sales tax rate for sales to residents of that state.

Thus, if this or another federal law authorizing such use tax collections is enacted, it seems likely it will provide some exemption for smaller retailers and a simplified, statewide tax rate and payment method for sellers who have only minimal sales in each of a number of states. Otherwise, most small mail order sellers would instantly be forced out of business without such an exemption, due to the impossible complexity and enormous cost of filing sales or use tax returns for every state and local taxing district where a sale is made.

9.9 Environmental Laws Affecting Your Business

As the world becomes more crowded and as the damaging effects of two centuries of unrestrained industrial development becomes more apparent on the environment, political attempts to remedy these problems, particularly the problems of pollution and toxic emissions, have resulted in a flood of legislation, regulations, and litigation involving environmental matters. While this is probably all to the good in the larger sense, some of the immediate effects of these new environmental restrictions have been to create another whole layer of complex and often conflicting government regulations on business, plus a virtual minefield of legal exposure for companies of all sizes.

For small businesses — most of which do not have in-house legal staffs and can hardly afford the large legal fees needed for professional guidance through this maze of regulations — the effect of the growing body of environmental laws is especially harsh. Small businesses are also disproportionately affected by the heavy costs of complying with various mandated emissions requirements, which often require large capital expenditures for sophisticated new pollution control equipment.

While this section cannot do much more than scratch the surface of the environmental law exposure and increased operational complexities most businesses are going to face, the discussion below explains some of the main problem areas you need to be at least passingly familiar with. This section also provides a capsule description of the major areas of federal environmental law that may currently apply to your business or which may apply at some time in the future.

Environmental Clean-up Laws

Perhaps the most pervasive of the environmental laws, with the most devastating potential consequences for the unwary, are the environmental clean-up laws, and the legal liability these laws attach to real estate that has been contaminated by hazardous substances. The main laws that apply in this area are the Comprehensive Environmental Response, Compensation and Liability Act[11] (CERCLA or the Superfund law) and the Resource Conservation and Recovery Act (RCRA).[12]

CERCLA and RCRA apply to virtually every real estate transaction. While RCRA applies primarily to currently generated hazardous waste, including limits on creation of waste and requirements for disposing of it, CERCLA is more focused on cleaning up hazardous substances that have been spilled or dumped in the past.

CERCLA Liability

CERCLA deals with all kinds of pollution: air, surface water, groundwater, and soil. It covers virtually every type of hazardous substances as defined under CERCLA, the Clean Water Act, the Clean Air Act, or the Toxic Substances Control Act. There are, however, major exceptions for petroleum and certain petroleum derivatives. The main thrust of CERCLA is to impose liability on private owners of property to clean up hazardous wastes they have created. CERCLA would also apply to owners of the inherited property, if the property in question was already contaminated when it was acquired.

In short, even if you were not responsible for creating a contamination problem, if you acquire real estate that is already contaminated — and it later becomes apparent there has been a spill or dumping that requires an environmental cleanup, possibly at astronomical cost — you are liable for the costs of the cleanup, if you are the current owner. You can't simply walk away from the property and let the government take it in lieu of paying the clean-up costs.

Once the owner, you are the responsible party and may be held liable for costs that exceed the value of the property many times over. You may even become liable somewhere down the road if you sell a business — an existing corporation, for instance — that has formerly owned contaminated property. The government could eventually institute environmental proceedings against the current property owner, who then sues all the prior legal owners of the property, including you, for indemnity or reimbursement.

Of course, you may be able to sue the prior owner or anyone in the chain of prior owners for indemnification, if they are still in existence and can be found. However, since that is a pretty slim thread upon which to hang your financial survival, you need to take precautions up front, before acquiring any real property, to protect yourself from possible environmental liability for cleanup under CERCLA.

The following are some things you can and should do to reduce your risk in any real estate or existing business acquisition:

- Exercise considerable diligence concerning the current condition and past uses of any real estate involved in a transaction. Also, if buying an existing corporation, you need to find out what properties it owned in the past and be concerned whether any such properties may have been contaminated by hazardous substances.

- Be particularly wary of any sites that have been used as gas stations, landfill areas, locations of dry cleaners, chemical or other industrial production processes, battery production, recycling, or metal plating. Be extremely cautious if the site contains underground storage tanks.

- Consider retaining an environmental audit firm to do detailed site inspections and evaluations to determine if there may be a contamination problem.

- In a business or real estate purchase agreement, require written representations and warranties about the site from the seller and include provisions under which he or she will indemnify you if there is a problem. Be mindful of the seller's financial viability, in case you should be forced to seek indemnity from him or her. A promise isn't worth the paper it is written on, if the seller doesn't have the wherewithal to make good on it.

Even though under the Superfund law there is an innocent purchaser defense, you must be able to demonstrate that you made appropriate inquiry before acquiring the property to determine any pre-existing contamination problem. There is little guidance in the law at this point as to what constitutes an appropriate inquiry, so perhaps you should not expect to escape liability under that rule. The best defense is to avoid purchasing property that is contaminated by taking the steps outlined above. Even if such steps fail to discover a lurking environmental problem, at least you will have a much stronger argument to make under the innocent purchaser defense if you have done a due-diligence survey and had an environmental audit performed by a reputable firm.

RCRA Requirements

RCRA contains a comprehensive set of rules for managing hazardous wastes, including petroleum-based substances, and regulating those who generate hazardous wastes, transport them, and store, treat, or dispose of them. Penalties for violations include fines of up to $25,000 a day, plus imprisonment.

One important focus of RCRA is on underground storage tanks (USTs), many of which are known to be leaking gasoline or other contaminants into the surrounding soil and groundwater. Under RCRA, much of the regulation of USTs is left to state governments. Thus, under federal regulations, the owner of a UST must notify the state of the tank's existence, including tanks that were taken out of service after January 1, 1974.[13]

New USTs must satisfy federal performance standards, which generally require that they be constructed of fiberglass-reinforced plastic or steel that is cathodically protected from corrosion.[14] Furthermore, all existing USTs must be upgraded to federal standards by December 22, 1998,[15] which will result in some major expenditures for many small businesses, such as service stations.

Clean Water Act

Under the Clean Water Act, the federal Environmental Protection Agency (EPA) and individual states are the watchdogs of water pollution standards.[16] It also allows private citizens to sue to enforce the act. Penalties for violations can be as high as $50,000 a day, and even negligent, but unintentional violations can result in imprisonment. For certain existing facilities, this law provides for a system of EPA permits for discharging certain amounts of water pollutants.

Wetlands Development

Portions of the Clean Water Act require that all proposed development activities, which involve the dredging or filling of wetlands, obtain permits from the U.S. Army Corps of Engineers.[17] Thus, before you acquire real property that you plan to develop in any way, you need to do a careful survey to determine if the property lies within an area that is considered to be a wetland. Otherwise, you may end up with a piece of property which is undevelopable and which can hardly be sold at all, even for a huge loss.

This has been a trap for more than one unwitting buyer of land in wetlands districts, since wetlands include much more than swamps and marshes. Many dry-looking parcels may also fall within the regulatory definition. Furthermore, be aware that many states have adopted wetlands restrictions, which may require you to also obtain state development permits.

Clean Air Act

The Clean Air Act of 1970, which was substantially amended and strengthened by the Clean Air Act of 1991, among other things, restricts the ability of stationary sources of air pollutants to emit various pollutants into the atmosphere at new or modified facilities.[18] States are allowed to implement their own rules for controlling air pollution levels. The Clean Air Act of 1991 has greatly expanded the impact on small businesses. As this act's amendments go into effect, they will require a diverse number of air pollution controls. Some will include:

- Gasoline stations will need vapor-recovery devices on gasoline pumps.
- Furniture makers may need incinerators to burn off hydrocarbons released from spray-paint booths.
- Restaurants in smoggy areas will have to install containment units that collect hydrocarbon emissions from charcoal grills.
- Many bakeries will have to install oxidation devices or catalytic converters to neutralize the gases produced by fermenting yeast when dough is baked.
- Auto-body paint and repair shops will have to install extremely expensive equipment to catch hydrocarbon emissions from spray painting.
- Print shops will have to neutralize or eliminate use of chemicals that contribute to ozone formation.

As the above examples indicate, the requirements under the Clean Air Act of 1991 are very pervasive and will affect many nonindustrial types of businesses who would never have considered themselves to be polluters in the past. Companies that are sources of air pollutant emissions will have to obtain state-issued construction and operating permits under EPA rules. Small businesses will have to apply for permits at least every five years and file reports of their compliance with the law every six months, if they produce more than 100 tons per year of any ozone-forming pollutant. Ozone-forming pollutants are the main targets of the act.

According to some experts, once these rules go into effect, a small business' main cost of complying with the clean air regulations is likely to be all the required paperwork. Penalties for violations are also very severe, with civil penalties as high as $25,000 a day for each violation, plus felony imprisonment and huge fines for willful or negligent releases of hazardous air pollutants. In addition, the EPA has set emissions fees of $25 a ton for every ton of regulated pollutants that a firm emits, up to $4,000 per year.

Toxic Substances Control Act

If your business is one that engages in the manufacturing, processing, or distribution of chemical substances, you may be required under the federal Toxic Substances Control Act (TSCA) to report certain information to the EPA regarding the chemical substances and mixtures you use.[19] The TSCA requires manufacturers to give a 90-day notification before producing a new chemical substance and, in some cases, for older chemicals. The EPA may require safety testing before approval of such a chemical. The TSCA also has extensive recordkeeping rules regarding use and disposal of toxic chemicals.

There are severe penalties for failing to make the required reports to the EPA, including civil and criminal penalties of $25,000 and up, plus up to a year's imprisonment for each violation. Each day the violation continues is considered a separate violation for purposes of the fines levied under the TSCA.

Pesticide Regulations

The Federal Insecticide, Fungicide and Rodenticide Act (FIFRA),which amends the Federal Environmental Pesticides Control Act of 1972 (FEPCA), regulates both the manufacture and distribution of pesticides.[20]

Environmental Impact Statements

The National Environmental Policy Act of 1969 (NEPA) requires an environmental impact statement (EIS) to be prepared with respect to major federal actions that significantly affect the quality of the human environment.[21] While this would not, at first impression, seem to directly affect you, as a small business owner, the EIS requirement also applies in any situation where a federal agency approves some action by other persons, such as a private company.

In addition, many states have adopted similar EIS requirements; for instance, when a local planning board approves a real estate development, an EIS may be required under state law, if not federal.

Asbestos Regulation

As lung disease, cancer, and other health risks attributed to the exposure to asbestos have come to light, a number of state and federal laws have been enacted to deal with this problem. In addition, huge numbers of individual damage suits for alleged harm to individuals, who were exposed to asbestos in the workplace and elsewhere, have resulted in enormous judgments against many companies, even forcing a giant building materials firm, Johns-Manville Corporation, into Chapter 11 bankruptcy to protect itself from a host of asbestos-related lawsuits.

Federal amendments to the TSCA and the Asbestos Hazard Emergency Response Act of 1986 (AHERA) have given the EPA power to issue regulations regarding asbestos in school buildings. In addition, Occupational Safety and Health Administration (OSHA) regulations have been issued to limit asbestos exposure in the workplace and to set construction standards regarding use of asbestos.[22]

Noise Control

Both OSHA and the EPA have issued regulations on noise emission standards, ranging from aircraft noise to protections of workers from hearing impairment in the workplace.

9.10 Consumer Credit Laws and Regulations

Many of the largest and most successful companies in America have gotten where they are, in part, by providing consumer credit to persons who buy their products. Classic examples would include such giant companies as Sears and General Motors, although countless smaller companies have also found that financing their customers' purchases can be a major boon to sales and that the interest earned on such credit can also become an important profit center in its own right.

The definition of consumer credit does not refer to the practice of allowing a client or customer to charge it and pay you at the end of the month, which is largely unregulated by the government. Instead, the following discussion deals with the situation where your business extends credit and charges interest during the period over which the loan amount (or amount financed) is being paid off by the customer.

The three main areas of the law regulating the extension of consumer credit, which affects nearly all businesses that grant such credit, are the federal Equal Credit Opportunity Act, the federal Truth-in-Lending Act, and state laws that prohibit usury.

If your business is engaged in providing consumer credit, you will most likely be subject to the provisions of the federal Equal Credit Opportunity Act (ECOA).[23] In general, the ECOA prohibits discrimination in credit transactions on the basis of race, color, religion, national origin, sex, age, or marital status.

The basic principle of this law is that each person applying for credit must be considered as an individual. This means, primarily, that there are very strict limits regarding what you may ask about marital status and about the spouse of the applicant. You may ask about marital status, but only to determine what rights and remedies you might have as a creditor — such as in a community property state — to refuse an applicant's credit.

The ECOA also forbids discrimination in providing credit because some or all of the applicant's income derives from public assistance programs, or because a person exercised a right, in good faith, under the Consumer Credit Protection Act.

Equal Credit Opportunity Act

If your business activities involve lending money, or if you sell to consumers on credit terms, you may have to comply with the federal Truth-in-Lending Act and state laws such as those that prohibit the charging of usurious interest rates on loans or other credit transactions.[24]

Regulations under the Truth-in-Lending Simplification and Reform Act provide that a business is not subject to the truth-in-lending rules unless it extended consumer credit at least 25 times in either the previous year or the current calendar year.[25] For loan transactions, required disclosures include:

Truth-in-Lending Act

- The annual percentage rate of interest;
- When the finance charge begins to accrue;
- The total amount of the finance charge;
- The number of payments to be made and the dollar amount of each payment;
- When payments are to be made;
- The total dollar amount of all payments;
- How any prepayment penalty and any late charges are to be computed;
- The amount of any prepaid finance charges and any deposit, plus the sum of the two;
- The amount financed;
- The existence of any balloon payment and its dollar amount;
- Annual statements of billing rights;
- Other information regarding security interests and rights to rescind; and
- Periodic billings to credit customers must include a number of disclosures regarding outstanding balances, how finance charges have been computed, and other items.

The rules regarding the Truth-in-Lending Act are far too complex to cover satisfactorily in a book of this nature; it can only alert you to the possibility that you may be required to comply with those rules and give you some sense of what will be required if the rules do apply to you. If you plan to extend credit to consumers — other than sending out bills requesting payment in full, without interest charge, after you have provided goods or services — you need to consult an attorney experienced in this area.

Fortunately, legislation has considerably simplified the truth-in-lending rules, and the Federal Reserve Board has published model disclosure statements and billing rights statements that can be used to satisfy the requirements of the truth-in-lending regulations.

Cash Discount Act

The Cash Discount Act permits sellers to offer a discount of any amount to customers who pay in cash or by check without running afoul of the truth-in-lending rules. The discount, in this case, has to be clearly disclosed and made available to all customers.[26] In the past, if you offered more than a 5% cash discount, you were considered to be imposing a finance charge on credit customers and had to give them all the required truth-in-lending disclosures.

Usury Laws

See Section 11.9 for a brief description of how this state's usury laws may apply to your business.

9.11 Employee or Independent Contractor?

As was pointed out in Section 5.2, there are some major advantages in hiring independent contractors rather than employees to work in your business. Not only do you gain considerable payroll tax savings by retaining independent contractors, but there are far fewer administrative headaches.

Unfortunately, just because you hire someone and you agree that he or she will be an independent contractor, it does not necessarily make it so for tax and legal purposes. So before you hire anyone to work for you as an independent contractor, you need to take a hard look at whether the IRS or a court of law would consider that person to be your employee rather than an independent contractor. While the IRS uses a 20-factor test to evaluate whether a person is or is not an employee, a few major warning flags will indicate to you whether or not the person is your employee. These include:

- The person works mostly or only for your firm. That is, the person is not like a lawyer, for example, who has a number of clients besides you that he or she works for.
- The worker is subject to your control, and you have the right to direct how the work is done, not just to demand a particular result.

- The person works in your office or establishment and does not have his or her own place of business, business cards, business name, etc.
- The kind of work the person does for you is normally done by employees, such as secretarial work.
- The person is not a licensed professional of any type.

Unless you are quite clear that the work relationship will not be considered that of employer/employee, be very careful about hiring someone as a so-called independent contractor. The consequences of being wrong can be severe. Here are just a few of the things that can happen if your independent contractor is determined to be an employee:

- You are liable for not only the employer payroll taxes you failed to pay, but also for a portion of the employee taxes you failed to withhold, for example, income taxes and FICA tax.
- If you treat someone as an independent contractor, report payments of $600 or more a year to that person on IRS *Form 1099-MISC*. If you do, and the IRS later determines the person was really an employee, the back taxes you are liable for are limited to the employer payroll taxes, 20% of the employee's FICA tax you failed to withhold, and income tax withholding equal to only 1.5% of the wages you paid the person.

   If you do not file *Form 1099-MISC* and the person is reclassified as an employee, you are liable for 40% of the employee's FICA tax and income tax withholding equal to 3% of the wages — twice as much as if you would have filed *Form 1099-MISC*. Furthermore, there is a $100 penalty for failure to file *Form 1099-MISC* and you will owe interest on the taxes due. It is no longer a bargain to "borrow" from the IRS.

   You may also be assessed other penalties if you did not have a reasonable basis for treating the person as a nonemployee and may be liable for up to 100% of the employee's FICA and income tax which you failed to withhold.

- If the person is hurt on the job and you have not provided workers' compensation insurance coverage, you will be liable for extensive legal damages.
- If your business has a qualified retirement plan and you have not contributed to the plan on behalf of the person because he or she was not thought to be an employee at the time, the retirement plan could be disqualified for tax purposes for failing to cover the employee in question.

Thus, do not get stampeded into the independent contractor game by your friends and business associates who tell you how simple it is to avoid all those payroll taxes.

The above discussion of independent contractors summarizes federal rules only. Many states take an even more restrictive view than the IRS on the employee versus independent contractor issue.

Independent Contractor Treatment Tips

There are a number of steps you may be able to take to make a stronger case for someone who works for you to be treated as an independent contractor. Obviously, not all of the following will necessarily be feasible in every case, and a number of these steps, if implemented, may require some significant changes in the way you do business.

But if you can follow most of the suggestions below with regard to a given worker, you will improve your odds against having that worker reclassified as an employee by the IRS.

- Have a written agreement, signed by both parties, that makes it clear the company doesn't have the right to control the methods or procedures for the worker to accomplish the work contracted for. Include language in the agreement that states it is the worker's obligation to pay income and self-employment taxes on amounts earned, and that he or she will receive a *Form 1099* reflecting amounts earned, if the amount earned is $600 or more.

- Try to avoid setting working hours by hour or week. It would be all right to specify starting and completion dates for the work.

- Make it clear that if additional workers are needed to help, the contractor will hire and pay them.

- The arrangement should make it clear that the contractor is not limited to working exclusively for you, but is free to take on other work from other customers.

- Compensation should be based on what work is performed rather than the time spent to do it. This may require careful estimates so that the worker is fairly paid, not overpaid, for the work done.

- Avoid providing office space to the contractor on a regular basis.

- Let the workers be responsible for their own training, if that is possible.

- Each worker should be advised, in writing, to provide for their own liability, workers' compensation, health, and disability insurance coverage.

- Costs such as meals, transportation, and clothing should be built into the contract price of the job, rather than being billed directly to your account.

- It should be clear in your agreement with the worker that he or she can't be fired and can't quit. The worker's job is to fulfill a given work contract.

- Don't give the worker other work to fill in during downtime. This may mean, of course, that you will have to pay the worker somewhat more for the work done than you otherwise would, if you wish to keep him or her happy.

- Don't pay bonuses to a person you treat as an independent contractor.

Other Alternatives

Hiring individuals as your own employees or treating them as independent contractors may sometimes pose a difficult choice. Fortunately, you have other available options. You could:

- Hire temporary employees from a temporary help agency; or

■ Lease employees from an employee leasing company.

An increasing number of companies are utilizing these two worthwhile alternatives.

Hiring "temps" is usually quite straightforward, at least for many kinds of positions, but it may cost you a bit more than straight hiring. A temporary help agency has to charge you enough to make a profit, as well as pay for any benefits it provides to the temps, who are the agency's employees — not yours. One benefit to you, other than the simplicity of having someone else handle payroll, benefits, workers' compensation, and other costs of retaining such workers, is that you can send such workers home the moment you no longer need them, with no adverse consequences.

Of even greater importance to many companies is the opportunity to try out temps and offer permanent jobs to those whose performance they like. In effect, you get to "test out" such individuals for as long as you wish, before deciding if you want to offer them employment as your own employee, not the agency's, which is exactly what many temps are seeking.

Employee leasing is a bit more complicated, because in many cases, you do the hiring. In some cases, you may even transfer your existing staff over to the payroll of the leasing company, which then leases them back to you for a fee equal to the salaries, taxes, and benefits paid by the leasing company, plus its mark-up percentage.

Leasing tends to be more of a long-term solution than hiring temps. Do your homework in checking out the reputation and background of any leasing company you will be dealing with. A number of leasing companies have gone broke or absconded with the payroll taxes withheld from employees' salaries, frequently leaving the firms that leased from them holding the bag. While there are many reputable leasing firms, they tend not to be as large and well known as the major temp firms, such as Kelly Services, Manpower, and other well-established firms in the industry.

Similar to hiring temps, leasing can be a major time- and energy-saving convenience. For example, if you lease all of your employees, you may be freed up to do what you do best, such as selling, rather than spending much of your time bogged down with payroll, benefits, and other employee-related paperwork.

You may also actually save money on your costs for workers, particularly if the leasing company is large and has been able to negotiate much less expensive, pooled rates for health insurance or workers' compensation than you could as a small employer.

Thus, leasing can offer substantial advantages to small companies, and usually avoids the problems and risks involved in seeking to treat workers as independent contractors, where such status is somewhat questionable. Be sure you deal with a reputable, established, financially responsible employee leasing company.

9.12 Whether You Should Incorporate Outside Your State

For most small businesses, there is little reason to consider incorporating your business under the laws of some state other than where you live. In fact, there are a few good reasons why you should not incorporate in a different state.

- Your corporation may have to pay a qualification fee to transact business in your home state as a foreign corporation. See Section 11.2 on this point.

- If your attorney is a local lawyer, he or she is likely to be much less familiar with the corporate laws of some other state than those of your state. Thus, your attorney is likely to either charge you more for corporate law advice if he or she has to research the law of an unfamiliar jurisdiction or give you less accurate advice than he or she could about your state's corporate laws.

- In many states, your corporation will have to pay some sort of minimum annual franchise tax or capital tax to the state of incorporation, even if you do no business there.

Don't believe the newspaper ads that tell you to incorporate in wonderful, tax-free Nevada or some other state and avoid your state's corporation income or franchise taxes. It doesn't work. If your corporation does business in your state, it pays the same taxes on its taxable income regardless of whether it is incorporated in your state, Nevada, or in the Grand Duchy of Luxembourg.

Perhaps the only valid reason why you might want to incorporate elsewhere would be to take advantage of some particular provision or flexibility available under the corporate laws of a particular state. If you own all the stock of your company, it is unlikely you would ever need to take advantage of any such provisions, which are usually more important where different groups are struggling for control of a corporation's board of directors or the like.

9.13 Foreign Investment in U.S. Businesses

Under the Foreign Direct Investment and International Financial Data Improvements Act of 1990, foreign individuals owning or acquiring 10% or more voting interest in U.S. businesses, including interests in U.S. real estate, must report certain information, including annual financial and operating data, to the U.S. Department of Commerce. Failure to file can result in civil penalties of $2,500 to $25,000.[27] For more information on this law, write to:

Bureau of Economic Analysis
U.S. Department of Commerce
BE-50 (IN)
Washington, DC 20230
(202) 606-5577

9.14 Emerging Trends and Issues

Today, businesses of every size and type are being buffeted by the ever-accelerating rate of change in the business, economic, social, and political environment in which they must operate. Part of the reason is that Congress, along with 50 state legislatures and countless government agencies, spew out reams of new laws and regulations all year long, in ever greater volume. As Benjamin Franklin once put it, "No man is safe in his bed when the Congress is in session."

To blame all of the disorienting changes that are occurring on lawmakers, however, is unfair since it seems that life in general is becoming more complex and unpredictable by the day. Accordingly, this section attempts to provide you, as a business owner, with a brief overview of developing and current trends in the business environment.

Labor Rates

Low labor rates abroad are causing the permanent shutdown of many large and small U.S. manufacturers, who can no longer keep up with foreign competition or U.S. manufacturers who move their operations overseas where wages are lower. This trend seems likely to continue and will have a rippling effect throughout the U.S. economy, adversely affecting many of the small firms that are either suppliers to large U.S. manufacturers or whose service operations will be drastically affected as larger companies close plants and make massive and permanent layoffs of thousands of employees.

Automation

Increasing automation, both here and abroad, is also likely to have a dramatic effect on employment and competitiveness in this country and throughout the world. Automation has been a factor in replacing blue-collar labor for decades. With the continual explosion in computing power and sophistication, vast numbers of middle managers and other white-collar workers are beginning to be displaced. With the advent of expert systems and "artificial intelligence," which are still in their infancy, but rapidly coming into their own, it is difficult to say whose job, if anyone's, will be safe in a few years.

While the ability to replace workers with computers or computer-driven machinery may be very attractive from a cost-savings standpoint to an employer, its societal effects are hard to predict and may prove to be very adverse to the overall business environment. The field of information processing is moving rapidly, and it is difficult to visualize how the world and the U.S. economy may look in as little as five or six years.

Downsizing

According to an American Management Association (AMA) survey for the year ending in June 1991, 55.5% of the organizations polled engaged in downsizing and 60% of those firms had also made significant staff cutbacks in the previous year, suggesting that firms are now cutting even deeper and deeper. The survey revealed that the cuts were heaviest on the Pacific Coast, averaging 12.6% of the workforce among firms reporting downsizing. Middle management jobs, which are estimated to make up something like 5% to 8% of the total workforce, accounted for more than 16% of the jobs cut in the 1991 survey period.

This trend has continued into 1994, as many of the nation's largest, most successful corporations, including IBM, General Motors, and Boeing, have announced one round of massive layoffs after another. Challenger, Gray & Christmas, a placement firm, says the pace of layoffs among large companies in 1993 ran well ahead of 1991, which was supposedly the bottom of the recent recession.[28]

While much of this change seems frightening to businesspeople, as well as to their employees, it may also give rise to fantastic new opportunities. Many of these people are likely to start their own smaller businesses due to the permanent disappearance of so many middle management or automatable jobs. Many may even keep working for their former firms as independent contractors or consultants.

In addition to enriching the overall business environment by creating a major upsurge in the formation of new, small, and flexible business entities, firms that cater to the needs of other small businesses may find the coming decade to be one of explosive growth and unparalleled opportunity.

Telecommuting

One of the most predictable trends, which is already well under way, is the growth of telecommuting, where more and more people work out of their homes, communicating with their clients or employers by use of personal computers, modems, faxes, or multiple phone lines. Already, some employers, like certain government agencies in Washington, D.C., are taking an intermediate step by setting up satellite telecommuting offices in suburban areas. By going to these nearby satellite offices, equipped with computer workstations, many workers can, on most days, avoid long and arduous commutes to downtown offices by piping their work product electronically to the main office instead.

A 1992 survey by Link Resources Corporation, a research and consulting firm, showed telecommuting has become a major factor in the economy almost overnight. The survey estimated that company employees who work at home part- or full-time increased in 1992 by 39%, over 1991, to

39 million individuals, most of whom are believed to be telecommuting. The survey apparently did not even take into account home-based businesses, which are also believed to be proliferating at startling rates.

Not all the consequences of increased telecommuting are positive. Some unforeseen side effects are already beginning to surface, such as rising workers' compensation costs for employers who have substantial numbers of employees working at home.

Apparently, employees who injure themselves at home tend to claim in many cases that such injuries are work-related, and therefore compensable under the workers' compensation system. In addition, injuries sustained while commuting are also more likely to be compensable, where such workers are constantly taking work back and forth between the office and home.

As a result, workers' compensation insurers have already begun to raise their rates for telecommuting employees. Don't overlook this potential expense when analyzing the costs and benefits of having more of your workforce telecommute.

Pending Law Changes

Now that one political party controls both the White House and Congress, look for significant law changes in 1994 and during the remainder of the Clinton administration. Many of these future law changes are sure to affect your business, for better or worse. Major new legislation to look for in the near future may include:

- Mandatory health care coverage — This is currently the Clinton administration's number one priority. The exact shape of change in this area is anyone's guess at this time. However, it is possible that the initial proposal to pay for universal health care with a payroll tax will not be part of the final plan, due to the enormous opposition to such a tax. Instead, look for some sort of mandated insurance coverage, probably with insurance rates and medical coverage terms set by the government.

  Part of the final package may also include a limit on deductions for medical insurance. Under such a limit, excess premiums paid for health care plans providing more than a defined "standard" level of benefits would not be deductible by employers and the excess payments would also be taxable income to the covered employee. Some portion of the additional costs of universal health care will be borne by the government. It seems likely the government will seek to fund the costs by imposing increased "sin" taxes on alcohol and cigarettes, and a national sales tax or value-added tax (VAT) of some kind cannot be ruled out as a possibility

- Full deductibility of health insurance for the self-employed — The Clinton health care reform plan and several competing proposals have all endorsed an increase in the percentage of self-employed persons' health insurance deduction from the current 25% to 100%.

Such plans call for this deduction — which has expired and been renewed after the fact several times in recent years — to be made permanent. Such provisions, if enacted, would finally put self-employed business owners on a par with those who are incorporated, with regard to deductibility of their medical insurance costs.

- Taxation of S corporation taxable income as self-employment income — Another proposal that has surfaced in connection with the Clinton health care reform proposals is to tax the income of S corporation shareholders as self-employment income, as has long been the case with partners in partnerships. This would close what has long been perceived as a loophole in the taxation of S corporations, by subjecting owners to self-employment tax on their share of the net taxable income of the S corporation — presumably with exceptions being made for rental income and interest income, which have never been considered self-employment income for owners of unincorporated businesses.

- States may be allowed to tax out-of-state mail order vendors — Legislation is pending in Congress that would authorize states, for the first time, to enact legislation requiring out-of-state sellers to collect sales or use tax on interstate sales for goods shipped to residents of the state in question. For details, see the discussion of this proposed legislation in Section 9.8.

- Federal legislation regarding limited liability companies (LLCs) — Now that some four-fifths of the states have adopted LLC laws and the tax benefits of LLCs threaten to reduce federal income tax revenues, one congressional committee is already looking into the possibility of requiring LLCs to be taxed as corporations. LLCs are generally taxed as partnerships under current federal tax law.

- Striker replacement law — The Clinton Administration supported a striker replacement law in Congress in 1994, which was defeated in July by seven votes in the U.S. Senate. The intent of this proposed law is to overturn a 1938 Supreme Court decision that allows employers to fire workers who go on strike over economic issues, such as wages. If enacted, the proposed legislation will both prohibit employers from hiring permanent replacement workers during a strike and require them to rehire strikers after the strike ends. The proposed bill contains other provisions that tend to shift the balance of economic power to labor unions and impose major burdens on small, nonunion employers by making it easier for labor unions to organize the workforce of smaller firms. Although the bill was defeated in 1994, a Congressional election year, look for it to be reintroduced in the 1995–96 Congressional session.

- Information returns (1099s) for payments to corporations — Under current law, businesses do not have to file 1099 information return forms for most payments they make to corporations; however, Congress may soon eliminate this important exemption. Doing so would greatly increase the paperwork burden on nearly all businesses.

- Increase estimated tax "safe harbor" to 115% — The ink is hardly dry on the 1993 Deficit Reduction Act, which allows high-income individual taxpayers to base-their estimated tax payments on 110% of the prior year tax, and the House Ways and Means Committee is already considering raising the "safe harbor" percentage to 115% of the prior year tax liability.

Other Legal Trends and New or Pending Legislation

Listed and discussed below are some other legal trends and new or pending legislation you should know about for future reference. This information provides possible tips for issues or rules which may affect your business.

Minimum Wage

From all indications, the Clinton administration will support an early increase in the federal minimum wage, which is currently $4.25 an hour. Look for an increase in the $5.00-an-hour range before the end of 1995.

While changes in the minimum wage in the past have usually occurred only at intervals of several years, depending upon the mood and makeup of Congress, current proposals call for indexing the minimum wage so it would automatically increase each year with the cost-of-living or other index.

Repeal of Bulk Sales Law

In 1988 and 1989, the National Conference of Commissioners on Uniform State Laws and the American Law Institute, respectively, both recommended that states should abolish or repeal their bulk sale or bulk transfer laws, which previously were in effect in all states. Both of these prestigious organizations concluded that bulk sale laws — originally adopted in most states in the late nineteenth century for the purpose of protecting creditors from fraud — no longer serve any useful purpose, but are instead a significant burden upon persons buying existing businesses.

Since these recommendations were made, about half the states have repealed their bulk sales laws, and several have amended and simplified theirs. This trend is likely to continue in the next few years. For information on whether your state still has a bulk sale law in effect, contact your state's secretary of state's office.

Video Display Terminals

Until recently, white-collar workplaces or offices generally created very little liability exposure for employers, with regard to hazardous working conditions. This, too, is beginning to change.

In recent years, there have been an increasing number of lawsuits filed by employees in connection with hazards of working long hours on computers; and the city of San Francisco has adopted an ordinance that provides regulatory safeguards for workers using video display terminals (VDTs) for four or more hours per shift. A number of other city and state governments around the nation are also considering similar laws or ordinances because the use of computers in the workplace is such a universal phenomenon and because a number of threats to employees' health have arisen in connection with the heavy use of computers.

These threats range from excessive exposure to radiation emitted by VDTs to carpal tunnel syndrome, a common and debilitating nerve entrapment disorder that can cause severe pain and weakness in the wrist. Carpal tunnel syndrome can result from too many hours spent typing on a computer keyboard — as well as from many other tasks requiring repetitive flexing and extensions of the wrist.

Laws regulating VDTs are likely to begin appearing all over the country in the near future, and offices that don't pay attention to ergonomics — the study of equipment design to reduce workplace injury — may well become sitting ducks for lawsuits or fines. While most legal claims by employees regarding VDT usage have been imposed on workers' compensation insurers thus far, employers may become directly liable:

- If they participate actively in the design of computer systems or workstations that allegedly caused the injury to an employee; or
- If new state legislation removes such claims from the workers' compensation system and places financial responsibility directly upon employers.

Helpful Organizations

Communicate your thoughts on government policy and pending legislation to groups like the National Federation of Independent Business (NFIB), the U.S. Chamber of Commerce, your local chamber of commerce, or a trade association for your industry. It also can be helpful to call or write your senator, U.S. representative, or state legislator to voice your opinion in favor of or opposition to pending legislation or regulations that will affect your business.

Small business has been hit very hard by the government at all levels in recent years, and the more small business owners join and work together through helpful organizations, the better the chances of shaping the future.

Endnotes

1. I.R.C. § 168.
2. I.R.C. § 179(b)(1).
3. I.R.C. § 6425.
4. 15 U.S.C. §§ 1051–1128.
5. I.R.C. § 1244(c). The Tax Reform Act of 1984 § 481(a).
6. I.R.C. § 1211(b).
7. I.R.C. § 1244(c)(1)(C).
8. I.R.C. § 1244(c)(3).
9. I.R.C. § 1244(d)(1)(B).
10. 16 C.F.R. § 435.1.
11. 42 U.S.C.A. §§ 9601 *et seq.*
12. 42 U.S.C.A. §§ 6901 *et seq.*
13. 40 C.F.R. § 280.22(a) and (b).
14. 40 C.F.R. § 280.20.
15. 40 C.F.R. § 280.21.
16. 33 U.S.C.A. §§ 1251–1376.
17. 33 U.S.C.A. § 1344(a).
18. 42 U.S.C.A. §§ 7401–7626.
19. 15 U.S.C.A. §§ 2601–2629.
20. 7 U.S.C.A. §§ 135 *et seq.*
21. 42 U.S.C.A. §§ 4321–4347.
22. 29 C.F.R. §§ 1910 and 1926.58.
23. 15 U.S.C. § 1691.
24. 15 U.S.C. §§ 1601 *et seq.*
25. 12 C.F.R. § 226.2(a)(17).
26. 12 C.F.R. § 226.4(c)(8).
27. 15 C.F.R. § 806.
28. *Barron's National Financial Weekly.* August 30, 1993.

Internal Accounting Controls Checklist

☐ The same person who handles your cash receipts should not be the same person who makes the bank deposits. Cash is too easily misappropriated. Don't tempt an employee by letting him or her handle both of these duties.

☐ The person who writes checks should not also sign them or have the authority to sign checks. A different person should sign checks.

☐ Whoever signs checks should only sign them when the bill that is being paid is presented at the same time. The check number should be written on the bill to avoid double payments or payments to a nonexistent vendor. When you sign the check, be sure you know what the bill is for.

☐ Consider using some type of mechanical check imprinting equipment for all checks that are written, as a further means of preventing unauthorized payments. Such machines keep a record of the amount of any checks written.

☐ Use only prenumbered checks and keep all of the cancelled or voided checks in your records. This will help make it readily apparent if any additional checks are written without your knowledge.

☐ Complete a monthly bank reconciliation yourself or have your outside accountant do it. Never let the person who writes checks do the reconciliation.

☐ Deposit your daily cash receipts in the bank each day. Do not let cash collections for one day get mingled with the next day's collections.

☐ Use prenumbered sets of sales checks, invoices, and receipts to keep control of payments made and received. Duplicates will be kept track of by the individuals making sales, etc., and the master copy will enable you to make sure they account for all of their transactions.

☐ Use a petty cash fund and voucher system for stamps, small bills, and other small cash outlays. Do not use cash from the day's receipts to pay bills! Put a voucher or bill in the petty cash box each time money is taken out. When the fund is depleted, write a check to bring it back up to the maximum amount (say $50), and record all the vouchers at the time the check is cashed to replenish the fund.

☐ Maintain a master or control account for all of your accounts receivable, and reconcile it each month to the subsidiary accounts receivable. If someone is stealing money from customer payments, it will be easier to spot if the master and subsidiary accounts are reconciled regularly.

Chapter 10

Sources of Help and Information

If you're going to sin, sin against God, not the bureaucracy.
God will forgive you, but the bureaucracy won't.

— Admiral Hyman G. Rickover

10.1 General Considerations

Many government and private organizations provide free or low-cost services and publications to small business. Unfortunately, most small business owners only find out about a few of these sources and then only on a haphazard basis. This chapter summarizes many of the services and publications you may need to draw on as an owner or operator of a small business.

10.2 Professional Services

Accountants

Select your accountant carefully. This is the one person outside your business who is most likely to be closely in touch with almost everything going on in your operation. Besides helping to set up your books and to establish systems for handling cash receipts and disbursements, a good accountant can provide a wealth of practical advice on a wide range of subjects that are important to your business, including planning for taxes, managing your money, obtaining financing, and evaluating business opportunities. Attorneys and bankers are often in a good position to recommend accountants.

Attorneys

Unless you are starting out as a sole proprietor, you will usually need an attorney to prepare a partnership agreement or to set up a corporation. You will probably do well to consult an attorney anyway to make sure you are obtaining necessary licenses and permits or to help you obtain them in some cases. In most parts of the country, local bar associations have lawyer referral services that can put you in touch with attorneys in your area. In most cases, you will do better to ask an accountant or banker to recommend a good business lawyer. If you need highly specialized legal advice or representation, ask an attorney you know to recommend a specialist.

Bankers

Establish a good relationship with officers of the bank branch where you open an account for your business. While you may find it tough to borrow from your banker when you first go into business, he or she will be interested in keeping an eye on your business to see how it develops. It pays to cultivate the relationship to create a good impression before you want to apply for a business loan from the bank. Ask around before opening an account; find out if there is a bank in your area that is well known for lending to small businesses. Many of the large banks tend to be more interested in larger accounts, although different branch managers of the same bank may have very different ideas about working with small businesses. Your banker can be a useful source of free financial advice and a good connection when wanting to meet other business owners in your community.

Benefit Consultants

If you intend to establish a corporate pension or profit-sharing plan — or Keogh plan, if you have a number of employees — you may want to seek out a benefit consulting firm and obtain its proposals as to the type of benefit plan you need and how it should be structured. Since many such firms are primarily engaged in selling insurance products, such as life insurance, annuities, and investment contracts, designed for pension plans, the plan these firms design for you will almost invariably involve building in their products. Since an insured retirement plan may not necessarily make sense in your particular situation, ask your attorney or accountant to recommend a benefit consulting firm that does not have products to sell other than its consulting and plan administration services.

10.3 U.S. Small Business Administration and Other Helpful Agencies

The federal Small Business Administration (SBA) is one government agency that is genuinely helpful to small businesses. The SBA not only guarantees financing for many small businesses (see Section 9.7), but it also provides a number of valuable services.

One service you might find helpful is the Service Corps of Retired Executives (SCORE). SCORE is a program in which retired executives with many years of business experience volunteer their services as consultants to small businesses and charge only for their out-of-pocket expenses. Other SBA programs designed to provide assistance to small businesses include:

- Small Business Development Centers (SBDCs) — SBDCs are local centers operated by the state or community, with SBA assistance, to provide a wide range of business counseling and training. To see if your state has an SBDC network, refer to Section 11.10.
- Small Business Institutes (SBIs) — SBIs provide in-depth business counseling at hundreds of universities across the country.

In addition, SBA offices perform a variety of seminars and workshops on topics of interest to people who are starting or operating small businesses. Here are some of the seminars offered by the SBA.

- *Building a Business Plan*
- *Starting a New Business*
- *Preparing the Loan Proposal*

Contact your local SBA office for more information.

Business Information Centers

The SBA has also opened new Business Information Centers — each of which has a full set of all 51 of the books in this *Starting and Operating a Business* series — in Seattle, Houston, and Atlanta, with more coming soon in St. Louis, Los Angeles, and elsewhere. Each of these centers is designed to assist in disseminating helpful information to small business.

Telephone Hotlines

The SBA and several other government agencies maintain toll-free telephone hotline information services to assist businesses and taxpayers. Some of the more important ones to know about are listed below.

SBA Answer Desk

The SBA Answer Desk has a toll-free number of a small business information and referral service offered by the SBA, which you can call from anywhere in the continental United States, except Washington, D.C. For the number in D.C., check the local directory. The telephone Answer Desk offers a wide range of prerecorded, informational messages, any of which you may access if you have a touch-tone phone.

SBA Answer Desk
(800) U-ASK-SBA or 827-5722

SBA Online

The SBA has set up an electronic bulletin board system (BBS), called *SBA Online*, to help distribute information about its services and publications to anyone with a personal computer and modem. Since the service is sponsored by several major corporations, including Sprint, a huge variety of information is available toll-free nationwide via an 800-number. Typical SBA information available at no cost includes:

- Business development
- Financing services
- Government contracting opportunities
- Small business facts and programs
- Local Small Business Development Center and Business Information Center access
- Legislation and regulations
- SBA acquired assets for resale

In addition, the *SBA Online* established two new access numbers for 1994 that offer full usage of electronic mail services, as well as providing gateways to other government agencies and on-line services, including the Internet. The Internet is a world-wide computer database established by the government and research agencies to allow mail and information sharing. It has grown to become a popular backbone of the recently promoted "information superhighway."

Other outside services of *SBA Online* include access to Census Bureau data, the Internal Revenue Service, and the U.S. Patent and Trademark Office, as well as news from NASA, the Environmental Protection Agency, and other regulatory agencies. Internet services include the ability to write and receive Internet e-mail, and access to newsgroups.

Although full usage does require either 900 number charges per minute or a regular Washington D.C. toll call, the BBS provides a helpful *Offline Mail Reader* and estimates of file download time at various modem speeds. In addition, the BBS is well-designed for efficient usage, is accessible from virtually any computer set up, and provides numerous quick access utilities.

To log on to *SBA Online* for the first time:

- Set the following parameters for your modem's communication program:
  - No parity
  - Eight data bits
  - One stop bit
  - VT 102 terminal emulation

- Dial 1-800-697-4636 at any modem speed (2400 to 19.2K)
- Press Control key + "C" after you see a "Connect" message. You will see the SBA logo and be prompted to type in your name and business address.

The BBS then provides easy-to-use menu choices for navigation around the service. Be sure to read the "Help" menu for an excellent explanation of general BBS and computer terminology, as well *SBA Online* access tips.

After you are comfortable with the 800 number service, try the other access numbers:

SBA Online
Direct Dial
(202) 401-9600

900 Service
(900) 463-4636

Technical Support (for questions or problems)
(202) 205-6400

The Small Business Hotline is a specialized free service offered by the Export-Import Bank to small exporters needing general information or problem-solving assistance relating to doing business abroad. It provides information on export credit and on assistance available from other government agencies and the private sector.

Small Business Hotline

Small Business Hotline – Automated Info System
(800) 424-5201

The IRS has an assistance program called Tele-Tax. The program allows you to call a toll-free number in your state to listen to pre-recorded tax information that will answer many federal tax questions.

Internal Revenue Service

About 140 topics are available, including information on the Small Business Tax Education Program (STEP), business income, sole proprietorships, and the self-employment tax.

For more information on Tele-Tax, call the IRS's toll-free number to request *Publication 910, Guide to Free Tax Services*. This publication not only lists the many tax publications you can order, but it also lists the Tele-Tax phone numbers and topic numbers in your state.

Internal Revenue Service
(800) 829-3676

The Trade Information Center has a hotline where you can receive general information on exporting that is provided by various U.S. government agencies.

Trade Information Center

Trade Information Center
U.S. Department of Commerce
(800) USA-TRADE or 872-8723

Like certain Scandinavian countries, the Environmental Protection Agency (EPA) has a small business ombudsman who gives easier access to the EPA, helps you comply with EPA regulations, and makes sure you are treated fairly in any EPA disputes.

**Environmental Protection
Agency Ombudsman**

EPA Small Business Ombudsman
(703) 305-5938
(800) 368-5888

Social Security Administration

If you want to find out what records the Social Security Administration (SSA) has on your earnings and your projected benefits at retirement age, you can file a simple form requesting a detailed printout of this information. This is something everyone should do once every few years because if the SSA has made a serious mistake in your earnings record, you have only a limited number of years in which you can contact them and have your record corrected.

To obtain the request form, call the SSA's toll-free number or write the SSA for this form at the Consumer Information Center address below.

Social Security Administration
(800) 772-1213

Consumer Information Center
Department 72
Pueblo, CO 81009

Corporate Agents, Inc.

There are also companies who can assist in the incorporation process, providing a variety of incorporation kits and services. One such company, Corporate Agents, Inc., can help you form your corporation in any state for as little as $39 (plus state fees), depending on the state. Some examples of complete costs for other states are $115 for Delaware, $169 for Florida, $331 for New York, and $1,014 for California.

The fees cover all costs, including all state filing fees and recording costs, preparing and filing articles of incorporation, and a registered agent's service fee for the first six months. Also available for a nominal additional cost are the corporate kits, which include the corporate seal, minute book, stock certificates, and sample forms and bylaws.

For more information on this company, you can send the preaddressed post card located at the back of this book or call Corporate Agents at the toll-free number below:

Corporate Agents, Inc.
1013 Centre Road
P.O. Box 1281
Wilmington, DE 19899
(800) 877-4224
FAX (302) 998-7078

10.4 Publications Regarding Small Business Operations

U.S. Small Business Administration

The U.S. Small Business Administration (SBA) has more than 50 helpful booklets and other publications on subjects of importance to new and existing small businesses. The publications, which sell for a nominal fee — usually about $0.50 (50 cents) to $1.00 each, and never more than $2.00 — can be obtained through your nearest SBA office or by calling the SBA Answer Desk and asking for a list of publications.

SBA Answer Desk
(800) U-ASK-SBA or 827-5722

You can also use the preaddressed post card in the back of this book to request lists of SBA publications.

Small Business Institutes (SBIs) are located on university campuses throughout the United States. Part of a cooperative program with the SBA, SBIs offer you business assistance while furthering the education of college students. Students, supervised by faculty members, provide your business with:

Small Business Institutes

- Free confidential consulting;
- In-depth analysis of your firm's business situation;
- Alternatives and recommendations to business problems; and
- Written and oral reports.

Headquartered at the University of Central Arkansas, the Small Business Institute Directors' Association (SBIDA) National Center and the Small Business Advancement Network perform research and gather information on small business. The SBIDA National Center is the link between all SBI universities and the government. The SBIDA also:

- Is the center of correspondence for SBI schools;
- Keeps records on all SBI schools;
- Publishes the *SBIDA News*;
- Processes SBIDA membership; and
- Is a center for advocacy.

The Small Business Advancement Network is an electronic bulletin board which provides information on grant opportunities, cooperative ventures between the SBA and SBI, and small business research. The network is available during regular business hours and is updated daily. For information on the SBI nearest you, contact:

SBIDA National Center
University of Central Arkansas
College of Business
UCA P.O. Box 4983
Conway, AR 72035-5002
(501) 450-5300

For more on the Small Business Advancement Network, contact:

Small Business Advancement National Center
University of Central Arkansas
College of Business
UCA P.O. Box 5018
Conway, AR 72035-0001
(501) 450-5377

The Oasis Press

The publisher of this book, The Oasis Press, has a number of how-to business guides and software programs targeted toward small businesses. Some of the most recent titles published by The Oasis Press include:

- *Bottom Line Basics: Understand and Control Business Finances.* This guide goes beyond accounting to help you plan, manage, and control your company's finances. (Paper, $19.95)
- *The Business Environmental Handbook.* Your company can be both environment-friendly and -profitable. This comprehensive guide tells you how. (Paper, $19.95)
- *Buyer's Guide to Business Insurance.* A step-by-step guide that gives you advice and tips for improving your business insurance costs, coverage, and service. (Paper, $19.95) A companion software, The Insurance Assistant, is also available from the publisher.
- *People Investment.* An up-to-date guide for staffing a business and avoiding today's legal hurdles. (Paper, $19.95)
- *Power Marketing.* A comprehensive guide that details successful marketing strategies for your business. (Paper, $19.95)
- *The Secrets to Buying and Selling a Business.* A guide designed to help both buyers and sellers in their quest to make the best deal possible. (Paper, $19.95)
- *Start Your Business: A Beginner's Guide.* This guide is the perfect companion to this *Starting and Operating a Business* book, helping you answer the essential questions regarding money matters, marketing, staffing, business plans, and other important start-up issues. (Paper, $8.95)

Information on these and other related resources from The Oasis Press is provided at the back of this book or it can be obtained by calling:

The Oasis Press
(800) 228-2275

Magazines

Here are some magazines that provide continuing information for businesses in general and small businesses in particular. There are also a number of specialized publications you may find helpful. Most of these publications can be located through your local library or news stand.

The Wall Street Journal
200 Liberty Street
New York, NY 10281
(212) 416-2898

D&B Reports
299 Park Avenue
New York, NY 10171-0002
(212) 593-6723

In Business
419 State Avenue
Emmaus, PA 18049-3717
(215) 967-4135

Success Magazine
P.O. Box 3038
Harlin, IA 51537
(212) 551-9500
(800) 234-7324

**Entrepreneur Magazine
Business Start-ups**
Subscriber Service
P.O. Box 58808
Boulder, CO 80322
(800) 421-2300

Business Review
P.O. Box 777
Cypress, TX 77429-0777
(713) 373-3535

Business Week
Subscriber Service
P.O. Box 506
Hightstown, NJ 08520
(800) 635-1200

Nation's Business
U.S. Chamber of Commerce
1615 H. Street, NW
Washington, DC 20062
(202) 463-5650

Inc.
Subscriber Service
P.O. Box 54129
Boulder, CO 80322-4129
(800) 234-0999

Small Business Opportunities
1115 Broadway, 8th Floor
New York, NY 10010-2803
(212) 807-7100

Small Business Reports
Subscriber Services
P.O. Box 53140
Boulder, CO 80322-3140
(800) 234-1094

Independent Business
National Federation of Independent Business
Membership Development Office
600 Maryland Avenue, SW, Suite 700
Washington, DC 20024
(202) 554-9000

Home Business Opportunities
P.O. Box 1606
Ozark, AL 36360
(205) 774-0990

Statistical Information

Some of the more important sources of statistical information that you will need if you do your own marketing research are:

Title

Publisher

Survey of Buying Power
Sales and Marketing Management Magazine
Comprehensive data on population, retail sales, and consumer buying income for states, counties, and cities.

Bill Communications, Inc.
355 Park Avenue South
New York, NY 10010
(212) 592-6200

Publication Price List
Titles on corporate relations, human resources, management, economic and business environments, and consumer research.

Conference Board
845 Third Avenue
New York, NY 10022
(800) 872-6273

Survey of Current Business
U.S. Department of Commerce's monthly survey of business trends and conditions.

Superintendent of Documents
U.S. Government Printing Office
Washington, DC 20402
(202) 783-3238

The Complete Information Bank for Entrepreneurs & Small Business Managers, Second Edition
An excellent sourcebook which lists and describes hundreds of leading business books and other sources of help and information for small businesses.

Center for Entrepreneurship
Wichita State University
1845 Fairmont
Wichita, KS 67260-0147
(316) 689-3000

Encyclopedia of Business Information Sources, Ninth Edition
Arranged by industry, this guide lists trade associations and major sources of statistical information.

Gale Research, Inc.
835 Penobscott Building
Detroit, MI 48226
(313) 961-2242

U.S. Occupational Safety and Health Administration

The U.S. Occupational Safety and Health Administration (OSHA) provides a number of useful, free publications on OSHA requirements for small businesses. Two of the more important ones are listed below. Each is available from one of OSHA's ten regional offices or from one or more local OSHA offices in every state.

OSHA Handbook for Small Business (OSHA 2209)	Helpful handbook designed to assist small business employers to meet their legal requirements under the OSHA laws and regulations.
Recordkeeping Guidelines for Occupational Injuries and Illness (O.M.B. No. 1220-0029)	Provides useful summary of what records must be kept, who must keep them, and for how long.

OSHA offices can also provide you with a package or folder entitled, *Information from the Occupational Safety and Health Administration,* which includes the above publications, plus required posters and about a dozen other OSHA informational booklets and pamphlets. See the pre-addressed postcard at the back of the book for ordering booklets and required posters.

Securities and Exchange Commission

The SEC's Office of Small Business Policy publishes *Q & A: Small Business and the SEC*, which is a guide to special services, rules, regulations, and suggestions regarding a company's first public offering of stock. It is available from:

Office of Small Business Policy
Securities and Exchange Commission
450 Fifth Street NW
Washington, DC 20549
(202) 942-4040 (publications)

Equal Employment Opportunity Commission

The Equal Employment Opportunity Commission (EEOC) publishes a useful and comprehensive publication on all the discrimination laws that it enforces, such as civil rights, age discrimination, and equal pay. To obtain the publication that is entitled, *Laws Enforced by EEOC*, contact:

Office of Communications and Legislative Affairs
Equal Employment Opportunity Commission
1800 L Street NW
Washington, DC 20507
(202) 663-4900
(800) 669-3362

10.5 Do-It-Yourself Incorporation

If you want to form your own corporation and save several hundred dollars in legal fees, there are books that tell you how to do it and provide the forms you need; however, think carefully before you attempt to do this on your own. In some cases, setting up a corporation is not that complicated, and if you follow the instructions in a self-incorporation book precisely — if one is available for your state — you should be able to do it properly. But you will have to spend many hours carefully figuring out and then doing all that is required. Your time might be worth much more than the money you would save in legal fees because you could concentrate more on getting the business off to a good start. Check Section 11.10 to see if there is an incorporation book for your state.

10.6 Information Regarding Payroll Taxes and Withholding

Major offices of the IRS frequently put on seminars for new employers regarding payroll tax requirements. Call your local IRS office for information as to when such seminars will be held in your area. In addition, you may want to obtain *Circular E, Employer's Tax Guide,* and *Notice 109, Information About Depositing Employment and Excise Taxes.* Both can be obtained from the IRS office nearest you. In addition, the Matthew Bender Company publishes an excellent book called the *Payroll Tax Guide*, which covers almost every aspect of federal payroll tax returns.

Matthew Bender Company
(800) 223-1940

10.7 Other Useful Tax Publications

The publications below can also be obtained from your local IRS office:

Publication	Subject
Publication 334	*Tax Guide For Small Business Income and other Federal Taxes*
Publication 349	*Federal Highway Use Taxes on Heavy Vehicles*
Publication 378	*Fuel Tax Credits and Refunds*
Publication 463	*Travel, Entertainment, and Gift Expenses*
Publication 510	*Federal Excise Taxes*
Publication 541	*Tax Information on Partnerships*
Publication 542	*Tax Information on Corporations*

Publication	Subject
Publication 544	*Sales and Other Dispositions of Assets*
Publication 552	*Recordkeeping Requirements*
Publication 583	*Taxpayers Starting a Business*
Publication 587	*Business Use of Your Home*
Publication 589	*Tax Information on S Corporations*
Publication 910	*Guide to Free Tax Services*
Publication 937	*Business Reporting*

To order these free tax publications or other tax forms, call:

Internal Revenue Service
(800) 829-3676

10.8 ERISA Compliance

If your business has a pension or profit-sharing plan and you wish to handle your own Employee Retirement Income Security Act (ERISA) filings for the plan, obtain a copy of Charles D. Spencer & Associates' publication, *5500 Annual Reports for Employee Benefit Plans*. This publication will help you prepare the necessary *Form 5500* series through its easy-to-understand, step-by-step instructions. For ordering information, contact:

Charles D. Spencer & Associates, Inc.
250 South Wacker Drive, Suite 600
Chicago, IL 60606
(312) 993-7900

10.9 Information on Franchising

Title and Author	Publisher
Franchise Bible Erwin J. Keup	**The Oasis Press** 300 North Valley Drive Grants Pass, OR 97526 (800) 228-2275
Miscellaneous titles on franchise topics. Write for a catalog.	**International Franchise Association** 1350 New York Avenue, NW, Suite 900 Washington, DC 20005
Business Franchise Guide	**Commerce Clearing House, Inc.** 4025 West Peterson Avenue Chicago, IL 60646
Miscellaneous titles on franchise topics. Write for a catalog.	**Pilot Books** 103 Cooper Street Babylon, NY 11702

Title and Author	Publisher
Franchise Opportunities Handbook U.S. Department of Commerce	**Superintendent of Documents** **U.S. Government Printing Office** Washington, DC 20402
Franchising in the U.S. Michael M. Coltman	**Self-Counsel Press Inc.** 1704 North State Street Bellingham, WA 98225 (800) 663-3007
Franchisee Rights — A Self-Defense Manual for The Franchisee Alex Hammond	**Hammond & Morton** 1185 Avenue of the Americas New York, NY 10036
Franchising: Regulation of Buying and Selling A Franchise Philip F. Zeidman, Perry C. Ausbrook, and H. Bret Lowell	**Bureau of National Affairs, Inc.** 9435 Key West Avenue Rockville, MD 20850 (800) 372-1033
The Info Franchise Newsletter *The Franchise Annual*	**Info Press** 728 Center Street Lewiston, NY 14092-0550 (716) 754-4669
Survey of Foreign Laws and Regulations Affecting International Franchising Compiled by the Franchising Committee of the Section of Antitrust Law of the American Bar Association	**Publications Planning and Marketing** **American Bar Association** 705 North Lake Shore Drive Chicago, IL 60611

Notes

State Laws & Related Resources

Notes to California State Chapter

What's New

This update, through March 1995, of the California state chapter features new information and additions in several areas. The list below will help you locate the most significant changes by chapter–section number.

- Limited Liability Company (LLC) law enacted, but all LLCs in California will have to pay at least $800 annual minimum tax – 11.2

- Latest sales tax rate changes in various cities and counties included – 11.4

- Major 1995 changes in California employer withholding and unemployment tax requirements added – 11.5

- New California smoke-free workplace rules for employers, effective January 1, 1995, is discussed – 11.5

- New requirement for most California employers to report information on newly hired employees to the California Employment Development Department within 30 days is described – 11.5

- 1994 law changes in California Family Rights Act, regarding employee's rights to family and medical leave, explained – 11.5

- Information added on California's pregnancy leave law requirements for employers – 11.5

- Manufacturers and certain other businesses may now file for a sales tax refund (at a 6% rate) for sales tax paid on purchases of qualified equipment and machinery, in lieu of claiming the 6% income tax investment credit – 11.8

If changes have occurred since publication of this update, contact the state office listed below for assistance or referral to the appropriate agency.

Office of Small Business
California Trade and Commerce Agency
801 K Street, Suite 1700
Sacramento, CA 95814
(916) 324-1295

About the Author

The author of *Starting and Operating a Business in California*, as well as the principal author and technical editor of the entire *Starting and Operating a Business* series, is Michael D. Jenkins.

Mr. Jenkins, an attorney at law and a certified public accountant, is a graduate of Harvard Law School. He has worked in Los Angeles and San Francisco as an accountant and as an attorney with a prominent San Francisco firm well-known in the venture capital arena. He is a member of the State Bar of California, the American Bar Association, the American Institute of Certified Public Accountants, the California Society of Certified Public Accountants, and the Washington Society of Certified Public Accountants. He currently resides in Issaquah, Washington.

Chapter 11

State Laws and Taxes

11.1 Introduction

California, which has by far the largest population of any state in the union, with approximately 30 million consumers, offers an almost boundless market for all types of businesses. Its highly developed economy is the nation's largest and richest and is also one of the most diverse of any state. For several decades, the words "California" and "growth" have almost become synonymous, and it was common knowledge that the California economy and the price of California real estate could never go in any other direction but up. This, however, is no longer the case.

Old myths die hard, but those days of unbridled optimism and growth in California came to an abrupt halt for a rough period lasting more than three years. It began in 1990 with a sudden decline in real estate values, after more than a decade of a seemingly endless upward price spiral. The decline in property values was quickly followed by a sharp contraction in most segments of the California economy, as the long boom cooled and massive layoffs spread into a number of key industries — such as construction and defense-related areas. For a state that had long felt it was immune to the periodic recessions that affected the rest of the country, it was a rude shock to experience net out-migration of individuals and businesses to other states for the first time within memory. Many residents moved to other western states in search of lower taxes, fewer environmental problems and restrictions, and lower housing and living costs.

The already difficult situation was exacerbated by a series of natural and societal calamities, starting with the San Francisco Bay Area earthquake in late 1989. This natural disaster was followed in quick succession by a severe and unprecedented freeze in 1990, the Oakland/Berkeley firestorm in 1991, riots in Los Angeles in 1992, a huge earthquake in Southern California in 1994, and the shocking and sudden governmental bankruptcy of one of the nation's richest counties — Orange County — in 1995. California was also hit with a prolonged drought, fires and mudslides in Malibu, and unparalleled, widespread floods.

Almost equally shocking was an increase in the state's usually low unemployment rate to nearly 11% at the depth of the recent recession. Also, many proud Californians were appalled to find their state government running huge budget deficits since 1991, despite sharp tax increases. To add insult to injury, the budget situation reached such crisis proportions in 1992, that, for an extended period of time, California was unable to pay its bills, and had to issue "IOUs" instead of checks.

However, in 1994, the state's economy began to take a turn for the better. The California unemployment rate dropped sharply from 10.7% in January to 7.4% by year end — although still a full 2.0% above the national unemployment rate, which has been at 5.5% or less for the first quarter of 1995.

The worst seems to be over, as are most of the layoffs in construction, aerospace, and defense. However, the Business Forecasting Project, conducted by the University of California at Los Angeles, estimates that California has lost about 720,000 jobs in recent years — including 100,000 construction jobs and 380,000 defense and aerospace jobs. The project's findings still expect the state to lose another 50,000 aerospace jobs before the process finishes unwinding.

The good news is that overall employment growth has occurred since at least early 1994, albeit at a moderate pace, and Governor Pete Wilson has already promised significant tax cuts, based on estimates of an increase of nearly 200,000 jobs in 1994 and projections of a continuing recovery during 1995 and subsequent years. Federal Reserve Chairman Alan Greenspan noted of late that even Southern California, an economic basket case until recently, "is picking up."

California's employment growth now seems more focused on what most economists refer to as "the industries of the future," such as high-tech manufacturing and research, foreign exports, motion pictures and entertainment, and professional services. While this suggests a more stable, less cyclical growth than the old boom-and-bust cycles of construction and aerospace, the downside is that these new growth industries tend to be the most productivity-driven ones. In other words, because of their very efficiency, these industries don't create new jobs nearly as fast as their rapid growth rates might suggest. Thus, most economic forecasters feel that California may finally be over the economic hump, but unemployment is likely to remain fairly high, and the state probably will not soon return to anything like the kind of broad-based economic growth and low unemployment rates it routinely experienced until the '90s.

One lingering after-effect of the recent unpleasantness is a much more unattractive tax structure in California. In an attempt to balance the state budget in the midst of the recession, the business climate was cooled considerably by:

- An increase to the top state income tax rate from 9.3 to 11%;
- A 1.25% statewide hike in the sales tax rate, as well as authorization of local governments to raise local sales tax rates; and
- A drastic increase in alcoholic beverage excise taxes.

With these and other tax increases, California has some of the highest sales taxes in the country, as high as 8.5% in some of the major metropolitan areas, and no lower than 7.25% anywhere in the state. This is in addition to relatively high income tax rates.

For a state that was rated by *Inc.* magazine as having one of the best and friendliest business climates in the nation only a few years ago, things have changed considerably, and generally not for the better.

In part, California is now paying for its own past success in attracting people and businesses to the state. The rapid growth in economy and population has proved to be a mixed blessing for California. With the growth have come problems of environmental pollution; an aging infrastructure unable to keep up with the needs of a growing population; crowded freeways; growing budgetary problems at both the state and local government levels; and a loss of some of the allure of the California lifestyle that has drawn so many to the state over the years.

To deal with what has become the most serious air pollution problem in the country, Southern California is moving toward some of the most stringent and far-reaching environmental restrictions that will have ever been implemented in any developed society. These restrictions will be phased in over the next decade or more, despite uncertainty regarding their economic and social effects. These restrictions include everything from mandating that a certain percentage of cars sold in the state be "zero-emission vehicles" to requiring expensive air pollution control equipment for even the smallest businesses — such as bakeries and dry cleaning shops — which are already feeling the impact of these new rules.

Due to the high degree of business regulation by the state, doing business in California demands attention to many issues, which include:

- State labor laws;
- Job safety and health rules;
- Tax regulations enforced by taxing agencies that are very aggressive in their enforcement;
- Anti-discrimination laws that are broader than most states; and
- Environmental protection restrictions that are increasingly stringent.

Notwithstanding its current severe economic difficulties and the complexities of doing business in the state, California is still a "must" place to be for most businesses, as it remains by far the largest and richest market in the United States. It leads the nation in a great many categories, including total employment, direct exports, small business profits, wine production, solar and wind energy, aerospace, agriculture, venture capital spending, women-owned businesses, freeway mileage, tourist spending, high-tech manufacturing, and Ph.D.s awarded.

Even the drastic collapse of the Mexican peso and ensuing economic contraction south of the border since January, 1995, probably will not affect the California economy, which now amounts to some $800 billion. Since the state's exports to Mexico were only $5.6 billion in the first nine months of 1994, even a complete loss of all exports to Mexico would have only a modest effect on California's enormous economy, with its gross domestic product larger than any but the five largest national economies in the world.

The state, strategically located on the Pacific Rim, is very well positioned in relation to the large and fast-growing economies of Asia, as well as Australia, New Zealand, Alaska, Western Canada, and the Pacific Northwest. Perhaps even more important when it comes to industries of the future, California is almost synonymous with high-tech, with its electronics, biosciences, solar, and space-related industries.

While the Santa Clara Valley — known worldwide as the Silicon Valley — may have lost some of its edge over the rest of the high-tech world in recent years to places like the Pacific Northwest and Utah, it continues to boast the largest concentration of high-technology firms in the world. In addition, several of the most important new rival areas competing for worldwide high-tech supremacy are in Los Angeles, Orange, and San Diego counties.

While the current budget crisis has led to major tax increases and other increases in the cost of doing business, there is also a positive side to the tax picture. California has relatively low property tax rates — limited, in general, to one percent of property value, with certain exceptions — no inheritance or gift taxes, and no property tax whatsoever on business inventories or intangible property. Also, the annual wage base on which unemployment taxes are imposed, at $7,000 per worker, is much lower than in a number of other states and has not been increased in several years.

Even in the midst of the current budget crunch, California has recently expanded the number and size of enterprise zones throughout the state, where firms can do business with drastically reduced tax burdens. In fact, California's enterprise zone laws are rated as being the best, in terms of incentives offered to businesses, of any in the country.

In addition, the state had the courage and wisdom, in the face of all its fiscal woes in 1993 and 1994, to enact a number of significant business tax incentives, which are discussed in greater detail throughout the remainder of this chapter. These new or restored tax incentives, most of which apply to tax years that begin in 1994, include:

- The research and development (R&D) tax credit has been made permanent;

- A 6% investment tax credit on purchases of production equipment in most manufacturing industries, for R&D, and in the bio-tech industry;
- In lieu of the above credit, certain new businesses are allowed a refund of the state portion (6%) of the sales tax on their purchases of qualified equipment;
- The California franchise income tax on the income of S corporations was reduced from 2.5 to 1.5%;
- The deduction for net operating losses for purposes of the California franchise tax on corporations has been restored, but with certain limitations that did not apply under the old law;
- A 50% exclusion for capital gains on sales of certain "small business stock" has been enacted, with rules and definitions that are very similar to the newly-enacted federal tax break for gains on sale of stock in certain small corporations;
- The reporting requirements have been simplified for multinational companies that file "water's edge" elections for California franchise tax purposes, with the requirement to file a "water's edge spreadsheet" eliminated; and
- A limited liability company law was enacted, permitting companies to be organized that have the corporate benefits of limited liability with regard to creditors, but which retain most of the tax benefits and flexibility of a partnership.[1]

California continues to attract huge numbers of immigrants from Asia and Latin America, many of whom bring with them an ingrained entrepreneurial spirit and a strong work ethic. While the state's economy may continue to have its ups and downs for a while yet, its continued status as a magnet for immigrants and growth in new small business start ups should eventually turn things around.

Even the terrible damage done by the latest Los Angeles earthquake has a silver lining: the billions of dollars of insurance money and federal disaster relief gave a significant boost in 1994 to the long-depressed construction and building materials industries.

Finally, aside from purely economic considerations, California remains a world leader in business sophistication, innovation, and technology thanks to its existing infrastructure of high-tech businesses, a highly skilled and educated workforce, and world-class universities, such as Stanford, Berkeley, and Cal Tech. California is definitely "big-time," and businesses that can make it in California can often make it anywhere. As mystery writer, Ross MacDonald, put it, "I live here because California is to the 20th Century what London was to the 19th Century — the center of world culture, a place filled with activity and motion."

Despite the apocalyptic, doom-and-gloom media headlines about this state's decline in recent years, this huge, rich, quintessentially modern state of California is getting back on track and still has much to offer anyone wishing to start, relocate, or operate a business.

11.2 Choosing the Legal Form of the Business

One of the first decisions you must make when starting your new business is to choose which legal form of business organization you will adopt. There have traditionally been three basic forms: the sole proprietorship, the partnership, and the corporation. California has a fourth form of business — the limited liability company. General considerations for choosing a legal form of business are located in sections 2.1–2.6.

More state-specific considerations for California are discussed below. Other requirements, such as business name registration, taxes, wage-hour, and labor laws, are discussed in sections 11.4–11.7.

Sole Proprietorships

A sole proprietorship is a business that is owned by one person. Because there are no formal legal requirements for setting up a sole proprietorship, you will find it relatively simple to form and operate. A sole proprietorship offers you greater personal control of your business, fewer tax requirements and filings than other forms of business, and all the profits or losses. You will be personally liable for all your business' debts and obligations, as discussed in Section 2.2.

Similar to federal tax law, as an owner of a sole proprietorship in California, your business earnings or losses will be subject to state income taxes, and you report them on your personal individual income tax returns, *Form 540, California Resident Income Tax Return – Individuals*, and its schedules. You must also attach a copy of your federal *Schedule C*.

Tax rates are indexed for inflation and are announced late each year by the Franchise Tax Board (FTB), which is the state agency that administers and enforces the state income, corporation income, and franchise taxes.

Although California personal income tax rates are not the highest in the nation, they are still higher than many other states. Rates for 1993 begin at 1.0% and are graduated up to a maximum of 9.3% on taxable income of more than $61,240 for married couples filing jointly, and $30,620 for single taxpayers.

For some high-income taxpayers, however, rates are above this 9.3% maximum. These high-income brackets and rates are:

- A 10% bracket, starting at $107,464 for individuals other than heads of households or joint filers; and
- An 11% bracket on taxable income of more than $214,929.

For married taxpayers filing jointly, the 10% bracket starts at taxable income levels of $214,929, and the 11% bracket applies to taxable income of more than $429,858. California personal exemption credits are phased out for single taxpayers with taxable income of more than $107,464 and for joint filers with more than $214,929 of federal adjusted gross income (AGI).

Similarly, itemized deductions begin to phase out at the rate of 6% of federal AGI over the same income amounts for the California personal exemption credits just mentioned. Thus, the top marginal California tax rate in certain ranges of income for some high-income individuals was significantly higher in 1994 than the top rate in the recent past, which was only 9.3%.

In addition, the California alternative minimum tax has been increased from 7.0 to 8.5% for individuals. Tax brackets for 1995 will not be announced until September or October 1995.

For additional information on sole proprietorship taxes and requirements, refer to sections 11.4 and 11.5.

Partnerships

Any two or more individuals or entities who agree to contribute money, labor, property, or skill to a business and who agree to share in its profits, losses, and management are considered to have a partnership.

General Partnerships

As a partner in a general partnership, you have the right to share in management and have unlimited personal liability for the partnership's debts, taxes, and other obligations. Partnership agreements are not required by law, but it is sound business practice for you and your partner(s) to draw up a partnership agreement that, at a minimum, outlines basic business issues. Consider consulting an attorney when writing your partnership agreement.

A general partnership in itself is not subject to an income tax; however, it is required to report income and expenses of the partnership on federal and state information returns. The state informational return, *Form 565, Partnership Return of Income*, must be filed with the FTB.

In addition, you and your partner(s) are required to report your share of the partnership's profit or loss on your personal individual income tax returns, *Form 540, California Resident Income Tax Return – Individuals*. If you have nonresident partners, you can file a group return for them.

If your partnership owns real property in the state, you need to file a statement of partnership for the real property in each county where the property is located.[2] The statement must be signed by you and your partners and must include a verification and notarial acknowledgment.

For additional information on requirements for partnerships, refer to sections 11.3 and 11.5.

Limited Partnerships

A limited partnership can be formed between two or more individuals, partnerships, corporations, or other entities. In this type of partnership, limited partners have limited liability and are only liable for the amount of their investment in the partnership.[3] In exchange for this limited liability, limited partners cannot participate in the day-to-day management of the business. That responsibility is left to the general partners who have unlimited liability.[4] A limited partnership must always have at least one general partner and at least one limited partner. There must be a written limited partnership agreement.

In California, limited partnerships follow the California Revised Partnership Act.[5] The act departs from other limited partnership laws in the areas of management and control. For example, under the laws of many states, limited partners who participate in management can lose their limited liability status. In California, however, you can only lose limited liability status, with respect to general creditors of the partnership, if the creditor can prove that your "control" action led him or her to reasonably, but wrongly, believe that you were liable as a general partner.[6] In addition, the revised act allows a limited partner to:

- Consult with and advise the general partner;
- Act as a surety or guarantor of partnership debts or for a general partner;
- Own or direct a general partner;
- Serve on an audit committee;
- Serve on a committee of limited partners for the purpose of approving actions of the general partner; and
- Vote on certain extraordinary matters concerning the partnership.[7]

Another benefit of the revised act is that you, as a limited partner, can lend money to the partnership without automatically subordinating your loans to those of other creditors. If you receive a distribution from a limited partnership, however, you will be liable for repaying the distribution if it didn't leave enough in the partnership to pay existing claims of creditors.

At the time of distribution, the partnership's remaining assets must be worth more than the total of its full-recourse debts. In determining this, for example, the partnership is allowed to count the excess value of real estate secured by a trust deed over the amount of the loan on the property — if, as usual, the loan is nonrecourse.[8]

To form a limited partnership in California, you are required to file a *Certificate of Limited Partnership, Form LP-1*, with the California Secretary of State in Sacramento.[9] The certificate, which must disclose the names of the general partners, does not have to disclose the identities of the limited partners or the amounts contributed to capital. The filing fee is $70.[10]

A California limited partnership should also file copies, certified by the secretary of state, in each county where it does business or owns real estate.[11] Further, a limited partnership cannot bring or maintain a lawsuit in the state courts of California until it files a *Certificate of Limited Partnership*.[12]

Foreign limited partnerships — those formed under the laws of a state other than California — pay a $70 filing fee and file *Form LP-5* with the secretary of state. *Form LP-5* is an application for registering your foreign limited partnership to do business in the state. *Form LP-5* can be obtained from the secretary of state.

Under legislation that went into effect in 1993, every limited partnership that is "doing business" in California or is registered with the secretary of state is liable for an $800 annual minimum tax. This tax is equal to the corporate minimum franchise tax of $800 a year.[13]

This creates a potential tax trap for many limited partnerships that have gone out of business, even if the business dissolved before 1993 when the franchise tax legislation went into effect. Although your limited partnership has dissolved and has filed a "final" tax return, the FTB will now bill the partnership's former general partner for each subsequent year for the $800 minimum tax, plus applicable penalties and interest, until the limited partnership is formally dissolved by filing either *Form LP-3, Certificate of Dissolution – Limited Partnership*, or *Form LP-4, Certificate of Cancellation – Limited Partnership*, with the secretary of state.

Do not overlook this technical detail, particularly if you were a general partner in a now-defunct limited partnership that had registered with the secretary of state and later dissolved, but has not filed one of the above dissolution forms with the California Secretary of State. As a former general partner, you will be held personally liable for the tax, which the FTB will aggressively collect.

Recently, the California Legislature provided some relief from this harsh rule. For a limited partnership that ceased doing business and filed a final tax return before 1993, the FTB will excuse any franchise tax liability if the limited partnership filed a certificate of dissolution or certificate of cancellation with the secretary of state no later than December 31, 1994.[14] For more information on limited partnerships, contact:

Limited Partnerships Division
California Secretary of State
923 12th Street, Suite 301
P.O. Box 944225
Sacramento, CA 95814
(916) 653-3365

Corporations

A corporation is a more complicated form of business because it is considered a distinct legal entity and has a legal status or existence separate from you, the incorporator or owner. One of the main advantages to incorporating your business is that you are not personally liable for the corporation's debts, as long as you comply with all the necessary corporate formalities and recordkeeping requirements.

To learn more about corporate formalities, obtain a copy of *The Essential Corporation Handbook* by Carl Sniffen from your local bookstore or through The Oasis Press.

If you are considering incorporating your business, consult an attorney to be sure you know and understand your responsibilities and options. To form a corporation, you will need to know how to file articles of incorporation, what types of taxes to expect, and how to comply with state securities laws.

A brief overview of some of these issues is presented below. Other requirements are discussed in sections 11.4 and 11.5. Keep in mind, you will need to research more details once you make your decision to incorporate. One office that can help you with state requirements is:

Corporate Division
California Secretary of State
1500 11th Street
Sacramento, CA 95814
(916) 657-5448

For tax questions on corporations, contact your local Franchise Tax Board, or call:

Franchise Tax Board
P.O. Box 942857
Sacramento, CA 94257-0500
(916) 845-6600
(800) 852-5711 (in United States)

Domestic Corporations

If yours is a domestic corporation — one that will be incorporated in California — apply to the secretary of state and:

- Adopt bylaws;
- File your articles of incorporation;
- Pay the $100 filing fee;[15] and
- Make a prepayment of the annual $800 minimum franchise tax.

Legal fees for setting up a corporation will typically run between $500 and $1,000, even for a simple incorporation. If it is necessary to obtain a permit from the California commissioner of corporations to issue stock or securities, legal fees can be much more; however, if a number of conditions for exemptions are met — such as a maximum of 35 stockholders or offering securities only to qualified or financially sophisticated purchasers — a permit from the commissioner of corporations won't be necessary. If such exemption requirements are met, you will only need to file a notice and pay a minimum $25 fee with the commissioner to issue stock and activate your corporation.[16]

Even for the simplest incorporation, the minimum cost of incorporating will be $925 — $100 for the filing fee, $800 for the franchise tax, and $25 for the activation fee. This is in addition to any legal fees.

If you are doing business in California but choose to incorporate outside the state to avoid California taxes and requirements, check with your accountant or attorney. One of the drawbacks of incorporating in another state is that your corporation will have to pay a one-time $350 qualification fee to legally transact business in California.[17] In addition, you will pay all the same taxes and fees as a California corporation and may also be subject to franchise or capital stock taxes in the other states where you incorporate.

If your business is incorporated in another state and you seek to do business in California as a foreign corporation, your corporation is required to file an application for a certificate of qualification and pay a $350 filing fee.[18] The application should state the:

Foreign Corporations

- Name and address of the corporation;
- Address of the principal executive office;
- Address of the principal California office, if any;
- A certificate of good standing from the state of incorporation;
- Name of an agent within the state on whom legal process can be served, if sued; and
- Other information, including consent to service of process on the secretary of state — if the registered agent cannot be located.

California recognizes S corporations and, as a general rule, affords them the same tax treatment as is afforded to S corporations under federal law. An S corporation's income is taxed directly to the shareholders.[19] In addition to taxing the shareholders, there is also a 1.5% franchise tax on its income that must be paid by the corporation. Even if this annual tax is less than $800, an S corporation must still pay the $800 minimum tax. Nevertheless, S corporations that pay out a majority of their income as dividends will considerably reduce their tax burden as compared to a C corporation.

S Corporations

A corporation wishing to elect S corporation status or change from a regular, or C corporation, to an S corporation for tax purposes in a particular tax year is required to file *Form FTB 3560, S Corporation Election or Termination/Revocation*, by the 15th day of the third month of that tax year. S corporations must also file an annual return, *Form 100S, California S Corporation Franchise or Income Tax Return*, with the FTB. For general information on S corporations, see Section 2.5.

California recognizes professional corporations as corporate entities. In professional corporations, only members of the particular profession involved — such as medical, legal, or accounting — may be shareholders. A professional corporation in California is taxed as a corporation and shareholders enjoy limited liability against most creditors.

Professional Corporations

One major exception to this limited liability status, however, is that shareholders do not share limited liability protection against professional malpractice claims.

Once your corporation has completed its initial filings and registered for a business account number, you will have to remember to file its annual report, *Form SO-200, Statement by Domestic Stock Corporation*,[20] and

Annual Reports

pay an annual $5 filing fee.[21] This annual report must be filed with the Corporate Division of the California Secretary of State within 90 days after your articles of incorporation are filed.

After this initial filing, you will need to file the annual report in the six-month period preceding the anniversary date of when your articles were filed. Failure to file this report on time could result in your corporation's charter being revoked or suspended. A similar annual report and $5 fee must be filed by foreign corporations.[22]

Corporate Taxation

In addition to federal taxes affecting corporations, as discussed in Section 2.4, California corporations are subject to several taxes.

The California income and franchise taxes are closely related to each other. They both apply to corporations and they tax a corporation's California income at 9.3%. A corporation, however, is usually only responsible for one or the other.

The franchise tax applies to any corporation that is incorporated in California or doing business within the state. These corporations are subject to the 9.3% franchise tax on the income that is apportioned or allocable to California. Even if all of a domestic corporation's business is conducted elsewhere, the franchise tax still applies. Even if a corporation has little or no income, there is an annual minimum franchise tax of $800 that must be paid.

The income tax applies to corporations incorporated outside California who are not considered to be doing business in the state, but who do receive income from sources within California, such as rental income. This California income is subject to the 9.3% rate. The $800 minimum franchise tax generally does not apply to corporations that are subject to the corporate income tax.

Corporations subject to either the franchise tax or the income tax must file an annual tax return, *Form 100, California Corporation Franchise or Income Tax Return*, with the FTB by the 15th day of the third month following the end of their taxable year.

In addition to applicable income and franchise taxes, domestic and foreign corporations that do business both within and outside of California must apportion their business income between California and elsewhere by using a three-factor formula based on sales, property, and payroll. A California percentage is determined for each of the three factors.

Until California legislation passed in late 1993,[23] the old apportionment method had provided for adding up the three unweighted percentages and dividing their sum by three to arrive at the apportionment percentage that determines the amount of business income subject to California tax. However, for most taxpayers, the formula has been amended, for tax years that began on or after January 1, 1993, to double-weight the sales factor.

Thus, the new formula is:

$$\frac{(2 \ \times \ \text{sales factor}) \ + \ (\text{property factor}) \ + \ (\text{payroll factor})}{4}$$

Double-weighting the sales factor in the formula considerably increases the amount of taxable income that must be apportioned to California for out-of-state companies that have substantial sales in the state, but which have only a small percentage of their property and payroll in California.

If your business will be operating as a corporation, you may be affected by two other taxing methods.

- Unitary Tax System — If you do business in California and have another business under common ownership that does business out-of-state, you need to be aware of the California unitary tax. Like several other states, California's unitary franchise tax is applied not only to a corporation doing business in California, but often it is extended to parent, subsidiary, and brother/sister corporations worldwide.

- "Water's Edge" Unitary Tax System — California has reacted to external pressures and adopted legislation that permits unitary businesses to elect to be taxed under a more limited "water's edge" unitary method rather than the normal, worldwide unitary method that is discussed above. A water's edge election, if permitted, imposes taxes only on a multinational group's U.S. operations and not on its overseas business; thus, taxability extends only to the "water's edge."

For more information concerning the unitary tax and disclosures, contact:

Franchise Tax Board
(916) 845-6600
(800) 852-5711 (in United States)

State Securities Laws

When your newly formed corporation issues shares of its stock to you or to any other shareholders, you must be very careful to comply with both federal and state securities laws. Otherwise, you could be a target for lawsuits from disgruntled investors in your corporation or even criminal prosecution.

In general, when your corporation issues stock in California, the issuance must be approved, or qualified, by the corporations commissioner, unless the stock issuance meets one of the exemptions provided under the California securities laws. There are three separate exemptions from qualification that may apply to your issuance of stock. Most new corporations issuing their original shares of stock can qualify under at least one of these exemptions.

The first two exemptions — the Limited Offering Exemption and the Small Offering Exemption — pertain to an initial issuance of stock by a corporation. These exemptions are primarily for the benefit of small businesses, and a small filing fee of $25 or more must accompany the notice that is filed with the secretary of state, in both cases. If your corporation wishes to issue more stock at some point after its initial issuance of shares, these exemptions may not apply, and you should consult an attorney with expertise in securities law before issuing more stock. The third exemption — the Subsection N exemption — is a new provision enacted in 1994, that exempts any offering of securities from qualification, if a number of conditions are met.

Any issuance of securities under California law, whether under one of the above exemptions or not, is subject to Section 25401 of the California Corporations Code. This section makes it unlawful to offer or sell a security in the state by means of any written or oral communication that includes an untrue statement of a material fact or fails to state a material fact that is necessary to ensure the statements made are not misleading. In short, be completely honest and don't withhold any unfavorable information from any prospective investor in your company's stock, or you will be in big trouble from a securities law standpoint.

In the case of the typical small corporation start up, you will probably be able to qualify for exemption from registering with the Securities and Exchange Commission (SEC), under federal laws, as described in Section 4.14.

For more information about state registration of stock, exemptions, and state securities (or blue sky) laws in general, consult your attorney, or contact the California Secretary of State, Corporate Division.

Limited Liability Companies

California offers you a fourth and relatively new legal form of business organization: the limited liability company (LLC). California was the 46th state to enact LLC legislation, which went into effect September 30, 1994.[24] An LLC, as described in Section 2.6, is not a corporation or a partnership, yet it combines the corporate characteristic of limited liability for owners with partnership-type taxation. Advantages of selecting LLC status, as compared to other legal forms, include:

- Pass-through tax treatment — LLCs are treated as partnerships for federal income tax purposes, as well as for California income tax purposes — taxable income or loss of an LLC "passes through" to you, as one of the owners. Thus, if your business expects to generate taxable losses for some time, your ability to pass through those losses to offset your taxable income from other sources could be an important reason to select LLC status. On the other hand, if your business generates large profits, LLC status will prevent the possible double taxation that can occur when a regular corporation distributes some of its profits to the owners as dividends. However, note that California unlike most other states, does impose some taxes on an LLC, as discussed below. When losses or substantial profits are generated, an LLC can provide tax advantages. In intermediate situations, a regular corporation will probably remain a good choice since it can be used as a separate taxpayer to split taxable income between the firm and its owners.
- Limited liability — Like a corporation, an LLC limits the personal liability of its owners to the amount they have invested or promised to

invest. Unlike a general partnership, you are not liable for the debts of the business beyond that.

- No maximum limitations on number or type of owners — Although most states require an LLC to have at least two owners, it does not have to meet the numerous S corporation requirements — such as no more than 35 shareholders and no corporations or partnerships or certain other types of entities or persons allowed as shareholders.

- Simpler to operate than S corporations — While LLCs are in many ways equivalent to S corporations, they are much simpler to maintain and operate from a tax-compliance and tax-planning perspective. The tax requirements for S corporations are notorious for their complexities and numerous pitfalls which can inadvertently result in loss of S corporation tax status or unpleasant tax surprises.

- Active management participation — Like general partnerships, LLCs may permit all owners to participate in day-to-day management of the business.

To form an LLC under California law, one or more persons, not necessarily members of the LLC, must execute and file articles of organization with the California Secretary of State. Before or after filing articles, the members of the LLC must enter into an operating agreement — preferably in writing — as to how the LLC will be run.[25] An LLC in California must have at least two members.[26] In the case of a sole owner of a business, this is one minor disadvantage of an LLC, as compared to a corporation. However, this restriction could be easily avoided in many cases, by making your spouse a second owner or member of the LLC.

The legal name of an LLC must contain either the words "limited liability company" or "LLC" as the last words in the name. "Limited" and "Company" may be abbreviated to "Ltd." and "Co.," respectively.[27]

An $80 fee must be paid when filing articles of organization with the secretary of state, or, in the case of a foreign LLC, when "qualifying" to do business in California.[28]

Depending upon how an LLC is organized, it will either be treated as a corporation, or in a manner similar to a partnership for California state tax purposes. Accordingly, since most persons setting up an LLC will prefer partnership treatment, it is important that the articles of organization be drafted or reviewed by a competent tax adviser.

If your LLC is structured to qualify for partnership tax treatment, you must file a federal partnership tax return. However, instead of filing a California partnership tax return, *Form 565*, this type of LLC must file a *Form 568* with the FTB, beginning with the 1994 tax year. *Form 568*, which is in many ways very similar to a partnership return, is due by the 15th day of the fourth month after the end of the tax year.[29]

However, two California taxes are imposed on the LLC itself, even though it is otherwise treated like a partnership. First, California LLCs are subject to an $800 annual LLC tax or minimum tax.[30] Also, California LLCs must pay an LLC fee based on its total income — not net — for the year from all sources according to the following table.

Total Income	LLC Fee
Less than $250,000	None
$250,000–499,999	$ 500
$500,000–999,999	1,000
$1,000,000–4,999,999	2,000
More than $5 million	4,000[31]

The LLC fee tax schedule above is for tax years beginning between January 1, 1994 and December 31, 1995. Somewhat higher tax rates will apply in 1996 and later years, and will be subject to annual adjustment by the FTB beginning in 1999.

An LLC that is treated as a corporation is not subject to the above requirements, but instead is subject to the regular corporate franchise tax on its income and must file a California corporation franchise tax return, *Form 100*, or income tax return *Form 200* each year.[32]

LLCs are not necessarily for everyone. Most states have adopted a Limited Liability Company Act, and others are considering similar legislation. While your firm, if set up in the form of an LLC, will have limited liability under California law, and presumably under the law of other states that have adopted LLC laws, there are still unanswered questions about how LLCs will be treated from state to state.

If your firm will be doing business in other states that have not adopted LLC laws, it is unclear at this time whether those states will respect the limited liability provisions of California's LLC law. It is also not clear whether other states will treat your LLC as a partnership for tax purposes, although it seems likely that most other states will as long as the Internal Revenue Service does.

While there are numerous benefits to setting up your business in the form of an LLC in California, a warning is in order. An obscure section of the legislation that established the California Limited Liability Company Law states that no professional person required to be licensed or certified by the state may operate in the form of an LLC.[33]

This seems to clearly prohibit physicians, dentists, lawyers, accountants, and other professionals from practicing in LLC form. However, the California Secretary of State's office is broadly interpreting this limitation to also apply to all manner of licensed businesses, such as auto mechanics, beauty operators, and real estate brokers, and will not accept articles of organization if filed on behalf of such a state-licensed business.

If this strict interpretation is upheld, a great number of businesses in California will be barred from using the LLC as their form of business organization. As of early April 1995, this policy is still in effect, but a change or possible corrective legislation is under active consideration.

To determine whether the advantages of operating as an LLC — if you will be doing business in other states — will outweigh the potential legal and tax risks, consult with your tax attorney and accountant. For more information on LLCs in California, contact:

Limited Liability Company Unit
California Secretary of State
923 12th Street, Suite 300
P.O. Box 944228
Sacramento, CA 94244-2280
(916) 653-3795

11.3 Buying an Existing Business — State Legal Requirements

Buying a business is always a significant undertaking, and as a prospective purchaser, you must investigate the business being acquired as thoroughly as possible to avoid hidden liabilities and pitfalls. Be sure your investigation includes:

- A review of business books and records, including tax returns, payroll records, current receivables and payables, and minute books;
- A physical inventory of all furniture, fixtures, equipment, inventory, and tangible personal or real property being acquired;
- A review of the status of any leases, contracts, or pending litigation;
- A search to determine if the seller has any overdue taxes, such as unemployment tax, owed to the state or federal governments;
- A review of all intangible property rights, such as patent, trade or service marks, and copyrights; and
- Discussions with customers and suppliers of the business.

In many instances, you or the seller may want to keep the potential sale confidential, so your discussions with customers and suppliers may be limited. Any purchase agreement should contain a detailed set of representations and warranties concerning the business being acquired. You may also wish to consider using an escrow or set-off provisions to provide recourse in the event a hidden liability is discovered after closing.

Purchasing an existing business is one endeavor you should not attempt without the assistance of an attorney. For more information on buying a business, refer to Chapter 3. Important environmental laws you need to be aware of when purchasing an existing business are discussed in sections 9.9 and 11.9.

Bulk Sale Law

Although most states have repealed their bulk sale law, California's law is still in effect. When a business sells all or over half of its assets through a major transaction that is not part of its ordinary business activities, or through a sale by an auction or one conducted by a liquidator, the bulk sale law is used to protect the rights of creditors — such as suppliers and others — who have advanced goods or money to a business and have not yet been paid. Most sales involving less than $10,000 or more than $5 million are exempt.[34]

Like most other states that still have such a law, California's bulk sale law follows the general requirements outlined in the Uniform Commercial Code (UCC). This law is of particular importance to you, because as purchaser of an existing business, you are required to perform certain duties under this law to ensure that the rights of the seller's creditors are protected. To comply with this law, both you and the seller have certain responsibilities.

- The seller must provide you with a list of all the business names and addresses used by the seller in the last three years.
- You must give notice of the bulk sale by publication, filing, and by delivery or certified mailing of notice to the county tax collector, as described below.
- You must comply with special additional requirements in the case of certain bulk sales that involve no more than $2 million, where payment is substantially all in cash or a promise to pay cash at a future date.[35]

For transactions subject to the bulk sale law, the seller is required to prepare a notice to creditors of bulk transfer and file it with the county recorder and county tax collector in the county where the business is located. This filing must be made at least twelve days before the sale.[36]

If a copy of the notice is delivered to the county tax collector between March 1 and the last Friday in May, it must be accompanied by a completed business personal property statement covering the property involved in the bulk sale.

The notice must also be published in a general circulation newspaper in both the judicial district where the property is located and where the seller's main California office is located. Publication must occur twelve or more days before the transfer.[37]

Once you have complied with the state requirements above, the burden shifts to the seller's creditors to take some action to protect their rights. Compliance will also protect you from later claims against the assets you have purchased. If you fail to comply with these provisions, it could cause you major financial hardship. To be sure you meet the requirements of the bulk sale law, consult with your attorney.

Recorded Security Interests

Before closing a deal, you should know if there are any security interests or liens against any of the assets of the business that would interfere with your receiving clear title to any part of it. To protect yourself, have your attorney check with the secretary of state's office for any recorded security interests and thoroughly research county, state, and federal records for any judgment liens or other liens, before you finalize your agreement to acquire the property. For a fee, the secretary of state's office will provide a listing of any security interests that have been recorded as a lien against the assets of the business you are buying.

Uniform Commercial Code
Index and Record Division
California Secretary of State
P.O. Box 1738
Sacramento, CA 95812
(916) 445-8062

Of course, if the transaction involves a purchase of real property, you should also have a title search performed to find out if the seller has good title and if there are any recorded deeds of trust or other claims against the property that the seller has not disclosed to you. You also need to make sure that you have adequate means of access to the property.

Unemployment Tax Experience Rating

A company's unemployment tax experience rating determines the amount that must be contributed to the state unemployment insurance fund. If the seller has earned a better state unemployment tax experience rating than you would receive as a new employer, you may wish to explore the option of taking over the seller's rate when you acquire the business.

In California, you have 90 days after the business changes hands to apply to the California Employment Development Department (EDD) for a reserve-account transfer. By doing so, you may be able to succeed to an unemployment tax rate substantially below the new employer rate of 3.4%. Your application should be made on EDD *Form DE 4453*. For more information on unemployment tax experience ratings, contact:

California Employment Development Department
(916) 322-0507

Unemployment Tax Release

In addition to investigating your seller's tax experience rating when you purchase an existing business, look into its history of activity with unemployment taxes. You will want to be sure that the seller has made all the required unemployment reports and payments. If you fail to withhold enough of the purchase price to cover the unpaid employment taxes, you may be held liable for any unpaid taxes.[38]

As a condition of closing the sale, require the seller to obtain a *Certificate of Release of Buyer, Form DE 2220*, from the EDD certifying that all unemployment taxes due the state have been paid by the seller. For more information on the *Certificate of Release of Buyer*, contact your local EDD employment tax district office.

Payroll Tax Release

As purchaser of a business, you should review the payroll liabilities of the business to make certain that all payroll taxes have been paid and withholding deposits have been made. Failure to obtain proper releases may cause you to be liable for unpaid payroll or withholding taxes owed by the seller.

Sales Tax Release

Like the unemployment tax release, you will want to be sure the seller provides you with a sales tax release ensuring that he or she has paid all sales tax obligations before closing the deal. To do this, you must obtain a sales and use tax certificate of no tax due from the State Board of Equalization.

With this certificate's information, you will not be liable for failure to withhold any amount of unpaid taxes from the purchase price because the certificate will tell you if withholding is necessary or not.[39] Your request for the certificate must be made in writing. There is no required form or format for making the request, but be sure to send it by certified mail.

Sale Price Allocation

In California, unlike most states, much of the purchase price for acquiring a business' assets is typically subject to sales tax to the extent that the sale includes tangible assets, such as furniture, equipment, or machinery. Even an otherwise tax-free, stock-for-assets merger transaction — a "Type C reorganization" in tax jargon — between two corporations can result in a sales tax on the assets transferred by the acquired corporation. This is a serious potential sales tax trap, unique to California.

Purchases of inventory for resale, however, are exempt from sales tax. So, to reduce the sales tax on the transaction, you and the seller may decide to allocate more of the purchase price to inventory and less to equipment and machinery in your agreement of sale. Such an allocation may also save on income taxes because you will have a higher tax cost for the inventory, which may be preferable to obtaining a higher depreciation basis for the equipment and machinery.

In addition, allocating more of the sales price to inventory will save personal property taxes because inventory is exempt from the personal property tax in California, while furniture, equipment, and machinery used in the business are not.

Real Estate Transfer

If you are purchasing a business that owns real property in California, be aware that the change of ownership must be reported to the county tax assessor on a timely basis. Your real property taxes may be much higher than the seller's when the property is reassessed at its current value versus the Proposition-13-assessed value upon which the seller's tax was based. Also, if the seller is not a California resident, you may be required to withhold California income tax or franchise tax from the purchase price.

Environmental Warranties

Today, many purchasers of businesses are being held liable for the environmental problems created by their predecessors. There are many federal and state laws and regulations regarding the environment you must consider. Environmental laws pertain to air, water, storage of hazardous materials — including some very common household-type products — waste disposal, underground storage tanks, and other matters. Clean-up costs can sometimes exceed the cost of the property acquired.

As a result, you may want to consider an environmental audit of the property before you buy it. The audit would test the soil and water of any real estate being acquired to determine the environmental condition of the property. The purchase agreement should contain detailed representations and warranties of the seller stating that:

- The seller has not violated any environmental law or regulation; and
- The seller will reimburse you against any cost or liability imposed for environmental problems occurring before the acquisition.

For additional information about environmental matters, refer to sections 9.9 and 11.9.

11.4 State Requirements that Apply to Nearly All New Businesses

Regardless of the legal form of business organization you choose, your business will be required to comply with a number of state requirements, such as obtaining business licenses, paying various taxes, and registering your fictitious business name.

There are also local requirements, taxes, and restrictions that may apply to your business. Like state requirements and taxes, local requirements can change every year. Before starting your business, contact the appropriate state or local government agencies to make sure your business complies with state and local laws. This section introduces you to several basic state requirements and offers further information on what you need to do.

Business Licenses and Permits

If you start a business in California, you may need at least one license from the state and others from the city or county in which you conduct business. To find out what type of local license you may need, contact your city hall or county clerk's office. As stated in sections 4.3 and 9.9, make sure your business also conforms to local zoning laws, building codes, health and environmental requirements, and fire and police regulations by obtaining the necessary permits.

State Licenses

Many occupations and businesses are required to be licensed in California. Fees vary widely among the different types of businesses and occupations. The more than 100 different types of licenses and permits are usually granted based on a combination of requirements, such as registration, bonding, education, experience, and passage of licensing exams.

Because it is illegal to engage in any of these regulated businesses or professions without being licensed, find out whether there is a state licensing requirement for the business you plan to start and, if so, determine whether and how you will be able to comply with the licensing requirements.

While a number of businesses and occupations are regulated by other state agencies, most licenses are granted by departments or divisions of the California Department of Consumer Affairs or the California Trade and Commerce Agency. Either of these agencies will generally be able to advise you as to which division or department, if any, you must apply to for a state license.

California Department of Consumer Affairs
(916) 445-1254

California Trade and Commerce Agency
(916) 322-1394

For a detailed listing of occupations and businesses that require state licenses, and for the applicable agency contacts, refer to Section 11.6.

Estimated Income Taxes

One of the most surprising concepts to new entrepreneurs is that, as a business owner, you will have to estimate how much money you will make before you make it. Then several times each year, you must pay taxes on the amount you have estimated.

No matter which business form you choose, filing and paying California estimated taxes must now become part of your regular agenda. If you don't have the money to pay estimated income taxes, get your accountant's advice on whether you should get a loan to cover the tax when due or pay underpayment penalties to the government after the end of the year. Note that any state tax penalties you pay — unlike the state tax itself — will not be allowed as a deduction on your federal tax return.

If your business is a sole proprietorship or partnership, you must report the business income — whether it is actually distributed to you or not — on your personal tax return. If you are just starting your business, contact your state income tax office to get estimated tax forms. To be sure you handle the estimating, filing, and paying correctly, consult your accountant.

After your first year of paying estimated taxes to the state, you will probably automatically receive forms to use in future years, but even if the forms don't come, you are still responsible for filing and paying on time.

Individual

California individual estimated tax filing requirements for a sole proprietor or partner are virtually identical to federal estimated tax requirements. One difference between the two, however, is that federal tax law requires estimated tax equal to 90% of the tax for the year be paid during the year, while California generally only requires 80% be paid.[40] Section 4.6 discusses federal estimated income taxes.

Similar to federal law, California individual estimated tax vouchers, *Form 540-ES*, are due on April 15, June 15, September 15, and January 15 of the following year. Any remaining unpaid California personal income tax is due on April 15 of the following year with your California personal income tax return, *Form 540*, for California residents, or *Form 540-NR*, for nonresidents.

Corporate

As mentioned in Section 11.2, if your business is incorporated in California, you are required to pay an initial $800 minimum franchise tax at the time of incorporation. Approximately three and a half months after your date of incorporation, you will have to pay your first estimated tax payment, even if your corporation does not have taxable income. This first payment must also be at least $800. After this, California corporate estimated tax rules generally follow the federal estimated tax rules for corporations. Each subsequent year, the minimum California estimated tax due for the first quarter must be at least equal to the annual $800 minimum franchise tax.

Payments of estimated franchise tax can be mailed in with the estimated tax voucher, *Form 100-ES*. To avoid underpayment penalties, California generally requires corporations to pay 95% of the estimated franchise tax each quarter.[41] Tax payments are due in four installments, based on this schedule:

Estimated Tax Payment Schedule for Corporations

1st Payment – 25% of estimated tax is due on the 15th day of the fourth month of the fiscal year (April 15 for calendar-year corporations).

2nd Payment – 25% of estimated tax is due on the 15th day of the sixth month of the fiscal year (June 15 for calendar-year corporations).

3rd Payment – 25% of estimated tax is due on the 15th day of the ninth month of the fiscal year (September 15 for calendar-year corporations).

4th Payment – 25% of estimated tax is due on the 15th day of the twelfth month of the fiscal year (December 15 for calendar-year corporations).

Both individuals and corporations send their estimated tax payments to the Franchise Tax Board.

Electronic Payments

California requires corporate taxpayers paying $20,000 or more of estimated tax in a quarter, or having $80,000 or more of tax liability for the year, to make the tax payments by electronic funds transfer (EFT). If you are required to make your payments using EFT, there is an EFT Helpline.

Franchise Tax Board
(916) 369-4025

Penalties

If you do not make your estimated tax payments on time, you will be charged interest. If 100% of the previous year's tax liability was paid in a timely manner during the current year, generally there is not a penalty for underpayment of estimated tax, except for certain large corporations or banks that had taxable income of one million dollars or more during any one of the three tax years preceding the current year.[42]

Sales and Use Taxes

If your business is involved in retail sales, you are required to pay tax on sales or rentals of tangible personal property (not real estate). The tax is legally imposed on the seller and must be collected from the purchaser by the seller.

Tax Rates

The statewide sales tax rate in California is 7.25%. Six percent goes to the state and 1.25% to local governments. In addition to the statewide rate of 7.25%, local taxing districts in many urbanized counties may enact public transit and other local district sales taxes of up to a maximum of 1.5%. Combined sales tax rates in the counties that have additional local sales taxes are as follows:

Counties	Tax Rate
San Francisco	8.50%
Alameda, Contra Costa, Los Angeles, San Benito, Santa Cruz, and San Mateo counties	8.25
Del Norte, Fresno, Imperial, Inyo, Madera, Orange, Riverside, Sacramento, San Bernardino, San Joaquin, and Santa Barbara counties	7.75
Santa Clara	7.75**
Sonoma County	7.50
San Diego	7.00*
Monterey	6.50*

* Temporary tax rate due to refund of unconstitutional tax. Contact any State Board of Equalization office for current rates.

** Voter approved transportation authority tax of 0.5% will not go into effect until approval by courts.

In addition, the city of Calexico in Imperial County has adopted a 0.5% sales tax, raising the rate in Calexico to 8.25%, and portions of Fresno have a 7.85% rate. An additional 0.5% tax goes into effect in Clearlake City in Lake County in July 1995.

Knowing when a local district sales tax applies to a particular transaction is important and can be tricky to determine. In general, a retailer located in a taxing district (such as a transit district) must collect sales tax at that district's tax rate unless the property is shipped outside the district — as per the contract of sale — by a common carrier (such as a trucking company) or the seller's own vehicle.

On the other hand, a retailer who ships merchandise into another local tax district is only required to collect that district's tax if the retailer is considered to be doing business within that district.

To be considered doing business within a district, you need to:

- Maintain an office, warehouse, or other place in that district;
- Own or lease property in the district; or
- Use your own vehicle to deliver the goods there.

Exemptions

A considerable number of transaction categories are exempt from the state's sales and use tax. Probably the most significant exemption is for food products, although this does not apply to restaurant meals and sales of liquor. Detailed information regarding sales tax exemptions is available from your local State Board of Equalization (SBE) office.

Seller's Permit

With a limited number of exceptions, every business that will sell tangible personal property, such as merchandise, is required to obtain a seller's permit from the SBE. A separate seller's permit must be obtained for each place of business that sells property subject to tax. To obtain a permit, submit a completed application form, *Form BT-400-MIP*, or *Form BT-400-MCO*, to the SBE. Applications may be submitted in person or by mail. A sample copy of *Form BT-400-MIP* is included at the end of this book. There is no fee for obtaining a seller's permit, and depending on the type of business and conditions surrounding ownership, you may not have to post a security deposit.

Pamphlet 73 outlines your sales and use tax obligations as a seller's permit holder and provides a list of sales and use tax regulations you can obtain from the board. These various regulations cover almost every conceivable kind of business subject to sales and use taxes. You can request this form from any SBE office.

Use Tax

Use tax is intended to tax the use of all property purchased outside the state but actually used within California. Use tax also applies to items that were exempt from sales tax when purchased — such as items bought for resale — that you end up using instead of reselling.

In general, federal law has prevented states from collecting use tax on mail order sales occurring in interstate commerce where the out-of-state mail order company had no activity in the taxing state other than solicitation by catalog or flyer and delivery of the purchased items by common carrier or the mail.

In 1987, the California Legislature attempted to maneuver around these federal restrictions, by extending the definition of "retailer" to include most out-of-state mail order sellers. In 1992, the U.S. Supreme Court held that a North Dakota law attempting to do the same thing was invalid under U.S. law, so it now appears that California will no longer be able to enforce these far-reaching mail order provisions.[13]

The California law, however, does provide that out-of-state retailers owned or controlled by California retailers in the same or similar line of business are considered to be engaging in business in California and must collect use tax on sales destined for California. The same provision applies to franchise or license owners with franchisees or licensees operating under a trade name in California. The state will apparently continue to attempt to enforce most of these provisions.

Resale Certificate

When you purchase merchandise your business will resell, lease, or rent to others, you are exempt from paying sales tax on it if you have given the seller a resale certificate to keep on file. This certificate shows the seller that the state has authorized your business to resell that merchandise, so sales tax does not have to be collected on the merchandise until you resell it later.

A blank form of a resale certificate, which you may reproduce, is provided for your use at the end of this book, along with a copy of *Sales and Use Tax Regulations* for more specifics on resale certificates. You may also buy blank resale certificate forms at most stationery or office supply stores in California.

Even if you will be selling at wholesale only, you must obtain a seller's permit. As a wholesaler or manufacturer, you will not have to collect sales tax on goods you sell to a retailer or wholesaler for resale if the retailer or wholesaler holds a valid seller's permit and provides you with a resale certificate during the transaction.

The SBE implemented a program that allows you to check whether a seller who gives you a resale certificate holds a valid seller's permit. You can now quickly check the validity of any resale certificate number by telephoning the SBE, Monday through Friday, 8:30 A.M. to 4:30 P.M. To do so, call the SBE district office that handles your sales and use tax account.

State Board of Equalization Resale Verification Offices

Oakland	(510) 286-4321	**San Jose**	(408) 277-1003
Sacramento	(916) 324-2397	**Santa Ana**	(714) 558-4296
San Diego	(619) 525-4532	**Van Nuys**	(818) 901-5525

Sales Tax Returns

Sales and use tax returns are usually required to be filed and any taxes paid within one month after the end of each calendar quarter. Larger businesses may be required to make more frequent payments. Sales and use taxes collected generally are reported on *Form BT-401*. A new and simplified sales and use tax form, *Form BT-401EZ*, is now available for some businesses. Those eligible to use the new, simpler form include businesses that operate from a single location in the county, and do not:

- Sell fuel, automobiles, boats, aircraft, or make sales to aircraft common carriers;
- Claim a credit on the return for prepayments or for sales tax paid to other states;
- Engage in fixed-price contracts or leases; and

- Claim exemptions for returned merchandise, tax-paid purchases that are resold, cash discounts, bad debts, or a manufacturer's state tax exemption or other exempt transactions that are not provided for on the simplified form.

Recordkeeping

If you sell or lease tangible personal property, the sales and use tax law requires you to keep complete records of the gross receipts from sales or rentals, whether or not the receipts are believed to be taxable. You also are required to keep adequate and complete records to substantiate all deductions claimed on sales and use tax returns and of the total purchase price of all tangible personal property bought for sale, lease, or consumption in California.

For more information on sales taxes and requirements, contact your nearest State Board of Equalization office. There are 47 field offices statewide. Check your local phone directory under government listings or see the list at the back of this book.

Property Taxes

You do not need to contact the county tax assessor's office regarding payment of any real property taxes on real estate acquired for your business. The office will contact you by mailing a property tax bill to the owner of record; however, when you purchase real estate — including real estate held by a corporation, if you buy more than 50% of the corporation's stock — you should notify the county assessor of the change in property ownership.

The county assessor's office will reassess the property at its current value under the Jarvis-Gann Amendment to the California Constitution: Proposition 13. In most counties, the tax assessor will automatically pick up the transaction when the deed is recorded. If they fail to do so and you haven't given timely notice, you will be subject to penalty. Real property taxes are due in two installments each year, on April 10 and December 10.

Business Personal Property Tax Statement

If your business owns $30,000 or more (at cost) of taxable personal property in its initial assessment year, or $100,000, at cost, in any subsequent year, you must file a business personal property tax statement each year. The tax statement is based on the personal property your business owns, claims, possesses, controls, or manages in its respective county as of 12:01 A.M. on the first day of March.[44] Persons with less than $30,000 of taxable personal property must file a business personal property tax statement only if requested by the county assessor.

The statement is due between April 1 and the last Friday in May each year, depending upon the deadline adopted by the particular county. There is a 10% penalty assessment on any unreported property.[45]

Exemptions

The personal property tax applies to most types of tangible personal property of a business, except inventory, which is exempt from the property tax. Intangible personal property items, such as stocks, bonds, money, and insurance policies, are not subject to property taxes in California.

Information Returns

California has a whole body of tax information reporting requirements practically identical to those for the IRS *Form 1099* series of information returns. In fact, to meet these state reporting requirements, California has taxpayers file copies of federal 1099 forms with the Franchise Tax Board (FTB). The *Form 1099* series is used to report any payments of $600 or more made to any person during the calendar year for items such as rent, compensation for services, commissions, interest, plus other items of fixed or determinable income. To learn more about the *Form 1099* series, refer to Section 4.7.

In addition, trades and businesses in California receiving cash payments in excess of $10,000 are required to file a copy of the IRS information return, *Form 8300*, with the FTB. Note that, under both the federal and California cash reporting laws, "cash" generally includes most kinds of monetary instruments, including checks other than personal checks. A copy of the federal *Form 8300* must be filed with the FTB within 15 days after a reportable transaction.

California requires that certain information returns be filed on magnetic media rather than on paper. These include: forms *1099-DIV, 1099-INT, 1099-OID,* and *1099-PATR* when there are more than 50 payees; and forms *1099-G, 1099-R, 1099-MISC, 5498,* and *W-2G,* if there are more than 250 payees. All *Form 1099-B* returns must be filed on magnetic media.

FIRPTA Withholding

In addition to the income tax withholding that is required on employee wages — see Section 11.5 — California tax law has developed a trend toward requiring income tax withholding in various other business situations.

For example, California has enacted a withholding tax requirement based on the federal Foreign Investment in Real Property Tax Act (FIRPTA) that applies to the purchase of California real estate from persons living outside the United States or out-of-state residents.[46] Under this California law, you, as the California purchaser, must withhold California income tax on a real estate transaction when:

- The seller is a foreign person;
- Such withholding is required under the federal FIRPTA rules (see Section 4.9); or
- The seller has an out-of-state address.

The amount of California income or franchise tax that must be withheld is equal to one-third of the federal tax required to be withheld on the transaction. The California tax must be paid to the FTB along with *Form 597* within 20 days after the transaction, with a copy of the federal *Form 8288* attached. Some smaller transactions are exempt.

Out-of-State Contractors

Another example of this income tax withholding trend deals with out-of-state, independent contractors. If you pay a nonresident, independent contractor more than $1,500 in a calendar year for services performed in California, the FTB requires you to withhold California income tax — generally at the rate of 7% — on these payments.[47] Examples of these types of independent contractors include construction workers and professional athletes.

This withholding applies only to payments made to an independent contractor that are reported on federal *Form 1099*. Amounts withheld are to be remitted to the FTB on *Form FTB 591* and *Form 592*. Legislation has been pending to extend withholding to all payments to independent contractors, resident and nonresident. This would result in an enormous administrative burden on every California business that uses independent contractors.

Partners Outside California

Partnerships doing business in California must also withhold personal income tax on distributions to partners who do not reside in California.

- For foreign (non-U.S.) partners, partnerships should withhold at the maximum California personal or corporation income tax rate.[48]
- For domestic partners living in other states, partnerships should withhold 7%, if total California-source income distributed to that partner exceeded $1,500 during the calendar year.

Fictitious or Assumed Business Name

An assumed, fictitious, or trade name is any name used in the course of business that does not include the full legal name of all the owners of the business. If your business goes by any name other than your own real name, your business is operating under a fictitious name. A fictitious name might also suggest the existence of additional owners by using such words as "company," "associates," or "group."

If you operate a sole proprietorship and use your own true name in the business name, you do not have to register the name. This is also true for a partnership whose business name includes the last names of all the general partners. A corporation is not considered to be using a fictitious name unless it does business under a name other than the exact corporate name that is stated in its articles of incorporation. No one may adopt a fictitious business name that includes the complete words or abbreviations of "Limited Liability Company," "LLC," or "LC," except for an entity that is, in fact, organized as a limited liability company under the laws of either California or another jurisdiction.[49]

Why register your trade name? The purpose of trade or fictitious business name registration is to provide a public record of all the owners of a business. If you don't register, you will not be able to bring a lawsuit on your behalf to the state's courts. This includes any lawsuit, not just suits related to the use of a business name. Another reason to register your trade or business name is to ensure no one else can use that name in the future, assuming, of course, you are the first user of that name. Although being the first to register a certain name probably keeps any other business in your industry from using that name in the state, it is not a universal guarantee. If name protection is critical to your business — especially if you will be marketing in more than one state — it is best to discuss your situation with an attorney who specializes in this area of law.

To register your trade or fictitious business name, file a fictitious business name statement within 40 days of opening your business with the county clerk of the county where your principal place of business is located.[50] Most county clerks furnish fictitious business name statement forms without charge. There is, however, a $10 filing fee for the first business name, and $2 for each additional name.[51]

Within 30 days after filing the statement with the county clerk, it must be published in a newspaper of general circulation in the same county.[52] This notice must appear once a week for four consecutive weeks with not less than five days between publishing dates. An affidavit showing that it was published must be filed with the county clerk not more than 30 days after the last date of publication.[53]

Many area newspapers provide the form for filing, publish the notice, and file the affidavit. An easier way to obtain these services may be to contact the California Newspaper Service Bureau. For a fee, this bureau will send you all the necessary forms — complete with instructions on how to fill them out — and once you fill out and return these forms to the bureau, they will then file and publish the fictitious business name statement for you. For an additional fee, they will also make a preliminary check of your proposed business name before the filing.

California Newspaper Service Bureau
Fictitious Business Name Department
915 East First Street
Los Angeles, CA 90012
(213) 229-5500
(800) 788-7840 (in United States)

Trademarks and Service Marks

Trademarks and service marks used in interstate commerce can be registered with the United States Patent Office, Washington, D.C. See Section 9.5. You can register your local trademark or service mark in California by filing with the secretary of state's office, who can issue a certificate of registration. For more information, contact:

Trademark Division
California Secretary of State
923 12th Street, Room 301
Sacramento, CA 95814
(916) 445-9872

Checklist of State Requirements

In addition to those requirements listed in Section 4.13, the following checklist summarizes the primary requirements you will need to satisfy to start a business in California whether or not you have employees. If

you have employees, the following section describes additional requirements for your business.

☐ Determine if your particular business requires a state license to operate. If in doubt, check with the California Department of Consumer
Affairs or the California Trade and Commerce Agency.

☐ Be prepared to make California estimated income tax payments —
franchise tax in the case of a corporation — immediately.

☐ Apply for a sales and use tax seller's permit from the State Board of
Equalization office nearest you.

☐ File quarterly or more frequent sales and use tax returns, if sales or use
tax must be collected, on *Form BT-401* or, if eligible, on *Form BT-401EZ*.

☐ File change of ownership statement with the county assessor, if your
business has acquired real estate, even if you bought the stock of an
incorporated business that already owned real estate in California.

☐ File with the county clerk and publish a fictitious business name statement. Then, file an affidavit of publication with the county clerk.

☐ File a business personal property tax statement with the county assessor, if requested, or if the cost of your business' taxable personal property on March 1 equals or exceeds $30,000 ($100,000 after initial year).

☐ If you acquire California real estate from a foreign person or out-of-
state resident, withhold California income tax or franchise tax.

☐ For a sole proprietorship, report any income or loss on your California
personal income tax return, *Form 540*.

☐ Withhold California income tax if you make total yearly payments
that exceed $1,500 to a nonresident, independent contractor for ser-
vices performed within the state.

☐ For a partnership, withhold California income tax on distributions to
foreign partners and to domestic (U.S.) nonresident partners.

☐ For a partnership, file a statement of partnership in each county where
the partnership owns real property.

☐ Your partnership must file *Form 565* and each partner must report his
or her share of the partnership's income or loss on *Form 540*.

☐ For a limited partnership, file *Certificate of Limited Partnership, Form
LP-1*, with the secretary of state and copies in counties where the partnership has places of business or real estate. Pay $800 annual mini-
mum tax.

☐ For a limited liability company, file articles of organization with the
secretary of state and adopt an operating agreement. If the LLC is taxable as a partnership, pay an annual LLC tax of $800 plus applicable
LLC fee, based on gross receipts, if any. Also, file LLC annual tax
return *Form 568*. If the LLC is taxable as a corporation, file corporation franchise tax return *Form 100* and pay regular corporate franchise
tax, instead of the LLC tax or the LLC fee.

☐ For a corporation, file articles of incorporation, adopt bylaws, and observe necessary corporate formalities. Also file *Form 100*, the franchise income tax return, annually. S corporations file *Form 100S*.

☐ File annual state tax information returns, using copies of the federal *Form 1099* series.

11.5 Additional Requirements for Businesses with Employees

Once you hire an employee to work in your business, you take on several additional responsibilities. In California, you will need to withhold and pay certain payroll taxes, obtain workers' compensation insurance, comply with safety and health regulations, and know your rights and those of your employees under various labor laws. This section discusses these requirements in further detail and recommends publications and assistance programs offered by various agencies. General considerations and federal requirements are covered in Chapter 5.

Withholding Taxes

Like the federal government, the state of California requires you to withhold and pay state personal income tax (PIT) on wages paid to your employees.[54] When you hire an employee, you need him or her to complete either federal *Form W-4* or state *Form DE 4, Employee's Withholding Allowance Certificate*. These forms tell you the appropriate rate to withhold from his or her wages. To find out when and what forms to use to file your PIT withholdings, refer to the California Tax Withholding Summary below. For information on California's withholding tax tables, contact the California Employment Development Department (EDD).

State Disability Insurance Contributions

In addition to PIT withholding, you must withhold state disability insurance (SDI) contributions from your employees' wages. The SDI contribution rate for 1995 is 1.0% of an employee's wages up to the first $31,767.00 paid in a calendar year,[55] or a maximum SDI withholding obligation of $317.67 per year, per employee.

You, as the employer, are not subject to SDI, but you are required to collect the tax from your employees. SDI contributions are paid to the state together with PIT withholdings whenever a PIT payment is required. *Form DE 88* is used to make payments by all employers except those making electronic payments. As occurs almost every year, California has significantly revamped its employer withholding rules. Effective for 1995, a new quarterly payroll tax return, *Form DE 6*, was introduced for employers required to withhold PIT or SDI. *Form DE 6* requires you to report the following items on each employee:

▪ Name;
▪ Social security number;

- Total wages paid; and
- Total California personal income tax withheld.[56]

You must continue to pay PIT on a quarterly, monthly, or more frequent basis. These payments will be reconciled at the end of the year by filing either a new annual reconciliation return, *Form DE 7* for annual filers[57] no later than January 31 of the following year, or *Form DE 43 Annual Reconciliation* for quarterly filers, due by February 28. Also, many employers will no longer be required to file copies of the employee wage statements (W-2 forms) with the EDD — at least not for 1995.[58]

Under the new withholding deposit rules, as a California employer that is required to make federal withholding tax deposits, you must remit withheld PIT and SDI once the accumulated amount of PIT exceeds $500 — within the same number of banking days as is required for deposits of federal withholding.[59]

Starting in 1996, the $500 threshold will be adjusted annually, to an amount as low as $75 if interest rates earned on the state Pooled Investment Fund are over 9%, or remain at the current $500 level if interest rates are under 4%. The deposit threshold remains at $350, as in 1994, if you are not required to make federal withholding deposits. In this case, you must make payments by the 15th day of the month after a month in which $350 of withheld PIT has accumulated.[60]

The following table summarizes how the new California payroll tax deposit rules mesh with the federal tax deposit requirements, for employers who are required to withhold state PIT and SDI.

1995 California Withholding Tax Summary

Your Federal Deposit Schedule	And You Have Accumulated State PIT Withholding	SDI & PIT Deposit Required	If Pay Day Is	Deposit Due By
Next banking day	$500 or less	No	N/A	N/A
Next banking day	More than $500	Yes	N/A	Next banking day
Semi-weekly	$500 or less	No	N/A	N/A
Semi-weekly	More than $500	Yes	Wed., Thur., or Friday	Following Wednesday
Semi-weekly	More than $500	Yes	Sat., Sun., Mon., or Tue.	Following Friday
Monthly	$500 or less	No	N/A	N/A
Monthly	More than $500	Yes	N/A	15th of the next month
Quarterly	Less than $350	No	N/A	Remit with quarterly report
Quarterly	$350 or more	Yes	N/A	15th of the next month

The rules outlined in the table are likely to change every year, as well as the fluctuating $500 threshold amount. Large employers are subject to different rules. You may wish to contact EDD for more information on current filing and deposit requirements after 1995.

If you make deposits averaging $20,000 or more over any one year period ending June 30th, you are required to make payment by electronic funds transfer (EFT) during the following calendar year.

New employers are required to register with the EDD on *Form DE 1* for commercial employers and obtain an eight-digit employer identification number. See the following discussion of unemployment taxes for details on when and where to register.

Once you have registered as an employer with the EDD, you should automatically receive an initial supply of *Form DE 88* tax payment forms; however, it is your responsibility to order more DE 88 forms in time to file, before you run out of them. You will also need to obtain *Form DE 1857, Notice to Employees of Unemployment Insurance and Disability Insurance*. This notice must be posted if you are subject to disability and unemployment insurance taxes. *Form DE 1857* is available through the California Employment Development Department.

State Unemployment Tax

If your business employs one or more individuals and your payroll totals $100 in any calendar quarter in the current or preceding year, you will be responsible for registering for and paying unemployment insurance tax.[61] These payments or contributions provide unemployment compensation for workers who become involuntarily unemployed. If you are required to pay California unemployment tax, you must register as an employer with the EDD.[62]

The tax ranges from 1.1 to a maximum of 5.4% and is imposed on the first $7,000 of wages per employee. The current rate for new employers is 3.4%, a rate that will apply until you establish your own tax experience rating. You must also pay an additional 0.1% employment training tax (ETT) on the first $7,000 of wages per employee if you have a positive reserve account balance — more was contributed than claimed in benefits.

The taxes are imposed on your employees' covered wages, but it is illegal to deduct this tax from their wages. You, as the employer, are responsible for paying the state unemployment tax and, if applicable, the employment training tax.

If you are the owner of a sole proprietorship or a partner in a partnership, you do not have to pay unemployment tax for yourself since you are not considered an employee of the business.

If your business is subject to this tax, you must obtain a registration number from the California Employment Development Department (EDD). This must be done within 15 days after having paid more than $100 in wages for the first time.

To register, complete *Form DE-1* and submit it to the EDD office listed below. There are different types of DE-1's for different types of businesses. The EDD will help you choose the form that best suits your type of business. A sample copy of the DE-1 for commercial employers is included at the end of this book.

California Employment Development Department – MIC-28
P.O. Box 826880
Sacramento, CA 94280-0001
(916) 654-7041

Tax Experience Rating

The rate at which you will have to pay unemployment tax is called an unemployment tax experience rating. This rate is a risk-based system depending upon the amount of unemployment benefits paid to your former employees as it relates to the total wages your company has paid over a period of years. For example, the more former employees who claim benefits, the higher your experience rating. Conversely, the fewer former employees claiming benefits, the lower your rate. To find out how you can save on unemployment taxes, see Section 11.8.

If you are a new employer, you will be assigned a standard rate by the state. This rate may increase or decrease over the course of time, depending in large part on your unemployment experience history. If you are purchasing a business and you would like to take over the previous employer's rate, see Section 11.3.

State Employer ID Number

If you have already applied for a sales tax seller's permit on *Form BT-400* with the State Board of Equalization, and if you indicated on the application that you will pay wages in excess of $100 in a calendar quarter, the EDD will use that application to assign an eight-digit state employer identification number to your business. The EDD will then send you a notice with your new account number along with a DE-1 registration form to complete and return to the EDD.

This new account number will be used on all state employment tax returns and forms. The EDD is responsible for administering the state Personal Income Tax (PIT) withholding, the state disability insurance (SDI) contributions, the state unemployment insurance (UI) tax, and employment training tax contributions. All required forms and payments are sent to this department.

Publications

You can request a copy of the *California Employer's Guide, Form DE 44,* which is available at no cost, from any local EDD Employment Tax District Office.

To receive the DE 44 or other EDD forms and publications (25 or less) you may also contact the EDD forms request line. If you would like to receive more than 25 forms, please request the preprinted EDD form *Requisition for Employment Development Department Publications.* A sample of this form is located in the back of this book.

California Employment Development Department
805 R Street, Warehouse
Sacramento, CA 95814-6497
(916) 654-7043 (Forms request line)

Workers' Compensation Insurance

Workers' compensation insurance is a state-mandated insurance require-ment for most companies.[63] As the owner of a sole proprietorship, a part-ner in a partnership, or the sole stockholder of an employer corporation, you do not have to obtain workers' compensation for yourself.[64] You are, however, required to provide it for your employees.

Workers' compensation insurance provides wage loss and medical bene-fits to employees injured on the job and it protects you from legal action for damages for injuries or job-related illnesses suffered by your employ-ees. Be aware that neither general liability nor health and accident insur-ance can properly substitute for workers' compensation insurance.

Although many insurance companies offer workers' compensation cover-age in California, some companies may be reluctant to write a policy that covers only one or a few employees, unless it is tied to other types of insurance policies.

If you experience difficulty in obtaining the necessary coverage, contact your local workers' compensation insurance commission office for the names of insurance carriers. If that fails, you might try the State Com-pensation Insurance Fund, an organization created by the California Legislature to provide this line of insurance at competitive rates. To con-tact this organization, check your local phone directory for the office nearest you.

As an employer, you are also required by California law to:

- Notify new employees in writing, by the end of their first pay period, of their right to workers' compensation in case they incur a job-related injury or illness;[65]
- Notify injured employees of their benefits and give them a claim form, *Form DWC-1*, within 24 hours of an injury;[66]
- Post the *Notice of Compensation Carrier* that provides the insurance carrier's name and advises employees of their rights to compensation if injured on the job and to select their own physician;[67] and
- Report all work-related injuries.

For more information on workers' compensation, contact:

State Compensation Insurance Fund
2275 Gateway Oaks Drive
Sacramento, CA 95833
(916) 924-5155

Safety and Health Regulations

As an employer in California, you will have to comply with state and federal job safety laws designed to prevent injuries resulting from unsafe or unhealthy working conditions. California administers its own occupational safety and health programs through the California Department of Industrial Relations, Division of Occupational Safety and Health (DOSH).

California has its own extensive body of laws and regulations dealing with on-the-job employee health and safety — similar to the federal Occupational Safety and Health Administration (OSHA) provisions — as well as a large enforcement staff.

The Cal/OSHA provisions are far too extensive and complex to deal with in a book of this nature; however, there are several general points listed on the next few pages regarding your legal obligations as an employer under Cal/OSHA provisions. For further information, contact:

Division of Occupational Safety and Health (DOSH)
California Department of Industrial Relations
455 Golden Gate Avenue, Room 5205
San Francisco, CA 94102
(415) 703-4341

Written Safety Program

Senate Bill 198 — known as the Injury and Illness Prevention Program (IIPP) law — requires every California business, regardless of size, to implement and maintain a written injury and illness prevention program.

Among other requirements, your program must include the seven specific components listed below.

- A demonstrated management commitment and assignment of responsibilities;
- A system for assuring employee compliance with safe work practices;
- A safety communication system with employees;
- A scheduled inspection and evaluation system;
- Abatement procedures to fix unsafe and unhealthy conditions;
- An accident investigation program; and
- Safety/health training and instruction.[68]

DOSH strictly enforces the requirements of the IIPP law. If even one of the requirements is missing or improperly implemented, your business will be cited for noncompliance and fined a substantial amount of money.

For help in complying with the IIPP law, obtain a copy of the *Safety Law Compliance Manual for California Businesses* by John R. Spooner, available from The Oasis Press. This step-by-step guide explains in easy-to-understand language exactly what the IIPP law is about. It addresses each requirement and walks you through the process of developing a program, writing a plan, training an employee to conduct the program, and preparing the required notices for distribution.

A companion workbook, *Our Company Injury & Illness Prevention Program Binder*, is also available from The Oasis Press. This workbook includes ready-made forms, logs, checklists, and sample documents to help you implement your program. For ordering information, contact:

The Oasis Press
(800) 228-2275

Another helpful resource is the *SB 198 Handbook*, available for $45 from the California Chamber of Commerce. A 25% discount is available for chamber members.

California Chamber of Commerce
P.O. Box 1736
Sacramento, CA 95812-1736
(800) 331-8877

Notice to Employees

Your business must post a permanent job safety notice to employees in each place of employment.[69] A fine of up to $7,000 may be imposed for failure to post this notice.[70] A copy of the notice *Safety and Health Protection on the Job – CAL/OSHA Form 1000* can be obtained by contacting the California Department of Industrial Relations, Communications Division. You can also contact the EDD.

Communications Division – Posters
California Department of Industrial Relations
P.O. Box 420603
San Francisco, CA 94142-0603
(415) 703-5281

Recordkeeping Requirements

Virtually every employer in California is required by state law to keep a log of all employee work-related illnesses and injuries, as well as a supplementary record of such illnesses or injuries, on one of several prescribed forms.[71] However, small employers are generally exempt from all Cal/OSHA recordkeeping requirements.[72] Your business will qualify for the small employer exemption if you never had more than ten employees on the payroll during any 24-hour period in the previous calendar year.

If your business will be subject to Cal/OSHA recordkeeping requirements, request the *Cal/OSHA Recordkeeping Booklet*, and a *Log and Summary of Occupational Injuries and Illnesses – Cal/OSHA Form 200* from the California Department of Industrial Relations.

Form 200 generally does not have to be filed with any agency; however, the California Division of Labor Statistics and Research selects a number of employers each year — including otherwise exempt small employers — who must keep *Form 200* and report certain information requested on a survey form.[73]

As indicated above, if any occupational injury or illness results in lost work-time beyond the day of injury, or in medical treatment other than first aid, you must report the injury or illness to your insurance carrier within five working days by filing *Form 5020*, in duplicate, or by filing on the carrier's own form supplied for that purpose. Your copy of this completed form will also constitute the required supplementary record. In case of a work-related death or severe injury to an employee, you must immediately report it by phone or telegram to the nearest DOSH district office.[74]

An additional supplementary record of occupational injuries and illnesses is available to complement *Form 200* by providing more detailed records of each recordable occupational injury or illness. For California employers, any of the following forms can be used as the supplementary record:

- California Division of Labor Statistics and Research *Form 5020* (Rev. 3), *Employer's Report of Occupational Injury or Illness*;
- A version of the *Employer's Report of Occupational Injury or Illness* form supplied by your workers' compensation insurance carrier; or
- Federal OSHA *Form 101*.

Two copies of one of these forms must also be filed with the insurance carrier within five days after any serious industrial injury or illness. There is no requirement to maintain or even have these forms until an employee incurs an occupational injury or illness. Although, consider keeping the forms on hand anyway because you must record a reportable injury or illness within six working days to DOSH, in addition to filing with your insurance carrier within five days.

Special Permits

Employers in the construction business must obtain special Cal/OSHA permits if erecting or demolishing a structure more than three stories high or doing excavations five feet or deeper in which a person is required to descend.[75]

Consultations

California also provides free consultation services to employers who request assistance with their safety and health programs. The consultations are confidential and independent of the compliance aspect of DOSH. For more information about consultation services, contact:

Division of Occupational Safety and Health (DOSH)
California Department of Industrial Relations
(415) 703-4341

California Smoke-Free Workplace Rules

Beginning January 1, 1995, California law prohibited smoking in most enclosed workplaces in the state.[76] For the purpose of this law, an enclosed workplace is broadly defined to include almost any place of employment that has a ceiling and four walls, such as offices or restaurants. The state law provides the following exemptions for employers — but doesn't prevent such regulations from being promulgated by local governments:

- Small businesses with 5 or fewer employees are exempt, if they meet all four of the following conditions:
  - A smoking area must not be accessible to minors;
  - Air from any smoking areas must be vented directly outside the building by an exhaust fan;
  - Employees may not be required to work in smoking areas against their will; and
  - The employer must comply with all applicable federal and state ventilation standards.

- Hotels and motels may allow smoking in up to 65% of their guest rooms. Smoking is also permitted in designated portions of hotel or motel lobbies — up to 25% of the entire space in large lobbies, 50% in lobbies with less than 2,000 square feet of floor space.

- Bars, taverns and gaming clubs are exempt from the new rules until January 1, 1997, unless federal or state agencies set smoke-limited standards for them before such date.

- Smoking need not be banned in meeting and banquet rooms in hotels, motels, restaurants, and convention centers, except when used for exhibit purposes or when meals are being served. During such times, smoking may still be allowed in anterooms or corridors if employees are not stationed in such places.

- Smoking is permitted in warehouses with more than 100,000 square feet of floor space and 20 or fewer full-time employees. But any office space within a warehouse must be kept smoke-free.

- Tobacco shops and attached private smokers' lounges are exempt from the no-smoking rules.

- "Break" rooms for employees that are designated for smoking are allowed, subject to strict ventilation rules, like those for small businesses.

- Smoking is allowed in truck cabs and tractors, except when a non-smoking employee is present.

- Various other exempt places include private residences — except when used as a licensed child-care facility, theatrical production sites (if smoking is critical to the production), medical research or treatment sites (if necessary for research), and patient smoking areas of long-term healthcare facilities.

If you designate a smoking area, you are required to post signs at each building entrance, stating that "Smoking is Prohibited Except in Designated Areas." Or, if a building is to be entirely smoke-free, you must clearly post "No Smoking" signs at all building entrances. If a nonemployee is seen smoking in an enclosed work area where smoking is not permitted, you must ask that person to refrain from doing so when appropriate.

Wage-Hour Laws

California's wage-hour laws are somewhat similar to the federal standards; however, the California standards do not exempt as many employees as the Fair Labor Standards Act (FLSA). The main employee exemption from the California labor standards is for administrative, executive, and professional employees who are either paid more than certain amounts per month, or who are licensed in certain professions.[77]

The California Labor Code requires you to display an official poster regarding the state's wage and hour laws and working conditions in an area frequented by employees.[78] The Industrial Welfare Commission (IWC) publishes an official poster entitled *Orders Regulating Wages,*

Working Conditions, and Hours, Form 1104. A copy of IWC *Form 1104*, or other posters most frequently required for nonagricultural employers, can be requested by mailing the preprinted post card provided in the back of this book. The card also requests the *Pay Day Notice* that you must also display.[79]

In addition to the wage and hour requirements discussed below, you should be aware of two other important rules under the California Labor Code:

- Wages must be paid at least twice a month, with the exception of exempt executive, administrative, and professional employees.[80]

- A terminated employee must be paid up to the time employment terminates. If you discharge an employee, the employee must receive his or her final paycheck immediately, or else wages will continue to accrue until paid, for up to 30 days.[81] Similarly, an employee who quits must be paid on the termination date, if he or she has given 72 hours advance notice. Otherwise, payment must be made within 72 hours if an employee quits without giving notice.

Minimum Wage

The state's minimum wage law requires that you pay all your covered employees at least $4.25 per hour.[82] This wage is the same as the federal minimum wage, as set by the FLSA. The California minimum wage law will generally apply to your business, even if some or all of your employees are exempt from the federal minimum wage law.

The minimum wage is reduced to 85% of the basic minimum wage rate for employees who are learners — during their first 160 hours of employment — and for minors under certain very limited conditions.[83] A reduced minimum wage may also apply for disabled workers, if a special license is obtained.

The California Labor Code also requires that an employee working a split shift — that is, four hours in the morning and four hours in the evening — be paid one additional hour's pay at the minimum wage for each day a split shift is worked.[84]

Equal Pay

Federal and state equal opportunity statutes require equal pay for comparable worth for men and women performing similar services. Failure to do so can result in a claim based on wage or sex discrimination.

Overtime Pay

Like the FLSA, California law requires you to pay employees — other than exempt employees or executives — one and one-half times the regular rate of pay for all hours worked more than 40 in a workweek.[85] In addition, California requires payment of overtime premium pay if an employee works more than 8 hours in one day, or more than six days in a week, as follows:

- An employee must receive time and a half for each hour worked in excess of 8 (up to 12) hours in a single workday and for each hour (up to 8) worked on the seventh workday in a given workweek.

- If an employee works more than 12 hours in a day or more than 8 hours on the seventh workday in a week, he or she must be paid at double the regular hourly pay rate for hours worked in excess of 12 a day, or in excess of 8 hours on the seventh day of a week.[86]

Under certain conditions, however, employees can be hired to work a four-day, ten-hours-a-day workweek, without treating the ninth and tenth hours worked on those days as overtime.[87]

Child Labor

Like most states, California regulates the employment of children. If you intend to hire children in your business, check with the California Department of Industrial Relations to find out what specific restrictions and exemptions there are relating to acceptable occupations and conditions and to allowable hours of employment. Below is a partial discussion of the states' child labor regulations.

In general, the California child labor laws prohibit hiring children under 16 years of age from working in manufacturing establishments.[88] There are also a number of other prohibitions against hiring children under 16 years of age to work with various types of dangerous machinery or with toxic chemicals.

In addition, children cannot work in a number of occupations, situations, and industries considered hazardous to their health, such as railroads, vessels, or mining operations.[89]

Minors, except 16- and 17-year-olds not required to be in school, are not permitted to work more than eight hours a day; work more than six days in a workweek; and except for delivery of newspapers, minors may not work before 5:00 A.M. or after 10:00 P.M. — after 12:30 A.M. if the next day is not a school day.[90]

If you intend to employ children under 18 years of age in a business, you will probably need legal guidance as to the conditions under which they may work, under both the federal and California child labor laws. Refer also to Section 5.7 for a discussion of federal laws that apply to the employment of minors.

Other State Labor Laws

As an employer, you will also have to deal with other employee-related state requirements, which may vary depending upon how many employees you have. To correctly determine your policies on issues such as family leave and the time for paying wages, review the general guidelines below.

To learn more about the state's labor laws, check your local phone directory for the nearest location of the California Department of Industrial Relation's Division of Labor Standards Enforcement. This division will be able to provide you with forms, information, and referrals.

Breaks, Holidays, and Sick Leave

Most employers allow employees breaks for meals and rest. Generally, employees also receive at least seven paid holidays a year and are granted sick leave, which is paid time off for an employee who is temporarily incapacitated. In California, an employee must be given at least a 10 minute paid break for every four hours worked. A 30-minute meal break must be given to an employee no more than five hours into a workshift. Those in the motion picture industry must receive a meal break of 30 minutes, no more than six hours into workshift. Contact the division of labor standards to find out exactly what the state law requires.

Family and Medical Leave

In addition to the federal Family and Medical Leave Act requirements, California has its own Family Rights Act leave law that requires businesses that employ 50 or more workers, within 75 miles of a worksite, to grant twelve weeks of unpaid leave of absence to employees for family or medical purposes, such as:

- The birth or adoption of a child; or
- A serious health condition of the employee, spouse, child, or parent.[91]

Under the California Family Rights Act, an employee must have worked twelve months — and 1,250 hours within those twelve months — to be eligible for the leave.

Under the Family Rights Act, if need for such a leave is foreseeable, the employee must give reasonable advance notice and, where possible, must make reasonable efforts to schedule the leave to avoid disruption of company operations. Upon returning from such a leave, the employee is entitled to the same or a comparable position that he or she held before the leave, with only limited exceptions.

During the period an employee is taking family leave, he or she is entitled to continue to participate in the group health plan of the employer at the employer's expense, for up to 12 weeks. But if the employee fails to return after the leave has expired, the employer may seek to recover the premiums paid on the employee's behalf.

The employee may also continue to participate in other employee welfare and retirement plans of the employer while on leave, but the employer is not required to contribute to a retirement plan on behalf of the employee during the period of leave, or to count the leave time as a period of service earned under the retirement plan.

As an employer, you are not required to grant leave in certain situations, such as:

- When the employee is one of the 5 highest paid employees, or among the top 10% of employees, in terms of gross salary; or
- When the leave, if granted, would result in undue hardship to the business' operations.

In addition to the Family Rights Act, California also has a pregnancy disability leave. Any company with five or more employees must grant a leave of absence of up to 16 weeks to a pregnant employee if a doctor determines the leave is necessary. The leave can be used during or after pregnancy, or a combination of both. The employee must be given the same or a comparable job when she returns to work.[92]

Refer to Section 5.12 for information on the federal Family and Medical Leave Act of 1993. To find out more about California's leave laws, you can contact:

California Department of Fair Employment and Housing
(916) 445-9918

Reporting New Hires

Many California employers with five or more employees are now required to report all new hires, rehires, or returning employees to the California Employment Development Department (EDD) within 30 days of their being hired or rehired, or returning.[93] The purpose of this new reporting requirement is to help the state track down parents who are delinquent on their child support payments and reduce welfare fraud.

The new reporting requirement applies to employers of five or more employees, in any of the following categories:

- Automotive dealers and gasoline service stations;
- Automotive repair, services, and parking;
- Building construction — general contractors and operative builders;
- Business services;
- Construction — special trade contractors;
- Eating and drinking places;
- Engineering, accounting, research, management, and related services;
- Health services;
- Heavy construction other than building construction — contractors;
- Holding companies and other investment offices;
- Hotels, rooming houses, camps, and other places of lodging;
- Landscaping and horticultural services;
- Motion pictures;
- Motor freight transportation and warehousing;
- Water transportation; or
- Wholesale trade — durable goods or nondurable goods.

A report is not required for an employee to whom you pay less than $300 a month in wages, or for any employee who is under 18 years of age.

As a California employer, you may choose one of several methods to report your new employees. *Report of New Employee(s), Form DE 34,* is provided by the EDD for your convenience. However, you may choose to use your own reporting form. The following information must be included on the reporting form:

- Employer name, address, and account number; and
- Employee's first name initial, last name, and social security number.

Mail or fax your reporting forms to the EDD address below.

In place of the form provided, you can also report using magnetic media. For additional information on magnetic media reporting, contact the Magnetic Media Unit.

A prerecorded telephone message has been provided to answer common new employee registry questions. At the end of the message, you can leave your name and telephone number, and your call will be returned as soon as possible. You can contact your local EDD Employment Tax District Office also.

Data Capture Group – MIC 23
California Employment Development Department
P.O. Box 997016
West Sacramento, CA 95799-7016
(916) 657-0529 (Pre-recorded message)
(916) 654-6845 (Magnetic media)
FAX (916) 653-5214

Right-to-Work

Right-to-work laws guarantee that a person may not be denied employment for refusing to join a union. Many of these right-to-work laws also prohibit mandatory payment of union dues by non-union workers in order to retain employment.

California does not have a right-to-work law and allows "union shop" or "agency shop" contracts, or both, between a company and a union. In a union shop, an employee not belonging to a union may be hired but then must join the union, usually within 30 days. In an agency shop, an employee need not join the union but, to remain employed, must pay dues to the union.

Fair Employment Practices

California has a fair employment practices law that in many respects is even broader in coverage than the federal anti-discrimination laws that are discussed in Section 5.8. In addition, some local governments in California, such as San Francisco, have enacted gay rights ordinances, prohibiting discrimination based on sexual preference. Both Los Angeles and San Francisco have also enacted ordinances that prohibit discrimination against persons with AIDS in employment situations and otherwise.

The California law applies to any employer that regularly employs five or more persons.[94] The law makes it illegal to discriminate because of race, color, religious creed, national origin, ancestry, physical disability (including AIDS or HIV), mental disability, medical condition, marital status, or sex — which includes pregnancy — in hiring, firing, compensation, or conditions of employment.[95] California has also adopted a law that prohibits age discrimination in employment against persons more than 40 years old.[96]

In addition, California law expressly prohibits sexual harassment by employers and by others where the employer knows of the situation and fails to take immediate and appropriate action to correct it. You must take all reasonable steps to prevent sexual harassment from occurring in your workplace, including providing an information sheet explaining the nature and illegality of sexual harassment.[97]

Further, employers with five or more employees are required to display an official poster regarding equal employment opportunity. The poster, called *Discrimination in Employment is Prohibited by Law*, is available in both English and Spanish. Copies of this poster can be obtained from any office of the California Department of Fair Employment and Housing. A copy of this official notice can be requested by using the preprinted post card provided at the end of this book. To receive more state-specific information on anti-discrimination laws, contact:

Communications Center
California Department of Fair Employment and Housing
2014 T Street, Suite 210
Sacramento, CA 95814
(916) 227-0511

Independent Contractors

If you have only occasional needs for particular skills or services, you might want to engage independent contractors, rather than hire more employees. When you have work performed by independent contractors, you have fewer governmental regulations and taxes to deal with and you can disengage the relationship when the contract is completed.

It is critical that you don't unknowingly misclassify, as independent contractors, individuals who should be treated as employees — you could be held liable for back taxes and penalties. As discussed in sections 5.2 and 9.11, it is sometimes difficult to determine whether an individual qualifies as an independent contractor. As a general rule, if your company is the individual's only customer or client, the government will probably maintain that the person is your employee and expect your firm to withhold taxes and comply with other employer regulations.

Although the criteria are not precisely defined, contractors have the freedom to choose what work they will do and when, where, and how it will be done. Contractors maintain a separate business location and usually furnish their own tools and supplies. Contractors report income to the IRS on *Schedule C* or *Schedule F* and the IRS compares it to the *Form 1099*s it receives from you and the contractors' other clients.

Depending on their industry and size of business, contractors also provide their own licenses, permits, performance bonds, insurance, advertising, business cards, and stationery. Contractors can hire and fire their own employees and subcontractors.

To avoid the ramifications of a wrong determination between an employee and independent contractor, or if you have workers and are unsure whether they are properly classified, you may request a written determination from the California Employment Development Department by submitting a completed *Determination of Employment Taxes and Personal Income Tax Withholding, Form DE 1870*. You may obtain this form from your local Employment Tax District Office, which can be found in your local telephone directory. The department will respond with a written determination within 60 days of receiving your request. Mail completed forms to:

California Employment Development Department – Audit Section, MIC-94
P.O. Box 826880
Sacramento, CA 94280-0001

11.6 State Licenses

As noted in Chapter 6, many businesses and professions are required to obtain licenses before engaging in business. State governments have traditionally licensed professionals, such as doctors, lawyers, and accountants. To further protect consumers, California has expanded the list to include other occupations.

Licensing Agencies

Most licenses are administered by the California Department of Consumer Affairs, but several important licensing departments are divisions of the California Trade and Commerce Agency. For more information, contact:

California Department of Consumer Affairs
400 R Street, Suite 1080
Sacramento, CA 95814
(916) 445-1254

California Trade and Commerce Agency
801 K Street, Suite 1700
Sacramento, CA 95814
(916) 322-1394

Listed below are the major California licensing agencies and various activities subject to licensing. The businesses or occupations below are grouped under the major departments and agencies that administer them. Because this is not a complete list, licensing agencies should be called to obtain more information on general businesses or occupations.

Department of Consumer Affairs

Business or Occupation	Licensing Agency
Accountants, certified public	State Board of Accountancy
Adult day care center	Department of Health Services
Alarm companies	Bureau of Collection and Investigative Services
Architects and building designers	State Board of Architectural Examiners
Automobile repair shops; official lamp, brake, and smog adjusting stations	Bureau of Automotive Repair
Building designers	State Board of Architectural Examiners
Barber shops and colleges	Board of Barber Examiners
Boxing and wrestling	State Athletic Commission

Department of Consumer Affairs (continued)	**Business or Occupation**	**Licensing Agency**
	Cemeteries, cemetery brokers, and salespersons	Cemetery Board
	Chiropractors	Board of Chiropractic Examiners
	Contractors (construction)	Contractors State License Board
	Counselors (marriage, family, and child)	Board of Behavioral Science Examiners
	Cosmetologists, manicurists, and electrologists	Board of Barbering and Cosmetology
	Court and shorthand reporters	Certified Shorthand Reporters Board
	Dentists, dental assistants, and hygienists	Board of Dental Examiners
	Educational psychologists	Board of Behavioral Science Examiners
	Electronic equipment repair dealers and appliance repair dealers	Bureau of Electronic and Appliance Repair
	Employment agencies	Bureau of Employment Agencies
	Engineers and land surveyors	Board of Registration for Professional Engineers and Land Surveyors
	Funeral directors and embalmers	Board of Funeral Directors and Embalmers
	Furniture (upholstered) manufacturers, bedding manufacturers, and furniture and bedding sellers	Bureau of Home Furnishings and Thermal Insulation
	Geologists and geophysicists	Board of Registration for Geologists and Geophysicists
	Guide dog schools and trainers	Board of Guide Dogs for the Blind
	Landscape architects	Board of Landscape Architects
	Locksmiths	Board of Security and Investigative Services

	Medical professions:
	  Acupuncturists
	  Audiologists
	  Hearing aid dispensers
	  Midwives
	  Physical therapists
	  Physicians and surgeons
	  Physician's assistants
	  Podiatrists and chiropodists
	  Professional corporations in the health field
	  Psychologists
	  Registered dispensing opticians
	  Respiratory care practitioners
	  Speech and language pathologists
		Medical Board of California

Business or Occupation	Licensing Agency	**Department of Consumer Affairs** (continued)
Nurses	Board of Registered Nursing	
Nurses (vocational) and psychiatric technicians	Board of Vocational Nurse and Psychiatric Technician Examiners	
Nursing home administrators	Board of Examiners of Nursing Home Administrators	
Optometrists	State Board of Optometry	
Pest control operators	Structural Pest Control Board	
Pharmacies and pharmacists; drug distributors	Board of Pharmacy	
Private investigators	Bureau of Security and Investigative Services	
Protection dog operators	Bureau of Security and Investigative Services	
Repossessors	Bureau of Security and Investigative Services	
Security guards; training schools	Bureau of Security and Investigative Services	
Tax preparers	Tax Preparer Program	
Veterinarians	Board of Examiners in Veterinary Medicine	

Business or Occupation	Licensing Agency	**Trade and Commerce Agency**
Alcoholic beverage manufacturers, distributors, and retailers	Department of Alcoholic Beverage Control	
Banks and trust companies	State Banking Department	
Business opportunity brokers	Department of Real Estate	
Mineral, oil, and gas brokers and salespersons	Department of Real Estate	
Real estate brokers and salespersons	Department of Real Estate	
Real estate subdivisions, security dealers, and syndicates	Department of Real Estate	
Savings and loan associations	Department of Savings and Loan	

Business or Occupation	Licensing Agency	**Independent Boards, Agencies, and Commissions**
Attorneys	State Bar of California	
Day-care centers	Department of Health Services	
Horse racing: parimutuel wagering, horse owners, jockeys, trainers, grooms, exercise boys	California Horse Racing Board	
Hospitals	Department of Health Services	
Osteopaths	Board of Osteopathic Examiners	
Public utilities and transportation	Public Utilities Commission	
Rehabilitation facilities	Department of Health Services	
Skilled nursing facilities	Department of Health Services	

Your business may have to obtain several different licenses from various federal, state, and local government agencies. For more detailed information on licensing requirements and fees, refer to the *California License Handbook*, which you can obtain from this office for a fee of $20. This fee includes postage, tax, and handling.

California Office of Small Business
California Trade and Commerce Agency
Attention: Mr. Koki Tanaka
801 K Street, Suite 1700
Sacramento, CA 95814
(916) 324-1295
FAX (916) 322-5084

You may also want to obtain the *California Permit Handbook*, which contains information on areas that affect your business, such as pollution control or the use of natural resources. The book, which currently costs $18, is available from:

Publication Section
California Department of General Services
4675 Watt Avenue
P.O. Box 1015
North Highland, CA 95660
(916) 574-2256

Many local governments in California have business license taxes, many of which are taxes on gross receipts, as is the case in Los Angeles, San Francisco, Sacramento, Oakland, and Fresno. Often, the tax rate in a particular city or county will depend upon your type of business. For more information, contact your local city hall.

11.7 State Excise Taxes

California imposes a number of excise taxes and certain license fees. Some excise taxes are imposed on the production, importation, use, or sale of certain goods. Others are imposed on services and certain types of businesses. Excise taxes that may apply to your business are listed below. Refer to Chapter 7 for information on federal excise taxes. For additional information on state excise taxes, contact:

Excise Taxes
California State Board of Equalization
(916) 327-4208

Alcoholic Beverages

If you are engaged in producing, handling, or distributing alcoholic beverages in California, you may be subject to monthly license taxes. Fees vary according to the types of licenses that are held. In addition, there are state excise taxes based on the quantity sold of liquor, beer, and wine.[98] Tax rates are as follows:

Type of Beverage	Tax Rate per Gallon
Beer	$0.20
Distilled spirits	3.30
Sparkling wines	0.30
Spirits (over 50% alcohol)	6.60
Still wines	0.20

For questions concerning tax rates, call the State Board of Equalization (SBE) at the number listed above. For information on licensing, contact the Department of Alcoholic Beverage Control.

Department of Alcoholic Beverage Control
Statewide Headquarters
(916) 263-6900

Tobacco Products

If you are a distributor of cigarettes and other tobacco products in California, you are required to file monthly reports with the SBE by the 25th of each month for the preceding month's cigarette sales.

California imposes a tax of $0.37 (37 cents) per pack of 20 cigarettes. A wholesale tax on other tobacco products is set annually by the SBE. For the period of July 1, 1994 to June 30, 1995, the tax rate for tobacco products is 31.2% of the wholesale cost to the distributor.

Gasoline and Special Fuels

If you are a distributor of gasoline or user of motor fuels in California, you are required to pay gasoline or other fuel taxes. The 1995 gasoline and diesel tax rate is $0.18 (18 cents) per gallon. In addition, a tax of $0.007 ($^7/_{10}$ of a cent) per gallon applies to businesses that store petroleum products in underground storage tanks. This rate will increase to $0.008 ($^8/_{10}$ of a cent) in 1996 and $0.009 ($^9/_{10}$ of a cent) in 1997.[99] Various rates or annual fees apply to fuels other than gasoline. Distributors and others required to pay tax must report and pay to the SBE monthly.

Motor Vehicle Registration

Registration fees are imposed on motor vehicles, including trailers and semitrailers, and are collected by the California Department of Motor Vehicles (DMV). The fees are based on classifications by weight for commercial vehicles and by value for other vehicles. For commercial vehicles, annual fees are determined from a set of weight tables.

Severance Taxes

If you produce oil and gas[100] or harvest timber[101] in California, you will be subject to state severance taxes, with rates for oil and gas taxes set annually by the California Department of Conservation. Rates for the timber yield tax are set annually by the State Board of Equalization.

Hazardous Substances Taxes

If you operate a hazardous waste disposal facility, generate hazardous waste, or dispose of hazardous substances, you may be subject to California's hazardous waste regulations.

In 1993, the California legislature completely revised most of the taxes and laws regarding hazardous wastes and waste disposal. All of these changes went into effect on January 1, 1994 or earlier. The new rules provide for a $12 per ton disposal fee for hazardous waste that is generated in a cleanup, removal, or remediation of a hazardous substance, which is classified as non-RCRA hazardous waste.

Non-RCRA hazardous waste is hazardous waste that is regulated under California law, but is not classified as hazardous waste under the federal Resource Conservation and Recovery Act regulations. Out-of-state disposals of hazardous waste are now excluded from the California hazardous waste disposal fee.

Substantial fixed fees — adjusted annually for inflation — are imposed on a potentially responsible party for hazardous waste cleanup and on generators of hazardous wastes, as well as on the operator of any facility receiving non-RCRA hazardous waste imported into California for treatment, recycling, or disposal.[102]

Various other fees are set by the new law for hazardous waste facility fees, permits for offsite hazardous waste storage or treatment facilities, and managing extremely hazardous wastes. Household hazardous waste collection facilities that are operated in accordance with the law are generally exempted from the above waste disposal fees and facility and generator fees.

Environmental Fee

If your corporation has 50 or more employees and is considered to be in an industry that uses, generates, or stores hazardous materials in California, it must file an environmental fee return and pay an annual environmental fee based on its number of employees.

Number of Employees	Fee
1–49	$ 0
50–74	100
75–99	300
100–249	500
250–499	750
500 or more	1,000 [103]

While you might not think your business has anything to do with hazardous materials, the state aggressively interprets this law to apply to nearly all corporations with 50 or more employees. Because of the extreme interpretation of this law, you may want to pay the fee and file for a refund at some point in the future, if you think your corporation should not be subject to the tax. This may, however, mean a fight in the courts.

For more information on the environmental fee for corporations, contact:

California State Board of Equalization
(916) 324-5998

In addition to the taxes mentioned above, your business may be subject to:

Miscellaneous Taxes

- A 2% (of value) annual tax, plus a registration fee, on automobiles registered with the DMV.[104] Annual registration and weight fees are also imposed on commercial vehicles and trailer coaches;
- Taxes on racehorses, including stallions and brood mares;[105]
- A tax on the value of privately owned railcars operated on railroads in California,[106] that is due by December 10th each year and payable to the SBE.[107]

11.8 Planning for Tax Savings in a Business — State Tax Laws

As discussed in Chapter 8, there are effective legal ways to reduce your taxes. This section continues that discussion and provides you with state specifics on those tax strategies that can help you in your business. Before implementing any of the following tax-saving tips, be sure to consult your tax adviser or accountant.

Unemployment Tax Savings

Your best strategy for reducing the unemployment tax your company pays is to plan and hire carefully, so you have minimal layoffs. Over time, this will lower your unemployment tax rating. An effective way to pre-screen employees and to test your long-term need for a new position is to use a temporary help agency as a source for workers at all skill levels.

If you operate your business as a sole proprietorship, some minor tax advantages exist in hiring certain family members as employees in your business. In California, any wages your sole proprietorship pays to your father, mother, spouse, or children under 18 years of age, are exempt from state and federal unemployment tax. Keep in mind, however, that because you don't pay unemployment tax for them, they are not eligible to collect benefits if they are fired or laid off. However, you are still subject to withhold state Personal Income Tax (PIT) for them.

Because the owner of a sole proprietorship is not considered an employee of the business, you do not have to pay any unemployment tax on your own salary, and you are not subject to California state disability insurance (SDI) tax. Thus, you can save up to $317.67 in California taxes based on the 1995 SDI rate of 1.0% on the first $31,767.00 of wages. You can also save on the unemployment insurance tax rate of 3.4% for new employers and the employment training tax (ETT) of 0.1% on the first $7,000 of wages.

State Tax Credits and Exemptions

California provides a wide array of tax credits and exemptions for businesses. In 1993, the California legislature responded to a growing exodus of small and large businesses from the state by enacting a number of major tax credits and other business tax incentives, all of which are designed to encourage firms to make investments and create jobs in California. Some of the available credits that might apply to your business are discussed below.

Research and Development Tax Credit

Research and development tax credits, equal to 8% of qualified research expenses — 12%, in the case of basic research — in excess of specified base levels are available to businesses conducting research and development in California.[108]

Investment Tax Credit

Effective January 1, 1994, a California investment tax credit (ITC) is allowed, equal to 6% of the cost of certain equipment used in:

- Manufacturing, processing, refining, fabricating, or recycling of property;
- Research and development; and
- Services that repair, maintain, measure or test qualifying equipment.[109]

Any 1994 ITCs on eligible equipment purchases must be claimed on and used to offset income or franchise taxes on the 1995, or later, tax returns, rather than on the 1994 returns. The ITC is available to both large and small businesses that meet the above requirements, provided the equipment is purchased for and used in California for at least one year after purchase.

Sales Tax Refund In Lieu of Credit

Effective September 11, 1994, if you pay sales or use tax on the purchase of equipment that would qualify for the investment tax credit, you may elect to receive a refund of the sales or use tax, in lieu of claiming the 6% investment credit on your income or franchise tax return.[110] Your claim for refund must include the date, description, and purchase price of the items eligible for the credit as well as proof that you paid the sales or use tax on the purchase. If yours is a new business or is not yet operating at a profit, claiming a sales tax refund may be of more immediate benefit than taking an income tax credit, since the income tax credit could be greater than your current year's income or franchise tax liability, and thus would not be fully useable in the current tax year.

Small Business Stock

Noncorporate investors in stock of certain small corporations, excluding the stock of any S corporation, who purchase stock issued by the corporation on or after August 10, 1993, and before January 1, 1999, may exclude up to 50% of the gain realized on a subsequent sale or other taxable disposition of the stock, if they have held it for more than five years.[111] For stock to qualify for this favorable tax treatment, the issuing corporation must, at all times after June 30, 1993 and before the issuance of the stock to the investor, have assets of $50 million or less and must operate in a trade or business other than:

- Service businesses, such as law, medicine, banking finance, insurance, or other services;
- Farming;
- Oil and gas extraction; or
- Hotels, motels, and restaurants.

Thus, the only businesses whose stock will qualify, for the most part, are generally those in the manufacturing, wholesale, retail, and some extractive industries, other than oil and gas. A number of other requirements must also be met, including a requirement that the corporation have at least 80% of the total dollar value of its payroll in California.

Mass Transit Pass Tax Credit

A credit is available for employer-subsidized public mass transit passes that are bought for employees. The credit is equal to:

- Forty percent of the cost of the pass if employee parking is not subsidized;
- Twenty percent if parking is subsidized; or
- Ten percent if employee parking is provided free.[112]

This credit expires December 1, 1996.

Net Operating Losses

The California tax reform provisions of 1993 generally allow corporations and individuals to carry forward, for a five-year period, 50% of their business net operating losses and to deduct those losses in subsequent profitable years. The net operating loss (NOL) deductions from previous tax reform provisions were temporarily suspended in 1991–92. However, taxpayers were able to accrue NOLs during that period, which may be carried over an additional one or two years beyond the five-year period. The prior law had allowed a fifteen-year carryover period for NOLs.[113]

One of the business incentives legislation enacted in 1993 is a 100% carryover of NOLs for both new and small businesses, for years beginning on or after January 1, 1994. However, for a new business to qualify for the 100% carryover, the losses must be incurred in its first three years of operation.[114] Losses incurred in the first year of operation carry forward for eight years; those incurred in the second year carry forward seven years; and losses incurred in the third year carry forward six years.[115]

Even if it is not a new business, your small businesses, defined as "a taxpayer with total receipts of less than $1 million during the taxable or income year,"[116] may still qualify for the 100% carryover of losses,[117] but with only a five-year carryover period.

Enterprise Zone Program

California has designated certain areas in the state as Enterprise Zones and Employment and Economic Incentive Areas (EEIA). The Enterprise Zone Program, a partnership between the state, local government, and the private sector, is available to businesses expanding or located in the more than 30 designated areas in California. According to a survey published in *Site Selection Magazine*, California's enterprise zones provide more incentives than those of any other state. The incentives, designed to encourage business development, include:

- A tax credit for sales and use tax paid on the first $20 million of equipment or machinery purchased;
- An expanded hiring credit for wages paid to qualified employees during the employee's first 60 months on the job;
- A 15-year carryover of net operating losses;
- Expensing of certain depreciable property; and
- Lender interest income deductions for loans made to zone businesses.

Keep in mind, however, the provisions of the temporary suspension in 1991–92 of the California net operating loss deduction mentioned earlier do not apply to certain firms operating in enterprise zones.[118]

Other local incentives may include waivers or reductions of fees, streamlined review of permits, reduced land costs, and low-cost financing. For more detailed information on tax incentives for locating your business in an enterprise zone or program area, request the free Franchise Tax Board booklets, *Form FTB 1047, Guidelines for Enterprise Zone Tax Incentives*, and *Form FTB 1048, Guidelines for Program Area Tax Incentives*, from:

Franchise Tax Board
P.O. Box 942840
Sacramento, CA 94240-0070
(916) 854-6600

For information on geographical locations and boundaries and other technical, nontax information regarding enterprise zones and program areas, contact:

California Trade and Commerce Agency
Attention: Enterprise Zone Programs
801 K Street, Suite 1700
Sacramento, CA 95814-3908
(916) 322-3502

Disaster Area Recovery Incentives

In 1992 and 1993, responding to the ongoing series of natural and societal disasters that have adversely impacted the California economy in recent years, the state adopted two major target area investment incentive programs for affected areas.

The two new programs are in addition to the already existing depressed economic area programs for enterprise zones and program areas, discussed above.

- Los Angeles Revitalization Zone Program — In the wake of the April and May, 1992 civil disturbances and resulting widespread destruction in the Los Angeles and nearby communities, a comprehensive program of tax and other incentives were adopted to expedite economic recovery in the riot areas, now called the Los Angeles Revitalization Zone (LARZ). These incentives include:

- A 50% tax credit for wages paid in the LARZ, on wages of up to 150% of the minimum wage — that is, 150% of $4.25 or $6.37 an hour;[119]

- A full income or franchise tax credit for any sales taxes paid on building materials used to replace or repair buildings in the LARZ or to purchase depreciable tangible personal property for use exclusively in the LARZ;[120]

- A 100% first-year deduction for the cost of such tangible personal property, with no upper limit;[121] and

- A tax deduction for lenders on interest they receive on loans made to businesses that operate in the LARZ, making such interest tax-exempt to the banks for California franchise tax purposes.[122]

- Local Agency Military Base Recovery Area Program — To stimulate business and industrial growth in areas heavily impacted by military base closures, the California legislature in 1993 adopted another comprehensive set of tax incentives very similar to those described above for the LARZ. The Local Agency Military Base Recovery Area (LAMBRA) incentives include:

  - Employers' wage credits;

  - Sales tax credits;

  - First-year expensing of depreciable tangible personal property; and

  - A 15-year carryover of net operating losses incurred in affected areas for certain employers.[123]

However, the LAMBRA incentives generally do not go into effect until taxable years beginning on or after January 1, 1995 and before January 1, 2003. The areas to be designated as LAMBRA zones will be selected by the California Trade and Commerce Agency.

Estate Planning and Marital Deduction

Estate planning for your business and personal assets is easier for married couples because of the unlimited marital deduction for federal estate tax purposes, as discussed in Chapter 8, which permits postponement of all federal estate tax until the death of the surviving spouse.

California does not have an inheritance tax, so your estate planning can be based almost entirely on federal estate tax considerations for passing assets to a surviving spouse. There is, however, an estate or "pick-up" tax in California. This tax must be paid at death on estates that are subject to federal estate tax, even though it reduces the federal estate tax dollar for dollar. It is not usually relevant for planning purposes since it merely shifts estate tax dollars from the federal government to the state.

California also follows the long-time federal rule that when one spouse dies, the other spouse's half of the community property is also entitled to a "step up" in tax basis to the property's value at the date of death.

Do-It-Yourself Wills

If you want to complete your own will, the state of California law provides for a standard do-it-yourself will form. The law is intended to reduce the large percentage of people in California who die without valid wills, or who write their own crude wills that lead to legal disputes over their meaning. California is the first state to provide such standard wills for its citizens.

You can obtain the will form by sending a check or money order for $2 and a stamped, self-addressed, legal-sized envelope to:

Will Forms
P.O. Box 420411
San Francisco, CA 94142-0411

For more information, you can call the State Bar of California and request to hear a tape-recorded message regarding wills.

State Bar of California
(415) 561-8858 (Pre-recorded message)

Sheltering Profits on Export Sales

If your company does significant export business, you may want to form a separate Domestic International Sales Corporation (DISC) or Foreign Sales Corporation (FSC) to take advantage of the federal export incentives described in Section 8.4.

You should keep in mind, however, that California does not grant any special tax benefits for either DISCs or FSCs. Thus, a DISC will typically be fully taxable in California, to the same extent as any other corporation subject to California's taxing jurisdiction.

On the other hand, California law provides no "deemed distribution" of any of the DISC's income to its shareholder or shareholders. Only an actual distribution of DISC earnings is taxable to shareholders as a dividend under California law.

For FSCs, California's tax rules also differ from the federal law. California may be constitutionally prohibited from directly taxing the earnings of FSCs who have foreign management; however, where an FSC is a subsidiary of, or under common control with, a U.S. corporation doing business in California, the state may be able to compel the two companies to file a combined report and pay tax on a unitary basis. Hence, any profits of an FSC in such a case would be indirectly subjected to tax in California.

For additional discussion of California's unitary franchise tax system, see Section 11.2.

Dividends Received Deduction

If your corporation owns stock in another corporation, your company may qualify for a dividends received deduction, which could reduce the income tax it has to pay on the dividends it receives. To find out if your corporation can take advantage of the federal dividends received deduction, consult with your accountant.

There are significant differences between California and federal tax treatment of dividends received by a corporation on an investment in stock of another corporation. California allows:

- A 100% dividends received deduction, if the corporation that receives the dividend owns more than 50% of the stock of the paying corporation;
- An 80% deduction, if it owns 20% or more of the stock, but not more than 50% of the stock; and
- A 70% deduction, if it owns less than 20% of the stock of the payor corporation.[124]

This assumes that 100% of the income of the payor of the dividends is subject to taxation in California. If the actual percentage of the payor's income that is subject to tax in California is less than 100%, then that percentage must be multiplied times 100%, 80%, or 70% to determine the portion of the total dividend that is nontaxable to the recipient corporation.

Depreciation Rules

One of the most important differences between California and federal tax law is depreciation. California has not conformed to the federal Accelerated Cost Recovery System (ACRS) of rapid depreciation that went into effect in 1981 or, for corporations, with the modified ACRS (MACRS) system that went into effect in 1987.

Thus, for California tax purposes, any depreciable assets a corporation acquires generally must be depreciated under a set of rules that are basically the same as the federal tax depreciation rules that existed before 1981. S corporations, however, may now use the MACRS system for California tax purposes.

An immediate write-off or rapid depreciation of certain depreciable assets is permitted for businesses operating in enterprise zones, program areas, the Los Angeles Revitalization Zone (LARZ), and for tax years beginning in or after 1995, in Local Agency Military Base Recovery Areas under the LAMBRA provisions.

Corporate Earnings and Interest

Unlike the federal law, California's tax law for corporations does not contain any penalty tax provisions like the federal personal holding company tax or accumulated earnings tax.

California does not exempt the interest earned on state or municipal bonds, with the exception of those issued by the state of California or its political subdivisions. Individual taxpayers, however, are not taxed on interest from U.S. Treasury obligations, such as treasury bills or treasury bonds, or from securities issued by certain U.S. government agencies.

However, corporations subject to the California franchise tax must pay tax on interest from all sources, including interest on U.S. Treasury obligations and interest on state or municipal bonds — including those issued by California and its political subdivisions.

11.9 Miscellaneous Business Pointers

This section provides general business information on such topics as financial assistance, usury laws, and emerging trends in California. Refer to Chapter 9 for information on federal assistance programs and other basic business pointers.

State Business Loan Programs

A wide variety of financial incentive programs are available in California for new or expanding businesses. In addition to the tax credits, enterprise zone programs, and disaster area recovery incentives discussed in Section 11.8, the state has several other loan and financing programs, which are listed below. For more information about these and other programs contact:

Office of Small Business
California Trade and Commerce Agency
801 K Street, Suite 1700
Sacramento, CA 95814
(916) 327-4357

Industrial Development Bonds

California cities and counties can offer financing to businesses through the issuance of industrial development bonds. The business assumes the obligation of paying off the debt, often over a term of 20 to 30 years. Interest rates your business would pay on such bonds will usually be substantially below the current prime lending rate charged by banks.

Where such bonds are taxable to bondholders, the proceeds can be used by a business for a variety of projects. They can be used for financing purchases of land, buildings, or equipment, as well as for permanent working capital. Such taxable bonds can be issued for amounts as low as $250,000 with no maximum limit.

Export Finance Program

The California Export Finance Program provides working capital loan guarantees to California businesses seeking to complete export sales. To qualify for these loan guarantees, applicants must have been in business for at least one year, and the export products must have a 51% California content.

For more information or assistance regarding this program, contact:

California Export Finance Office
(714) 562-5519
FAX (714) 562-5530

Pollution Control Financing

California Loans for Environmental Assistance Now (CLEAN) is a loan program designed to help California small businesses finance the cost of production equipment and pollution control devices needed to comply with environmental restrictions. Financing is available in amounts up to $750,000, for terms of up to seven years. There is a 2% loan processing fee, and interest rates are comparable to commercial loans.

For more information or assistance, contact the Office of Small Business at the address listed above, or one of the regional California Financial Corporations listed below.

The Small Business Loan Guarantee Program is operated under the supervision of the Office of Small Business, California Trade and Commerce Agency. The loan guarantee program operates through the twelve regional California Financial Corporations that are listed below.

Small Business Loan Guarantee Program

These regional corporations are organized to receive and review business and agricultural applications for guarantees of financial assistance. Unlike the federal U.S. Small Business Loan Guarantee program, the Small Business Loan Guarantee program is not limited as to the types of loans or financial assistance that can be made available to eligible borrowers. Guarantees have been issued on short- and long-term loans, revolving lines of credit, seasonal inventory, and accounts receivable loans.

To qualify for such a loan guarantee, your firm must demonstrate that financing is not available from conventional sources. In addition, the financial assistance must conform to policy and guidelines, and there must be a reasonable prospect of repayment. The guaranteed portion of the loan is generally no more than 85 to 90% of the required total financing. The loan term period varies from one to seven years, at interest rates typically one to two points above the bank prime rate.

To be eligible for one of these loans, a business or farm must not exceed the size limitations of a small business or farm as defined in the SBA regulations. A loan, however, can be made to a firm exceeding the SBA size limitation if it results in employment or continued employment of 15 or more persons who live in economically disadvantaged areas or who are youths, or both.

Business or farming start ups can qualify for assistance, but due to the much higher risks involved, it is much more difficult for a start up to obtain such financing than for an existing operation that needs financing to expand. Applications are reviewed by one of the regional corporations rather than the Office of Small Business.

For more information, contact one of the California Financial Corporations listed below.

California Capital Financial Corporation
926 J Street, Suite 1500
Sacramento, CA 95814
(916) 442-1729
FAX (916) 442-7852

California Coastal Financial Corporation
5 East Gavilan Street, Suite 215
Salinas, CA 93902
(408) 424-1099
FAX (408) 424-1094

Bay Area Financial Corporation
3932 Harrison Street
Oakland, CA 94611
(510) 652-5262
FAX (510) 652-6017

Pacific Coast Regional Financial Corporation
3255 Wilshire Boulevard, Suite 1501
Los Angeles, CA 90010
(213) 739-2999
FAX (213) 739-0639

Hancock Financial Corporation
3600 Wilshire Boulevard, Suite 926
Los Angeles, CA 90010
(213) 382-4300
FAX (213) 382-4732

Valley Financial Corporation
3417 West Shaw Avenue, Suite 100
Fresno, CA 93711
(209) 271-9030
FAX (209) 271-9078

California Southern Financial Corporation
600 B Street, Suite 2450
San Diego, CA 92101
(619) 232-7771
FAX (619) 232-6743

SAFE-BIDCO
145 Wikiup Drive
Santa Rosa, CA 95403
(707) 577-8621
FAX (707) 577-7348

California Coastal – Santa Barbara Financial Corporation
924 Anacapa Street, Suite 3B
Santa Barbara, CA 93101
(805) 962-9251
FAX (805) 966-5849

California Coastal – Arroyo Grande Financial Corporation
378 South Halcyon Road
Arroyo Grande, CA 93420
(805) 473-8925
FAX (805) 473-8927

Inland Empire SBDO Financial Corporation
201 North East Street, Suite 204
San Bernardino, CA 92401
(909) 384-9006
FAX (909) 384-5151

Valley/Bakersfield Financial Corporation
5330 Office Center Court, Suite 61
Bakersfield, CA 93309
(805) 322-7889
FAX (805) 322-7892

Small Business Investment Companies

A Small Business Investment Company (SBIC) is a privately owned and operated company that has been licensed by the U.S. Small Business Administration (SBA) to provide equity capital and long-term loans to small firms. Often, an SBIC also provides management assistance to the companies it finances.

SBICs invest in all types of manufacturing and service industries and a wide variety of other businesses, including construction, retail, and whole-sale concerns. Many investment companies seek out small businesses that offer new products or services because these small businesses usually have the growth potential that is attractive to SBICs. For a list of the SBICs in California, contact the SBA at one of the offices listed in Section 11.10.

Local Government Loan Programs

In addition to the state loan assistance programs described above, there are additional local government sources of financing that may assist your company with expansion plans. At the city and county level in many communities, there are redevelopment agencies, local economic development corporations, and special assessment districts, all of which are possible sources of financing designed to encourage companies to expand. For more information, contact:

Office of Business Development
California Trade and Commerce Agency
801 K Street, Suite 1700
Sacramento, CA 95814
(916) 322-3520

Usury Laws

Usury laws define the maximum amount of interest that may be charged on a credit transaction, such as a promissory note or other instrument, that requires the payment of interest.

The California Constitution, as amended by the voters in 1979,[125] prohibits individuals and businesses from charging usurious interest on loans or other extensions of credit. Unless there is a written agreement, any interest in excess of 7% per annum is considered usurious. With a written agreement, you can generally charge 10% or more, and some types of loans are exempt from the usury law.

Section 1244 Stock

As discussed in Section 9.6, if you take a loss on small business corporation stock that qualifies as Section 1244 stock, you get favorable tax treatment from the IRS. California law closely follows the federal law in allowing ordinary loss treatment of up to $100,000 on the sale or worthlessness of Section 1244 stock owned by individual taxpayers.[126]

Environmental Regulations

If your business will have any impact on the surrounding environment, such as erecting a new building or renovating an existing structure, contact the U.S. Environmental Protection Agency (EPA) to make sure you meet their requirements.

California has some of the broadest-reaching environmental laws in the world, many of which go well beyond federal environmental standards and those enacted by other states. These include statewide rules as well as local restrictions and permitting requirements for businesses. Requirements are particularly stiff in the Los Angeles air basin, which is in the process of gradually phasing in the strictest air pollution rules to be found anywhere in the nation.

While these environmental restrictions may make the air easier to breathe and water safer to drink, the extreme complexity of the various state, regional, county, and city environmental regulations are making life increasingly complex for all except the simplest, least-polluting businesses.

If you are starting a new business or expanding an existing one in California, you will probably need to consult an attorney with expertise in environmental law requirements in your locality to determine what environmental permits, fees, and taxes may be required and to find out what kind of special pollution-control or pollution-free equipment, if any, you may have to install, either now or at some time in the next few years as even stricter rules are phased in.

One agency that can help you meet environmental requirements is the Business Environmental Assistance Center (BEAC). The agency's environmental professionals will:

- Provide individual counseling on regulations specific to your business;
- Assist you in obtaining environmental permits;

- Give you a site inspection at your business and make recommendations;
- Help you locate financial assistance for pollution prevention equipment;
- Identify training and certificate programs and specialized environmental consultation services;
- Assist you in locating new information on the latest technology; and
- Provide current federal, state, and regional environmental regulations.

For more information, or to receive some of its helpful publications and services, contact either:

Business Environmental Assistance Center
100 South Anaheim Boulevard, Suite 125
Anaheim, CA 92805
(800) 662-BEAC

Business Environmental Assistance Center
3120 De La Cruz
Santa Clara, CA 95054
(800) 799-BEAC

Emerging Trends and Issues

To keep you as up-to-date as possible on state-specific issues and trends that may affect you and your business, this subsection discusses potential and pending legislation or public concerns in California.

- A recovering, but still not buoyant California economy — Ever-increasing state government regulation of business and a high-tax environment may continue to make it difficult for the state to return to growth rates that were considered normal in the 1970s and 1980s. Continued out-migration of educated and skilled workers — many of whom are being replaced by an increasing inflow of mostly unskilled immigrant workers — is causing fiscal strains on the state government. This migration is making it more difficult for California employers to find qualified employees, as well as leading to social tensions, as reflected by the recent passage of Proposition 187. The recent troubles of the Mexican economy, unless corrected quickly, are likely to lead to major increases in emigration from that country, much of which will be into neighboring California.

- Lower state taxes — California boosted tax rates significantly during the depths of the recent recession, and while it has adopted a number of business tax incentives — including a manufacturer's investment tax credit, a permanent R&D credit, and a limited liability company law — tax rates remain high, compared to most other western states. As the economy and employment continue to rebound, look for government tax revenues to pick up substantially. This should permit the state to offer more across-the-board tax relief for businesses and individual taxpayers, making California more competitive with neighboring states in attracting business investment.

- Mandatory health care coverage — With the demise of President Clinton's national health care reform proposals in 1994, and California voter's rejection of a similar state initiative proposal in November 1994, the idea of employer-mandated health care coverage seems to be dead for now. However, the problems of inadequate or unaffordable health care coverage for large parts of the population remain, so it is likely that similar attempts to make employers foot the bill will resurface in the near future.

- Increasingly aggressive tax collection by the state — The Franchise Tax Board (FTB) has begun assessing collection cost fees against taxpayers who fail to file returns or pay taxes on time. Currently, these fees are $88 for personal income taxpayers and $166 for corporate taxpayers. They are assessed when the tax collection process reaches a certain point, usually after first mailing the taxpayer a notice that the fee will be charged if payment is not forthcoming. Filing enforcement fees of $51 for individual income tax and $560 for corporations are also being assessed, where a taxpayer fails to file a delinquent tax return within 25 days after the FTB makes a formal demand that they file.

  In addition, the state is using private collection agencies to collect taxes owed by nonresident taxpayers. The collection fees charged by these agencies, generally 20 to 25%, are then added to the amount of taxes due.

- Withholding taxes on payments to independent contractors — California has already begun to require businesses to withhold on payments made to out-of-state independent contractors for services rendered within the state. Significant tax revenue is being raised from this withholding, and bills have already been proposed in the legislature to extend such withholding to in-state independent contractors. This would create a tremendous additional paperwork burden on California businesses. Keep an eye on the newspapers for possible enactment of such a bill. If it happens, your life is going to suddenly become a lot more complicated if you use independent contractors.

National Federation of Independent Business

If you would like to keep abreast of emerging trends and issues that will affect your business, consider joining the National Federation of Independent Business (NFIB). The NFIB is this nation's largest organization representing the interests of small business owners. Through NFIB, you will learn more about pending state and federal legislation, regulations, and taxes that will affect you and, more importantly, you will be able to speak out on these issues through NFIB's state and national lobbying efforts. As an NFIB member, you would receive:

- *Independent Business (IB)*, the bimonthly national magazine for small business owners; and
- *State Reports*, that specifically cover issues in California.

For more information on NFIB, contact:

National Federation of Independent Business
Attn: Membership Services
53 Century Boulevard
Nashville, TN 37214
(800) NFIB NOW (634-2669)

11.10 State Sources of Help and Information

Throughout the state, you will be able to find many public and private agencies and organizations that can assist you with your business. For your convenience, many of these sources of help and information are listed below.

Do-It-Yourself Incorporation

You can incorporate your business on your own in California, but if you have an existing partnership or sole proprietorship that you want to convert to a corporation, see your accountant first. There may be important tax consequences that will influence the way you transfer assets and structure the corporation.

Your tax accountant, attorney, or secretary of state's office may also be able to refer you to a do-it-yourself incorporation book that can assist you through the incorporation process, providing state-specific information, ready-to-use forms, and stock certificates.

You might also want to check Kevin Finck's *California Corporation Formation Package and Minute Book*. The book's eighth edition, currently being revised for 1995, includes step-by-step instructions, stock certificates, and forms for incorporating in California.

For a basic, yet realistic overview of what owning and operating a corporation will require, you may be interested in Carl Sniffen's *The Essential Corporation Handbook*. This book is a comprehensive reference to the hows and whys of being a corporation, maintaining your corporation in good standing, and avoiding personal liability as a director, officer, or shareholder. Both *California Corporation Formation Package and Minute Book* and *The Essential Corporation Handbook* are available from The Oasis Press. For more information, contact:

The Oasis Press
(800) 228-2275

State Agency Assistance

Many state offices are available to help you find the information you need or at least refer you to the appropriate office. Unfortunately, due to the magnitude of the California state government, you will be hardpressed to find the right office to get the proper referral if you do not connect with an information specialist or a telephone receptionist who is familiar with the area of information you are seeking.

Many state agencies now have sophisticated answering systems that provide prerecorded messages and allow you to leave your query to be answered at a later time. Unfortunately, if you just need a referral to the appropriate agency, you are stuck. To combat this maze, try to contact the State Information Operator.

State Information Operator
(916) 322-9900

If you are outside the state capitol of Sacramento, you might want to reduce your phone bill by contacting the nearest Small Business Development Center (SBDC) in your area. A list of SBDCs is provided at the end of this section.

Office of Small Business

The key office you need to be aware of is the Office of Small Business (OSB), which provides management, financial, and technical assistance. The OSB also provides:

- Assistance with licensing requirements;
- Assistance with starting a small business;
- Sources of reference literature;
- Procedures for government contracting;
- Available consultant services; and
- Conferences, seminars, and workshops.

The OSB provides one-stop assistance through the its Small Business Development Centers (SBDCs), which are listed at the end of this section. The OSB also provides financial assistance through regional development corporations, which are listed in Section 11.9.

Some helpful pamphlets and booklets you may want to request from the OSB include:

- *California License Handbook* — costs $20
- *California Business Notice and Posting Handbook* — costs $6

Additionally, the Office of Small Business has a Help-Line that provides assistance through tape-recorded messages. All you need is a touch-tone phone and you can access nearly 90 topics that concern small business. The information is basic, so you can use it to ask more specific questions from the offices the Help-Line refers you to.

Topics include:

- Financial assistance to small businesses;
- Management and technical assistance to small businesses;
- Referrals to state agencies that assist small businesses, minority and women-owned businesses, and disabled veteran business enterprise programs;
- Small business publications;
- Selling to state agencies;
- Federal Small Business Administration financial assistance programs; and
- Selling to federal agencies.

A more complete list of topics and their code numbers is located in the Appendix. As its primary responsibility, the Office of Small Business will also help you settle disputes with state or federal agencies. For more information, contact:

Office of Small Business
California Trade and Commerce Agency
801 K Street, 17th Floor
Sacramento, CA 95814
(916) 324-1295
(916) 327-HELP (Help-Line)
(800) 303-6600 (Toll-free Help-Line)

State Board of Equalization

The State Board of Equalization (SBE) is the main revenue agency of the state of California. The SBE has 47 field offices throughout the state to answer your questions regarding the taxes it administers and to provide tax publications upon your request.

The information pamphlets and tax tip booklets, many of which are available at no cost, include:

- *Your California Seller's Permit, Pamphlet 73*
- *Tax Tips for Construction and Building Contractors, Publication 9*
- *Sales and Use Tax Law, Publication 1*
- *Cigarette Tax Law, Publication 4*
- *Instructions for Reporting State-Assessed Property, Publication 67*

You can also request *Pamphlet 77, Publications*, a brochure from the Document Design and Control Unit of the SBE. This brochure lists the various tax schedules, newsletters, calendars, reports, and tax laws and regulations also available. For a complete list of publications, contact the nearest SBE office or use the preaddressed post card at the back of this book to request *Pamphlet 77*. A list of the SBE field offices is located in the Appendix.

Franchise Tax Board

For personal income tax and corporate franchise tax matters, contact your local office of the Franchise Tax Board (FTB), or call:

Franchise Tax Board
P.O. Box 942840
Sacramento, CA 94240-0040
(916) 854-6600
(800) 852-5711 (Nationwide)

Employment Development Department

If you hire employees, you will have to contact the California Employment Development Department (EDD). Once you have registered with the EDD, you will receive all the materials you will need, including the *California Employer's Guide*. For more information, check your local phone directory under "Government Listings – State" for the employment tax district office nearest you.

The EDD also offers free information seminars to the public that help employers comply with state employment tax laws. Many successful businesses have already benefited by correcting noncompliance as a result of information presented in these seminars. Topics featured in the seminars include:

- State payroll reporting requirements;
- Preparing payroll tax returns;
- Avoiding unnecessary tax liabilities;
- Distinguishing between independent contractors and employees;
- New laws and emerging issues;
- Services provided by EDD; and
- Customized topics to meet specific needs.

The EDD has developed an informational brochure to help answer questions regarding these seminars. To make reservations to attend a seminar, or to obtain a copy of the information brochure, contact your local EDD Employment Tax District Office.

Employment Tax Problem Resolution Office

The EDD established the Employment Tax Problem Resolution Office (ETPRO) to ensure that employer rights are protected during the employment tax assessment and collection process. As an impartial entity within EDD, ETPRO is dedicated to helping taxpayers resolve problems that cannot be resolved through the normal chain of command. If at any time an employer is unable to resolve an employment tax problem with an EDD representative and the office manager of the EDD, he or she may contact ETPRO for assistance. ETPRO will review the issues and surrounding facts to ensure the department has properly protected the rights of the employer. To contact ETPRO, call or write to:

Employment Tax Problem Resolution Office
California Employment Development Department – Tax Branch, MIC-93
P.O. Box 826880
Sacramento, CA 94280-0001
(916) 654-8957

Also, the EDD has developed the brochure *Employers' Bill of Rights* to increase employers' awareness of their rights during the employment taxation process. To obtain a copy of the *Employers' Bill of Rights* brochure, contact your local EDD Employment Tax District Office.

Office of Business Development

If you are relocating from another state or expanding your existing business, you will want to contact the Office of Business Development. This office can assist you with information on site selection, labor supply, incentives, permits and regulations, and taxation. Two helpful publications the office provides on the above topics are:

- *The Climate's Right*
- *California Trade and Commerce Agency Sources Directory*

To obtain these publications, or for general information, contact:

Office of Business Development
California Trade and Commerce Agency
801 K Street, Suite 1700
Sacramento, CA 95814
(916) 322-3520

Cal/OSHA

If you are an employer looking for more information on California's health and safety regulations, Cal/OSHA offers two publications that will help you answer some of your questions regarding safety programs and recordkeeping requirements.

- *Developing a Workplace Safety and Health Program*
- *Recordkeeping and Reporting Requirements Under the California Occupational Safety and Health Act*

To obtain these publications, or learn more about Cal/OSHA, contact:

Communications Division
California Department of Industrial Relations
P.O. Box 420603
San Francisco, CA 94142-0603
(415) 703-4981

Federal Agency Assistance

The federal agencies described in Chapter 10 also have regional and local offices in California.

U.S. Small Business Administration

The U.S. Small Business Administration (SBA) publishes pamphlets and books covering the myriad aspects of business and provides limited financing for qualified borrowers. Instead of contacting the SBA Washington office, you can contact any of the state offices listed below.

Fresno	(209) 487-5189	**San Diego**	(619) 557-7250
Los Angeles	(818) 552-3210	**Santa Ana**	(714) 550-7420
Sacramento	(916) 498-6420	**San Francisco**	(415) 744-6820

Service Corps of Retired Executives

Sponsored by the SBA, the Service Corps of Retired Executives (SCORE) is an association of retired businesspeople in your area who provide counseling. To find the nearest chapter, write or call SCORE at one of the SBA offices above.

Small Business Institute

The Small Business Institute (SBI) program is a joint effort of the SBA and California universities. As part of their course work, senior-level college students, under the direction of faculty members, provide management consulting, market surveys, and other assistance for small business owners. To learn more about this program, contact one of the SBA offices above.

Internal Revenue Service

To ask questions or request forms from the Internal Revenue Service, you can call the toll-free information number below. You can also hear prerecorded tax information from the IRS Tele-Tax number. The codes and topics that may interest you include:

- 101 – IRS help available
- 103 – Small Business Tax Education Program
- 309 – Business use of home

- 310 – Business use of car
- 311 – Business travel expense
- 312 – Business entertainment expenses
- 352 – Self-employment tax
- 455 – Forms/Publications – How to order

For a complete list of codes, contact the IRS forms and publications number and request *Publication 910, Guide to Free Tax Services.*

Internal Revenue Service
(800) 829-1040 (Questions)
(800) 829-3676 (Forms and publications)
(213) 617-3177 (Tele-Tax, Los Angeles)
(800) 829 4477 (Tele-Tax)

Local Sources

Most communities throughout the state provide additional resources that can be invaluable to your business whether you are currently operating, just starting, or relocating a business.

Chambers of Commerce

Local chambers of commerce can be excellent resources to learn more about the area or community in which you plan to locate your business. These offices are usually very helpful sources of information and referrals. Any chamber of commerce can provide information about general business conditions, available space and rentals, and local business organizations and associations. These offices are usually listed in the White Pages of the local telephone directory.

Public Libraries

Your local public library offers a wealth of useful information. You can locate the answer to a number of business-related questions in the reference section. Statistics available on your industry and your competition can contribute to your market research and business plan. In the periodical section, you will find publications that can provide information on emerging trends and issues in the business world. Telephone and specialized directories, available in libraries, can help you locate hard-to-find suppliers, potential buyers, associations, and organizations.

Many of the larger libraries also offer a reference assistance section. If a library in your area has this service, you may even be able to call the reference librarian for the information you need. Specialized, private, or college libraries may be available in your area, as well. To find a library near you, look under the Yellow Pages or the Government Section of your phone directory.

Bank of America

Bank of America has produced an excellent series of booklets on small business operations called the *Small Business Reporter*. Titles include:

- *How to Buy or Sell a Business*
- *Understanding Financial Statements*

- *Business Financing*
- *Marketing Small Business*
- *Financial Records for Small Business*
- *Management Transitions*

Free copies of the *Small Business Reporter* can be obtained at any California branch of Bank of America.

State Business Publications

Business journals can keep you up-to-date on business-related activities and issues in California. Daily newspapers are also helpful since they cover state and local news and information that could affect your business. There may be a business journal or publication that you can subscribe to in your respective area. Here is a current listing for your convenience.

Los Angeles Business Journal
5700 Wilshire Boulevard, Suite 170
Los Angeles, CA 90036
(213) 549-5225

Santa Clara Valley Business Journal
96 North Third Street, Suite 100
San Jose, CA 95112
(408) 295-3800

Orange County Business Journal
4590 MacArthur Boulevard, Suite 100
Newport Beach, CA 92660
(714) 833-8373

San Diego Business Journal
4909 Murphy Canyon Road, Suite 200
San Diego, CA 92123
(619) 277-6359

Sacramento Business Journal
1401 21st Street, Suite 200
Sacramento, CA 95814
(916) 447-7661

San Francisco Business Times
275 Battery Street, Suite 940
San Francisco, CA 94111
(415) 989-2522

Small Business Development Centers

Small Business Development Centers (SBDCs) are located throughout the state to assist you. These centers, usually located on college campuses, provide start-up information and sponsor business-oriented seminars. Review the addresses below for the SBDC office nearest you.

SBDC: State Director's Office
801 K Street, Suite 1700
Sacramento, CA 95814
(916) 324-5068
FAX (916) 322-5084

SBDC: Napa Valley College
1556 First Street, Suite 103
Napa, CA 94559
(707) 253-3210
FAX (707) 253-3068

SBDC: North Coast (serving Del Norte and
  Humboldt counties)
779 9th Street
Crescent City, CA 95531
(707) 464-2168
FAX (707) 465-6008

SBDC: Solano County
320 Campus Lane
Suisun, CA 94585
(707) 864-3382
FAX (707) 864-3386

SBDC: Satellite Operation
408 7th Street, Suite E
Eureka, CA 95501
(707) 445-9720
FAX (707) 445-9652

SBDC: East Bay
2201 Broadway, Suite 701
Oakland, CA 94612
(510) 893-4114
FAX (510) 893-5532

SBDC: Silicon Valley, San Mateo County
111 North Market Street, Suite 150
San Jose, CA 95113
(408) 298-7694
FAX (408) 971-0680

SBDC: Satellite Operation (serving San
Mateo and Northern Santa Clara counties)
1730 South Amphlett Boulevard, Suite 208
San Mateo, CA 94402
(415) 358-0271
FAX (415) 358-9450

SBDC: Gavilan College (serving Southern
Santa Clara, San Benito, and Monterey
east of Highway 101)
7436 Monterey Street
Gilroy, CA 95020
(408) 847-0373
FAX (408) 847-0393

SBDC: Central Coast (serving Santa Cruz
and Monterey counties west of Highway 101)
6500 Soquel Drive
Aptos, CA 95003
(408) 479-6136
FAX (408) 479-5743

SBDC: Butte College Tri-County (serving
Butte, Glenn, and Tehama counties)
260 Cohasset Road, Suite A
Chico, CA 95926
(916) 895-9017
FAX (916) 895-9099

SBDC: Sierra College (serving Sierra,
Placer, and Nevada counties)
560 Wall Street, Suite J
Auburn, CA 95603
(916) 885-5488
FAX (916) 823-4704

SBDC: Greater Sacramento Area (serving
Sacramento, El Dorado, and Yolo counties)
1787 Tribute Road, Suite A
Sacramento, CA 95815
(916) 263-6580
FAX (916) 263-6571

SBDC: San Joaquin Delta College (serving
San Joaquin, Calaveras, Amador, and
Alpine counties)
814 North Hunter
Stockton, CA 95202
(209) 474-5089
FAX (209) 474-5605

SBDC: Valley Sierra
1012 Eleventh Street, Suite 300
Modesto, CA 95354
(209) 521-6177
FAX (209) 521-9373

SBDC: Satellite Operation (serving
Merced, Mariposa, Stanislaus, and
Tuolumne counties)
1632 N Street
Merced, CA 95340
(209) 385-7312
FAX (209) 383-4959

SBDC: Eastern Los Angeles County (serving
East Los Angeles, Pasadena, Glendale,
West Covina, and Pomona)
363 South Park Avenue, Suite 100
Pomona, CA 91766
(909) 629-2247
FAX (909) 629-8310

SBDC: Weill Institute (serving Kern, Mono,
and Inyo counties)
1330 22nd Street, Suite B
Bakersfield, CA 93301
(805) 322-5881
FAX (805) 322-5663

SBDC: Northern Los Angeles (serving
Burbank, Van Nuys, and San Fernando
Valley)
14540 Victory Boulevard, Suite 206
Van Nuys, CA 91411-1618
(818) 373-7092
FAX (818) 373-7740

Export SBDC of Southern California
110 East 9th, Suite A669
Los Angeles, CA 90079
(213) 892-1111
FAX (213) 892-8232

SBDC: Satellite Operation (serving Los
Angeles, Ventura, and Santa Barbara
counties)
300 Esplanade Drive, Suite 1010
Oxnard, CA 93030
(805) 981-4633
FAX (805) 988-1862

SBDC: Orange County
901 East Santa Ana Boulevard, Suite 101
Santa Ana, CA 92701
(714) 647-1172
FAX (714) 835-9008

SBDC: Inland Empire (serving Riverside and San Bernardino counties)
2002 Iowa Avenue, Suite 110
Riverside, CA 92507
(909) 781-2345
FAX (909) 781-2353

SBDC: Greater San Diego Chamber of Commerce (serving northern San Diego County)
4275 Executive Square, Suite 920
La Jolla, CA 92037
(619) 453-9388
FAX (619) 450-1997

SBDC: Accelerate Technology
Graduate School of Management, Room 230
University of California, Irvine
Irvine, CA 92717-3125
(714) 856-8366
FAX (714) 725-2978

SBDC: Southwest Los Angeles County
21221 Western Avenue, Suite 110
Torrance, CA 90501
(310) 782-3861
FAX (310) 782-8607

SBDC: Redwood Empire
520 Mendocino Avenue, Suite 210
Santa Rosa, CA 95401
(707) 524-1770
FAX (707) 524-1772

SBDC: Satellite Operation (serving Sonoma, Lake, and Mendocino counties)
Hilltop Professional Center
15322 Lakeshore Drive, Suite 205
P.O. Box 4550
Clearlake, CA 95422
(707) 995-3440
FAX (707) 995-3605

SBDC: Central California (serving Fresno, Madera, Kings, and Tulare counties)
1999 Tuolumne Street, Suite 650
Fresno, CA 93721
(209) 237-0660
FAX (209) 237-1417

SBDC: Satellite Operation
430 West Caldwell, Suite D
Visalia, CA 93277
(209) 625-3051
(209) 625-3052
FAX (209) 625-3053

SBDC: Southwestern College Small Business Development and International Trade Center
(serving southern San Diego County)
900 Otay Lakes Road, Building 1600
Chula Vista, CA 91910
(619) 482-6393
FAX (619) 482-6402

Endnotes

1. CAL. CORP. CODE § 17000 *et seq.*
2. CAL. CORP. CODE § 15010.5.
3. CAL. CORP. CODE § 15632.
4. CAL. CORP. CODE § 15643(b).
5. CAL. CORP. CODE §§ 15611–15723.
6. CAL. CORP. CODE § 15632.
7. CAL. CORP. CODE §§ 15632(b)(5) and 15636.
8. CAL. CORP. CODE § 15666.
9. CAL. CORP. CODE § 15621.
10. CAL. CORP. CODE § 15621; CAL. GOV'T. CODE § 12213.
11. CAL. CORP. CODE § 15621(d).
12. CAL. CORP. CODE § 15712(b)(4).
13. CAL. REV. & TAX. CODE § 23081.
14. CAL. REV. & TAX. CODE § 23081(e).
15. CAL. GOV'T. CODE § 12201.
16. CAL. CORP. CODE §§ 25102(h), 25102(f), or 25102(n).
17. CAL. GOV'T. CODE § 12204.
18. CAL. CORP. CODE § 2105.
19. CAL. REV. & TAX. CODE § 23800 *et seq.*
20. CAL. CORP. CODE § 1502.
21. CAL. GOV'T. CODE § 12210(a).
22. CAL. CORP. CODE § 2117.
23. CAL. REV. & TAX. CODE § 25128.
24. CAL. REV & TAX. CODE § 17000 *et seq.*
25. CAL. CORP. CODE § 17050(a).
26. CAL. CORP. CODE § 17050(b).
27. CAL. CORP. CODE § 17052(a).
28. CAL. CORP. CODE § 17701.
29. CAL. REV. & TAX. CODE § 18633.5(a).
30. CAL. REV. & TAX. CODE § 23091.
31. CAL. REV. & TAX. CODE § 23092.
32. CAL. REV. & TAX. CODE § 18633.5(h).
33. Section 93 of the Beverly-Killea Limited Liability Company Act (S.B. 469).
34. CAL. COM. CODE § 6103(c)(12).
35. CAL. COM. CODE § 6104.
36. CAL. COM. CODE § 6105(b).
37. Id.
38. CAL. UNEMP. INS. CODE § 1733.
39. CAL. REV. & TAX. CODE § 6812.
40. CAL. REV. & TAX. CODE § 19136.
41. CAL. REV. & TAX. CODE § 19144.
42. CAL. REV. & TAX. CODE § 19147.
43. *Quill Corp. vs. North Dakota,* Sup. Ct. 1904 (1992).
44. CAL. REV. & TAX. CODE § 441.
45. CAL. REV. & TAX. CODE § 463.
46. CAL. REV. & TAX. CODE § 18662(e).
47. CAL. ADMIN. CODE tit. 18, § 18805-3 and CAL. REV. & TAX. CODE § 18662.
48. CAL. REV. & TAX. CODE § 18666.
49. CAL. BUS. & PROF. CODE § 17910.5.
50. CAL. BUS. & PROF. CODE § 17910.
51. CAL. BUS. & PROF. CODE § 17929(a).
52. CAL. BUS. & PROF. CODE § 17917(a).
53. CAL. BUS. & PROF. CODE § 17917(d).
54. CAL. UNEMP. INS. CODE § 13020.
55. CAL. UNEMP. INS. CODE §§ 984–985.
56. CAL. UNEMP. INS. CODE § 13021(a).
57. CAL. UNEMP. INS. CODE § 13021(j).
58. CAL. UNEMP. INS. CODE § 13050(c)(2).
59. CAL. UNEMP. INS. CODE § 13021(c).
60. CAL. UNEMP. INS. CODE § 13021(h).
61. CAL. UNEMP. INS. CODE § 675.
62. CAL. UNEMP. INS. CODE § 1086.
63. CAL. LAB. CODE § 3700.
64. CAL. LAB. CODE § 3351(c).
65. CAL. LAB. CODE § 3551.
66. CAL. LAB. CODE § 5401.
67. CAL. LAB. CODE § 3550.
68. CAL. LAB. CODE § 6401.7.
69. CAL. LAB. CODE § 6408.
70. CAL. LAB. CODE § 6431.
71. CAL. LAB. CODE § 6410.
72. CALIFORNIA DEPARTMENT OF INDUSTRIAL RELATIONS, *A Guide to Cal/OSHA,* June 1985.
73. CAL. LAB. CODE § 6411.
74. CAL. ADMIN. CODE tit. 8, § 342.
75. CAL. LAB. CODE § 6500.
76. CAL. LAB. CODE § 6404.5.
77. Cal. I.W.C. Orders 1-89, 4-89, 5-89, 7-90, and 10-89.
78. CAL. LAB. CODE § 1183.
79. CAL. LAB. CODE § 207.
80. CAL. LAB. CODE § 204.
81. CAL. LAB. CODE §§ 201–202.
82. Cal. I.W.C. Order no. MW-88, pursuant to CAL. LAB. CODE § 1182.
83. Cal. I.W.C. Orders 1-89, 4-89, 5-89, 7-90, and 10-89.

84. Id.

85. Id.

86. Id.

87. Id.

88. Cal. Lab. Code § 1290.

89. Cal. Lab. Code §§ 1291–1294.

90. Cal. Lab. Code § 1391(a)(3).

91. Cal. Gov't. Code § 12945.2.

92. Cal. Gov't. Code § 12945(b)(2).

93. Cal. Unemp. Ins. Code § 1088.5.

94. Cal. Gov't. Code § 12926(d).

95. Cal. Gov't. Code § 12940(a).

96. Cal. Gov't. Code § 12941.

97. Cal. Gov't. Code § 12950(b).

98. Cal. Bus. & Prof. Code §§ 23000–24082.

99. Cal. Health & Safety Code §§ 25299.41 and 25299.43.

100. Cal. Pub. Res. Code ch. 93, Laws (1939).

101. Cal. Rev. & Tax. Code §§ 38101–38805.

102. Cal. Health & Safety Code § 25205.5.

103. Cal. Health & Safety Code § 25205.6.

104. Cal. Rev. & Tax. Code §§ 10701–11005.6.

105. Cal. Rev. & Tax. Code § 5721.

106. Cal. Rev. & Tax. Code § 11401.

107. Cal. Rev. & Tax. Code § 11404.

108. Cal. Rev. & Tax. Code § 23609.

109. Cal. Rev. & Tax. Code § 17053.49.

110. Cal. Rev. & Tax. Code § 6902.2.

111. Cal. Rev. & Tax. Code § 18152.5.

112. Cal. Rev. & Tax. Code § 23605.

113. Cal. Rev. & Tax. Code § 24416.

114. Cal. Rev. & Tax. Code § 24416(b)(2).

115. Cal. Rev. & Tax. Code § 24416(e)(2).

116. Cal. Rev. & Tax. Code § 24416(f)(1).

117. Cal. Rev. & Tax. Code § 24416(b)(3).

118. Cal. Rev. & Tax. Code § 24416.3(c).

119. Cal. Rev. & Tax. Code § 17053.10.

120. Cal. Rev. & Tax. Code § 17052.15.

121. Cal. Rev. & Tax. Code § 17266.

122. Cal. Rev. & Tax. Code § 17233.

123. Cal. Rev. & Tax. Code §§ 17053.45, 17053.46, 17268, and 17276.2(d).

124. Cal. Rev. & Tax. Code § 24402.

125. Cal. Const. art. XV, § 1.

126. Cal. Rev. & Tax. Code § 18151.

Index

(continued)

Appendix

Checklist of Tax and Other Major Requirements for Nearly All Small Businesses

Requirement	Number of Employees of Business:							Section Reference
	None	1–4	5–10	11–14	15–19	20–99	100+	
Federal estimated taxes	√	√	√	√	√	√	√	Sec. 4.6
Federal income tax returns	√	√	√	√	√	√	√	Sec. 4.12
Form SS-4, Application for Federal I.D. Number:								
Sole Proprietorships		√	√	√	√	√	√	Sec. 5.2
Partnerships	√	√	√	√	√	√	√	Sec. 5.2
Corporations	√	√	√	√	√	√	√	Sec. 5.2
Form 1099 returns	√	√	√	√	√	√	√	Sec. 4.7
Federal payroll tax returns		√	√	√	√	√	√	Sec. 5.2, 5.3
Provide and file W-2's to employees at year-end		√	√	√	√	√	√	Sec. 5.2
ERISA compliance:								
For unfunded or insured employees' welfare plan:								
Provide a Summary Plan Description to employees		√	√	√	√	√	√	Sec. 5.5
File a Summary Plan Description							√	Sec. 5.5
File *Form 5500, Annual Report*							√	Sec. 5.5
Provide a Summary Annual Report to employees							√	Sec. 5.5
File and provide to employees a Summary of Material Plan Modifications							√	Sec. 5.5
File a Terminal Report, if plan terminated							√	Sec. 5.5
For funded employee welfare plan:								
File and provide all items described in ERISA list		√	√	√	√	√	√	Sec. 5.5
For employees' pension or profit-sharing plan:								
Provide a Summary Plan Description to employees and file with U.S. Department of Labor		√	√	√	√	√	√	Sec. 5.5
File *Form 5500, Annual Report*							√	Sec. 5.5
File *Form 5500-EZ* or *Form 5500-C/R*		√	√	√	√	√		Sec. 5.5
Provide to employees and file a Summary of Material Modifications		√	√	√	√	√	√	Sec. 5.5
File a Terminal Report, if plan terminated		√	√	√	√	√	√	Sec. 5.5
Provide a Summary Annual Report to employees		√	√	√	√	√	√	Sec. 5.5
Bonding requirement for plan officials		√	√	√	√	√	√	Sec. 5.5
Federal Wage and Hour Laws and Regulations — coverage depends on nature of business and employee types not covered		√	√	√	√	√	√	Sec. 5.7

Checklist of Tax and Other Major Requirements for Nearly All Small Businesses (continued)

Requirement	None	1–4	5–10	11–14	15–19	20–99	100+	Section Reference
Federal Fair Employment Laws:								
Americans with Disabilities Act anti-discrimination rules					√	√	√	Sec. 5.8
Anti-discrimination laws regarding race, color, sex, etc.					√	√	√	Sec. 5.8, 11.5
Anti-discrimination laws regarding age						√	√	Sec. 5.8
Anti-discrimination laws regarding federal contracts		√	√	√	√	√	√	Sec. 5.8
Discrimination in Employment is Prohibited			√	√	√	√	√	Sec. 11.5
Equal Pay Act for Women		√	√	√	√	√	√	Sec. 5.8
File *Form EEO-1*							√	Sec. 5.8
Post notice regarding discrimination: racial, sexual, etc.					√	√	√	Sec. 5.8
Post notice regarding age anti-discrimination laws						√	√	Sec. 5.8
Post other anti-discrimination notices by certain federal contractors		√	√	√	√	√	√	Sec. 5.8
Federal Family and Medical Leave Act						√*	√	Sec. 5.12
Post notice regarding family and medical leave						√*	√	Sec. 5.12
Immigration Laws:								
Complete *INS Form I-9* for each new hire		√	√	√	√	√	√	Sec. 5.9
OSHA Job Safety Regulations:								
Health and safety		√	√	√	√	√	√	Sec. 5.6
Post *Job Safety and Health Notice*		√	√	√	√	√	√	Sec. 5.6
Post *Employee Rights Notice* regarding OSHA		√	√	√	√	√	√	Sec. 5.6
Record industrial injuries and illnesses				√	√	√	√	Sec. 5.6
Report job fatalities or multiple injuries to OSHA		√	√	√	√	√	√	Sec. 5.6
Federal and State Child Labor Laws		√	√	√	√	√	√	Sec. 5.7, 11.5
Local business licenses	√	√	√	√	√	√	√	Sec. 4.3, 11.4
Sales and use tax permit and returns, if selling tangible personal property	√	√	√	√	√	√	√	Sec. 11.4
Fictitious business name statement, if using fictitious business name	√	√	√	√	√	√	√	Sec. 11.4
California estimated taxes	√	√	√	√	√	√	√	Sec. 11.4
California income taxes	√	√	√	√	√	√	√	Sec. 11.2, 11.4
California Wage and Hour Laws and Regulations — most employees are covered, yet some types are not		√	√	√	√	√	√	Sec. 11.5
Workers' compensation insurance		√	√	√	√	√	√	Sec. 11.5
California Fair Employment Laws: General prohibition of discrimination		√	√	√	√	√	√	Sec. 11.5

* Only applies to companies with 50 or more employees.

Checklist of Official Government Posters and Notices Required to be Displayed by Businesses

Type of Poster or Notice	Who Must Post	Where to Obtain
Local business license	Nearly all businesses operating in a particular locality.	Local city hall or county courthouse
Sales tax permit	Each place of business where tangible personal property is sold.	State tax office
OSHA poster regarding job safety and health	All employers.	U.S. Department of Labor, Occupational Safety and Health Administration
U.S. Fair Labor Standards Act Federal Minimum Wage poster *(WH Publication 1088)*	Employers with employees whose wages and working conditions are subject to the U.S. Fair Labor Standards Act.	U.S. Department of Labor, Employment Standards Administration, Wage and Hour Division
Federal Equal Employment Opportunity poster	All employers with 15 or more employees 20 weeks of a calendar year or with federal contracts or subcontracts of $10,000 or more.	Federal Equal Employment Opportunity Commission
Federal Age Discrimination poster	All employers with 20 or more employees, 20 or more weeks in a calendar year.	U.S. Department of Labor, Wage and Hour Division
Federal Rehabilitation Act poster regarding hiring of disabled persons	Employers with federal contracts or subcontracts of $2,500 or more.	Assistant Secretary for Employment Standards, U.S. Department of Labor, Washington, D.C.
Poster regarding hiring of Vietnam-era veterans	Employers with federal contracts or subcontracts of $10,000 or more.	The government contracting officer on the federal contract
Employee Polygraph Protection Act notice	Most private employers.	U.S. Department of Labor, Wage and Hour Division
Poster explaining the Family and Medical Leave Act of 1993	Employers with 50 or more employees during 20 weeks of the year.	U.S. Department of Labor, Wage and Hour Division

Checklist of Official Government Posters and Notices Required to be Displayed

Type of Poster or Notice	When required	Where to obtain
Notice to Employees of Unemployment Insurance and Disability Insurance (DE 1857)	Required to be posted by all employers subject to California unemployment insurance and disability insurance taxes.	California Employment Development Department
Notice regarding workers' compensation insurance, *Notice of Compensation Carrier*	Required to be posted by nearly all California employers and must give the insurance carrier's name, the date coverage expires, and the phone number of the nearest State Labor Commissioner's office.	Your workers' compensation carrier
Cal/OSHA poster: *Safety and Health Protection on the Job —* Cal/OSHA *Form 1000*	Required to be posted by all California employers.	**Communications Division – Posters California Department of Industrial Relations** P.O. Box 420603 San Francisco, CA 94101-0603
California Industrial Welfare Commission *Orders Regulating Wages, Working Conditions, and Hours* (IWC *Form 1104*)	Required to be posted by all California employers.	Fifteen different orders applicable to various industries and businesses are available. To receive the appropriate poster, contact the California Department of Industrial Relations and indicate the nature of your business.
Pay Day Notice	Required to be posted by all California employers.	**Communications Division – Posters California Department of Industrial Relations** P.O. Box 420603 San Francisco, CA 94101-0603
Discrimination in Employment is Prohibited by Law	Required to be posted by all California employers with five or more employees. To request this poster, send a self-addressed stamped envelope to the address at right.	**Communications Center California Department of Fair Employment and Housing** 2014 T Street, Suite 210 Sacramento, CA 95814

California Small Business Help-Line — Topics and Code Numbers

(800) 303-6600

(916) 327-HELP

Help-Line Brochure
To receive a brochure of the Help-Line Menu, press 3 and the # sign and leave your name and address.

California Small Business Development Center Program
- [1][0] California Small Business Development Centers (SBDCs)
- [1][1] Types of small business assistance
- [1][2] Business licensing and permit assistance
- [1][3] Workshops and seminars
- [1][4] One-on-one business counseling services
- [1][5] Referrals to financial resources
- [1][6] Business plans and marketing assistance
- [1][7] Business Environmental Assistance Center (BEAC)
- [1][8] Technology transfer information and assistance
- [1][9] Export financing & business development

Telephone Numbers to Centers & Market Areas of California Financial Corporations
- [2][0] Alameda County to Kern County
- [2][1] Kings County to Modoc County
- [2][2] Mono County to San Diego County
- [2][3] San Francisco County to Siskiyou County
- [2][4] Solano County to Yuba County
- [2][5] California Financial Corporations

State Financial Assistance Programs Sponsored by California Office of Small Business
- [3][0] Overview of Programs
- [3][1] California Loan Guarantee Program
- [3][2] California Bond Guarantee Program
- [3][3] California Loans for Environmental Assistance Now (CLEAN)
- [3][4] RUST Loans: Repair/Replacement of Underground Storage Tanks
- [3][5] Hazardous Waste Loan Program
- [3][6] Fishing Fleet Loan Program
- [3][7] Farm Loan Program
- [3][8] California Export Loan Assistance Program

Telephone Numbers and Addresses to State Financial Assistance Programs
- [4][0] Bay Area Financial Corporation
- [4][1] California Capital Financial Corporation
- [4][2] California Coastal Financial Corporation
- [4][3] California Southern Financial Corporation
- [4][4] Hancock Financial Corporation
- [4][5] Pacific Coast Regional Financial Corporation
- [4][6] SAFE-BIDCO
- [4][7] Valley Financial Corporation

[5][0] California Small Business Publications
- [6][1] California License Handbook
- [6][2] California Business Posting and Notice Handbook
- [6][3] And More!

[7][0] State Certification & Registration
- [7][1] Small Business Preference Program
- [7][2] Women-Owned Business Certification
- [7][3] Minority-Owned Business Certification
- [7][4] Disabled Veteran Business Certification
- [7][5] Selling to state agencies

[8][0] Federal Small Business Programs
- [8][1] Small Business Administration (SBA)
- [8][2] Loan Guarantee & Bonding Programs
- [8][3] Export Loan Guarantee Program
- [8][4] Viet Nam Veteran Era Loans
- [8][5] Small Business Investment Companies
- [8][6] Small Business Innovative Research
- [8][7] Fixed Assets Loans (504 Loan Program)
- [8][8] Small Business/Minority Certification, selling to federal agencies

If you are sponsoring or know of small business events, such as conferences, workshops, or seminars, please send the details to:

The California Small Business Advocate
801 K Street, 17th Floor
Sacramento, CA 95814

Instructions for Requisition for Employment Development Department Publications

REQUISITION FOR EMPLOYMENT DEVELOPMENT DEPARTMENT PUBLICATIONS

Use the order blank on the reverse to request Employment Development Department forms and publications. Indicate the quantity requested on the line preceding the form number.

After completing the information on the reverse side of this form, mail it back to the EDD by simply folding the form on the indicated fold lines so that the EDD address appears on the outside, tape the form closed (**do not tape sides**), and affix proper postage. A new requisition form will be sent with each shipment of supplies.

Order no more than a six month's supply of forms since overstocking may result in your having obsolete forms.

Do not use this form to reorder preprinted Report of Contributions Booklet (DE 88) use the reorder form enclosed *with your* DE 88 booklet. If you have not received a DE 88 coupon booklet, contact your nearest Employment Tax District Office.

Do not use this form to order the First Claim for Disability Insurance (DE 2501). These forms are preprinted with the appropriate field office address, and may be conveniently obtained by phone order. Consult the white pages of your local telephone book under "State Government/Employment Development Department" for the telephone number of the nearest Disability Insurance office.

fold here first

Place
Stamp
Here

Employment Development Department
805 R Street
Sacramento   CA   95814-6497

fold here last

Requisition for Employment Development Department Publications

EDD

Serving the People of California

REQUISITION FOR EMPLOYMENT DEVELOPMENT DEPARTMENT PUBLICATIONS

See instructions on reverse side before completing this requisition form.

___	DE 1	Registration Form for Commercial Employers	___	DE 4	Employee's Withholding Allowance Certificate
___	DE 1AG	Registration Form for Agricultural Employers	___	DE 4P	Withholding Certificate for Pension or
___	DE 1GS	Registration Form for Governmental			Annuity Payments
		Organizations & Public Schools	___	DE 6	Annual Contribution Return
___	DE 1HW	Registration Form for Employers of House-	___	DE 7	Annual Reconciliation Form
		hold Workers	___	DE 34	Report of New Employee(s)
___	DE 1NP	Registration Form for Nonprofit Employers	___	DE 43	Annual Reconciliation of California Personal
___	DE 1P	Registration Form for Employers Depositing			Income Tax Withheld
		Only Personal Income Tax Withholding	___	DE 43 I	DE 43 Information Sheet
___	DE 3B	Report of Wages	___	DE 44	California Employer's Guide
___	DE 3D	Quarterly Contribution Return (Voluntary	___	DE 938	Quarterly Return Adjustment Form
		Plan)	___	DE 2566	Elective Coverage
___	DE 3DP	Quarterly Contribution Return			

___	DE 231	Employment	___	DE 231SC	Specialized Coverage
___	DE 231A	Wages	___	DE 231SE	Statutory Employees (Agent/Commission
___	DE 231B	Automotive Repair Industry			Drivers, Traveling/City Salespersons,
___	DE 231C	Beauty and Barber Shops			Construction Workers, Homeworkers, Artists,
___	DE 231CF	Commercial Fishing			and Authors)
___	DE 231D	Multi-State Employment	___	DE 231T	Tips
___	DE 231E	Restaurant and Hotel Industry	___	DE 231TA	Employment Tax Audit Process
___	DE 231EB	Taxability of Employee Benefits	___	DE 231V	Election Campaign Workers
___	DE 231EC	Disability Insurance Elective Coverage (DIEC)	___	DE 231W	Personal Income Tax Abatement
___	DE 231EE	Exempt Employment	___	DE 231Y	Reporting New Employee Hiring
___	DE 231F	Temporary Services and Employee Leasing	___	DE 231Z	California System of Experience Rating
		Industries	___	DE 631	Employment Fraud Task Force
___	DE 231FE	Foreign Employment and Employment on	___	DE 631C	Offers in Compromise
		American Vessels or Aircraft	___	DE 631P	Payment Proposal
___	DE 231G	Construction Industry	___	DE 631TL	State Tax Lien
___	DE 231H	Manufacturing Industry	___	DE 159	Use Magnetic Media
___	DE 231 I	Services Industry	___	DE 195	Employer's Bill of Rights
___	DE 231J	Waiver of Penalty Policy	___	DE 195/S/	Employer's Bill of Rights (Spanish)
___	DE 231K	Casual Labor	___	DE 573	Avoid Unplanned Tax Liabilities
___	DE 231L	Domestic Services	___	DE 573/S/	Avoid Unplanned Tax Liabilities (Spanish)
___	DE 231M	Residential Care Facilities	___	DE 1857A	Notice to Employees
___	DE 231N	Salespersons	___	DE 1857A/S/	Notice to Employees (Spanish)
___	DE 231NP	Nonprofit Entities	___	DE 2320	Job Services, Unemployment, Disability
___	DE 231P	Withholding from Pensions, Annuities, and			Insurance
		Certain Other Deferred Income	___	DE 2320/S/	Job Services, Unemployment, Disability
___	DE 231PE	Public Entities			Insurance (Spanish)
___	DE 231PS	Personal Income Tax Withholding - Supple-	___	DE 2515	State Disability Insurance
		mental Wage Payments, Moving Expense	___	DE 2515/S/	State Disability Insurance
		Reimbursement	___	DE 8684	Work Sharing Program
___	DE 231Q	Employee FICA/SDI Taxes Paid by Employer	___	DE 8714CC	Disability Elective Coverage Fact Sheet
___	DE 231R	Third-Party Sick Pay	___	DE 8829	Household Employer's Guide
			___	EFT-I	Electronic Funds Transfer

State of California / Employment Development Department

State of California
Employment Development Department
805 R Street, Warehouse
Sacramento CA 95814-6497

(PLEASE PRINT OR TYPE)

ATTN:

COMPANY NAME:

STREET

CITY   STATE   ZIP

State of California
Employment Development Department
805 R Street, Warehouse
Sacramento CA 95814-6497

(PLEASE PRINT OR TYPE)

ATTN:

COMPANY NAME:

STREET

CITY   STATE   ZIP

State Board of Equalization Offices

CALIFORNIA STATE BOARD OF EQUALIZATION OFFICES

BOARD MEMBERS

DISTRICT	MEMBER	OFFICE ADDRESS	AREA CODE	TELEPHONE NUMBER
First	Member	450 N Street, PO Box 942879, Sacramento, 94279-0001	916	445-4081
Second	Brad Sherman	901 Wilshire Boulevard, Suite 210, Santa Monica, 90401-1856	310	451-5777
			818	360-3186
Third	Ernest J. Dronenburg, Jr.	110 West C Street, Suite 1709, San Diego, 92101-3966	619	237-7844
Fourth	Matthew K. Fong	13200 Crossroads Pkwy. No., Ste 450, City of Industry, 91746-3497	310	908-0524
EXECUTIVE DIRECTOR				
	Burton W. Oliver	450 N Street, PO Box 942879, Sacramento, 94279-0001	916	445-6464

SACRAMENTO HEADQUARTERS — **450 N Street, PO Box 942879, Sacramento 94279-0001** — **916** — **445-6464**

BUSINESS TAXES FIELD OFFICES

CALIFORNIA CITIES	OFFICE HOURS 8-5 UNLESS OTHERWISE LISTED BELOW	OFFICE ADDRESS	AREA CODE	TELEPHONE NUMBER
Arroyo Grande		1303 Grand Avenue, Suite 115, 93420-2461	805	489-6293
Auburn	8-12 & 1-5 M thru F	11714 Enterprise Drive, 95603	916	885-8408
Bakersfield		1800 30th Street, Suite 150, PO Box 1728, 93302-1728	805	395-2880
Bishop	8-12 & 1-5 M thru F	407 West Line Street, 93514-3321	619	872-3701
Chico	8-12 & 1-5 M thru F	8 Williamsburg Lane, 95926-2225	916	895-5322
Concord		1001 Galaxy Way, 94520 (PO Box 5965, Concord 94524)	510	687-6962
City of Industry		12820 Crossroads Parkway, PO Box 90818, 91715-0818	310	908-5280
Crescent City	8-12 & 1-5 M thru F	555 101 So. Highway, Suite B, PO Box 367, 95531-0367	707	464-2321
Culver City		5901 Green Valley Circle, PO Box 3652, 90231-3652	310	342-1000
El Centro		1295 State Street, Suite 201, 92243-2833	619	352-3431
Eureka	8-12 & 1-5 M thru F	134 D Street, Suite 301, PO Box 4884, 95502-4884	707	445-6500
Fresno		5070 N. Sixth Street, Suite 110, PO Box 28580, 93729-8580	209	248-4219
Grass Valley	8-12 & 1-5 M thru F	10375 Brunswick Road, Suite 100, 95945-9986	916	272-1347
Laguna Hills		23141 Moulton Parkway, Suite 100, PO Box 30890, 92654-0890	714	770-2157
Lancaster		43301 North Division Street, Suite 206, PO Box 5149, 93539-5149	805	940-7383
Marysville		922 G Street, PO Box 790, 95901-0790	916	741-4301
Merced	8-12 & 1-5 M thru F	635 Olivewood Drive, P.O. Box 192, 95341-0192	209	726-6527
Modesto		3340 Tully Road, Suite A, PO Box 5237, 95352-5237	209	576-6360
Norwalk		12440 E. Imperial Highway, PO Box 409, 90651-0409	310	466-1694
Oakland		2101 Webster Street, Suite 210, No. 46, 94612-3027	510	286-0347
Placerville	8-12 & 1-5 M thru F	344 Placerville Drive, Suite 12, PO Box 965, 95667-0965	916	622-1101
Quincy	9-1 M thru F	546 Lawrence Street, PO Box 938, 95971-0938	916	283-1070
Rancho Mirage		42-700 Bob Hope Drive, Suite 301, 92270-4473	619	346-8096
Redding		391 Hemstead Drive, PO Box 492529, 96049-2529	916	224-4729
Riverside		6700 Indiana Avenue, Suite 225, 92506-4204	909	782-4330
Sacramento		9823 Old Winery Place, Suite 1, 95827-1731	916	255-3350
Salinas		21 West Laurel Drive, Suite 79, 93906-3485	408	443-3008
San Bernardino		303 West Third Street, Suite 500, PO Box 1305, 92402-1305	909	383-4701
San Diego		1350 Front Street, Rm 5047, 92101-3612	619	525-4526
San Francisco		50 Fremont Street, Suite 1400, 94105-2234	415	396-9800
San Jose		100 Paseo de San Antonio, Rm 307, 95113-1477	408	277-1231
San Marcos		334 Via Vera Cruz, Suite 107, 92069-2637	619	744-1330
San Mateo		177 Bovet Road, Suite 250, PO Box 5530, 94402-5530	415	573-3800
San Rafael		7 Mt. Lassen Drive, Suite B136, 94903-0248	415	472-1513
Santa Ana		28 Civic Center Plaza, Rm 239, PO Box 12040, 92712-2040	714	558-4059
Santa Cruz		8030 Soquel Avenue, Suite 100, 95062-2094	408	462-9496
Santa Rosa		50 D Street, Rm 215, PO Box 730, 95402-0730	707	576-2100
Sonora	8-12 & 1-5 M thru F	1194 N. Highway 49, Suite 385, 95370-0385	209	532-6979
South Lake Tahoe	8-12 & 1-5 M thru F	2489 Lake Tahoe Boulevard, Suite 7, 96150-7729	916	544-4816
Stockton		31 East Channel Street, Rm 264, PO Box 1890, 95201-1890	209	948-7720
Torrance		680 W. Knox Street, PO Box T, 90507-0270	310	516-4300
Ukiah		620 Kings Court, Suite 110, 95482	707	463-4731
Union City		32145 Alvarado-Niles Road, PO Box 1887, 94587-6887	510	429-7090
Vallejo		704 Tuolumne Street, 94590-0625	707	648-4065
Van Nuys		6150 Van Nuys Boulevard, Rm 205, PO Box 7735, 91409-7735	818	901-5293
Ventura		1001 Partridge Drive, Suite 200, 93003-5599	805	654-4523
Visalia		4930 W. Kaweah Ct., Ste. 205, 93277	209	732-5641
Yreka	8-12 & 1-5 M thru F	1217 South Main Street, PO Box 435, 96097-0435	916	842-7439

OUT-OF-STATE FIELD OFFICES

Sacramento		450 N Street. PO Box 188268, 95818-0268	916	322-2010
Chicago, Illinois		150 North Wacker Drive, Rm 1400, 60606-1606	312	201-5300
New York, N.Y.		675 Third Avenue, Rm 520, 10017-4015	212	697-4680
Houston, Texas		9800 Northwest Freeway, Brookhollow Two, Suite 204, 77092-8807	713	681-1106

Addresses, office hours, and telephone numbers are current as of 12-1-94

Instructions for Form BT-400-MIP – Application for a Seller's Permit

BT-400-MIP (S1F) REV. 8 (9-94)

STATE OF CALIFORNIA
BOARD OF EQUALIZATION

APPLICATION FOR SELLER'S PERMIT AND REGISTRATION AS A RETAILER (INDIVIDUALS/PARTNERS)

WHO MUST HAVE A PERMIT

Generally, if you sell taxable merchandise or provide a taxable service in California, such as renting merchandise or fabrication labor, you must have a seller's permit. Wholesalers as well as retailers **must have a separate permit for each place of business.**

This application includes information you need to obtain a permit as well as a brief description of your rights and responsibilities once the permit is obtained.

If you have specific questions about information contained in this application, please contact any Board of Equalization office listed on the back of this page.

HOW TO OBTAIN A PERMIT

To obtain a seller's permit, you must complete the attached application. Directions for completing the application follow.

1. **Type or print neatly in ink.** The application is organized into sections. To help us issue your permit quickly and accurately, be sure the information you include in each section is correct and legible. Your application will become a part of your permanent file with us, and the information you included in your application — except for your name, business name and address, permit number, and status (active or closed out) — is confidential and may not be furnished to the public.

2. **Complete only the unshaded portions of the application.** In addition, the application is printed on both the front and reverse. Be sure to complete both sides.

3. **Be sure to indicate the type of ownership of your business.** If you check Partnership and if the Board requests, please include a copy of the partnership agreement with your application. If you do not supply the necessary documents, your permit may be delayed.

4. **Be sure the Certification Section is completed and signed by the owner or one partner.** The application should also be signed in Section I by the owner. In the case of a partnership all partners should also sign in Section I.

5. **Return the completed application to the Board office from which this application was obtained.** Locations, mailing addresses, and telephone numbers of Board offices may be found on the back of this page. Once your application is reviewed and found in order, you will be issued a permit without charge. In addition, copies of pertinent regulations, forms, and returns will be returned to you. However, depending on the type of business and conditions surrounding ownership, you may be required to post a security deposit.

YOUR RIGHTS AND RESPONSIBILITIES AS A SELLER

When you obtain a seller's permit, you acquire valuable rights and privileges as well as responsibilities. Information about some of those rights and responsibilities follows.

- **You may purchase property for resale without paying tax.** By providing the vendor with a completed resale certificate, you are not required to pay sales tax on tangible personal property you purchase for resale. However, you should not use a resale certificate if you intend to use the property prior to or instead of selling it. If you intend to use the property, you must pay sales tax

- **You must keep records.** To substantiate your sales, any deductions you report on your returns, and any purchases you have made for your business, you must keep adequate records. Generally, records must be kept for four years.

- **You must file returns.** Returns must be filed on or before the last day of the month following your reporting period. *You must file your return even if you did not sell any merchandise.*

- **You must pay taxes.** As a seller, you must pay taxes on gross receipts from retail sales. However, you are allowed by law to be reimbursed by collecting the tax from your customers.

- **You must notify the Board if you move, change ownership of, or sell your business.** Your permit is valid only at the address and for the type of ownership specified on the permit. Unless you notify the Board of any change in ownership, you could be held liable for the successor's operations. In addition, you should notify the Board immediately if you discontinue your business. Your notification will help us to close your account and return any security you may have deposited.

Form BT-400-MIP – Application for a Seller's Permit: Sample

BT-400-MIP (S2F) REV. 8 (9-94)

STATE OF CALIFORNIA
BOARD OF EQUALIZATION

**APPLICATION FOR SELLER'S PERMIT AND
REGISTRATION AS A RETAILER
(INDIVIDUALS/PARTNERS)**

SECTION I: OWNERSHIP INFORMATION	FOR BOARD USE ONLY		

1. PLEASE CHECK TYPE OF OWNERSHIP *(use additional sheet to include information about additional co-owners or partners)*

☐ Sole Owner
☐ Husband/Wife Co-ownership
☐ Partnership

FOR BOARD USE ONLY

TAX	OFFICE	NUMBER
S		

BUSINESS CODE   AREA CODE

PREPARER

	OWNER OR PARTNER	CO-OWNER OR PARTNER
2. FULL NAME *(first, middle, last)*		
3. RESIDENCE ADDRESS *(enter full address including zip code)*		
4. RESIDENCE TELEPHONE NO.	( )	( )
5. SOCIAL SECURITY NO.		
6. DRIVER'S LICENSE NO. & DATE OF BIRTH		
7. PRESENT/PAST EMPLOYER *(enter full address including zip code & telephone no.)*		
8. SPOUSE'S NAME		
9. SPOUSE'S SOCIAL SECURITY NO.		
10. SPOUSE'S DRIVER'S LICENSE NO. & DATE OF BIRTH		
11. NAME, ADDRESS & TELEPHONE NO. OF TWO PERSONAL REFERENCES	1. 2.	1. 2.
12. SIGNATURE		

SECTION II: BUSINESS INFORMATION

1. BUSINESS NAME	BUSINESS TELEPHONE ( )

2. BUSINESS ADDRESS *(do not list P.O. Box or mailing service)*	CITY	STATE	ZIP CODE

3. MAILING ADDRESS *(if different from No. 2 above)*	CITY	STATE	ZIP CODE

4. DATE YOU WILL BEGIN SALES *(month, day & year)*	5. DAYS & HOURS OF OPERATION	SUNDAY	MONDAY	TUESDAY	WEDNESDAY	THURSDAY	FRIDAY	SATURDAY

6. TYPE OF BUSINESS *(check one)*

☐ Retail ☐ Wholesale ☐ Mfg. ☐ Repair ☐ Service ☐ Construction Contractor

CHECK ONE

☐ Full Time ☐ Part Time ☐ Mail Order

7. TYPE OF ITEMS SOLD

8. ARE YOU

☐ Starting a new business? ☐ Adding/dropping partner? ☐ Other? _____

☐ Buying a business? *(indicate name & account number in area at right)*

FORMER OWNER'S NAME

ACCOUNT NUMBER

9. PURCHASE PRICE	10. VALUE OF FIXTURES & EQUIPMENT	11. NUMBER OF SELLING LOCATIONS *(if 2 or more attach list of all locations)*
$	$	

12. IF ALCOHOLIC BEVERAGES ARE SOLD, PLEASE LIST YOUR ALCOHOLIC BEVERAGE CONTROL LICENSE NO. AND TYPE

Form BT-400-MIP – Application for a Seller's Permit: Sample (continued)

BT-400-MIP (S2B) REV. 8 (9-94)

13. NAME, ADDRESS & TELEPHONE NUMBER OF ACCOUNTANT/BOOKKEEPER

14. NAME, ADDRESS & TELEPHONE NUMBER OF BUSINESS LANDLORD

15. NAME & LOCATION OF BANK OR OTHER FINANCIAL INSTITUTION	CHECKING AND SAVINGS ACCOUNT NUMBER

16. NAME & ADDRESS OF MAJOR SUPPLIERS	PRODUCTS PURCHASED

17. OTHER ACCOUNT NUMBERS ISSUED TO YOU BY THE BOARD

SECTION III: INCOME AND EXPENSES

1. PROJECTED MONTHLY BUSINESS EXPENSES	2. PROJECTED MONTHLY BUSINESS REVENUE	3. INFORMATION CONCERNING EMPLOYMENT DEVELOPMENT DEPARTMENT (EDD)		
		a. Are you registered with EDD?	☐ Yes	☐ No
RENT $_____	TOTAL GROSS REVENUE $_____	b. If no, will your payroll exceed $100 per quarter? If yes, you must make application with EDD. Number of employees See pamphlet DE 4525, "Employer Guide."	☐ Yes	☐ No
PAYROLL $_____	NON-TAXABLE $_____			
MISC. $_____	TAXABLE $_____	c. I have already received pamphlet DE 4525.	☐ Yes	☐ No
TOTAL $_____	TAX $_____	d. I have already received pamphlet DE 44, "Employer's Withholding Guide."	☐ Yes	☐ No

SECTION V: CERTIFICATION

The statements contained herein are hereby certified to be correct to the best knowledge and belief of the undersigned who is duly authorized to sign this application.

SIGNATURE	TITLE
NAME *(typed or printed)*	DATE

FOR BOARD USE ONLY
Furnished to Taxpayer

REPORTING BASIS			REGULATIONS
SECURITY REVIEW	☐ GA-324A	☐ DE-44	
	☐ BT-400Y	☐ DE-4525	
☐ BT-598 $_____	☐ BT-467	☐ OTHER	
☐ BT-1009	☐ BT-519		PAMPHLETS
BY	☐ BT-968		
APPROVED BY	☐ BT-1241C		
REMOTE INPUT DATE	☐ REG. 1668		RETURNS
BY	☐ REG. 1698		
	☐ REG. 1700		
☐ Permit Issued Date_____			

Instructions for Form DE-1 – Registration Form for Commercial Employers

INSTRUCTIONS FOR DE 1 REGISTRATION FORM FOR COMMERCIAL EMPLOYERS

An employer is required by law to file a registration form with the Employment Development Department (EDD) with any Employment Tax District Office (**ETDO**) within **fifteen (15) calendar days** after paying over $100 in wages for employment in a calendar quarter, or whenever a change in ownership occurs.

A. BUSINESS NAME — Give the name by which your business is known to the public. Enter "None" if no business name is used. Enter the date the new ownership began operating. Enter Federal Employer Identification Number(s). If not assigned, enter "Applied For."

B. OWNER OR CORPORATION NAME — Enter the full given name, middle initial, surname, title, social security account number, and driver's license number for each individual, partner or corporate office. If the business is a corporation, enter exactly as spelled and registered with the Secretary of State, include California corporate identification number.

C. BUSINESS LOCATION — Enter the California address and county where the business in A is physically conducted. If more than one California location, list on a separate sheet and attach to this form. In Mailing Address, enter the address where EDD correspondence and forms should be sent. If this address is the same as the business location, enter "Same." Provide daytime business phone number.

D. PRIOR REGISTRATION — If any part of the ownership in B is operating or has ever operated at another location, check "Yes" and provide account number, business name and address.

E. WAGES — Check the appropriate box when you first paid $100 or more in wages.

F. PIT WITHHOLDING — Check appropriate box. If you are not sure if you are subject to federal monthly/semi-weekly Personal Income Tax deposits, contact the local ETDO.

G. ORGANIZATION TYPE — Check the box which best describes the legal form of the ownership in B.

H. EMPLOYER TYPE — Check the box which best describes your employer type. Enter the total number of employees for the ownership in B.

I. BUSINESS TYPE — Check the box which best describes your business type. Describe the particular product or service rendered.

J. CONTACT PERSON — Enter the name and phone number of the person authorized by the ownership shown in B to provide information to EDD staff.

K. SUPPORTIVE SERVICES — Check the box which best describes the supportive services provided by B.

L. STATUS OF BUSINESS — Check the box that best describes why you are completing this form. If the business was previously owned, provide owner and business name, purchase price, date ownership was transferred to this ownership and EDD account number.

M. DECLARATION — This declaration should be signed by one of the names shown in B.

NEED MORE HELP OR INFORMATION? Contact one of the Employment Tax District Offices below or write to the Employment Development Department, P.O. Box 826880, Sacramento, CA 94280-0001.

We will **notify** you of your **EDD Identification Number** by mail. To help you understand your tax withholding and filing responsibilities, you will be sent a **California Employer's Guide, DE 44.**

EMPLOYMENT TAX DISTRICT OFFICES

Bakersfield ....(805) 395-2896	Modesto ....(209) 576-6207	San Jose ....(408) 452-7175
Capitola ....(408) 464-6293	Monterey ....(408) 649-2902	San Luis Obispo...........(805) 549-3512
Chico ....(916) 895-4401	Oakland ....(510) 577-2396	San Mateo ....(415) 358-4102
Downey ....(310) 923-1237	Orange ....(714) 288-2601	San Rafael ....(415) 472-5651
El Monte....................(818) 575-6751	Placerville....................(916) 622-2529	Santa Monica ....(310) 576-6400
Escondido ....(619) 737-2200	Pleasant Hill ....(510) 977-8265	Santa Rosa ....(707) 576-2094
Eureka ....(707) 445-6522	Redding ....(916) 225-2205	Stockton.....................(209) 956-1438
Fresno ....(209) 445-5132	Riverside.......................(909) 782-3260	Vallejo ....(707) 648-4040
Hollywood ....(213) 669-7670	Sacramento ....(916) 255-1965	Van Nuys ....(818) 901-5208
Interstate* ....(916) 464-1056	San Bernardino ....(909) 383-4176	Ventura ....(805) 654-4506
Laguna Hills ....(714) 768-6102	San Diego ....(619) 284-8615	Visalia..........................(209) 635-3220
Long Beach ....(310) 428-0021	San Francisco..............(415) 557-1898	Yuba City ....(916) 741-4020
Merced........................(209) 723-3061	*Out of State employers contact Interstate ETDO	

Form DE-1 – Registration Form for Commercial Employers: Sample

EDD
Serving the People of California

This form will be the basic record of YOUR ACCOUNT. **DO NOT FILE THIS FORM UNTIL YOU HAVE PAID WAGES WHICH EXCEED $100.00.** Please read the **INSTRUCTIONS** on the back before completing this form. **PLEASE PRINT OR TYPE.** Return this form to: ———▶

DE 1 REGISTRATION FORM FOR COMMERCIAL EMPLOYERS

ACCOUNT NUMBER	QUARTER	ETDO	FED CODE	ON-LINE PROCESS DATE	TAS CODE
				DEPT. USE ONLY	

A. BUSINESS NAME | OWNERSHIP BEGAN OPERATING — MONTH: DAY: YEAR | FEDERAL I.D. NUMBER

B. OWNER OR CORPORATION NAME | SSA NO./CORP. I.D. NO. | DRIVER'S LICENSE NUMBER

List all partners* or corporate officers names	TITLE — Indicate partner or officer title	SOCIAL SECURITY NUMBER	DRIVER'S LICENSE NUMBER

*If entity is a **Limited Partnership**, indicate General Partner with an (*). List additional partners on a separate sheet.

C. BUSINESS LOCATION Street and Number (see instructions) | CITY OR TOWN | STATE | ZIP CODE | COUNTY

MAILING ADDRESS (in care of P.O. Box or Street and Number) | CITY OR TOWN | STATE | ZIP CODE | PHONE NUMBER ( )

D. HAVE YOU EVER BEEN REGISTERED WITH THE DEPARTMENT? ☐ No ☐ Yes | IF YES, ENTER EMPLOYER ACCOUNT NUMBER, BUSINESS NAME AND ADDRESS — ACCT NUMBER   BUSINESS NAME   ADDRESS

E. INDICATE FIRST QUARTER AND YEAR IN WHICH WAGES EXCEEDED $100.
☐ Jan.-Mar. 19 ____ ☐ Apr.-June 19 ____ ☐ July-Sept. 19 ____ ☐ Oct.-Dec. 19 ____

F. WILL YOU BE SUBJECT TO FEDERAL MONTHLY/SEMI-WEEKLY DEPOSITS? ☐ No ☐ Yes

G. ORGANIZATION TYPE
☐ (IN) INDIVIDUAL OWNER ☐ (JV) JOINT VENTURE ☐ (LQ) LIQUIDATION ☐ (OT) OTHER (Specify)
☐ (HW) HUS/WIFE CO-OWNERSHIP ☐ (RC) RECEIVERSHIP ☐ (LP) LIMITED PARTNERSHIP ____
☐ (GP) GENERAL PARTNERSHIP ☐ (BK) BANKRUPTCY ☐ (TR) TRUSTEESHIP
☐ (CP) CORPORATION ☐ (AS) ASSOCIATION ☐ (EA) ESTATE ADMINISTRATION

H. EMPLOYER TYPE (see instructions)
☐ (01) Commercial ☐ (10) Church ☐ (11) Indian Reservation ☐ (22) Pacific Maritime ☐ (25) Fishing Boat | NUMBER OF EMPLOYEES

I. BUSINESS TYPE
☐ (N) Mining ☐ (F) Finance ☐ (I) Insurance
☐ (C) Construction ☐ (B) Communications ☐ (E) Real Estate
☐ (M) Manufacturing ☐ (S) Services ☐ (O) Other
☐ (T) Transportation ☐ (L) Utilities
☐ (R) Retail Trade ☐ (W) Wholesale Trade

1) Describe kind of product or type of service:

2) If MANUFACTURING, list principal products in order of importance

J. CONTACT PERSON FOR BUSINESS   NAME   ADDRESS   PHONE ( )

K. SUPPORTIVE SERVICES
If you are part of a larger organization and you are primarily engaged in providing supportive services to other establishments of the larger organization, check one of these boxes.
(1) ☐ Control Administrative (headquarters, etc.) (3) ☐ Storage (warehouse) (5) ☐ Does not apply
(2) ☐ Research, development, or testing (4) ☐ Other (specify)

L. IS THIS A(N):
☐ New business ☐ On-going business just purchased (☐ All ☐ Part) ☐ Other ____
☐ Change of partner(s) ☐ Change in form — (Sole proprietor to partnership; partnership to corporation; merger; etc.)
IF THE BUSINESS WAS PREVIOUSLY OWNED, PROVIDE THE FOLLOWING INFORMATION:
Previous Owner   Business Name   Purchase Price   Date of Transfer   EDD Account Number

M. DECLARATION
These Statements are hereby declared to be correct to the best knowledge and belief of the undersigned.

Signature ____ Date ____ Residence Phone ( )

Title ____ Residence Address ____
(Owner, Partner, Officer, etc.)   Street   City   State   ZIP Code

DE 1 Rev. 63 1-94 State of California Employment Development Department   93 24448   CU

Sales and Use Tax Regulations

Regulation 1668. RESALE CERTIFICATES. (Continued 1)

CALIFORNIA RESALE CERTIFICATE

. . . .
(Name of Purchaser)

. . . .
(Address of Purchaser)

I HEREBY CERTIFY: That I hold valid seller's permit No. . . . . issued pursuant to the Sales and Use Tax Law; That I am engaged in the business of selling . . . .

that the tangible personal property described herein which I shall purchase from: . . . .

will be resold by me in the form of tangible personal property; provided, however, that in the event any of such property is used for any purpose other than retention, demonstration, or display while holding it for sale in the regular course of business, it is understood that I am required by the Sales and Use Tax Law to report and pay tax, measured by the purchase price of such property or other authorized amount. Description of property to be purchased: . . . .

. . . .

Date: . . . . 19 . . . .
(Signature of Purchaser or Authorized Agent)

. . . .
(Title)

Under "Description of property to be purchased" there may appear:

    (A) Either an itemized list of the particular property to be purchased for resale, or

    (B) A general description of the kind of property to be purchased for resale. (A certificate, thus describing the property is good until revoked in writing.)

If the purchaser is not required to hold a permit because the purchaser sells only property of a kind the retail sale of which is not taxable, e.g., food products for human consumption, or because the purchaser makes no sales in this State, the purchaser should make an appropriate notation to that effect on the certificate in lieu of a seller's permit number.

    (3) If a purchaser issues a general (blanket) resale certificate which provides a general description of the items to be purchased, and subsequently issues a purchase order which indicates that the transaction covered by the purchase order is taxable, the resale certificate does not apply with respect to that transaction. However, the purchaser will bear the burden of establishing either that the purchase order was sent to and received by the seller or that the tax or tax reimbursement was paid to the seller. The purchaser may avoid this burden by using the procedure described in subsection (b)(4) below.

    (4) If a purchaser wishes to designate on each purchase order that the property is for resale, the seller should obtain a qualified resale certificate, i.e., one that states "see purchase order" in the space provided for a description of the property to be purchased. Each purchase order must then specify whether the property covered by the order is purchased for resale or whether tax applies to the order. If each purchase order does not so specify, it will be assumed that the property covered by that purchase order was purchased for use, and not for resale. If the purchase order includes both items to be resold and items to be used, the purchase order must specify which items are purchased for resale and which items are purchased for use. For example, a purchase order issued for produced parts for resale and also for tooling used to produce the parts should specify that the parts are purchased for resale and that the sale of the tooling is subject to tax.

    (5) If the seller does not timely obtain a resale certificate, the fact that the purchaser deletes the tax or tax reimbursement from the seller's billing, provides a seller's permit number to the seller, or informs the seller that the transaction is "not taxable" does not relieve the seller from liability for the tax nor from the burden of proving the sale was for resale.

Sales and Use Tax Regulations (continued)

State of California

BOARD OF EQUALIZATION

SALES AND USE TAX REGULATIONS

Regulation 1668. RESALE CERTIFICATES.

References: Sections 6012.8, 6012.9, 6072, 6091-6095, 6241-6245, Revenue and Taxation Code.
Automobile Dealers, effect of accepting from nondealer retailer, see Regulation 1566.
Construction Contractors, use by, see Regulation 1521.
Demonstration and Display, use of property purchased under resale certificates for, see Regulation 1669.
Drapery hardware installers accepting, see Regulation 1521.
Newspapers and Periodicals, for component parts of, see Regulation 1590.
Salt used by food processors, giving for, see Regulation 1525.
Vending machine operators furnishing, see Regulation 1574.

(a) EFFECT OF CERTIFICATE.

(1) The burden of proving that a sale of tangible personal property is not at retail is upon the seller unless the seller timely takes a certificate from the purchaser that the property is purchased for resale. If timely taken in good faith from a person who is engaged in the business of selling tangible personal property and who holds a California seller's permit, the certificate relieves the seller from liability for the sales tax and the duty of collecting the use tax. A certificate will be considered timely if it is taken at any time before the seller bills the purchaser for the property, or any time within the seller's normal billing and payment cycle, or any time at or prior to delivery of the property to the purchaser.

(2) If a purchaser who gives a resale certificate for property makes any storage or use of the property other than retention, demonstration, or display while holding it for sale in the regular course of business, the storage or use is taxable as of the time the property is first so stored or used. The use tax must be reported and paid by the purchaser with the purchaser's tax return for the period in which the property is first so stored or used. The purchaser cannot retroactively rescind or revoke the resale certificate and thereby cause the transaction to be subject to sales tax rather than use tax.

(b) FORM OF CERTIFICATE.

(1) Any document, such as a letter or purchase order, timely provided by the purchaser to the seller will be regarded as a resale certificate with respect to the sale of the property described in the document if it contains all of the following essential elements:

(A) The signature of the purchaser or an agent or employee of the purchaser.

(B) The name and address of the purchaser.

(C) The number of the seller's permit held by the purchaser, or if the purchaser is not required to hold a permit because the purchaser sells only property of a kind the retail sale of which is not taxable, e.g., food products for human consumption, or because the purchaser makes no sales in this State, an appropriate notation to that effect in lieu of a seller's permit number.

(D) A statement that the property described in the document is purchased for resale. The document must contain the phrase "for resale". The use of phrases such as "nontaxable", "exempt", or similar terminology is not acceptable.

(E) Date of execution of document. (An otherwise valid resale certificate will not be considered invalid solely on the ground that it is undated.)

(2) A document containing the essential elements described in (1) above is the minimum form which will be regarded as a resale certificate. However, in order to preclude potential controversy, the seller should timely obtain from the purchaser a certificate substantially in the following form:

Sales and Use Tax Regulations (continued)

Regulation 1668.   RESALE CERTIFICATES.   (Continued 2)

(c) OTHER EVIDENCE TO REBUT PRESUMPTION OF TAXABILITY.   A sale for resale is not subject to sales tax. However, a resale certificate which is not timely taken is not retroactive and will not relieve the seller of the liability for the tax. Consequently, if the seller does not timely obtain a resale certificate, the seller will be relieved of liability for the tax only if the seller presents satisfactory evidence that the specific property sold:

(1) Was in fact resold by the purchaser and was not used by the purchaser for any purpose other than retention, demonstration, or display while holding it for sale in the regular course of business, or

(2) Is being held for resale by the purchaser and has not been used by the purchaser for any purpose other than retention, demonstration, or display while holding it for sale in the regular course of business, or

(3) Has been used or consumed by the purchaser and the purchaser has paid the use tax directly to this State.

(d) GOOD FAITH.   A seller will be presumed to have taken a resale certificate in good faith in the absence of evidence to the contrary. If the purchaser insists that the purchaser is buying for resale property of a kind not normally resold in the purchaser's business, the seller should require a resale certificate containing a statement that the specific property is being purchased for resale in the regular course of business.

(e) MOBILEHOMES.   A mobilehome retailer who purchases a new mobilehome for sale to a customer for installation for occupancy as a residence on a foundation system pursuant to Section 18551 of the Health and Safety Code, or for installation for occupancy as a residence pursuant to Section 18613 of the Health and Safety Code, and which mobilehome is thereafter subject to property taxation, may issue a resale certificate to the mobilehome vendor even though the retailer is classified as a consumer of the mobilehome by Sections 6012.8 and 6012.9 of the Revenue and Taxation Code. Also, effective September 19, 1985, a mobilehome retailer, licensed as a mobilehome dealer under Section 18002.6 of the Health and Safety Code, who purchases a new mobilehome for sale to a customer for installation for occupancy as a residence on a foundation system pursuant to Section 18551 of the Health and Safety Code, may issue a resale certificate to the mobilehome vendor even though the mobilehome retailer may have the mobilehome installed on a foundation system as an improvement to realty prior to the retailer's sale of the mobilehome to the customer for occupancy as a residence.

Where the mobilehome is acquired by a mobilehome retailer, who is not licensed as a dealer pursuant to Section 18002.6 of the Health and Safety Code, for affixation by the retailer to a permanent foundation, or for other use or consumption (except demonstration or display while holding for sale in the regular course of business), prior to sale, the mobilehome retailer may not issue a resale certificate. The mobilehome retailer shall notify the vendor that the purchase is for consumption and not for resale. When a mobilehome manufacturer or other vendor is informed or has knowledge that the purchaser will install the mobilehome on a permanent foundation prior to its resale, the manufacturer or other vendor is not making a sale for resale. Such vendor is making a taxable retail sale and cannot accept a resale certificate in good faith.

(f) MOBILE TRANSPORTATION EQUIPMENT.   Any person, not exempt from use tax pursuant to Section 6352 of the Revenue and Taxation Code, who leases mobile transportation equipment and who is the consumer thereof, may issue a resale certificate to the equipment vendor for the limited purpose of reporting use tax on the fair rental value of the mobile transportation equipment.

(g) IMPROPER USE OF CERTIFICATE.   Except when a resale certificate is issued in accordance with the terms of subdivisions (e) or (f):

(1) A purchaser, including any officer or employee of a corporation, is guilty of a misdemeanor if the purchaser gives a resale certificate for property which the purchaser knows at the time of purchase will be used rather than resold. Such improper use of a certificate also may cause the purchaser to become liable for penalties called for by Sections 6072, 6094.5, 6484, or 6485.

Sales and Use Tax Regulations (continued)

Regulation 1668 RESALE CERTIFICATES. (Continued 3)

(2) Any person, including any officer or employee of a corporation, who gives a resale certificate for property which he or she knows at the time of purchase is not to be resold by him or her or the corporation in the regular course of business is liable to the state for the amount of tax that would be due if he or she had not given such resale certificate.

History: Effective July 1, 1939.

Adopted as of January 1, 1945, as a restatement of previous rulings.

Amended June 20, 1967, effective July 1, 1967.

Amended and renumbered November 3, 1969, effective December 5, 1969.

Amended April 6, 1977, effective July 1, 1977. Added new method of proof for resale, detailed what is adequate proof for resale, and clarified effect of purchase for use on a resale certificate.

Amended December 7, 1977, effective January 19, 1978. In (e) added the tax that would be due.

Amended July 28, 1982, effective June 26, 1983. Added new (e) and (f), renumbered (g) and (h), and added reference to Section 6072 to (g).

Amended April 9, 1985, effective June 27, 1985. In subdivision (g), amended to specify that the penalty provisions are also applicable to any officer or employee of a corporation who gives a resale certificate for property which he or she knows at the time of purchase will be used rather than resold. Added a reference to Section 6094.5 of the Revenue and Taxation Code with respect to the type of penalties a purchaser may be liable for if the purchaser makes an improper use of a resale certificate. Deleted subdivision (h) since it pertained to the effective date of amendments to the regulation which occurred in 1977.

Amended April 9, 1986, effective July 5, 1986. In subdivision (e), amended explanation under which mobilehome retailers may issue resale certificates to mobilehome vendors.

Regulations are issued by the State Board of Equalization to implement, interpret or make specific provisions of the California Sales and Use Tax Law and to aid in the administration and enforcement of that law. If you are in doubt about how the Sales and Use Tax Law applies to your specific activity or transaction, you should write the nearest State Board of Equalization office. Requests for advice regarding a specific activity or transaction should be in writing and should fully describe the facts and circumstances of the activity or transaction.

California Resale Certificate Cards

Copy and cut out these cards to send to the vendors from whom your firm buys the items you resell. With this card on file, your vendor does not have to charge you sales tax on those items, since your company will add the sales tax later when you resell them to other buyers. (However, vendors must add sales tax to any items your company purchases for its own use or the personal use of its owners or employees.)

FIRM NAME _____

I HEREBY CERTIFY,
That I hold valid seller's permit No. _____
issued pursuant to the Sales and Use Tax Law; that I am engaged in the business of selling

_____
that the tangible personal property described herein which I shall purchase from:

_____
will be resold by me in the form of tangible personal property; PROVIDED, however, that in the event any of such property is used for any purpose other than retention, demonstration, or display while holding it for sale in the regular course of business, it is understood that I am required by the Sales and Use Tax Law to report and pay for the tax, measured by the purchase price of such property.

Description of property to be purchased: _____

_____

Dated: _____ 19 _____ Purchaser _____

at_____ By and Title _____

Phone _____ Address _____

FIRM NAME _____

I HEREBY CERTIFY,
That I hold valid seller's permit No. _____
issued pursuant to the Sales and Use Tax Law; that I am engaged in the business of selling

_____
that the tangible personal property described herein which I shall purchase from:

_____
will be resold by me in the form of tangible personal property; PROVIDED, however, that in the event any of such property is used for any purpose other than retention, demonstration, or display while holding it for sale in the regular course of business, it is understood that I am required by the Sales and Use Tax Law to report and pay for the tax, measured by the purchase price of such property.

Description of property to be purchased: _____

_____

Dated: _____ 19 _____ Purchaser _____

at_____ By and Title _____

Phone _____ Address _____

Preview! New business books and tools from The Oasis Press.

Finally, a one-stop answer book for your questions about business corporations. Saves time with your attorney. Saves hours in the library. Tells what you need to know to avoid personal liability and legal pitfalls. A "must" whether you already own a small-business corporation, or plan to form one.
Paperback $19.95

From the editors at The Oasis Press comes this guide for the beginning business owner. This all-in-one book lists the major requirements and issues a new business owner needs to know:
- Start-up financing
- Creating a business plan
- Marketing strategies
- Environmental laws

Checklists and Plans of Action ensure that you have "all the bases" covered.
Paperback $8.95

New updated edition! Our best seller for 12 years — still your best source of practical business information. Find out what new laws affect your business. Now there's an edition for every state in the U.S., plus the District of Columbia.
Paperback $21.95
Binder Workbook Edition $29.95
Specify which state(s) you want on your order.

The old adage says that the only certainties in life are death and taxes. While one may be beyond your control, you can use recent tax law changes to your certain financial advantage. This new book covers every tax break now available in today's "reformed" tax environment.
Paperback $14.95

197 forms to get your people hired, your sales recorded, your product shipped, your cash flowing, your customers accounted for and your organization organized. Get the forms that pilot goods, people, services, and numbers through the business day.
Paperback $19.95
Expanded Binder Edition $49.95

Your people expect leadership. Let them know where you stand and where they stand using clear policies. This newly expanded book gives you 65 written model policies plus alternates. Covers sexual harassment, AIDS, privacy, and other sensitive issues. Includes 20 forms.
Paperback $29.95
Binder Edition $49.95
Software for IBM & MAC available, too.

Get business tips from over 157 seasoned experts.

Business Formation and Planning

**Start Your Business:
A Beginner's Guide**

 Book

This handy, easy-to-read book is full of checklists to help answer your start-up questions. Helps you ask the right questions and find out where you can get the answers. The Plan of Action Worksheets make it easy to compile and coordinate your to-do list. The book is divided into sections covering business, legal, marketing, human resources, sales, taxes, and other decisions.

**The Successful Business
Plan: Secrets & Strategies**

 Book and software
for IBM & compatibles

Start-to-finish guide on creating a successful business plan. Includes tips from venture capitalists, bankers, and successful CEOs. Features worksheets for ease in planning and budgeting with the Abrams Method of Flow-Through Financials. Gives a sample business plan, plus specialized help for retailers, service companies, manufacturers, and in-house corporate plans. Also tells how to find funding sources.

**Starting and Operating a
Business in... series**
Book available for each state in the
United States, plus District of Columbia

One-stop resource to current federal and state laws and regulations that affect businesses. Clear "human language" explanations of complex issues, plus samples of government forms, and sources for additional help or information. Helps seasoned business owners keep up with changing legislation, and guides new entrepreneurs step-by-step to start and run the business. Includes many checklists and worksheets to organize ideas, create action plans, and project financial scenarios.

**The Essential Corporation
Handbook**

 Book

This comprehensive reference for small business corporations in all 50 states and Washington, D.C. explains the legal requirements for maintaining a corporation in good standing. Features many sample corporate documents which are annotated by the author to show what to look for and what to look out for. Tells how to avoid personal liability as an officer, director, or shareholder.

**Surviving and Prospering
in a Business Partnership**

 Book

From evaluation of potential partners, through the drafting of agreements, to day-to-day management of working relationships, this book helps avoid classic partnership catastrophes. Discusses how to set up the partnership to reduce the financial and emotional consequences of unanticipated disputes, dishonesty, divorce, disability, or death of a partner.

**California Corporation
Formation Package and
Minute Book**

 Book and software
for IBM & Mac

Provides forms required for incorporating and maintaining closely held corporations, including: articles of incorporation; bylaws; stock certificates, stock transfer record sheets, bill of sale agreement; minutes form; plus many others. Addresses questions on fees, timing, notices, regulations, election of directors and other critical factors. Software has minutes, bylaws, and articles of incorporation already for you to edit and customize (using your own word processor).

**Franchise Bible:
A Comprehensive Guide**

 Book (New edition)

Complete guide to franchising for prospective franchisees or for business owners considering franchising their business. Includes actual sample documents, such as a complete offering circular, plus worksheets for evaluating franchise companies, locations, and organizing information before seeing an attorney. This book is helpful for lawyers as well as their clients.

Home Business Made Easy

 Book

Thinking of starting a business at home? This book is the easiest road to starting a home business. Shows you how to select and start a home business that fits your interests, lifestyle and pocketbook. Walks you through 153 different businesses you could operate from home full or part time. Author David Hanania has boiled the process down to simple steps so you can get started now to realize your dreams.

The Small Business Expert
Software for IBM-PC & compatibles

Generates comprehensive custom checklist of the state and federal laws and regulations based on your type and size of business. Allows comparison of doing business in each of the 50 states. Built-in worksheets create outlines for personnel policies, marketing feasibility studies, and a business plan draft. *Requires 256K RAM and hard disk.*

**Starting and Operating a
Business: U.S. Edition**
Set of eleven binders

The complete encyclopedia of how to do business in the U.S. Describes laws and regulations for each state, plus Washington, D.C., as well as the federal government. Includes lists of sources of help, plus post cards for requesting materials from government agencies. This set is valuable for businesses with locations or marketing activities in several states, plus franchisors, attorneys, and other consultants.

To order these business tools, use the enclosed order form, FAX 503-476-1479 or call us toll-free at 800-228-2275

IH 2 12 3

Step-by-step techniques for generating more profit.

Financial Management

Top Tax Saving Ideas for Today's Small Business

New Book

An extensive summary of every imaginable tax break that is still available in today's "reformed" tax environment. Deals with the various entities that the owner/manager may choose to operate a business. Identifies a wide assortment of tax deduction, fringe benefits, and tax deferrals. Includes a simplified checklist of recent tax law changes with an emphasis on tax breaks.

Financial Management Techniques for Small Business

Book and software for IBM-PC & compatibles

Clearly reveals the essential ingredients of sound financial management in detail. By monitoring trends in your financial activities, you will be able to uncover potential problems before they become crises. You'll understand why you can be making a profit and still not have the cash to meet expenses, and you'll learn the steps to change your business' cash behavior to get more return for your effort. Software makes your business' financial picture graphically clear, and lets you look at "what if" scenarios.

The Buyer's Guide to Business Insurance

New Book
(Available Spring 1994)

Straightforward advice on shopping for insurance, understanding types of coverage, comparing proposals and premium rates. Worksheets help identify and weigh the risks a particular business is likely to face, then determine if any of those might be safely self-insured or eliminated. Request for proposal form helps businesses avoid over-paying for protection.

Collection Techniques for Small Business

New Book
(Available Spring 1994)

Practical tips on how to turn receivables into cash. Worksheets and checklists help businesses establish credit policies, track accounts, and flag when it is necessary to bring in a collection agency, attorney, or go to court. This book advises how to deal with disputes, negotiate settlements, win in small claims court, and collect on judgments. Gives examples of telephone collection techniques and collection letters.

The Secrets to Buying and Selling a Business

New Book
(Available Spring 1994)

Prepares a business buyer or seller for negotiations that will achieve win-win results. Shows how to determine the real worth of a business, including intangible assets such as "goodwill." Over 36 checklists and worksheets on topics such as tax impact on buyers and sellers, escrow checklist, cash flow projections, evaluating potential buyers, financing options, and many others.

Business Owner's Guide to Accounting & Bookkeeping

Book

Makes understanding the economics of business simple. Explains the basic accounting principles that relate to any business. Step-by-step instructions for generating accounting statements and interpreting them, spotting errors, and recognizing warning signs. Discusses how banks and other creditors view financial statements.

Controlling Your Company's Freight Costs

Book

Shows how to increase company profits by trimming freight costs. Provides tips for comparing alternative methods and shippers, then negotiating contracts to receive the most favorable discounts. Tells how to package shipments for safe transport. Discusses freight insurance and dealing with claims for loss or damage. Appendices include directory of U.S. ports, shipper's guide, and sample bill of lading.

Financial Templates

Software for IBM-PC & compatibles

Calculates and graphs many business "what-if" scenarios and financial reports. Twenty-eight financial templates such as income statements, cash flow, and balance sheet comparisons, break-even analyses, product contribution comparisons, market share, net present value, sales model, pro formas, loan payment projections, etc. *Requires 512K RAM hard disk or two floppy drives, plus Lotus 1-2-3 or compatible spreadsheet program.*

Yes, we accept credit cards — VISA, MasterCard, American Express, Discover, or your personal or business check.

Proven tools and ideas to expand your business.

Marketing & Public Relations

Power Marketing

Book

A wealth of basic, how-to marketing information that easily takes a new or experienced business owner through the essentials of marketing and sales strategies, customer database marketing, advertising, public relations, budgeting, and follow-up marketing systems. Written in a friendly tone by a marketing educator, the book features worksheets with step-by-step instructions, a glossary of marketing terms, and a sample marketing plan. Also available: *Power Marketing Tools for Small Business*—two hours of audio tapes by author Jody Hornor that reveal 81 tools you can use to increase your market power.

How To Develop & Market Creative Business Ideas

Book

Step-by-step manual guides the inventor through all stages of new product development. Discusses patenting your invention, trademarks, copyrights, and how to construct your prototype. Gives information on financing, distribution, test marketing, and finding licensees. Plus, lists many useful sources for prototype resources, trade shows, funding, and more.

Cost-Effective Market Analysis

Book

Workbook explains how a small business can conduct its own market research. Shows how to set objectives, determine which techniques to use, create a schedule, and then monitor expenses. Encompasses primary research (trade shows, telephone interviews, mail surveys), plus secondary research (using available information in print).

Customer Information and Tracking System (CITS)
Software for IBM-PC & compatibles

 (Available Spring 1994)

Stores details of past activities plus future reminders on customers, clients, contacts, vendors, and employees, then gives instant access to that information when needed. "Tickler" fields keep reminders of dates for recontacts. "Type" fields categorize names for sorting as the user defines. "Other data" fields store information such as purchase and credit history, telephone call records, or interests.

Has massive storage capabilities. Holds up to 255 lines of comments for each name, plus unlimited time and date stamped notes. Features perpetual calendar, and automatic telephone dialing. Built-in word processing and merge gives the ability to pull in the information already keyed into the fields into individual or form letters. Prints mail labels, rotary file cards, and phone directories. This program is a great contact manager — call 1-800-228-2275 for information. *Requires a hard disk, 640K RAM and 80 column display. (Autodial feature requires modem.)*

International Business

Export Now

Book

Prepares a business to enter the export market. Clearly explains the basics, then articulates specific requirements for export licensing, preparation of documents, payment methods, packaging, and shipping. Includes advice on evaluating foreign representatives, planning international marketing strategies, and discovering official U.S. policy for various countries and regions. Lists sources.

EXECARDS®
International Communication Cards

EXECARDS offer unique cards you can send to businesspeople of many nationalities to help build and maintain lasting relationships. One distinguished EXECARD choice is a richly textured and embossed white card of substantial quality that expresses thank you in thirteen languages; Japanese, Russian, French, Chinese, Arabic, German, Swahili, Italian, Polish, Spanish, Hebrew, and Swedish, as well as English. Another handsome option is an ivory card with thank you embossed in Russian and English. To each, you can add a personal note or order a custom printed message. *Please call for more information.*

Now – Find Out How Your Business Can Profit By Being Environmentally Aware

The Business Environmental Handbook

Book

Save your business while you are saving the planet. Here's your chance to learn about the hundreds of ways any business can help secure its future by starting to conserve resources now. This book reveals little-understood but simple techniques for recycling, precycling, and conservation that can save your business money now, and help preserve resources. Also gives tips on "green marketing" to customers.

Give yourself and your business every chance to succeed. Order the business tools you need today. Call 800-228-2275.

Gain the power of increased knowledge — Oasis is your source.

Acquiring Outside Capital

Raising Capital: How to Write a Financing Proposal

 New Book

Valuable resource for writing and presenting a winning loan proposal. Includes professional tips on how to write the proposal. Presents detailed examples of the four most common types of proposals to secure venture capital and loans: Private Placement Circular; Prospectus or Public Offering; Financing Proposal; and Limited Partnership Offering.

The Money Connection: Where & How to Apply for Business Loans

 New Book

Comprehensive listing of funding sources. Lists hundreds of current nationally recognized business loan and venture capital firms. Describes the latest federal, state, county, and community loan, investment and assistance programs. Gives addresses and phone numbers of federal agency offices in each state.

Financing Your Small Business

 Book

Essential techniques to successfully identify, approach, attract, and manage sources of financing. Shows how to gain the full benefits of debt financing while minimizing its risks. Outlines all types of financing and walks you step by step through the process, from evaluating short-term credit options, through negotiating a long-term loan, to deciding whether to go public.

The Loan Package

 Book

Preparatory package for a business loan proposal. Worksheets help analyze cash needs and articulate business focus. Includes sample forms for balance sheets, income statements, projections, and budget reports. Screening sheets rank potential lenders to shorten the time involved in getting the loan.

The Successful Business Plan: Secrets & Strategies

 Book and software for IBM & compatibles

Now you can find out what venture capitalists and bankers really want to see before they will fund a company. This book gives you their personal tips and insights. The Abrams Method of Flow-Through Financials breaks down the chore into easy to manage steps, so you can end up with a fundable proposal. Software is available for this book—see the back page of this catalog or call 1-800-228-2275 for a free software catalog. *Software requires a hard drive.*

Financial Templates
Software for IBM & compatibles

Software speeds business calculations. Includes 28 financial templates including various projections, statements, ratios, histories, amortizations, and cash flows. This is just one of many useful software packages designed specifically for small businesses. Call 1-800-228-2275 for information. *Requires Lotus 1-2-3, Microsoft Excel 2.0 or higher.*

Human Resource Ideas

A Company Policy and Personnel Workbook

 Book and software for IBM & compatibles

Saves costly consultant or staff hours in creating company personnel policies. Provides model policies on topics such as employee safety, leave of absence, flextime, smoking, substance abuse, sexual harassment, performance improvement, grievance procedure. For each subject, practical and legal ramifications are explained, then a choice of alternate policies presented. Software is available for this book. Check our software catalog or call 1-800-228-2275 for more information.

People Investment

 Book

Written for the business owner or manager who is not a personnel specialist. Explains what you must know to make your hiring decisions pay off for everyone. Learn more about the Americans With Disabilities Act (ADA), Medical and Family Leave, and more.

Managing People: A Practical Guide

 Book

Focuses on developing the art of working with people to maximize the productivity and satisfaction of both manager and employees. Discussions, exercises, and self-tests boost skills in communicating, delegating, motivating, developing teams, goal-setting, adapting to change, and coping with stress.

Safety Law Compliance Manual for California Businesses

 Book

Now every California employer must have an Injury and Illness Prevention Program that meets the specific requirements of Senate Bill 198. Already, thousands of citations have been issued to companies who did not comply with all seven components of the complicated new law. Avoid fines by using this guide to set up a program that will meet Cal/OSHA standards. Includes forms.

Plus optional binder for your company's safety program

Also available — Company Injury and Illness Prevention Program Binder — Pre-organized and ready-to-use with forms, tabs, logs and sample documents. Saves your company time, work, and worry.

Why hesitate? If any product you order doesn't meet your needs, just return it for full refund or credit. 800-228-2275.

Unique cards get you noticed. Books & software save you time.

Business Communications

Proposal Development: How to Respond and Win the Bid

 Book

Orchestrates a successful proposal from preliminary planning to clinching the deal. Shows by explanation and example how to: determine what to include; create text, illustrations, tables, exhibits, and appendices; how to format (using either traditional methods or desktop publishing); meet the special requirements of government proposals; set up and follow a schedule.

Write Your Own Business Contracts

 Book

Explains the "do's" and "don'ts" of contract writing so any person in business can do the preparatory work in drafting contracts before hiring an attorney for final review. Gives a working knowledge of the various types of business agreements, plus tips on how to prepare for the unexpected.

Complete Book of Business Forms

 Book

Over 200 reproducible forms for all types of business needs: personnel, employment, finance, production flow, operations, sales, marketing, order entry, and general administration. Time-saving, uniform, coordinated way to record and locate important business information.

EXECARDS®
The Original Business-To-Business Communication Tools

EXECARDS, business-to-business message cards, are an effective vehicle for maintaining personal contacts in this era of rushed, highly-technical communications. A card takes only seconds and a few cents to send, but can memorably tell customers, clients, prospects, or co-workers that their relationship is valued. Many styles and messages to choose from for thanking, acknowledging, inviting, reminding, prospecting, following up, etc. *Please call 800-228-2275 for complete catalog.*

PlanningTools™
Paper pads, 3-hole punched

Handsome PlanningTools help organize thoughts and record notes, actions, plans, and deadlines, so important information and responsibilities do not get lost or forgotten. Specific PlanningTools organize different needs, such as Calendar Notes, Progress/Activity Record, Project Plan/Record, Week's Priority Planner, Make-A-Month Calendar, and Milestone Chart. *Please call 800-228-2275 for information.*

Business Relocation

Company Relocation Handbook: Making the Right Move

 Book

Comprehensive guide to moving a business. Begins with defining objectives for moving and evaluating whether relocating will actually solve more problems than it creates. Worksheets compare prospective locations, using rating scales for physical plant, equipment, personnel, and geographic considerations. Sets up a schedule for dealing with logistics.

Retirement Planning

Retirement & Estate Planning Handbook

 Book

Do-it-yourself workbook for setting up a retirement plan that can easily be maintained and followed. Covers establishing net worth, retirement goals, budgets, and a plan for asset acquisition, preservation, and growth. Discusses realistic expectations for Social Security, Medicare, and health care alternatives. Features special sections for business owners.

Mail Order

Mail Order Legal Guide

 New Book

For companies that use the mail to market their products or services, as well as for mail order businesses, this book clarifies complex regulations so penalties can be avoided. Gives state-by-state legal requirements, plus information on Federal Trade Commission guidelines and rules covering delivery dates, advertising, sales taxes, unfair trade practices, and consumer protection.

Need it tomorrow? In most cases that's possible if you order before noon, PST. Just give us a call at 800-228-2275.

IH 2 12 3

BOOKS FROM THE OASIS PRESS® Please check the edition (binder or paperback) of your choice

TITLE	BINDER	PAPERBACK	QUANTITY	COST
The Business Environmental Handbook		☐ $ 19.95		
Business Owner's Guide to Accounting & Bookkeeping		☐ $ 19.95		
Buyer's Guide to Business Insurance	☐ $ 39.95	☐ $ 19.95		
California Corporation Formation Package and Minute Book	☐ $ 39.95	☐ $ 29.95		
Collection Techniques for Small Business	☐ $ 39.95	☐ $ 19.95		
A Company Policy and Personnel Workbook	☐ $ 49.95	☐ $ 29.95		
Company Relocation Handbook	☐ $ 39.95	☐ $ 19.95		
Complete Book of Business Forms	☐ $ 49.95	☐ $ 19.95		
Controlling Your Company's Freight Costs	☐ $ 39.95			
Cost-Effective Market Analysis	☐ $ 39.95			
The Essential Corporation Handbook		☐ $ 19.95		
Export Now	☐ $ 39.95	☐ $ 19.95		
Financial Management Techniques For Small Business	☐ $ 39.95	☐ $ 19.95		
Financing Your Small Business		☐ $ 19.95		
Franchise Bible	☐ $ 39.95	☐ $ 19.95		
Home Business Made Easy		☐ $ 19.95		
How to Develop & Market Creative Business Ideas		☐ $ 14.95		
The Loan Package	☐ $ 39.95			
Mail Order Legal Guide	☐ $ 45.00	☐ $ 29.95		
Managing People: A Practical Guide	☐ $ 39.95	☐ $ 19.95		
The Money Connection	☐ $ 39.95	☐ $ 24.95		
People Investment	☐ $ 39.95	☐ $ 19.95		
Power Marketing for Small Business	☐ $ 39.95	☐ $ 19.95		
Proposal Development: How to Respond and Win the Bid (hardback book)	☐ $ 39.95	☐ $ 19.95		
Raising Capital	☐ $ 39.95	☐ $ 19.95		
Retirement & Estate Planning Handbook	☐ $ 39.95	☐ $ 19.95		
Safety Law Compliance Manual for California Businesses		☐ $ 24.95		
Company Illness & Injury Prevention Program Binder (OR Get kit WITH BOOK AND binder $49.95)	☐ $ 34.95	☐ $ 49.95 BOOK & BINDER KIT		
Secrets to Buying and Selling a Business	☐ $ 39.95	☐ $ 19.95		
Start Your Business		☐ $ 8.95		
Starting and Operating A Business in... book INCLUDES FEDERAL section PLUS ONE STATE SECTION —	☐ $ 29.95	☐ $ 24.95		
PLEASE SPECIFY WHICH STATE(S) YOU WANT:				
STATE SECTION ONLY (BINDER NOT INCLUDED) – SPECIFY STATES:	☐ $ 8.95			
U.S. EDITION (FEDERAL SECTION – 50 STATES AND WASHINGTON, D.C. IN 11-BINDER SET)	☐ $295.00			
Successful Business Plan: Secrets & Strategies (GET THE BINDER...IT'S A BUSINESS PLAN KIT)	☐ $ 49.95	☐ $ 21.95		
Surviving and Prospering in a Business Partnership	☐ $ 39.95	☐ $ 19.95		
Top Tax Saving Ideas for Today's Small Business		☐ $ 14.95		
Write Your Own Business Contracts (HARDBACK BOOK)	☐ $ 39.95	☐ $ 19.95		

BOOK TOTAL (Please enter on other side also for grand total)

SOFTWARE Please check whether you use Macintosh or 3-1/2" Disk for IBM-PC & Compatibles

TITLE	3-1/2" IBM Disk	Mac	Price	QUANTITY	COST
California Corporation Formation Package Software	☐	☐	$ 39.95		
★ California Corporation Formation Binder book & Software	☐	☐	$ 69.95		
Company Policy & Personnel Software (Standalone)	☐		$ 99.95		
★ Company Policy & Personnel Binder book & Software (Standalone)	☐		$125.95		
Customer Information & Tracking System	☐		$119.95		
Financial Management Techniques	☐		$ 99.95		
★ Financial Management Techniques Binder book & Software	☐		$129.95		
Financial Templates	☐	☐	$ 69.95		
The Small Business Expert	☐		$ 34.95		
Successful Business Plan (Full Standalone)	☐		$ 99.95		
★ Successful Business Plan Binder book & Software (Full Standalone)	☐		$125.95		

SOFTWARE TOTAL (Please enter on other side also for grand total)

Please add above totals on other side to complete your order. Thanks!

PSI Successful Business Library / Tools for Business Success Order Form (please see other side also)
Call, Mail or Fax to: PSI Research, 300 North Valley Drive, Grants Pass, OR 97526 USA
Order Phone USA (800) 228-2275   Inquiries and International Orders (503) 479-9464   FAX (503) 476-1479

Sold to: PLEASE GIVE STREET ADDRESS NOT P.O. BOX FOR SHIPPING

Name _____ Title: _____

Company _____ Daytime Telephone: _____

Street Address _____

City/State/Zip _____

☐   YES, I want to receive the PSI newsletter, *MEMO.
    Be sure to include: Name, address, and telephone number above.

Ship to: (if different) PLEASE GIVE STREET ADDRESS NOT P.O. BOX FOR SHIPPING

Name _____

Title _____

Company _____

Street Address _____

City/State/Zip _____

Daytime Telephone _____

Payment Information:

☐ Check enclosed payable to PSI Research (When you enclose a check, UPS ground shipping is free within the Continental U.S.A.)

Charge - ☐ VISA ☐ MASTERCARD ☐ AMEX ☐ DISCOVER   Card Number: _____ Expires _____

Signature: _____   Name on card: _____

EXECARDS — The Proven & Chosen Method of Personal Business Communications

ITEM	PRICE EACH	QUANTITY	COST
EXECARDS Thank You Assortment (12 assorted thank you cards)	$ 12.95		
EXECARDS Recognition Assortment (12 assorted appreciation cards)	$ 12.95		
EXECARDS Marketing Assortment (12 assorted marketing cards)	$ 12.95		
EXECARDS TOTAL (Please enter below also for grand total)			$

Many additional options available, including custom imprinting of your company's name, logo or message. Please request a complete catalog. 800-228-2275

PLANNING TOOLS — Action Tracking Note Pads — 8½" x 11"

ITEM		NUMBER OF PADS
Calendar Note Pad	☐ 1994	
	☐ 94/95	
	☐ 1995	
Total number of pads		
Multiply by unit price: x		
PLANNING TOOLS TOTAL	$	

UNIT PRICE FOR ANY COMBINATION OF PLANNING TOOLS
1-9 pads $3.95 each
10-49 pads $3.49 each

SAFETY PROGRAM FORMS

ITEM	PRICE EACH	QUANTITY
Employee Warning Notification (Package of 20)	$4.95	
Request for Safety Orientation (Package of 20)	$4.95	
Report of Potential Hazard (Package of 20)	$4.95	
SAFETY PROGRAM FORMS TOTAL	$	

YOUR GRAND TOTAL

BOOK TOTAL (from other side)	$
SOFTWARE TOTAL (from other side)	$
EXECARDS TOTAL	$
PLANNING TOOLS TOTAL	$
SAFETY PROGRAM FORMS TOTAL	$
TOTAL ORDER	$

Rush service is available. Please call us for details.

Please send me:

_____ EXECARDS Catalog

_____ Oasis Press Software Information

_____ Oasis Press Book Information

Use this form to register for advance notification of updates, new books and software releases, plus special customer discounts!

Please answer these questions to let us know how our products are working for you, and what we could do to serve you better.

Title of book or software purchased from us:_____

It is a:
- ☐ Binder book
- ☐ Paperback book
- ☐ Book/software combination
- ☐ Software only

Rate this product's overall quality of information:
- ☐ Excellent
- ☐ Good
- ☐ Fair
- ☐ Poor

Rate the quality of printed materials:
- ☐ Excellent
- ☐ Good
- ☐ Fair
- ☐ Poor

Rate the format:
- ☐ Excellent
- ☐ Good
- ☐ Fair
- ☐ Poor

Did the product provide what you needed?
- ☐ Yes ☐ No

If not, what should be added?_____
_____
_____
_____
_____

This product is:
- ☐ Clear and easy to follow
- ☐ Too complicated
- ☐ Too elementary

Were the worksheets (if any) easy to use?
- ☐ Yes ☐ No ☐ N/A

Should we include:
- ☐ More worksheets
- ☐ Fewer worksheets
- ☐ No worksheets

How do you feel about the price?
- ☐ Lower than expected
- ☐ About right
- ☐ Too expensive

How many employees are in your company?
- ☐ Under 10 employees
- ☐ 10 – 50 employees
- ☐ 51 – 99 employees
- ☐ 100 – 250 employees
- ☐ Over 250 employees

How many people in the city your company is in?
- ☐ 50,000 – 100,000
- ☐ 100,000 – 500,000
- ☐ 500,000 – 1,000,000
- ☐ Over 1,000,000
- ☐ Rural (under 50,000)

What is your type of business?
- ☐ Retail
- ☐ Service
- ☐ Government
- ☐ Manufacturing
- ☐ Distributor
- ☐ Education

What types of products or services do you sell?
_____
_____
_____

What is your position in the company?
(please check one)
- ☐ Owner
- ☐ Administration
- ☐ Sales/marketing
- ☐ Finance
- ☐ Human resources
- ☐ Production
- ☐ Operations
- ☐ Computer/MIS

How did you learn about this product?
- ☐ Recommended by a friend
- ☐ Used in a seminar or class
- ☐ Have used other PSI products
- ☐ Received a mailing
- ☐ Saw in bookstore
- ☐ Saw in library
- ☐ Saw review in:
  - ☐ Newspaper
  - ☐ Magazine
  - ☐ TV/Radio

Where did you buy this product?
- ☐ Catalog
- ☐ Bookstore
- ☐ Office supply
- ☐ Consultant
- ☐ Other_____

Would you purchase other business tools from us?
- ☐ Yes ☐ No

If so, which products interest you?
- ☐ EXECARDS® Communication Tools
- ☐ Books for business
- ☐ Software

Would you recommend this product to a friend?
- ☐ Yes ☐ No

If you'd like us to send associates or friends a catalog, just list names and addresses

☐ Yes ☐ No

If there is anything you think we should do to improve this product, please describe: _____
_____
_____
_____

on back.
Do you use a personal computer for business?
- ☐ Yes ☐ No

If yes, which?
- ☐ IBM/compatible
- ☐ Macintosh

Check all the ways you use computers:
- ☐ Word processing
- ☐ Accounting
- ☐ Spreadsheet
- ☐ Inventory
- ☐ Order processing
- ☐ Design/graphics
- ☐ General data base
- ☐ Customer information
- ☐ Scheduling

May we call you to follow up on your comments?
- ☐ Yes ☐ No

May we add your name to our mailing list?

Thank you for your patience in answering the above questions.
Just fill in your name and address here, fold (see back) and mail.

Name _____
Title _____
Company _____
Phone _____
Address _____

RR 244

If you have friends or associates who might appreciate receiving our catalogs, please list here. Thanks!

Name _____

Title _____

Company _____

Phone _____

Address _____

City/State/Zip _____

Name _____

Title _____

Company _____

Phone _____

Address _____

City/State/Zip _____

FOLD HERE FIRST

NO POSTAGE
NECESSARY
IF MAILED
IN THE
UNITED STATES

BUSINESS REPLY MAIL

FIRST CLASS MAIL PERMIT NO. 002 MERLIN, OREGON

POSTAGE WILL BE PAID BY ADDRESSEE

PSI Research
PO BOX 1414
Merlin OR 97532-9900

✂
Please cut
along this
vertical line,
fold twice,
tape together
and mail.
Thanks!

✂ Cut out these post cards along the dashed lines. Just write in the information on reverse side, add your return address, then apply the proper postage and drop in the mail.

Name

Title

Company

Address

City

State & Zip

Affix
Stamp
Here

**Communications Division – Posters
California Department of Industrial
Relations**

P.O. Box 420603

San Francisco, CA 94101-0603

Name

Title

Company

Address

City

State & Zip

Affix
Stamp
Here

**California Employment Development
Department**

805 R Street, Warehouse

Sacramento, CA 95814-6497

Name

Title

Company

Address

City

State & Zip

Affix
Stamp
Here

**Communications Center
California Department of Fair Employment
and Housing**

2014 T Street, Suite 210

Sacramento, CA 95814

Name

Title

Company

Address

City

State & Zip

Affix
Stamp
Here

**Document Design and Control Unit
California State Board of Equalization**

P.O. Box 942879

Sacramento, CA 94279-0001

Attn: Communications Division – Posters

Please send me:

- ☐ *Developing a Workplace Safety and Health Program (CS-1)*
- ☐ *Recordkeeping and Reporting Requirements Under the California Occupational Safety and Health Act*
- ☐ *Pay Day Notice*
- ☐ *Industrial Welfare Commission's Orders Regulating Wages, Working Conditions, and Hours (IWC Form 1104)*

Name _____

Title _____

Company _____

Address _____

City _____ State _____ Zip _____

Post card provided by The Oasis Press, 300 North Valley Drive, Grants Pass, OR 97526   5/95

Attn: Employment Tax District Office

Please send me:

- ☐ *California Employer's Guide, Form DE 44*

Name _____

Title _____

Company _____

Address _____

City _____ State _____ Zip _____

Post card provided by The Oasis Press, 300 North Valley Drive, Grants Pass, OR 97526   5/95

Attn: Communications Center

Please send me the poster, *Discrimination in Employment is Prohibited by Law,* in ☐ English

   ☐ Spanish

To obtain this poster, you must send a self-addressed, stamped envelope to the address on the back of this card.

Post card provided by The Oasis Press, 300 North Valley Drive, Grants Pass, OR 97526   5/95

Attn: Document Design and Control Unit

Please send me:

- ☐ *Pamphlet 77, Publications brochure*

Name _____

Title _____

Company _____

Address _____

City _____ State _____ Zip _____

Post card provided by The Oasis Press, 300 North Valley Drive, Grants Pass, OR 97526   5/95

✂ Cut out these post cards along the dashed lines. Just write in the information on reverse side, add your return address, then apply the proper postage and drop in the mail.

Affix
Stamp
Here

Name
Title
Company
Address
City
State & Zip

Attn: Communications Dept. – CWS4
Pacific Bell Directory
101 Spear Street, Room 429
San Francisco, CA 94105

Affix
Stamp
Here

Name
Title
Company
Address
City
State & Zip

Unicor Distribution Services
3150 Horton Road
Fort Worth, TX 76119

Affix
Stamp
Here

Name
Title
Company
Address
City
State & Zip

U.S. Department of Labor
ESA/Office of Public Affairs
Room C 4325
200 Constitution Avenue, NW
Washington, DC 20210

Affix
Stamp
Here

Name
Title
Company
Address
City
State & Zip

U.S. Department of Labor
OSHA Publications Office
200 Constitution Avenue, NW
Washington, DC 20210

Attn: Communications Dept. – CWS4

Please send me:

☐ A complimentary copy of *Small Business Success*

Name _____

Title _____

Company _____

Address _____

City _____ State _____ Zip _____

Post card provided by The Oasis Press, 300 North Valley Drive, Grants Pass, OR 97526   7/94

Attn: Unicor Distribution Services

Please send me:

☐ The Business Development list of publications (SBA 115A) offered by the U.S. Small Business Administration

Name _____

Title _____

Company _____

Address _____

City _____ State _____ Zip _____

Post card provided by The Oasis Press, 300 North Valley Drive, Grants Pass, OR 97526   7/94

Attn: U.S. Department of Labor – ESA/OPA

Please send me:

☐ Your most current version of *Your Rights Under the Fair Labor Standards Act* (WH Publication 1088)

Name _____

Title _____

Company _____

Address _____

City _____ State _____ Zip _____

Post card provided by The Oasis Press, 300 North Valley Drive, Grants Pass, OR 97526   7/94

Attn: U.S. Department of Labor – OSHA

Please send me:

☐ A list of free OSHA publications available from the OSHA Publications Office

☐ A list of OSHA publications available from the Government Printing Office for a small fee

Name _____

Title _____

Company _____

Address _____

City _____ State _____ Zip _____

Post card provided by The Oasis Press, 300 North Valley Drive, Grants Pass, OR 97526   7/94

Cut out these post cards along the dashed lines. Just write in the information on reverse side, add your return address, then apply the proper postage and drop in the mail.

Affix
Stamp
Here

Name

Title

Company

Address

City

State & Zip

Equal Employment Opportunity Commisssion
2401 E Street
Washington, DC 20507

Affix
Stamp
Here

Name

Title

Company

Address

City

State & Zip

PSI Research
300 North Valley Drive
Grants Pass, OR 97526

Affix
Stamp
Here

Name

Title

Company

Address

City

State & Zip

The Oasis Press
300 North Valley Drive
Grants Pass, OR 97526

Affix
Stamp
Here

Name

Title

Company

Address

City

State & Zip

The Oasis Press
300 North Valley Drive
Grants Pass, OR 97526

Attn: The Oasis Press

Please send me information about your resources on:

☐ **How to incorporate in** (list states) _____

☐ **How to form a Limited Liability Company**

☐ **How to form a partnership**

☐ **How to maintain a corporation**

Name _____

Title _____

Company _____

Address _____

City _____ State _____ Zip _____

Post card provided by The Oasis Press, 300 North Valley Drive, Grants Pass, OR 97526   7/94

Attn: The Oasis Press

Please send information on the Successful Business Library to these friends and associates:

Name _____

Title _____ Phone _____

Company _____

Address _____

City _____ State _____ Zip _____

Name _____

Title _____ Phone _____

Company _____

Address _____

City _____ State _____ Zip _____

Post card provided by The Oasis Press, 300 North Valley Drive, Grants Pass, OR 97526   7/94

Attn: Equal Employment Opportunity Commission

Please send me:

☐ **Free poster,** *Equal Employment Opportunity is the Law* (GPO 192 0 383798)

Name _____

Title _____

Company _____

Address _____

City _____ State _____ Zip _____

Post card provided by The Oasis Press, 300 North Valley Drive, Grants Pass, OR 97526   7/94

Attn: PSI Research

Please send me information on:

☐ **The next edition of** *Starting and Operating a Business in* (list states) _____

☐ **PSI Successful Business Software**

☐ *EXECARDS®* **Business-to-Business Communication Tools**

Name _____

Title _____ Phone _____

Company _____

Address _____

City _____ State _____ Zip _____

Post card provided by The Oasis Press, 300 North Valley Drive, Grants Pass, OR 97526   7/94